C.G. Jung and the Imagination

Stanton Marlan brings together writings which span the course of his career, examining Jungian psychology and the alchemical imagination as an opening to the mysteries of psyche and soul.

Several chapters describe a telos that aims at the mysterious goal of the Philosophers' Stone, a move replete with classical and postmodern ideas catalysed by prompts from the unconscious: dreams, images, fantasies, and paradoxical conundrums. Psyche and matter are seen with regard to soul, light, and darkness in terms of illumination, and order and chaos as linked in the image of *chaosmos*. Marlan explores the richness of the alchemical ideas of Carl Jung, James Hillman, and others and their value for a revisioning of psychology. In doing so, this volume challenges any tendency to literalism and essentialism, and contributes to an integration between Jung's classical vision of a psychology of alchemy and Hillman's *Alchemical Psychology*.

C.G. Jung and the Alchemical Imagination will be a valuable resource for academics, scholars, and students of Jungian and post-Jungian studies, Jungian analysis, and psychotherapy. It will also be of great interest to Jungian psychologists and Jungian analysts in practice and in training.

Stanton Marlan, PhD, ABPP, FABP is a Jungian analyst, President of the Pittsburgh Society of Jungian Analysts, and an Adjunct Professor in Clinical Psychology at Duquesne University, with long-time interests in alchemy and the psychology of dreams, and the author of *The Black Sun: Alchemy and the Art of Darkness*.

"Stanton Marlan's essays movingly mirror the steadily burning passion of the alchemists for their opus. With these critical ventures into alchemical psychology Marlan has forged an opus of his own that is more than an amalgam of other thinkers' insights. It is a singular work of creative scholarship and imagination and is thus another link in the golden chain of engagement with the mysteries of the human psyche."

Murray Stein, Ph.D., author of *Jung's Map of the Soul*

"To use an alchemical metaphor, in this collection of his writings, we find Stan Marlan having "taken another round in the container." That is, he works his material again and again, with it each time becoming more refined, sophisticated, and qualitatively transformed. The result is a series of deep insights and psychological wisdom, richly evolved and well worth the reader's time. I highly recommend this intellectually clarifying and emotionally satisfying book!"

Pat Berry, Ph.D., Jungian Analyst

"Over the years my own understanding of Jung has been deepened by Stan Marlan's own original and insightful essays on the pivotal place of alchemy in Jung's psychology. What a joy now to have the fifteen essays gathered in this volume. For the reader the book itself becomes an alchemical vessel whose fire attests to the radical depths and reveals the expansive reach of Jung's Alchemical Psychology beyond the narrow confines of what his psychology has become. Marlan's scholarship and elegant writing display Jung's alchemical imagination as a necessary and much needed recovery of the erotic coupling between psyche and nature, that dark desire of spirit to matter and for matter to be inspired. Read Marlan's book and learn to trust and to love the brilliance of the soul's dark light that illuminated the alchemists of old and beckons us to be with them today."

Robert D. Romanyshyn, Ph.D., author of *Victor Frankenstein, the Monster and the Shadows of Technology: The Frankenstein Prophecies*

C.G. Jung and the Alchemical Imagination
Passages into the Mysteries of Psyche and Soul

Stanton Marlan

The author's personal library. (Photo courtesy of the Marlan archives, with thanks to Dawn, Tori, and Brandon.)

LONDON AND NEW YORK

First published 2021
by Routledge
2 Park Square, Milton Park, Abingdon, Oxon OX14 4RN

and by Routledge
52 Vanderbilt Avenue, New York, NY 10017

Routledge is an imprint of the Taylor & Francis Group, an informa business

© 2021 Stanton Marlan

The right of Stanton Marlan to be identified as author of this work has been asserted by them in accordance with sections 77 and 78 of the Copyright, Designs and Patents Act 1988.

All rights reserved. No part of this book may be reprinted or reproduced or utilised in any form or by any electronic, mechanical, or other means, now known or hereafter invented, including photocopying and recording, or in any information storage or retrieval system, without permission in writing from the publishers.

Trademark notice: Product or corporate names may be trademarks or registered trademarks, and are used only for identification and explanation without intent to infringe.

British Library Cataloguing-in-Publication Data
A catalogue record for this book is available from the British Library

Library of Congress Cataloging-in-Publication Data
A catalog record has been requested for this book

ISBN: 978-0-367-40527-4 (hbk)
ISBN: 978-0-367-40528-1 (pbk)
ISBN: 978-0-429-35651-3 (ebk)

Typeset in Times New Roman
by codeMantra

Contents

List of figures vii
Foreword viii
Preface x
Acknowledgments xiv

Introduction 1

1 Jung's discovery of alchemy and its development in the Jungian tradition 8

2 Jung and alchemy: a daimonic reading 40

3 Fire in the stone: an inquiry into the alchemy of soul-making 58

4 Salt and the alchemical soul: Freudian, Jungian, and archetypal perspectives 81

5 The metaphor of light and renewal in Taoist alchemy and Jungian analysis 103

6 The metaphor of light and its deconstruction in Jung's alchemical vision 121

7 Facing the shadow: turning toward the darkness of the nigredo 137

8 The black sun	146
Part A. Archetypal image of the non-self	146
Part B. Epilogue to *The Black Sun: The Alchemy and Art of Darkness*	156
9 From the black sun to the Philosophers' Stone	160
10 A critique of Wolfgang Giegerich's move from imagination to the logical life of the soul	183
Part A. The psychologist who is not a psychologist: a deconstructive reading of Wolfgang Giegerich's idea of psychology proper	183
Part B. The absolute that is not absolute: an alchemical reflection on the *Caput Mortuum*, the dark other of logical light	197
11 What's the matter—with alchemical recipes? Philosophy and filth in the forging of Jung's alchemical psychology	213
12 The Philosophers' Stone as chaosmos: the Self and the dilemma of diversity	233
13 The Azure Vault: alchemy and the cosmological imagination	246
14 Divine Darkness and Divine Light: alchemical illumination and the mystical play between knowing and unknowing	253
Index	271

Figures

Frontispiece. The author's personal library		iii
Acknowledgements. The author in Jung's home library in Kusnacht		xv
2.1	The unification of air and earth, from Eleazar's *Uraltes Chymisches Werck*, 1735	53
3.1	The return of the soul. Revivification, from the *Rosarium philosophorum*	73
8.1	The black sun, *sol niger, nigredo, putrefactio*. From Mylius, *Philosophia reformata*, 1622	151
11.1	Pele, Goddess of Fire	224
11.2	The philosophical egg. From Codex Palatinus Latinus, 15th c	225
11.3	Illuminated tree	227
13.1	"Gates to the Garden." Acrylic on canvas	250
14.1	Alchemical homunculus by Franz Xaver Simm, 1899	255
14.2	*Rati-asana* (detail). Stone, Khajuraho, Vishvanatha temple, 1059–1087	256
14.3	*Illuminatio*. From *Artis Auriferae*, 1572	259
14.4	Nicolas de Locques: Les Rudiments de la Philosophie Naturelle. Paris, 1665, frontispiece (N. Bonnart)	263
14.5	Black jaguar	266

Foreword

In *Psychology and Alchemy*, Jung makes reference to a treasure that "is said to take nine years, nine months, and nine nights to come to the surface and, if not found in the last night, sinks down to start all again from the beginning."[1] Reading this always made me think of those invaluable things that remain buried, hidden, and forgotten until they are found.

The idea of this anthology came when I read one of Stanton Marlan's papers and was impressed by his clinical insights and the sophistication of his theoretical elaboration. I translated the paper into Portuguese, giving access to the Brazilian public. But still there were other papers that would be so interesting to the Jungian community; conversations began and the idea of this book emerged. And now these precious writings that could have been buried in the past, harder and harder to find, are brought to life again.

Anyone who knows Stan, has visited his library or read about it,[2] understands how alchemy is ingrained in his life and fundamental to his way of thinking and seeing the world. Some say that you know a man from his library and it comprises more than books. Stan's library is replete with mysterious objects that inspire inquiry, snakes and skulls and stones that open to a symbolic and numinous presence. They reveal one of the characteristics of the alchemists, a passionate curiosity into the unknown (see Frontispiece). There's no alchemical work without such passion and love for the sensuous embodiment of life and the surprising transformations that unfold before our eyes. Such is Stan's gaze, his curiosity leads the way into the depths, and he shares with us the mysteries revealed by them.

Stanton Marlan is an analyst whose eyes are at ease in the dark. Not unlike a true alchemist, he can navigate the depths of the unknown and bring us back treasures. This book should be celebrated. As many alchemical sayings advised: rejoyce!

Leticia Capriotti
Jungian Analyst
AJB/IAAP

Notes

1 Jung, C.G. *Psychology and Alchemy.* CW 12, par 111.
2 See the chapter "Transference, Friendship, and Other Mysteries: A Reverie" in the book *Archetypal Psychologies: Reflections in Honor of James Hillman*, edited by Stanton Marlan, New Orleans, LA: Spring Journal Books, 2008, 2–11.

Preface

This is a book about Jungian psychology and the alchemical imagination as an opening to the mysteries of psyche and soul. It is inspired by the work of Carl Jung and the developments in alchemical studies in the Jungian tradition. For Jung, it was alchemy that helped him come to terms with, "absorb" and "organize" his early and nearly overwhelming experiences into a new understanding of psychology, the process of transformation, the unconscious, individuation, and the Self. I have written about my own attempt to understand Jung's alchemical work for over two decades and have published many reflections in scattered books and journals, each article a kind of alchemical experiment aiming to distill my own perspective and to deepen my work as an analyst. For me, alchemy is a daimonic passion and its study has continued to inspire me.

Still, I had not imagined bringing these reflections together into a book until Leticia Capriotti, a Brazilian colleague, friend, and Jungian analyst, encouraged and inspired me to do so. Leticia's sensitive, informed, and enthusiastic reading of my work motivated me to look again at the trajectory of my thought as a whole and to consider my contribution with a fresh eye. What follows is a series of selected papers arranged in a way that best articulates the flow and development of my ideas as they emerged in the re-reading and re-thinking of my work.

Academic Acknowledgments

Versions of the following chapters have previously been published elsewhere. Some have been shortened and modified. I am grateful to each publisher for granting permission to republish.

Chapter 1. Jung's discovery of alchemy and its development in the Jungian tradition

Originally published as "Alchemy," in *The Handbook of Jungian Psychology: Theory, Practice and Applications*, edited by Renos Papadopoulos, 263–295. London, UK: Routledge, 2006.

Preface xi

Chapter 2. Jung and alchemy: a daimonic reading

Originally published under the same title in *How and Why We Still Read Jung: Personal and Professional Reflections*, edited by Jean Kirsh and Murray Stein, 46–65. London, UK: Routledge, 2013.

Chapter 3. Fire in the stone: an inquiry into the alchemy of soul-making

Originally published as "Fire in the Stone: An Inquiry into the Alchemy of Soul-Making," in *Fire in the Stone: The Alchemy of Desire*, edited by Stanton Marlan, 7–41. Wilmette, IL: Chiron, 1997. Reprinted by permission of Spring Journal and Books http://www.springjournalandbooks.com.

Chapter 4. Salt and the alchemical soul: Freudian, Jungian, and archetypal perspectives

Originally published as the Preface and the Introduction to *Salt and the Alchemical Soul*, edited by Stanton Marlan, XIII–XLV. Woodstock, CT: Spring Publications, 1995.

Chapter 5. The metaphor of light and renewal in Taoist alchemy and Jungian analysis

This paper was originally presented at the first international conference on Jungian Psychology and Chinese Culture in Guangzhou, China, December 16–20, 1998. It was originally published under the same title in *Quadrant*, Vol. XXXI, No. 2 (Summer 2001).

Chapter 6. The metaphor of light and its deconstruction in Jung's alchemical vision

This paper was first presented at the Inter-Regional Society of Jungian Analysts and later published in *Pathways into the Jungian World*, edited by Roger Brooke, 181–196. London, UK: Routledge, 2000.

Chapter 7. Facing the shadow: turning toward the darkness of the nigredo

Originally published as "Facing the Shadow," in *Jungian Psychoanalysis: Working in the Spirit of C.G. Jung*, edited by Murray Stein, 5–13. Chicago, IL: Open Court Publishers, 2010.

Chapter 8. The black sun:

A. *The black sun: archetypal image of the non-self*: Unpublished paper presented at "Psychology at the Threshold: An International Symposium of Archetypal Psychology, 31 August–4 September 2000; sponsored by the Pacifica Graduate Institute.

B. Epilogue to *The Black Sun: The Alchemy and Art of Darkness* Originally published as the Epilogue in *The Black Sun: The Alchemy and Art of Darkness*, College Station: Texas A&M University Press, 2005.

Chapter 9. From the black sun to the Philosophers' Stone

Originally published under the same title *in Spring: A Journal of Archetype and Culture*, 74 (2006): 1–30. http://www.springjournalandbooks.com.

Chapter 10. A Critique of Wolfgang Giegerich's move from imagination to the logical life of the soul:

Part A. The psychologist who is not a psychologist: a deconstructive reading of Wolfgang Giegerich's idea of psychology proper: This paper is a modified version of a paper "The psychologist who's not a psychologist," presented at the International Society for Psychology as the Discipline of Interiority Conference, Berlin, Germany, 24 July 2012. Originally published under the same title in *Journal of Analytical Psychology*, Vol. 61, No. 2 (2016), 223–238. Reprinted with permission of Wiley Publishing: 0021–8774/2016/6102/223 © 2016, The Society of Analytical Psychology Published by Wiley Publishing, 9600 Garsington Road, Oxford OX4 2DQ, UK and 350 Main Street, Malden, MA 02148, USA. DOI: 10.1111/1468–5922.12212.

Part B. The absolute that is not absolute: an alchemical reflection on the *Caput Mortuum*, the dark other of logical light: Originally published under the same title, in *International Journal of Jungian Studies*, Vol. 9, No. 1 (2017).

Chapter 11. What's the matter—with alchemical recipes? Philosophy and filth in the forging of Jung's *alchemical psychology*

Originally published under the same title, in *Jung and Philosophy*, edited by Jon Mills, 220–244. London, UK: Routledge, 2019.

Chapter 12. The Philosophers' Stone as chaosmos: the Self and the dilemma of diversity

The first part of this paper was presented at the 2010 IAAP Congress in Montreal. This paper was originally published under the same title in the

Jung Journal, Vol. 7, No. 2, 10–23, DOI: 10.1080/19342039.2013.787525. It is being reprinted here by permission of C.G. Jung Institute of San Francisco, www.sfjung.org.

Chapter 13. The Azure Vault: alchemy and the cosmological imagination

Originally published under the same title in *Conversing with James Hillman: Alchemical Psychology*, edited by Joanne H. Stroud and Robert Sardello, Dallas, TX: The Dallas Institute of Humanities and Culture, 2017.

Chapter 14. Divine Darkness and Divine Light: alchemical illumination and the mystical play between knowing and unknowing

This paper was first presented at the "*Ars alchemica:* The Art and Alchemy of Transformation" Conference held at Pacifica Graduate Institute, Santa Barbara, CA, USA, August 2017. Originally published under the same title in *Depth Psychology and Mysticism*, edited by T. Cattoi and D. M. Odorisio, Cham, SW: Springer International Publishing, 2018. Online at https://doi.org/10.1007/978-3-319-79096-113.

Acknowledgments

This book is a compilation of a select group of articles on alchemical themes written over a period of at least two decades. Many of these articles were written in response to invitations from individuals, universities, training programs, analytic institutes, and national and international conferences. I am grateful for the interest and support of these institutions, as well as to many academic and professional colleagues, writers, practitioners, publishers, editors, librarians, artists, patients, friends, and family members who have played an important role in inspiring and supporting my work over these many years. It feels nearly impossible to express the extent of appreciation I feel to all those who have, in so many ways, contributed to my thinking and this publication.

I would like to begin by acknowledging the deep gratitude I have for the contribution of C.G. Jung, whose revolutionary approach to alchemy has opened the door to a new era of understanding and whose work has been foundational to my ongoing reflections. Likewise, Maria-Louise von Franz's close collaboration with Jung has been a meaningful extension of his work and has provided inroads and access to the profundity of Jung's ideas. Closer to home, and more personally, I am grateful to my analyst and teacher Edward Edinger whose early lectures in New York, and whose book *Anatomy of the Psyche*, deepened and enriched my understanding of alchemy and its relationship to Jungian psychology. For many years, his work was a foundational and continuing source of inspiration.

My analytic relationship, and ultimately my friendship, with James Hillman has been the most influential source of my developing and new ideas about alchemy and alchemical psychology. Over the years, I have found Hillman's work to be the most original and challenging contribution to Jungian psychology. I met James after reading his groundbreaking book *Revisioning Psychology* and after completing my formal analytic training. I entered into a post-training analysis with him and ultimately into a collegial friendship. I was fortunate to work closely with James on alchemy and had many conversations, exchanges, and dialogues with him over the years, and his work continues to inspire me. I especially appreciate having had the privilege of helping him edit his work, *Alchemical Psychology*.

I would like to extend my thanks to Sonu Shamdasani. While I was visiting him in London and discussing my alchemical interests, he recommended that I visit Jung's library housed in his house in Kusnacht. This led me to contact Jung's grandson Andreas Jung and his wife Vreni. They graciously extended an invitation for me to visit. While in Jung's alchemical library, I had the opportunity to examine many alchemical works, to gather references, and to note sections of the texts that Jung underlined. Over two days, Andreas supported and helped me find materials of interest. It was nearly a numinous experience to sit at Jung's desk and have at my disposal his famous copies of the *Artis Auriferae* and the *Rosarium Philosophorum* as well as many obscure alchemical works.

The author in Jung's home library in Kusnacht. (Photo courtesy of Jan Marlan.)

I want to thank my friend and colleague Murray Stein, whose alchemical lectures and passion for Jungian studies have been an ongoing inspiration. While I was teaching in Zurich, Murray and his wife Jan graciously hosted my wife Jan and me and helped to guide me to many opportunities to meet other Zurich colleagues. It was a privilege to meet and spend some time with Alfred Ribi, a gnostic and alchemical scholar who kindly invited me to his home to exchange ideas and to see his alchemical library, which contained reproductions of Jung's copy books, in which we looked up references to the black sun and other images. I was also grateful to meet and spend some time with Theodore Abt of the Research and Training Centre for Depth Psychology according to C.G. Jung and Marie-Louise von Franz. His ongoing contributions to alchemy and Jungian psychology include his recovery of Arabic manuscripts and his recognition of their importance for alchemy and Jungian studies. I would also like to acknowledge Dorothea Türler, who was a candidate at the Zurich Institute and attended my classes. She generously gave me a copy of a rare text which included Rosicrucian and alchemical symbols that continue to stimulate my imagination.

Thanks as well to Adam McLean for his invitation to visit his library in Glasgow and to see his vast collection of alchemical images and his workshop. I am grateful for his permission to use a number of these images in my publications and appreciative to him for his exceptional website and for making images and alchemical manuscripts available to the public.

This book would not have come into existence if not for my good friend Leticia Capriotti, a Brazilian colleague and Jungian analyst. After reading my alchemical papers, she persuaded me of the value of bringing them together and publishing them in book form. Without her urging, generosity of spirit, and provocation, this project would not have occurred to me. I am grateful for our continuing conversations, her creative suggestions, her depth of soul, imagination, and sense of humor. Her work with Jung's *The Red Book* and knowledge of Hillman's archetypal psychology has been a continuing inspiration.

Likewise, this book would not have seen the light of day without the support of my longtime friend and colleague Claudette Kulkarni. Claudette has also been an invaluable resource and has supported my work over many years and publications. She has shared the work of preparing manuscripts, typing, helping with research and permissions, and writing letters. Her organizational ability, patience, and personal support kept the process going. Claudette's help in editing was essential. Claudette's rigor and tenacity led her to read every word with an eye to the reader's perspective and to offer creative alternatives. In addition, Claudette's passion for and study of philosophy and her feminist critical eye vitalize an enjoyable, engaging, and valuable friendship.

I'm grateful as well to Lorna Peachin, head librarian at the Kristine Mann Library, who, over many years, always went above and beyond expectations to find and provide me with obscure materials.Thanks as well to Susannah Frearson, my editor at Routledge, for her knowledgeable advice and patience in the process of completing this manuscript.

I'm grateful to many colleagues and friends who have invited me to speak at conferences and/or published my alchemical papers in their edited books.

My deep admiration also extends to colleagues and friends whose work, guidance, generosity, and depth have nourished my work over many years: Jean Kirsch, Heyong Shen, Renos Papadopoulos, David Rosen, Roger Brooke, Sanford Drob, Jon Mills, Joanne Stroud, Robert Sardello, David Odorisio, Thomas Cattoi, Dennis Hauke, Nancy Cater, Thomas Kapacinskas, Paul Kugler, David Miller, Robert Romanyshyn, Pat Berry, Lyn Cowan, James Hollis, Maury Krasnow, Wolfgang Giegerich, Greg Mogenson, Pamela Power, Michael Adams, Ed Casey, Gus Cwik, Janet Muff, Margot McLean, Brad DePaske, Arlene Landau, Jeff Raff, Robbie Bosnak, Dyane Sherwood, Scott Churchill, Donald Kalschad, Marcus Quintaes, Bitzalel Malamid, Thom Cavelli, Aaron Cheak, Tom Rockmore, James Swindal, and John Sallis.

I'd like to extend my profound thanks and appreciation to a number of colleagues, friends, and others who have contributed insights, art, discussions of dreams, and ideas that have richly enhanced my understanding of alchemy: Terry and Susan Pulver, David and Cate Perry, Dan Burston and Sharna Olfman, Sandy Miller, Vocata George, Diane Braden, John and Kristy White, Keith Knecht and Lynne Cannoy, Laura Chapman, Christopher McCann, Nancy Hayduke, Robert Fadden, Janice Towbin, Karl Bogarte, Richard Russell, Lynne de Gerenday, Courtney Padrutt, John Knapp, Robert Early, and Fan Honxia.

I offer my deepest gratitude to my family, whose many contributions to my life and work are an ongoing blessing and an irreplaceable foundation of my life. Their love and support, both intellectual and emotional, is a delight and a sustaining ground for all my endeavors. My deep love and appreciation to Dawn Marlan and Jeff Librett, Tori Marlan and Neil Pollner, Brandon Marlan and Bridget Cowan, and to my amazing grandchildren Malachi and Sasha Marlan-Librett, and Zia and Naomi Marlan-Pollner. Special thanks to my wife Jan for her love and intellectual companionship, her honest criticism and support—all of which have sustained me in my efforts to explore the depths of psyche.

Introduction

"Pray. Read, Read, Read. Read Again. Work and you shall find," says the *Mutus Liber*, an old alchemical text. Reading, re-reading, and re-thinking my work on alchemy is a stimulating and revelatory process. It has provided me with an opportunity to look again at my work as a whole and over time. It has allowed me to distill, examine, extract, coagulate, re-open, and re-imagine the ideas embedded in the following chapters. In a sense, this material serves as a *prima materia* for my continuing reflections and hopefully it can do so for others who choose to read and engage with this book and dream the work onward.

For me, reading Jung's alchemy is a daimonic passion, a way of reading that pays careful attention to what is written and also to the many voices of the unconscious. It is at once a reading and a listening. In a draft of *The Red Book*, Jung wrote, "Know that you attain yourself from what you read …. You read as much into a book as out of it."[1] In short, such a reading is itself already an alchemical process transforming the *prima materia* of what is written and allowing imagination to play a greater role in the formation of our ongoing understanding and perception of the cosmos. One might say that such a reading is personal yet strangely other, and that it both includes and surpasses the writer's intention and is carried forward by readers. It holds and goes beyond subject-object divides, melding them together in a creative tandem that self and soul require. In effect, it activates a way of thinking, a dialectic that comes to terms with both Jung and the unconscious, and inspires a continuing vitality of the alchemical imagination.

The sequence of chapters in this book brings to the fore a number of central psychological and alchemical themes that unfold and deepen our understanding of alchemy and Jung's psychology. Each chapter can be read in itself or as part of the whole—which, like alchemical experiments, repeats, extends, and amplifies it. My reflections begin with Jung's discovery and encounter with alchemy as an *opus divinum*, and as a psychological and symbolic art of transformation that provided a historical grounding for his psychology. This view of alchemy inspired many writers both in and outside of the Jungian tradition and, in my estimation, it was carried forward most prominently by classical analysts Marie-Louise von Franz and Edward Edinger, and uniquely imagined by revisionist analysts James Hillman and Wolfgang Giegerich. My own work has been inspired by all of them, but perhaps not surprisingly particularly by Edinger and Hillman, who were my analysts and teachers, and both of whom made major contributions to understanding the mysteries of alchemy opened up by Jung. Jung's profound engagement with the unconscious, Edinger's deep introversion and respect for the depths, and Hillman's originality and iconoclastic fidelity to the image and imagination—all played a role and helped animate my passion for a continuing exploration of the unconscious, the alchemical process, and its goal.

Hillman's question: "What Does the Soul Want?"[2] speaks to the importance of moving beyond any static conceptual rationalism to an ongoing inquiry into this question by a deep and sustained contact with the unconscious—its objectivity, its animation, its eros, and its mysteries. Such a contact requires a descent from the light of consciousness into the darkness of the unknown. I have described this process as a soul-making one, requiring an alchemical "turning the light around" and a deconstruction of the idea that light, as traditionally understood, is *the* best metaphor for consciousness. Moving beyond light into darkness can be explored in terms of facing the shadow and the alchemical *nigredo*. The linking of light and darkness sets the stage for a fundamental and recurring theme in both alchemy and Jungian psychology, namely, the *coniunctio oppositorum*, the unity of opposites, a bringing together of light and darkness into an illuminated vision.

For me, the engagement of consciousness with the unconscious reveals not simply a unity of opposites, but a multiplicity of intentions that challenge and oppose one another, as well as pull psyche toward unification—a fire in the stone and an alchemy of desire. When these tensions are held together, they catalyze a symbol-making process that produces complex archetypal images that exceed rational categories. The intercourse and linking together of passionate intentionalities has alchemically been described as an erotics of desire, a *hierosgamos* or sacred marriage, that gives birth to what the Taoist alchemists called a spiritual embryo, an image of rebirth and renewal, which ultimately leads to the epiphany of the secret of the Golden Flower—an unfolding illumination, a symbol of wholeness, and the goal of the work.

The black sun, *sol niger*, is an analogous image from Western alchemy that links consciousness with the unconscious, light with darkness, into a paradoxical oneness whose shine is an expression of the *lumen naturae*, the light of nature, a light of darkness itself. The alchemists considered it as a *prima materia*, but, like the Golden Flower, its illumination unfolds as a symbol and indication of the *ultima materia*, the mysterious Philosophers' Stone, and psychologically as the Self, the goal of the alchemical work. As a symbol of the Stone and the Self, the black sun avoids the tendency to view the goal as a static whole. Its dynamism is that it carries the darkness within itself as the deconstructive principle such that the Self is also Non-Self, and the Stone not a Stone. It is a oneness that is also other. There is no illumination without darkness, no wholeness without limit. It is also a oneness that does not require that differences subordinate themselves to a unifying principle. In fact, it breaks out of any idealism that situates all of reality in some form of subjectivity alone.

Moving on from the black sun to consider the Philosophers' Stone is not to leave the deconstructive principle of the black sun behind. The image is a *complexio oppositorum* and a *mysterium coniunctionis* that not only resonates with the Stone, but may well be considered another name for it. Hillman and Giegerich have each made valuable contributions to a psychological understanding of the Philosophers' Stone. Both are complex thinkers and in some ways overlap in their views—yet, there are critical differences between them. Both of them emphasize the importance of the link between image and thought, but each privileges one side of this syzygy over the other. For Hillman, as for Jung, image remains fundamental, while for Giegerich, thought is essential and goes dialectically beyond images and imagination. Both image and thought are important aspects of any vital notion of the Philosophers' Stone. For Giegerich, the imaginal requires continuing negative interiorization, but, just as he negates the literal residues of the imaginal, Hillman's imaginal psychology continues to give flesh to the unseen: "*Solve a coagula*," say the alchemists. In my work, I have found value in both perspectives, but ultimately I find myself critical of the idea that thought surpasses images and imagination on the way to what Giegerich calls "psychology proper" and the Absolute. My perspective, distilled from the work of Jung, Hillman, and others, is that thought and image each continually give rise to one another. Just as image gives rise to thought, so thought gives rise to image and the creative imagination. Perhaps in the end, thought and image may best be spoken of in a variety of ways: as an alchemical *circulatio*, as a monstrous *coniunctio*, and/or as a "trembling ground" of poetic undecidables (Derrida). All of the above might be thought/imagined as metaphors that attempt to speak the unspeakable, the unknown, and the paradoxical. Because we can think/imagine the Stone as both rational and non-rational, known and unknown, unity and diversity, order and disorder, cosmos and chaos, I have added the word "chaosmos" to the multiple names for the Stone, a term used by James Joyce to describe this structure in his alchemically relevant book *Finnegan's Wake*.

As Jung moved toward his idea of a psychology of alchemy and away from its literal, material practices, he recognized the importance of spiritual philosophy for understanding it and its goal, the Philosophers' Stone. For Jung, it was important that our spiritual and psychological understanding of alchemy did not degrade and leave matter and nature behind. The early spiritual alchemists considered many important aspects of psyche to be vulgar filth, while Jung and Hillman held them to be indispensable for alchemical recipes and practice. "As the alchemists insisted, the gold of possibility lies in the ugly waste of what is right to hand."[3] The alchemical *caput mortuum*, the dross of life, is part of the shadow of what Giegerich calls "psychology proper." While Giegerich's notion of sublation expresses itself in the "truth" of the logical life of the soul, Jung's idea of the transcendent function creatively produces symbols and imaginal results not reducible to logos.

My own view, following from Jung and from Hillman's Archetypal Psychology, is that what is expressed by the transcendent function is a dark illumination that is other than the "truth" of logical light and that produces a dynamically charged image which moves in a mercurial, erotic, and imaginal play between knowing and unknowing. For Romanyshyn, the "voice of things" is best served by the language of metaphor and imagination which "inhabits neither the brilliance of the day [spirit] nor the darkness of night [soul], but speaks simultaneously in light and shadow."[4] Hillman, like Jung, championed the importance of images and the imagination as fundamental, and advocated for this position with the notion of "sticking to the image," a position which Giegerich criticizes. Yet, strangely, Hillman critiques himself for being "stuck in the image" and also recognizes the soul's need to go beyond itself, moving skyward toward what he calls The Azure Vault. But for Hillman, this move is not simply the logic of spirit. Rather, it links soul and spirit in a vast bluing, an imaginal vivifying of psyche that does not leave images behind, but instead expands them in what he calls a living metaphysics and a cosmological praxis that express themselves in a polyadic cosmos, a pluralistic vision that has always been a mark of Archetypal Psychology's contribution to a revisioned psychology.

Although Hillman would deny that his vision is religious or mystical, he recognizes it as bordering on the transcendent and displaying a sense of "inexpressible sanctity"[5] that takes place in a "magical atmosphere."[6] As noted earlier in this Introduction, Jung *did* see alchemy as a religious, if not a mystical, philosophy, as an *opus divinum*, and as a path of transformation. It is interesting then to consider the relationship between psychoanalysis, alchemy, and mystical traditions—for some, a surprising connection between disciplines that seem to be as far apart as science and religion. For Jung, the connection is evident, but this recognition was not limited to him. It was also present in the work of Herbert Silberer, Jacques Lacan, and other analysts, as well as that of many philosophers and mystical theologians. In re-reading my work, I have noticed that many of the thinkers and systems of transformation I have studied describe a phenomenological process and a path that leads to the goals of these independent and yet overlapping approaches. A common and recurring element of these ideas is the importance of an initiation in the form of negation/deconstruction and an intimate link between this negation and some form of creative emergence—symbolic images and archetypal patterns that move the soul into greater depths and also reflect the goal of the work.[7]

In my judgment, the experiences of negation and their outcomes at best do not lend themselves to any static ontological fixity, but rather demonstrate an ongoing vital process, which, in the light of analysis, does not erase mystery but activates and enlivens it, making it a significant part of psychological and spiritual transformation. "[T]he stone does not allow itself to be held in meaning. It does not yield to understanding."[8] For me, mystery, imagination, and wonder are integral parts of psychological and analytic works, which keep alive the perennial play between knowing and unknowing.

> It is better that one accept each pole, e.g., both reason and unreason, both good and evil, into one's life, experience, and world-view, as only then can one experience the differentiated wholeness that will give rise to the individuated self.[9]

At the end of *Psychology and Alchemy*, Jung wrote, when dealing with alchemical processes:

> We are dealing with life-processes which, on account of their numinous character, have from time immemorial provided the strongest incentive for the formation of symbols. These processes are steeped in mystery; they pose riddles with which the human mind will long wrestle for a solution, and perhaps in vain. For, in the last analysis, it is exceedingly doubtful whether human reason is a suitable instrument for this purpose. Not for nothing did alchemy style itself an "art," feeling—and rightly so—that it was concerned with creative processes that can be truly grasped only by experience, though intellect may give them a name.[10]

I began this Introduction with a quote from the *Mutus Liber* about the importance of reading and would like to make one more negation, again quoting from Jung:

> The alchemists themselves warned us: …. "[R]end the books, lest your hearts be rent asunder," and this despite their insistence on study. Experience, not books, is what leads to understanding.[11]

In the end, my book may be best understood by going beyond it, by reading it and taking up its ideas to the extent that they are relevant to your own experience of life and soul. The *Mutus Liber* was called "the Silent or Mute book"—it is a book of mysteries, of secrets, aimed at creating the Philosophers' Stone, which is produced by the work of the alchemist with his *Soror Mystica*. Together, the alchemist and his mystical sister hold a secret with the intimate implications of an *opus erotica*. What the soul wants, Hillman concludes, is a re-thinking of it with the body and the world, which produces "a resurrection in beauty and pleasure," [12] a return to the world "[b]eautiful and glad,"[13] that heralds the alchemical *rubedo*, a vital reddening of life beyond abstract psychological life. For Hillman, the beauty of the imagination only makes sense if its desirousness is felt as a libidinal and Aphroditic reality, a "touch of Venus," and, like Voluptas, the goddess of sensual pleasure and delight.[14]

Once one goes beyond the limits of intellect alone, negates it, and turns to a deeper experience, it opens the potential for an abundant vitality which Lacan noted, "[b]egins with a tickle and ends with blaze of petrol."[15] Lacan's passionate metaphor speaks to the heat necessary for the transformation process, but for Hillman even Lacan's idea of *jouissance* falls short of describing the libidinal erotics of fire. For Hillman, "the libido [is] a cosmic erotic dynamic that permeates the world because it loves the world of matter ...."[16] Hillman's "Aphroditic language" drips with lust from

> the metabolic heats of the body that stew and digest and melt the loins. As the fire licks and clings to the logs it burns, so passion clings to the bodies of life. ... Like the claws of a cat, the paws of a lion, sulfuric fire attaches to the object of its desire or attaches itself to its desire. Intense internal heat as the moment of fertility.[17]

Initially, the heat of passion strives to possess life, the anima as soul. But life cannot be possessed by our grasp—we cannot own the objects of our lust without diminishing them or ourselves. Hillman traces the notion of libido to "a word cluster ... that includes ... to make liquid, melt ... to love, as well as [to] free ...."[18] Releasing and freeing the passion to possess implies a letting go of the self as well. I believe this is what Hillman means by "the psychotherapeutic cure of 'me.'"[19] Oddly, such a release does not diminish passion, but increases, tinctures, and matures it through considerable pain and struggle, returning the adept anew to the world of matter and nature. The return allows one to see in matter a display, an inner light (*innerlichkeit*), which illuminates the independence of the other. The Stone ripens in the fire and in the glow of the alchemical imagination.

For the alchemist, the art of fire is central to the opus, just as a psychoanalysis of fire is fundamental to the analytic transformation. Fire meets itself when the passions of the mind meet the passions of the body in the world. "The alchemist must be able to fight fire with fire, using his own fire to operate upon the fires with which he is operating. Working the fire by means of fire."[20] "The art of the fire and the key to alchemy means learning how to warm, excite, enthuse, ignite, inspire the material at hand ...."[21] It is my hope that reading this book ignites a spark in its readers and encourages them to attend to the intensity of this fire.

Notes

1. Jung, *The Red Book*, p. 244, Fn 145.
2. Hillman, *Healing Fictions*, p. 85.
3. Hillman, "Jung's Daimonic Inheritance," p. 18.
4. Romanyshyn, "Psychological Language," p. 79.
5. Hillman, *Alchemical Psychology*, p. 324, quoting Jung.
6. Ibid., p. 325, quoting Jung.
7. For some examples of initiatory negations and their goals, refer to Appendix A.
8. Hillman, *Alchemical Psychology*, p. 246, referring to insights from the work of David Miller.
9. Drob, *Reading the Red Book*, p. 246.
10. Jung, *Psychology and Alchemy, CW12*, para. 564.
11. Ibid.
12. Hillman, *Alchemical Psychology*, p. 258.
13. Ibid., p. 261.
14. Ibid.
15. Lacan, *The Other Side of Psychoanalysis*, p. 72.
16. Hillman, *Alchemical Psychology*, p. 257.
17. Ibid., pp. 21–22.
18. Ibid., p. 259.
19. Ibid., p. 255.
20. Ibid., p. 22.
21. Ibid., p. 20.

References

Drob, Sanford. *Reading the Red Book: An Interpretive Guide to C.G. Jung's Liber Novus*. New Orleans, LA: Spring Journal Books, 2012.

Hillman, James. *Alchemical Psychology, Uniform Edition of the Writings of James Hillman, Vol. 5*. Putnam, CT: Spring Publications, 2010.

———. *Healing Fictions*. Barrytown, NY: Station Hill Press, 1983.

———. "Jung's Daimonic Inheritance." *Sphinx: Journal of Archetypal Psychology*, Vol. 1, pp. 9–19, 1988.

Jung, C.G. *Psychology and Alchemy, The Collected Works of C.G. Jung, Vol. 12*, edited by Gerhard Adler and translated by Richard Francis Carrington Hull. Princeton, NJ: Princeton University Press, 1935/1944/1968.

———. *The Red Book: Liber Novus*, edited by Sonu Shamdasani and translated by Mark Kyburz, John Peck, and Sonu Shamdasani. New York: W.W. Norton & Co., 2009.

Lacan, Jacques. *The Other Side of Psychoanalysis: The Seminar of Jacques Lacan, Book XVII*, translated by Russell Grigg. New York: W.W. Norton & Co., 1991.

Romanyshyn, Robert. "Psychological Language and the Voice of Things." *Dragonflies: Studies in Imaginal Psychology*, Spring, Vol. 1, No. 2, pp. 73–79, 1979.

Chapter 1

Jung's discovery of alchemy and its development in the Jungian tradition

Jung considered alchemy in a way that few if any before him had imagined. Alchemy for the most part had been relegated to the status of a historical anachronism or hidden away within the confines of an esoteric occultism. To the contemporary mind, alchemists were viewed as odd, reclusive and strange old men in their laboratories hopelessly trying to change lead into gold. Their practice was seen as nonsense, or, at best, as a precursor to the modern science of chemistry.

Jung began his reflections with a similar attitude, as he describes in *Memories, Dreams, Reflections* (1963). There he notes that when he first desired to become more closely acquainted with alchemical texts, he procured the classic volume *Artis Auriferae Volumina Duo* (1593):

> I let this book lie almost untouched for nearly two years. Occasionally I would look at the pictures and each time I would think, 'Good Lord, what nonsense! This stuff is impossible to understand'.
> (Jung 1963: 204)

However, as his enquiry grew deeper, Jung concluded that the alchemists were speaking in symbols about the human soul and were working as much with the imagination as with the literal materials of their art. The gold that they were trying to produce was not the common or vulgar gold, but an *aurum non vulgi* or *aurum philosophicum*, a philosophical gold (Jung 1963). They were concerned with both the creation of the higher man and the perfection of nature. In a 1952 interview at the Eranos Conference, Jung stated:

> The alchemical operations were real, only this reality was not physical but psychological. Alchemy represents the projection of a drama both cosmic and spiritual in laboratory terms. The *opus magnum* had two aims: the rescue of the human soul and the salvation of the cosmos.
> (Jung, quoted in McGuire and Hull 1977: 228)

This move brought alchemy into the realm of contemporary thought and was the beginning of a sustained psychology of alchemy.

To see alchemy in this way—as a psychological and symbolic art—was a major breakthrough for Jung and a key to unlocking its mysteries. The exploration and development of this insight led Jung eventually to see in alchemy a fundamental source, background and confirmation of his psychology of the unconscious. The impact of alchemy on his continuing work was so great that: 'A good third of Jung's writings are directly or tangentially concerned with alchemy, proportionately far more than he wrote about typology, association experiments, eastern wisdom, or parapsychology' (Hillman 1980: 30, n. 3). As Schwartz-Salant (1995) has noted: 'C.G. Jung, perhaps more than any other modern researcher of alchemy, is responsible for resurrecting this body of thought as a respectable field of study' (Schwartz-Salant 1995: 2).

Jung's writings on alchemy

The English publication of Jung's *Collected Works* did not follow the order of his original writings or presentations. Some individual volumes have been arranged as collections of papers from different periods and not necessarily in terms of the unfolding of his ideas or the importance of his work. Editorial notes to each volume help to place his original writings back into chronological order. Although the historical unfolding of his ideas can be traced in his autobiography *Memories, Dreams, Reflections* (Jung 1963), it should be noted that Jung's works on alchemy are not simply systematic. The development of Jung's theoretical ideas might best be considered as a mosaic of discovery, elaboration and synthesis of his ongoing exploration of the unconscious and of its connection with alchemical thought.

As noted, Jung's work on alchemy constitutes a considerable field of research. The most obvious resources are to be found in those volumes of his *Collected Works* dedicated specifically to alchemy. These include *Psychology and Alchemy* (vol. 12), *Alchemical Studies* (vol. 13) and his magnum opus, *Mysterium Coniunctionis* (vol. 14). In addition to these major works, important alchemical reflections can be found in *Aion* (vol. 9ii) and in *The Practice of Psychotherapy* (vol. 16). The important paper in the latter volume related to alchemy is 'The psychology of the transference' (1946). Jung notes that this essay can also serve as an introduction to his more comprehensive account in *Mysterium Coniunctionis*. In addition, *The Symbolic Life* (vol. 18) contains a few short reflections: 'Foreword to a catalogue on alchemy' (1946), 'Faust and Alchemy' (1949) and 'Alchemy and psychology' (1950). The last piece was written initially for the *Encyclopedia Hebraica* and is a short synopsis of the alchemical work that is more fully elaborated in *Psychology and Alchemy*. Another short synopsis is also detailed in an interview with Jung in *C.G. Jung Speaking: Interviews and Encounters* (McGuire and Hull 1977). The interview was conducted by Mircea Eliade at the Eranos conference in 1952. These two synopses give a short but mature overview of Jung's alchemical process.

Beyond these materials, Jung's autobiography *Memories, Dreams, Reflections* (1963) contains his recollections of his discovery and elaboration of alchemy. These reflections are amplified in a considerable number of letters reproduced in *C.G. Jung Letters*, Volumes 1 and 2. These letters are a small treasure trove of correspondence with such figures as H.G. Baynes, Karl Kerenyi, Hermann Hesse, Erich Neumann, Victor White, Maud Oakes, John Trinick and others. In addition, there are also a collection of unpublished seminar notes containing 15 lectures from the winter of November 1940 to February 1941, which were compiled by Barbara Hannah with the help of a number of others including Marie-Louise von Franz, Toni Wolff and Jung himself. These notes, though reproduced, have not been made available to the public and were generally restricted to seminar members and analysts. Other tools for researching Jung's alchemical work include the *General Bibliography* (vol. 19, 1979a) and the *General Index* (vol. 20, 1979b) of the *Collected Works*. The index contains two sub-indices that focus on Renaissance collections of alchemical texts and their authors; it also contains alchemical themes and symbolic references that locate these ideas and images in Jung's overall alchemical writings. In addition, the student or researcher may find *The Abstracts of the Collected Works of C.G. Jung* (1976) to be of value, as it contains synopses of all of Jung's collected works.

Resources beyond Jung's writings

Beyond Jung's own works, a number of Jung's followers have written about alchemy in a way that helps the reader to enter the complexity of his work with greater ease. Both Marie-Louise von Franz and Edward Edinger have explicitly stated this goal in their works on alchemy. Specifically, von Franz's *Alchemy: An Introduction to the Symbolism and Psychology* (1980) and *Alchemical Active Imagination* (1979) serve as good introductory texts, as does Edinger's *Anatomy of the Psyche* (1985), as well as his other detailed studies which guide readers through Jung's most difficult works: *The Mystery of the Coniunctio: Alchemical Image of Individuation* (1994), *The Mysterium Lectures* (1995) and *The Aion Lectures: Exploring the Self in C.G. Jung's Aion* (1996a). In addition, Nathan Schwartz-Salant has compiled a work entitled *Jung on Alchemy* (1995) which, along with a scholarly introduction, contains carefully selected passages from Jung's major works.

Many Jungian analysts have written on and/or referenced Jung's work with important insights that lend themselves to understanding Jung's alchemical project. Andrew Samuels has dedicated a chapter of his book *The Plural Psyche* (1989) to helping others understand Jung's involvement with alchemy and to showing its relevance for current analytical theory and clinical application. David Holt's (1987–1988) article 'Alchemy: Jung and the historians of science' in *Harvest* provides a reference guide to the historical literature for those who have an interest in Jung's work in relation to the history of science and to scientific ideas. Holt has researched the important journal

Ambix, a periodical concerned with the history of chemistry and alchemy, which contains many responses to Jung's alchemical writings. Beverley Zabriskie (1996) has also addressed in her work the issue of the relationship of Jung's alchemy to modern science, particularly physics. The continuing importance of alchemy for current Jungian thinkers has been addressed by me in my edited book *Fire in the Stone: The Alchemy of Desire* (1997), which brings together a range of essays by Jungian analysts and scholars who have been inspired by the continuing vitality of the alchemical metaphor in their own work. Containing essays by James Hillman, Paul Kugler, Pat Berry, Don Kalsched, Lionel Corbett, Ron Schenk, Scott Churchill and myself, this collection can serve as introductory to the range of application of the alchemical metaphor. Finally, Murray Stein (1992) has produced a series of ten audiotapes entitled *Understanding the Meaning of Alchemy: Jung's Metaphor of the Transformative Process*, and Joseph Henderson (1987) has recorded a video on the alchemical text, *Splendor Solis*, with his commentary and discussion.

Beyond the references mentioned earlier, which survey the breadth of alchemy's application, there are a number of Jungian thinkers who have made contributions to the psychology of alchemy and who have addressed and elaborated specific alchemical themes. Each in his or her own way has been carrying on the work originally begun by Jung himself. It would be impossible within the scope of the present overview to include and elaborate every source or contribution from those who have applied Jung's theory to alchemy. However, a number of these contributors—including von Franz, Edinger, Hillman, Nathan Schwartz-Salant, Paul Kugler, Stanton Marlan, Jeffrey Raff, Walter Odajnyk, Hayao Kawai, Wolfgang Giegerich and Yasuhiro Tanaka—have been chosen to represent ideas that reflect a wide range of perspectives from classical application to contemporary revisionist themes. The work of these writers will therefore be more fully elaborated later in the text.

Many others have made important contributions, and their work can be pursued by readers interested in the particular themes of their writings as follows. Michael Fordham (1960) wrote about the relationship of analytical psychology to theory, alchemy, theology and mysticism. In 1967, Aniela Jaffé published an article entitled 'The influence of alchemy on the work of C.G. Jung'. Robert Grinnel's (1973) book *Alchemy in a Modern Woman* applied alchemy to a clinical case and followed its archetypal dynamics. In the same year, David Holt (1973) in 'Jung and Marx' continued his reflection on the importance of alchemy for understanding theory. Joe Henderson (1978) wrote on the 'Practical application of alchemical theory', which examines Solomon Trismosin's *Splendor Solis* and considers whether in theory or practice, we are 'always seeking to heal the split between Spirit and Matter' (Henderson 1978: 251), and in 2003, he and Dyane Sherwood published *Transformation of the Psyche: The Symbolic Alchemy of the Splendor Solis*. K.D. Newman (1981) in 'The riddle of the Vas Bene Clausum' amplified the idea of the closed container 'giving particular attention to the practical application it has for analytical psychotherapy' (Newman 1981: 239). Patrick McGoveran (1981) applied an alchemical model to a therapeutic milieu with psychotic borderline patients. Mario Jacoby (1984) in his book *The Analytic Encounter: Transference and Human Relationship* wrote about the application of alchemy to the analytic situation, focusing specifically on transference and erotic love. Barbara Stevens Sullivan (1989) in her book *Psychotherapy Grounded in the Feminine Principle* reflected on alchemy and the transference, as did Jean Kirsch (1995) in her paper 'Transference'—both adding important ideas about the nature of the dialectical relationship. Sullivan's particular contribution was to revise the masculine and feminine principles and to offer a renewed understanding of the *coniunctio*. Finally, Irene Gad (1999) published an introductory article on the continuing importance of alchemy entitled 'Alchemy: the language of the soul'.

Before going any further into the development of Jung's ideas about alchemy, it is important to turn to the origin of his engagement with alchemy.

Jung's discovery of alchemy

It is difficult to say precisely where the origin of an idea lies, but it is beyond doubt that Jung's engagement with alchemy was fundamental for the development of his mature psychological theory. The best description of Jung's early encounter with alchemy and his subsequent unfolding ideas about it comes from his autobiography, *Memories, Dreams, Reflections*.[1] In this work, it is evident that the role of his inner life—his images, dreams, visions and synchronistic experiences—was of paramount importance. These experiences were the *prima materia* of his scientific work, the 'fiery magma' out of which the goal of the work was to be crystallised and incorporated into a contemporary picture of the world.

Like the figure of Faust in Goethe's classic epic, Jung opened himself to the unconscious, out of which a radically new way of seeing emerged. This vision did not come easily and required an intense confrontation with the unconscious (1913–1917), which initiated him into a period of great uncertainty and isolation. In order to come to terms with his experiences, Jung began to draw mandalas (circular drawings) which he felt corresponded to the whole of his psyche actively at work. He did not know where the process was going, but felt the need to abandon himself to it. Over time, a sense of direction emerged, a path to a centre that seemed to have direction and aim, and to lead to a central and deeper structure of the personality. The existential recognition and articulation of this centre led Jung to postulate a structure of the psyche superordinate to the position of the *ego*, which he called the *Self*.

A number of Jung's dreams in the 1920s anticipated the receipt of a Taoist alchemical manuscript which would serve later to confirm his vision of the *Self* as the goal of psychic life. In 1928, Jung received a letter from

Richard Wilhelm asking if he would write a psychological commentary on a Chinese alchemical treatise, *The Secret of the Golden Flower*. This was Jung's first real and important contact with alchemy. This text gave further support to his developing idea of the *Self* and stirred him to become more acquainted with alchemical texts. He began a study of Western alchemy and soon obtained an important Latin treatise, *The Artis Auriferae Volumina Duo* (1593), containing a number of classical tracts on alchemy. Around that time, he remembered his crucial and now classic dream from 1926. At the end of this dream, he passed through some gates to a manor house and entered its courtyard. When he reached the middle of the courtyard, the gates flew shut. A peasant jumped down from a horse-drawn wagon and proclaimed, 'Now we are caught in the seventeenth century' (Jung 1963: 203). Jung connected this dream to alchemy, which had reached its height in that century, and concluded that he was meant to study alchemy from the ground up. This process of study absorbed Jung virtually for the rest of his life. For a long while before he found his way about in this labyrinth, and while studying another sixteenth-century text, the *Rosarium Philosophorum*, he noticed expressions that were used again and again. He attempted to decipher them, creating a lexicon of cross-references as if he were trying to solve the riddle of an unknown language. These studies convinced Jung of the parallels between alchemy and analytical psychology. He described this recognition in *Memories, Dreams, Reflections*:

> I had very soon seen that analytical psychology coincided in a most curious way with alchemy. The experiences of the alchemists were, in a sense, my experiences, and their world was my world. This was, of course, a momentous discovery: I had stumbled upon the historical counterpart of my psychology of the unconscious. The possibility of a comparison with alchemy, and the uninterrupted intellectual chain back to Gnosticism, gave substance to my psychology. When I pored over these old texts everything fell into place: the fantasy-images, the empirical material I had gathered in my practice, and the conclusions I had drawn from it. I now began to understand what these psychic contents meant when seen in historical perspective. My understanding of their typical character, which had already begun with my investigation of myths, was deepened. The primordial images and the nature of the archetype took a central place in my researches, and it became clear to me that without history there can be no psychology, and certainly no psychology of the unconscious.
>
> (Jung 1963: 205–206)

For Jung, a psychology of consciousness could be content with material from the personal life of the patient but, as soon as the processes went deeper and involved the unconscious, something else was needed. Working with the unconscious often required unusual decisions and the interpretation of dreams.

For Jung, this called for a source in addition to personal memories and associations, a contact with the 'objective psyche', Jung's term for psychic reality that goes beyond the limits of seeing psyche as simply a subjective phenomenon. Edinger's (1985) work *Anatomy of the Psyche: Alchemical Symbolism in Psychotherapy* is explicitly concerned with this point, and it is one of the reasons why alchemical images are so valuable, in so far as they give us an objective basis from which to interpret dreams and other unconscious material.

As Jung deepened his investigations, he came to realise that engaging the unconscious could bring about psychic change. His study of alchemy brought him to an understanding of the unconscious as a process, and he began to clarify his view that the psyche can be transformed in a positive way by the contact between the ego and the contents of the unconscious. This process of development can be seen in an individual's dreams and fantasies, and it leaves its mark on our collective lives in the various religious systems and their changing symbolic structures. Through a study of these collective transformation processes and through an understanding of alchemical symbolism, Jung arrived at the central concept of his psychology: the individuation process.

A vital part of Jung's work soon began to address a concern with the individual's worldview and thus the relationship of psychology and religion. He published these enquiries in his work *Psychology and Religion* (1937) and in a 'direct offshoot', *Paracelsica* (1942). Jung notes that the second essay in that book, 'Paracelsus as a spiritual phenomenon', is of particular importance. It was through this work on Paracelsus that Jung was finally led to discuss 'alchemy as a form of religious philosophy' (Jung 1962: 209). He took this up in his *Psychology and Alchemy* (1944) and thus felt that he had reached the ground that underlay his own experiences of the years 1913–1917. He noted that the process he had passed through corresponded to an alchemical transformation (Jung 1963: 209). It was a continuation of these thoughts that opened Jung further to the questions of religion and to his ongoing relationship to Christianity.

For Jung, the Christian message was of central importance for Western humankind, but it needed to be seen in a new light and in accord with the spirit of the times; otherwise, it would have no practical effect on human wholeness. He found many parallels between Christianity and alchemy and demonstrated a relationship between the dogma of the Trinity and the text of the Mass with the visions of Zosimos of Panopolis, a third-century Gnostic and alchemist. Jung's attempt to bring analytical psychology into relation with Christianity ultimately led to the question of Christ as a psychological figure. In *Psychology and Alchemy*, Jung (1944) demonstrated a parallel between Christ and the alchemist's notion of the 'lapis' or 'stone'. In the midst of these reflections, he had an important vision of a greenish/gold body of Christ. He felt that the image pointed to a central archetypal symbol and was the expression of the life spirit present in both man and inorganic nature. In this image, both are brought together in what amounts to an alchemical vision of Christ. Here, the Christ image is also the *filius macro cosmi*, the anthropos whose roots he saw in the Jewish tradition, on the one hand, and in the Egyptian Horus myth, on the other. This image was felt to animate the whole cosmos and was fundamental as an archetypal integration of spirit with matter, a conjunction that he felt was not adequately accomplished in Christianity (Jung 1963).

In the alchemical view, Christianity has saved humankind but not nature. Jung had critiqued Christianity for neglecting the body and 'the feminine' and, in so doing, ultimately devaluing 'nature'. Murray Stein takes up an extensive exploration of this issue in his book, *Jung's Treatment of Christianity* (1985). As noted earlier, the alchemist's dream was to save the world in its totality. Its *opus magnum* had two aims: the rescue of the human soul and the salvation of the cosmos. Alchemy with its emphasis on matter thus compensated for the lack in Christianity and held out the possibility of the further development of the religious psyche.

In *Aion*, Jung (1951) furthered his research, concerned now with the relationship of the Christ figure to psychology and to the structure of the Self. Here, he focused on the 'interplay between conscious and unconscious ... with the impact of the greater personality, the inner man, upon the life of every individual' (Jung 1963: 221). Jung noted that at the beginning of the Christian era, the ancient idea of the anthropos took possession of the people and that this archetype was then concretised in the Christ image. The image of God's own son stood opposed to the deified Augustus, ruler of the secular world, and represented hope and expectations that transcended the oppressive *Zeitgeist* of the times. In addition, Jung's aim was to demonstrate the full extent to which his psychology corresponded to alchemy or vice versa. He wanted to discover, side by side with religious questions, what special problems of psychotherapy were treated in the work of the alchemists.

Jung reflected on his earlier demonstration that the *coniunctio* in alchemy corresponded to the transference (1963: 212). This had already been taken up in *Psychology and Alchemy* (1944) and more particularly in his essay 'The psychology of the transference' (1946). In this essay, Jung established parallels between the alchemical process as seen in the illustrations of the *Rosarium Philosophorum* and the psychological problem of the opposites, transference and the *coniunctio*. A fuller treatment of these problems was taken up in Jung's final work, *Mysterium Coniunctionis* (1955–1956). In this work, he followed his original intention of representing the whole range of alchemy as a kind of 'psychology of alchemy', and as an 'alchemical basis for depth psychology' (Jung 1963: 221).

In *C. G. Jung Speaking*, Jung offered a synopsis of the alchemical process:

> This work is difficult and strewn with obstacles; the alchemical opus is dangerous. Right at the beginning you meet the "dragon," the chthonic spirit, the "devil" or, as the alchemists called it, the "blackness," the

nigredo, and this encounter produces suffering. "Matter" suffers right up to the final disappearance of the blackness; in psychological terms, the soul finds itself in the throes of melancholy, locked in a struggle with the "shadow." The mystery of the *coniunctio*, the central mystery of alchemy, aims precisely at the synthesis of the opposites, the assimilation of the blackness, the integration of the devil.... In the language of the alchemists, matter suffers until the *nigredo* disappears, when the "dawn" (*aurora*) will be announced by the "peacock's tail" (*cauda pavonis*) and a new day will break, the *leukosis* or *albedo*. But in this state of "whiteness" one does not *live* in the true sense of the word, it is a sort of abstract, ideal state. In order to make it come alive it must have "blood," it must have what the alchemists call the *rubedo*, the "redness" of life. Only the total experience of being can transform this ideal state of the *albedo* into a fully human mode of existence. Blood alone can reanimate a glorious state of consciousness in which the last trace of blackness is dissolved, in which the devil no longer has an autonomous existence but rejoins the profound unity of the psyche. Then the opus magnum is finished: the human soul is completed integrated [*sic*].

(Jung, quoted in McGuire and Hull 1977: 228–229)

At the conclusion of his work, Jung's imagination was captured by the ideas and metaphors of alchemy, with its dragons, suffering matter, peacock's tail, alembics and athanors; its red and green lions, kings and queens, fishes' eyes and inverted philosophical trees, salamanders and hermaphrodites; its black suns and white earth, and its metals—lead, silver and gold; its colours—black, white, yellow and red; and its distillations and coagulations, and rich array of Latin terms. All became the best possible expression of a psychic mystery as yet unknown which enunciated and amplified his maturing vision of the parallels between alchemy and his own psychology of the unconscious. All this and far more Jung saw as projected by the alchemists into matter. Their effort was to bring about unity from the disparate parts of the psyche, creating a 'chemical wedding'. This Jung saw as the moral task of alchemy: to unify the disparate elements of the soul, both personal and ultimately cosmic, and thus to create the goal, the lapis or philosopher's stone. Likewise, Jung's psychology works with the conflicts and dissociation of psychic life and attempts to bring about the mysterious 'unification' he called Wholeness.

Finally, with his *Mysterium Coniunctionis* (1955–1956), Jung noted that his psychology was at last 'given its place in reality and established on its historical foundations' (Jung 1962: 221). Thus, his task was finished. He felt that he had reached 'the bounds of scientific understanding, the transcendental, the nature of the archetype per se, concerning which no further scientific statement can be made' (1962: 221).

Classical development of Jung's ideas

The power of Jung's ideas strongly influenced his close followers, Marie-Louise von Franz (1915–1988) in Europe and Edward Edinger (1922–1998) in the United States. Both von Franz and Edinger held Jung's work to be fundamental and viewed themselves primarily as elaborators of his ideas, and as commentators who gave students easier access to the work of the master. These rather humble self-assessments do not adequately represent the extent to which their own contributions have extended and contributed to the field of analytical psychology and especially to our understanding of alchemy.

Von Franz has been considered to be the primary developer of Jung's alchemical legacy. She 'became world renowned among followers of Jung and after his death was an eloquent spokesperson for his ideas' (Kirsch 2000: 11). Von Franz met Jung when she was 18 years old in 1933, just around the time Jung's interest in alchemy was catalysing. He analysed her in exchange for her work on translations of texts from Greek and Latin. She continued as a close collaborator and eventually published what was in essence the third part of the *Mysterium Coniunctionis* called *The Aurora Consurgens* (1966). The *Aurora* is an account of and commentary on an alchemical text that dated roughly from the thirteenth century. The text has been ascribed to Thomas Aquinas, though its authorship is disputed. Jung chose this text as exemplary of medieval Christianity's attempt to come to terms with alchemical philosophy and as an instance of the alchemical problem of the opposites. Von Franz's (1966) commentary shows how Jung's analytical psychology may be used as a key to unlock the meaning of this difficult and very psychological text, and how the traditional practice of alchemy is best understood as a symbolic process.

Von Franz extended her work on alchemy through lectures to students at the Jung Institute in Zurich in 1959. These lectures were transcribed by Una Thomas, a member of the seminar, and published in 1980 under the title *Alchemy: An Introduction to the Symbolism and the Psychology*. The book was designed to be an introduction to Jung's more difficult study and is a 'practical account of what the alchemists were really looking for—emotional balance and wholeness' (Von Franz 1980). The text contains lectures on old Greek and Arabic alchemy as well as on later European alchemy and *The Aurora Consurgens*. In giving her course and publishing this book, von Franz hoped to enable students to read Jung with more comprehension. She recognised how dark and difficult his alchemical writings were and that even many of his closest students could not follow his work in this area. Nevertheless, she stressed the importance of this work. Her lectures continued in Zurich in January and February of 1969, and her book *Alchemical Active Imagination* was published in 1979. In addition to a short history of alchemy, von Franz concentrated on Gerhard Dorn, an alchemist and physician who lived probably in the sixteenth century. Following his work as a whole, and staying close to the original, she showed the similarity between the alchemist's practice and Jung's technique of active imagination, both of which promote a dialogue with the unconscious.

Von Franz's last direct work on alchemy is a historical introduction and psychological commentary on an Arabic alchemical text, *Hall ar-Rumuz*, or *Clearing of Enigmas*, alternatively translated *The Explanation of Symbols*, which was eventually published as *Corpus Alchemicum Arabicum: Book of the Explanation of the Symbols Kitab Hall ar-Rumuz* (2006). This text is attributed to Muhammad ibn Umail ('Senior'), who lived in the tenth century AD. Abt is in possession of a valuable collection of additional Arabic manuscripts, some of which have been published. These Arabic manuscripts represent the missing link within the mystical branch of alchemy, connecting Gnostic-Hermetic Greek alchemy to the mystical Latin alchemy of Europe.

Over the course of her long life, von Franz also contributed to the history of alchemy, the dialogue of alchemy with Christianity and the importance of a symbolic and psychological approach. She also furthered our thinking about the alchemical problem of the opposites and our understanding of the *Unus Mundus*, the unified field upon which the opposites rely. These themes are further elaborated in her book *Psyche and Matter* (1992). In it, she brings together reflections on number, time, synchronicity and the relationship between depth psychology, contemporary physics and quantum theory. She has also contributed to Jung's view of Christianity and an understanding of the importance of alchemy as a religious contribution to the Christian myth. In an interview (Wagner 1998), when asked what the main value was of Jung's and her own work on alchemy, she stated that:

> civilization needs a myth to live ... And I think that the Christian myth, on which we have lived, has degenerated and become one-sided and insufficient. I think alchemy is the complete myth. If our Western civilization has a possibility of survival, it would be by accepting the alchemical myth, which is a richer completion and continuation of the Christian myth ... The Christian myth is deficient in not including enough of the feminine. (Catholicism has the Virgin Mary, but it's only the purified feminine; it does not include the dark feminine). Christianity treats matter as dead and does not face the problem of the opposites—of evil. Alchemy faces the problem of the opposites, faces the problem of matter, and faces the problem of the feminine.
> (Marie-Louise von Franz, quoted in Wagner 1998: 15–16)

If von Franz can be considered to be the pre-eminent follower of Jung's in Europe, few would argue against the same status for Edward Edinger in the United States. For more than 40 years, 'in lectures, books, tapes and videos, he masterfully presented and distilled the essence of Jung's work, illuminating its relevance for both collective and individual psychology' (Sharp 1999: 18). Though Edinger wrote on a wide range of topics, including Moby Dick, Faust, Greek Philosophy, The Bible, the Apocalypse and the God image,[2] like von Franz, he had a special passion for alchemy. In the first issue of *Quadrant* (spring 1968), the New York Institute announced its final spring series of lectures by Edinger entitled 'Psychotherapy and alchemy', and the following issue contained a précis of Edinger's lectures by Gladys Taylor entitled 'Alchemy as a psychological process' (*Quadrant*, No. 2: 18–22). These lectures, given in New York and Los Angeles in the late 1970s and early 1980s, were serially published in *Quadrant, Journal of the C.G. Jung Foundation for Analytical Psychology*,[3] and were later collected for his book *Anatomy of the Psyche: Alchemical Symbolism in Psychotherapy* (1985). In these lectures and his book, Edinger focused on seven selected images, which he used to organise the typical stages of the alchemical process: *calcinatio, solutio, coagulatio, sublimatio, mortificatio, separatio* and *coniunctio*. By focusing on these images/operations, Edinger (1985: 14) attempts to bring order to 'the chaos of alchemy'. Each of these operations is found to be the centre of an elaborate symbol system. These central symbols of transformation 'provide basic categories by which to understand the life of the psyche, and they illustrate almost the full range of experiences that constitute individuation' (Edinger 1985: 15; cf. Robertson 1999: 54).

In his work, Edinger views Jung's discovery of the 'reality of the psyche' as a new approach to understanding alchemy and other pre- or pseudosciences such as astrology. For Edinger, these systems of thought are expressions of a phenomenology that can serve to illustrate patterns and regularities of the objective psyche. As such, they serve as archetypal images of transformation. What Edinger considers himself and Jung as presenting are psychic facts rather than 'theoretical constructs or philosophical speculations' (Edinger 1985: preface).

Edinger was also concerned with the practical problems of psychotherapy. His goal was to become familiar enough with archetypal images and to have sufficient enough knowledge drawn from personal analysis that we can discover an anatomy of the psyche, as 'objective as the anatomy of the body' (1985: preface). He contends that psychological theories are often too narrow and inadequate, and that when analysis goes deep, things are set in motion which are mysterious and profound. It is easy for both therapist and patient to lose their way. According to Edinger:

> What makes alchemy so valuable for psychotherapy is that its images concretize the experiences of transformation that one undergoes in psychotherapy. Taken as a whole, alchemy provides a kind of anatomy of individuation. Its images will be most meaningful ... to those who have had a personal experience of the unconscious.
>
> (Edinger 1985: 2)

For him, as for Jung, the work of alchemy can be equated with the individuation process, but the alchemical corpus exceeds any individual's process in richness and scope. In the end, for Edinger, alchemy was considered to be a sacred work, one that required a religious attitude; and like von Franz, he saw Jung's work in alchemy as a development of the Christian myth.

Edinger's examination of Jung's work on alchemy continued with a number of texts carefully devoted to explicating it. While the *Anatomy of the Psyche* (1985) is an overall look at alchemical processes and the symbolism of the individuation process, Edinger's further reflections focus on particular works of Jung in order to give us further access to and help in understanding them. In 1994, he published *The Mystery of Coniunctio: Alchemical Image of Individuation*. It contains both an introduction to Jung's *Mysterium Coniunctionis* and an essay on the psychological interpretation of the *Rosarium* pictures. These essays were first presented as lectures at the C.G. Jung Institute of San Francisco during 19–20 October 1984. In this work, Edinger takes a somewhat different stance from Jung, suggesting other ways to look at the pictures of the *Rosarium*. He does not oppose Jung's interpretations but suggests that the images have multiple facets, meanings and contexts in which they can be seen.

In 1995, Edinger published *The Mysterium Lectures* based on a course he gave to members of the Jung Society of Los Angeles during 1986–1987. In this text, he leads his readers through Jung's most difficult work. He follows his fundamental metaphor of the anatomy of the psyche, suggesting that this is a book of facts described in 'images'. He selects the major images throughout the *Mysterium* and elaborates them with amplificatory material and commentary. Edinger had the capacity to take difficult symbolic material and to translate it into clear, contemporary psychological statements, making it possible to integrate the material into our current psychological worldview.

In 1996, Edinger continued his elaboration of Jung's difficult work in *The Aion Lectures: Exploring the Self in C.G. Jung's Aion*. Here, he again worked through Jung's text, suggesting that the reader not approach it with a linear attitude. He stressed that Jung's way of thinking and writing is better understood as presentational and as a kind of 'cluster thinking', likening it to the way a dream presents itself. *Aion* examines the notion of the God image of Christianity and Jung's complex reflections on the archetype of the Self. These concerns are amplified in a number of his other commentaries and books beyond the scope of alchemy proper.

Innovations, criticism and developments

If von Franz and Edinger were major classical disciples of Jung's work, James Hillman is a major critic and innovator in his own right. From one perspective, Hillman fundamentally revised Jung's thoughts, but from another he returns to its radical essence, carrying its implications to a new level. His first organised attempts to present his alchemical reflections were in lectures given at the Zurich Institute in 1966. He states that he had been drawn by alchemy's 'obscure poetic language and strange images, and by its amazing insights especially in Jung's introduction to *The Secret of the Golden Flower* (Wilhelm 1931) and [in his essay on] "The philosophical tree"' (Hillman 2003: 101). Later, in 1968, while at the University of Chicago, Hillman continued his lectures and 'expanded [his] library research and collection of dreams with alchemical motifs' (Hillman 2003: 101). These lectures were given in an old wooden chemistry hall and entitled 'Analytic work – alchemical opus'. His approach in these lectures was 'to exhibit a background to analytical work that is metaphorical, even preposterous and so, less encumbered by clinical literalism' (Hillman 2003: 102). This theme had run through Hillman's papers on alchemical themes beginning in his 1970 publication 'On senex consciousness'. In 1978, Hillman published 'The therapeutic value of alchemical language' which set the stage for his continuing reflections. What followed was a series of papers: 'Silver and the white earth', parts 1 and 2 (Hillman 1980, 1981a), 'Alchemical blue and the *unio Mentalis*' (1981b), 'The imagination of air and the collapse of alchemy' (1981c), 'Salt: a chapter on alchemical psychology' (1981d), 'Notes on white supremacy: the alchemy of racism' (1986), 'The yellowing of the work' (1989a), 'Concerning the stone: alchemical images of the goal' (1993), 'The seduction of black' (1997) and 'The azure vault: the caelum as experience' (2004), a revision and elaboration of his paper on alchemical blue. Like alchemical texts themselves, the content of these papers is complex and difficult to summarise in any unified narrative, but if there are any themes that run through them, it is in his turn to the nuances of language and image, the importance of the imagination and attention to alchemical aesthetics, and to colour as an organising focus for reflection. Hillman continued to revise and add to his reflections and in 2010 published *Alchemical Psychology*, a book that integrates and expands his vision. For Hillman, images speak more directly when their metaphysical coverings can be set aside, then the

> level of collective consciousness can be peeled away, so that the material may speak more phenomenally. Then pagan images stand out: metals, planets, minerals, stars, plants, charms, animals, vessels, fires, and specific locales.
>
> (Hillman 2003: 102)

For Hillman, these alchemical images have been obscured by both Jung's psychology as well as its association with Christian metaphysics. He explained this awareness to the International Congress in Rome in 1977, noting that 'while Jung reclaimed alchemy for the psyche, he also claimed it for his psychology' (Hillman 2003: 102) and that its 'liberation of alchemy from the former traps (mysticism, charlatanism, and pre- or pseudoscience) entangled it in his system of opposites and Christian symbols and thought' (Hillman 2003: 102).

Jung's metapsychology and his reliance on Christian imagery led Hillman to make a distinction between an 'alchemy of spirit' and an 'alchemy of soul', and he noted that the transformation of the psyche can be distinguished from the Christian idea of redemption. He stated that when we make this distinction, then

> the subtle changes in color, heat, bodily forms and other qualities refer to the psyche's processes, useful to the practice of therapy for reflecting the changes going on in the psyche without linking these changes to a progressive program or redemptive vision.
>
> (Hillman 2003: 103)

In short, alchemy's curious images and sayings are valuable not so much because alchemy is a grand narrative of the stages of individuation and its conjunction of opposites, nor for its reflection on the Christian process of redemption, but 'rather because of alchemy's myriad, cryptic, arcane, paradoxical, and mainly conflicting texts [which] reveal the psyche phenomenally' (Hillman 2003: 103).

For Hillman, alchemy needs to be encountered with the 'least possible intrusion of metaphysics' (2003: 103). He saw Jung, von Franz and Edinger as informed consciously or unconsciously by a metaphysical attitude and attempted to examine alchemy in a scholarly manner in order to find objective meaning. He, on the other hand, saw himself as emphasising the 'matters' of alchemy as metaphorical substances and archetypal principles. He sought to activate alchemical language and images finding those qualities of human life which act on the very substance of personality.

> The work of soul-making requires corrosive acids, heavy earth, ascending birds; there are sweating kings, dogs, and bitches, stenches, urine, and blood ... I know that I am not composed of sulfur and salt, buried in horse dung, putrefying or congealing, turning white or green or yellow, encircled by a tail-biting serpent, rising on wings. And yet I am! I cannot take any of this literally, even if it is all accurate, descriptively true.
>
> (Hillman 1978: 37 and 39)

For Hillman, such passages resonate with the complex experiences of the soul. While Jung, von Franz and Edinger worked to develop and extend a 'psychology of alchemy', Hillman made a critical and innovative move and stylistic shift. His intention was less to extend a psychology of alchemy than to develop an alchemical way of psychologising and to restore an alchemical way of imagining. As noted, this alchemical psychology focuses on images and is highly sensitive to language. On the one hand, he didn't want to reduce alchemical metaphors to generalised abstractions, while on the other hand, he wanted to re-materialise our concepts, 'giving them body, sense and weight' (ibid.: 39).

Among those analysts most influenced by Hillman's work are Paul Kugler (1983) and myself (Marlan 1995). Kugler, picking up on Hillman's attention to language and his poetic metaphors in *The Dream and the Underworld* (1979), engages these metaphors through a careful attention to linguistics in his own book *The Alchemy of Discourse: An Archetypal Approach to Language* (1983). In this text, he integrates Jung's early research in his word association experiments with his later focus on the psychology of alchemy. He analyses the role language plays in the alchemical process of deliteralising matter, asking what is actually involved in the deliteralising of substance and notes that the process is similar to that of moving from an objective to a subjective level of interpretation (Kugler, personal communication, 13 March 2001). This movement from matter to soul is made possible by the inherent polysemy of sound patterns, which have multiple objects of reference, and allow interpretation to move back and forth between their implicit meanings. For Kugler, the acoustic image is the crucial intersection between external and internal, between the literal and the metaphoric. 'While the alchemists were working on the soul in matter they were simultaneously working on the "matters" of their soul' (ibid.). Alchemy thus works through the inherent polysemy of the phonetic patterns. In his book, Kugler demonstrates how through the acquisition of language we are separated from the external material world of reference and initiated into a shared archetypal system of meaning relations. The acquisition of language enabled man to take 'matters' out of life and transform them into imagination. Shifting the linguistic mode from semantic to phonetic consideration transforms the material of the 'day world' (objects of reference) into the insubstantial poetic images of the 'night world' (image—meanings).

Likewise influenced by Hillman, I have edited two books on the subject, *Salt and the Alchemical Soul* (Marlan 1995) and *Fire in the Stone: The Alchemy of Desire* (1997). The inspiration for the first book was Hillman's (1981d) essay 'Salt: a chapter in alchemical psychology'.[4] The goal of the work was an exercise in reflection on the image of salt, which has had a place in the history of depth psychology and in alchemy. In this work, a range of genres of depth psychology were explored, including a Freudian, a Jungian and a Hillmanian approach to the subject. The intention was not so much to juxtapose perspectives in order to find the right or best approach, but to appreciate the particular genius of each author. While this is true, the flavour of this approach draws heavily from the phenomenological/postmodern and archetypal perspectives in its sensitivity to a variety of perspectives and in its attempt to 'restore psychology to its widest, richest, and deepest volume, so that it would resonate with soul' (Hillman 1989b: 26). The second edited book (Marlan 1997b), *Fire in the Stone: The Alchemy of Desire*, was inspired by the continuing vitality of the alchemical metaphor. In my essay, 'Fire in the stone: an inquiry into the alchemy of soul-making' (Marlan 1997a),[5] the focus is on the psyche's intentionality and its complexity, emphasising its often conflicting and multiple intentionalities and reflecting on Hillman's (1983) question 'what does soul want?' My reflections on this question led to the metaphor of the 'alchemy of desire', which problematises any simple understanding of subjectivity and shifts the concern to a broader view of the dynamism of the soul. The essay seeks to look again at the soul's complexity and the danger of essentialism in psychological theory. It brings to bear the reflections of Hillman and Jacques Derrida, showing a relationship between their approaches, in so far as they share the medium of fictional space and articulate a postmodern voice. Both Hillman and Derrida revise our understanding of fiction and destabilise a literal understanding of psychological theory.

The complexity of the soul is not adequately understood by any of the forms of logocentrism but belong to a wider field of psyche (Hillman) or signs (Derrida). In this field, the hard and fast boundaries of the ego are progressively loosened. The essay goes on to reflect on the goal of both depth psychology and the opus of alchemy. The enquiry follows postmodern and archetypal sensibilities along the lines of Hillman's revisioning of the traditional concepts of telos and the goal, and opens a notion of fictional space in which an alchemy of desire is enacted, where we can 'speak meaningfully of a multiplicity of intentions in the play of desire, of a dialectic of desire in which … complex intentionalities encounter one another'. The alchemy of desire is 'a subtle field of traces, exchanges, and fictional enactments' from which 'we can develop an ear to the soul's desire' (Marlan 1997a: 14). This field of desire then articulates a shared psychological space opened by postmodernism and archetypal psychology.

Schwartz-Salant's *The Mystery of the Human Relationship* (1998) is both a theoretical and clinical contribution to the Jungian literature. His reflections bear on the philosophical foundation of Jungian analysis as well as on its clinical practice, on transference and beyond to human relationships in general. Schwartz-Salant (personal communication, 2000) notes that Jung employed alchemical symbolism to amplify his theory of the individuation process, and dealt with alchemical imagery from the point of view of projection. Projection as an idea requires a number of philosophical and metapsychological presuppositions which are taken for granted by classical analysts such as von Franz and Edinger. Going beyond these assumptions requires a fundamental shift in metapsychology if not ontology and it is this kind of shift that Schwartz-Salant intends to bring about. Rather than beginning with the idea of two separate individuals relating to one another, he emphasises an 'intermediate realm' between people in relationships as well as gives attention to the field between subject and object, mind and matter, psyche and body. His contribution is to focus on and deepen our understanding of this field as something more than an intersubjective event as it is often described in contemporary psychoanalysis (Schwartz-Salant, personal communication, 2000).

It is in his emphasis on the experiential rather than the causal relatedness of the alchemist and his or her work, and in an encouragement of the engagement with one's 'mad parts' and those of patients that Schwartz-Salant feels he goes beyond Jung (Schwartz-Salant, personal communication, 2000). He summarises his contribution as follows. He starts by noting that Jung employed alchemical symbolism to amplify his theory of individuation and that, in the process, he dealt with alchemical imagery from the point of view of projection, in other words, from the point of view that reified the subject–object dichotomy. Schwartz-Salant argues that this dualistic framework does not adequately capture the complexity of original alchemical imagery because this imagery is the 'residue of centuries of experiences that do not always, or even primarily, fit into an "inside-outside"' structure. To this end, he developed the idea of the interactive field, and in so doing he brings to bear 'correspondence theory, archetypal theory and subtle body theory' (Schwartz-Salant, personal communication, 2000). In addition, he draws on the phenomenologists Edmund Husserl and Maurice Merleau-Ponty as well as Jean Gebser and Henry Corbin, all who have contributed to understanding this realm (ibid.). For these thinkers, our traditional Cartesian understanding of an observing ego stands in the way of a deeper experiential awareness of what the alchemists were speaking about. Schwartz-Salant wants to capture this experience, which goes beyond a rational discursive approach and requires a kind of 'aperspectival consciousness' (ibid.).

Schwartz-Salant's continuing reflection on the human relationship led him to reimagine the model of transference found in Jung's 'Psychology of the Transference'. He was also the first one to analyse all 20 pictures of the *Rosarium*, the interpretation of which translates well to his field approach. Schwartz-Salant's work opened the door for a comparative psychoanalytic reflection showing how, for instance, what Kleinian analysts call projective identification can be seen more profoundly as the phenomenology of the field manifesting in a consciousness attuned to projection and causality (Schwartz-Salant, personal communication, 2000). This shows how the field is primary and how projective identification could be seen as part of alchemical imagery. He notes that from this perspective, one can see that Jung was working on the same issues as Melanie Klein. Beyond this, he has used alchemical texts to understand transformations in the field. Rather than seeing the field as an intersubjective product (Self-psychologists, Ogden, interpersonal approaches, etc.), he saw it like an actual field in physics, i.e. something with its own processes. That is why he used the term 'interactive'. In reimagining human relationships and the transference, and in encouraging an experiential entry into the interactive field, Schwartz-Salant goes beyond Jung.

Zabriskie in her own way but like Schwartz-Salant writes that her study of alchemy and its antecedents in Egyptian mythology have informed her 'understanding and approach to the psyche as a process capable of transformation and of its images in the dynamic interrelationships to each other and to the psychic "field" constellated around and within an individual' (personal communication, 2000). Zabriskie is also concerned with the relationship of this field to the issues of contemporary physics, and writes that the most compelling vector and amplification of the alchemical world has come from the 'themes and models of modern physics' (ibid.). She states that she came to this through studying the relationships between Jung and the Nobel physicist Wolfgang Pauli. This interest led to her paper 'Jung and Pauli: a subtle asymmetry' (1995a) and to her introduction in *Atom and Archetype: The Pauli/Jung Letters, 1932–1958* (2001). Zabriskie's other interest was in following Jung's study of the alchemist's hypothesis of the relation between the psychic and material dimensions and she wrote a review of von Franz's (1992) *Psyche and Matter* entitled 'The matter of psyche' (Zabriskie 1996). In addition, she is interested in the clinical and cultural contextualisation of alchemical imagery as in her 'Exiles and orphans: Jung, Paracelsus and the healing images of alchemy' (1995b) and 'Fermentation in Jung's alchemy' (1996). In the latter paper, she questioned why Jung inserted the eleventh engraving of an edition of the *Rosarium* between the fifth and sixth images and speculated on the philosophical and clinical values of this (Zabriskie, personal communication, 2000).

The question of Jung's relationship to contemporary clinical psychoanalysis was brought up by Andrew Samuels (1989). It was his concern to present Jung as a credible thinker in the mainstream of analytic discourse and his work as a reliable base for further contributions to analysis (Samuels 1989: 175). For Samuels, this concern requires some understanding of why Jung gave so much intellectual effort to a subject considered by many to be pejoratively mystical if not absurd. Samuels counters this judgement by pointing out that alchemy provides important if not central metaphors for psychological activity and that its imagery is well suited

> to capture the almost impossible essence of analysis or any other deep human condition; the play between interpersonal relatedness on the one hand and imaginal, intrapsychic activity on the other.
> (Samuels 1989: 176)

Samuels goes on to explore the fecundity of alchemical metaphors as a unique way of imagining psychological processes and their clinical application. To accomplish this, he, like many other Jungians, reflects on Jung's (1946) paper, 'Psychology of the transference', and elaborates how it is that Jung found in the obscure images of the *Rosarium Philosophorum* an important analogue of the archetypal level of experience. While Jung addressed the archetypal conceptions of the transference, Samuels noted that he also discussed its personal aspects. Thus for him, Jung contributed something new to the field that had not been picked up before as well as ideas that were later to become standard contemporary themes of psychoanalysis.[6]

Analysts have often split over the extent to which they feel that Jung should be understood in the tradition of psychoanalysis. Jeffrey Raff is one who would rather place Jung in the context of a larger spiritual perspective. In his book *Jung and the Alchemical Imagination* (2000), he picks up, renews and extends the classical tradition of Jung and von Franz. He sees alchemy as an expression of a long esoteric spiritual tradition of which Jung's work is a contemporary expression. Raff finds three major components of Jung's work important in extending this tradition of 'Jungian spirituality'. These are 'the transcendent function, active imagination, and the self' (Raff, personal communication, 2000). He is not so much interested in psychological interpretation as in 'developing a model for inner exploration and transformation'; and this is what, he feels, primarily connects him to the von Franz tradition (ibid.).

Like Hillman, but with very different conclusions, Raff puts special emphasis on the imagination and the nature of alchemy as an imaginal experience; and also like Hillman, he links imagination to the Sufi concept of an intermediate realm. He also emphasises the nature and development of inner figures that personify the unconscious and may be worked with in active imagination. Working with these figures moves psyche towards the manifestation of the Self, the classical goal of the individuation process. Up to this point, Raff is a 'very mainstream classical analyst though [he] emphasize[s] the inner figures more than is usual and also place[s] an extreme importance on active imagination' (ibid.).

Where Raff departs from Jung is in stating that Jung did not appreciate what the alchemists Dorn spoke about as a third *Coniunctio*, which is a union with the *unus mundus*. For Raff, Jung's work stopped with his interpretation of the second *Coniunctio*, which is the corporal union and 'which [he] interpret[s] as the point at which the Self comes fully alive within the psyche and begins to function more powerfully' (ibid.). Raff believes that Jung did not go far enough 'because of his bias that all is contained within the psyche' (ibid.). For Raff, the third *Coniunctio* occurs when the manifested Self, or the 'individuated' person, goes beyond the psyche to face the transpsychic world of the spirit (ibid.).

Though Jung intuited what he considered to be a metaphysical realm, he always claimed not to be a metaphysician and remained an empiricist. Raff, on the other hand, following the Sufi alchemists, argues that alchemy is really about the transpsychic world, the world of the Gnostic imagination. To access these spiritual dimensions, one must go beyond ordinary active imagination to enter what Raff considers the psychoid realm. In this state, body and spirit are one and spiritual beings manifest as psychoidal figures (ibid.). The most important of these figures he calls the Self of the psychoid or 'the ally', which is a personification of God. This figure is individually experienced as transcendental and not part of the psyche. For Raff, the alchemy of the psychoid is about the 'interaction of human awareness and feeling with spiritual entities that have taken on form in the psychoid world' (ibid.).

In his book, Raff talks about the third *coniunctio* as union of self and ally, and the inclusion of transpsychic forces as part of our worldview. On a personal note, he states that to his knowledge, no one has written about the ally in this way nor studied the third *coniunctio*. Hence, he feels that he differs from others in emphasising the spiritual nature of Jung's work and in putting less emphasis on clinical work or psychological interpretation. Raff extends his model to include the psychoid world as the place where spiritual entities manifest and take on form. For Raff, in the higher states of development, the human and divine worlds come together and one can imagine in this the Western equivalent of enlightenment.

Walter Odajnyk (1993) also takes up the theme of the spiritual importance of Jung's alchemical work in his book, *Gathering the Light: A Psychology of Meditation*. Odajnyk's focus is on the importance of the meditative tradition, which he feels has not been given adequate importance in serious psychological reflections. Thus, he turns to the East and to the psychological contributions that Jung has made to our understanding and appreciation of Eastern religious thought and practice. Throughout his book, he 'sought to demonstrate and, where necessary, to apply and extend, Jung's contribution to an understanding of psychology of meditation' (Odajnyk 1993: 166).

Odajnyk returns to Jung's commentary on *The Secret of the Golden Flower* (Wilhelm 1931) and thus also to the relationship between meditation and alchemy. He notes that while Western alchemy is more differentiated in its description of the earlier stages of development, the Eastern tradition is more developed in its description of its final goals. To develop this insight, Odajnyk takes up Jung's discussion of the *coniunctio*, as described in *Mysterium Coniunctionis*, and compares it to the goal of psycho-spiritual transformation in meditation. Odajnyk states that Jung had the tendency to lump together many images relating to the goal of the alchemical process, while for him there are many distinctions between these images which may refer to a further differentiation of the goal. In addition, there do not seem to be Western equivalents to certain descriptions found in Eastern alchemy. Jung concludes that psychic wholeness will never be attained empirically, but for Odajnyk, further acquaintance with Eastern alchemy and meditation practices raises the possibility of the actual psychological experience of these higher goals as taking place in what he has termed 'the meditation complex'. An additional amplification of this theme is taken up in Harold Coward's (1985) book, *Jung and Eastern Thought*, which also critiqued Jung for not going far enough. Coward (1985: 142) raises the question 'if there can be mystical experience without an individual ego?'

For Odajnyk (1993), this meditation complex is a way of seeing the new psychological and energetic field, and it is this perspective that forms a ground for innovative ways of interpreting Jung's ideas. In addition, this perspective lends itself to the consideration that apart from Jung's idea of the goal of wholeness, we can now also reconsider the idea of self-realisation and enlightenment. Besides his comparison of the Eastern and Western notions of the *coniunctio* and his introduction of the meditation complex, Odajnyk's assessment of Thomas Cleary's work is noteworthy. Cleary (1991) critiqued both Wilhelm's translation of *The Secret of the Golden Flower* and Jung's commentary of it (see Cleary 1991; Odajnyk 1993: 191–212).

The theme of Taoist alchemy is also addressed in my paper, 'The metaphor of light and renewal in Taoist alchemy and Jungian analysis' (Marlan 2001).[7] In this work, I noted that light and renewal are important if not fundamental metaphors in both Taoist alchemy and Jungian analysis, and the use of this metaphor is traced in the classical alchemical work, *The Secret of the Golden Flower*, mentioned earlier. In focusing on the metaphor of light and renewal in the two traditions, the relationship between analysis and spiritual discipline is addressed and a comparison is made between the images of 'turning the light around' and 'the emergence of the spiritual embryo', as well as further reflection on the unity of opposites or the *coniunctio*, themes important to both Taoist alchemy and Jungian analysis.

I continue a reflection on the theme of the metaphor of light in my paper 'The metaphor of light and its deconstruction in Jung's alchemical vision' (Marlan 2000a),[8] in which the interrelationship of light and consciousness and their privileged place in the development of Western metaphysics is challenged—by Jungian thought, archetypal psychology, postmodern theory, Eastern thought and alchemy—with the conclusion that consciousness and vision also have a shadow. A new understanding of light and its relation with darkness is essential for the development of consciousness in our time.

Reflections on this theme are deepened in 'The black sun: archetypal image of the non-self' (Marlan 2000b)[9] and in *The black sun: the alchemy and art of darkness* (Marlan 2005). The Black Sun, *Sol Niger*, is considered an archetypal phenomenon having two poles and multiple differentiations. At one end, the non-self can be seen in its most literal form, locked into the *nigredo* and mortification of the flesh, while its other pole opens the soul to the dark shine of sacred illumination.

Continued reflection of alchemy and Eastern thought is also taken up by Japanese analyst Hayao Kawai (1996) in *Buddhism and the Art of Psychotherapy*. In his book, Professor Kawai compares the classic series of

Ox Herding pictures with illustrations from the *Rosarium Philosophorum* (1996: 52). He notes that both sets of pictures illustrate the individuation process but while there are 'mysterious similarities' between them, he also sees important differences. For him, comparing these images amounts to contrasting Eastern and Western styles of consciousness. (He agrees with the conclusion of Marvin Spiegelman [Spiegelman and Miyuki 1985] who analyses the same sets of images.) Kawai notes that in the West, there is a tendency to emphasise a linear, developmental, goal-oriented tendency, while in the East, there is a leaning towards seeing the process as circular, archetypal and infinite. Likewise in the West, emphasis is placed on the individual person, while the East tends to focus on nature. These styles of consciousness are important with regard to how we see both the individuation and alchemical processes. It is possible to view these processes from either style of consciousness.

Kawai is masterful at resisting the temptation to simply fall into either perspective concluding that when working with a patient, it is necessary to be able to see from both orientations, with and without stages. For Kawai, it is important to carry and accept the paradox. In this way, the human person and nature can work in harmony. In concluding, Kawai, himself, ends with such a paradox. He reflects on the question of whether or not it is possible to integrate two orientations, linear/circular and developmental/archetypal, male and female, East and West, and concludes that it is both possible and impossible (Kawai 1996: 141). One is tempted to say that his orientation is typically Eastern, and perhaps comes more out of the recognition of the female principle than of the West's demands for either/or logos. But I believe that this would simply fall back into what Kawai deconstructs. His acute observation about the role of contemporary Japanese women in traditional society is a case in point. The soul's alchemy refuses to rigidify into traditional categories.

Wolfgang Giegerich's book *The Soul's Logical Life* (1998/2001) contains an important critical view of Jung's approach to alchemy. Giegerich elaborates both what he feels were Jung's contributions and where he feels Jung did not go far enough (Giegerich, personal communication, 2000). Reflecting on Jung's position, Giegerich acknowledges Jung's accomplishment in the discovery of alchemy as a basis for his depth psychology. He notes that using alchemy as a model had important and interrelated methodological advancements. Given this appreciation for Jung's contribution, Giegerich is nevertheless critical about some dimensions of Jung's alchemical conceptions. For him, as noted, but in a way different from others before him, Jung did not go far enough. Alchemy entered Jung's psychology only as a topic or content:

> while trying to hold the structure of psychology itself down in the total incompatible character of a modern science (the neutral empirical

observer standpoint). Its semantic content was not allowed to come home to (affect, infect) the logical or syntactical form of psychology.
(Giegerich, personal communication, 2000)

What Giegerich critiques is that Jung's scientific/modernist metapsychology seems to remain the same, maintaining a subject/object split, while at the same time making an object of alchemical ideas that themselves do not fit into these categories. Then, Jung would reduce alchemical processes to events 'in' the unconscious or the interior of the personality. Giegerich notes:

the individual, the personality, the inner, and 'the unconscious' are our names for the 'bottle' in which the mercurial 'substance' had to stay firmly enclosed for Jung.
(Giegerich, personal communication, 2000)

Giegerich continues his reflection by noting that 'because Mercurius remained enclosed in the above way "it" had to stay a substance, an object, and entity' and could not be true to its own nature as a spirit (something intangible and unrepresentable). This interpretation sets the stage for the fundamental thrust of Giegerich's emphasis in *The Soul's Logical Life*: namely, when Jung, and Hillman for that matter stick to 'images' as fundamental, they are in fact objectifying the spirit of alchemy. The image itself becomes objectified, while the true spirit of alchemy aims at realising the logical life of the soul, which is conceptual, subtle, non-positive, intangible. Throughout Giegerich's critique, he juxtaposes images as a 'pictorial form of thinking' (which valorises perception and imagination) with dialectical thought and logical expression (which he considers to be the true aim of alchemy). For Giegerich, when Jung opts to hold the image as fundamental, he steps over the goal of alchemy, namely, to release the spirit from its container, and thus ignores the 'self sublation' or death that the alchemical process requires. In doing so, he also skips 'over the successive psychological development of several centuries' (Giegerich, personal communication, 2000).

Jung pronounced his psychology of the unconscious to be the immediate successor and redemptor of alchemy. In this way he could declare the previous image-oriented (pictorial) mode of thinking, long overcome by the history of the soul, to still be 'the' psychological mode and decry the later development into which alchemy had dissolved as a mere rationalism, intellectualization, i.e. mere 'ego'. Jung excluded from his psychological reception of alchemy the fact that the telos of alchemy had been the overcoming of itself. He froze it, and psychology along with it, in an earlier phase.
(Giegerich, personal communication, 2000)

In short, for Giegerich, the task of alchemy was to deconstruct itself, or at least, in his terms, to surpass itself as a movement of the historical expression of the soul. Here, a Hegelian dialectical understanding of history influences Giegerich. Finally, for him, Jung did not give enough emphasis to the active dimensions of consciousness as constituting the reality of the psyche. That is, alchemy was an active human project, which meant that the observer of the alchemical process was not passive. He notes that even in the activity of 'registering, recording, maybe painting, the dream or fantasy images received and in thinking *about* them as a text' (ibid.), there was still the tendency to relate to this text as a finished 'product' delivered by the producing 'nature'. 'But consciousness had to refrain from entering the process of the production of images themselves'. Giegerich qualified this statement to note the 'exception' of active imagination, though even in this instance, 'what is to become active and enter the production process is not the reflecting mind, but the empirical ego'. In short, the mythos of Jungian work, psychological and alchemical, is that the 'natural process of the production of images was not to be interfered with'. For Giegerich, this was the vestige of fundamental naturalism left in Jung's psychology and in the end 'was contrary to the spirit of alchemy' (ibid.). Finally, one might say that Giegerich's reading is both Hegelian and deconstructive. He notes that in Jung: 'we have the curious spectacle ... of a singular dedication to and propagation of alchemy "and" its simultaneous repression. His advancement of alchemy as a psychological paradigm was "in itself" the substance of what it was intrinsically about' (ibid.).

Giegerich's ideas have begun to influence other Jungians. A case in point is the work of Yasuhiro Tanaka, a Japanese analyst. Tanaka (2001) has written a paper entitled 'The alchemical images and logic in analytical psychology'. He picks up on Giegerich's critique of 'images' and the limitations of an 'imaginal psychology'. For him, if we remain one-sidedly dependent on such a perspective, 'then we fall into the trap of remaining on the horizon of surface-psychology rather than depth psychology' (Tanaka, personal communication, 2000). For Tanaka as for Giegerich, 'we psychologists living after Jung, have to address the alchemical logic in analytical psychology'. His assessment of Jung is that while Jung on a personal level perceived the logical, paradoxical and dialectic dimension of alchemy, he could not 'interiorize it enough' or adequately apply it to his psychology as a theory. Thus, for Tanaka, our work now is 'not to fashion the bridge between alchemy and our clinical practice', but to examine the theoretical limitations of Jung's psychology:

> Alchemy was not only his [Jung's] historical background but also his logical background in the sense that for Jung it was none other than the theoria for sublating his own experience in to his psychology.
>
> (Tanaka, personal communication, 2000)

This then means that it was Jung's theory that could dispel the *massa confusa* and it is to this that we must now give our attention.

Current status and trends for future development

Jung's psychological reflections on alchemy helped to forge a number of his fundamental concepts. His idea of psychic reality, the centrality of the archetype, individuation, active imagination, the Self as a superordinate structure and the religious nature of psychic life were all developed and/or deepened through his engagement with alchemy. He linked his experiences with those of the alchemists and, as noted, alchemy became both the historical counterpart and confirmation of his thought. Jung thus brought alchemy out of obscurity and into the realm of modern psychology. In addition to the basic theoretical ideas noted earlier, alchemy provided Jung and Jungian psychology with a rich metaphoric language with which to describe the complex transactions of the unconscious and the transformations of analytical work.

The *prima materia* and *massa confusa* became an image of the disorganised beginnings of analytical work, the *vas hermeticum*, the container and sealed vessel of the analytical relationship. In this vessel, the matters of psyche could be heated up, cooked, coagulated, distilled and transformed. These psychological alchemical processes worked on the confusions and splits of the personality seeking to heal them through unifications, the *coniunctio* and the sacred marriage which eventually could result in a stabilised sense of wholeness, the Self or philosopher's stone. In this way, the metaphors of alchemy lend themselves to the newly developed psychology of the unconscious; the colours of alchemy became the colours of analytical psychology, as alchemy could now be seen in a psychological light.

Jung expressed his ideas in a non-dogmatic and tentative way. He thought of himself as a physician and empirical scientist who was discovering and documenting the objective facts of psychic reality. Classical analysts such as von Franz (1980) and Edinger (1985) epitomise this attitude. Edinger (1985: xix) has stated that what Jung presents are 'psychic facts rather than theoretical constructs or philosophical speculations'. Jung did in fact reject metaphysical claims but for many contemporary thinkers, such a rejection of the metaphysical implications of one's thought is considered naive. Even empirical science can be seen to carry ontological or at least theoretical implications. Although science claims to be free of philosophical assumptions, this position has been challenged by many philosophers of science as well in the larger hermeneutic tradition. Science, too, has ontological commitments that often remain unacknowledged. What we see is not simply a given; perspective and context are always part of what is seen. Jung knew this, but in most instances did not apply it to his own theory (Giegerich 1998/2001). Classical analysts have often held that Jung was ahead of his time, and our job is to understand him, amplify his ideas and apply them to new areas of research and practice, but for others, the implications in his thought are vestiges of metaphysical attitudes that must be seen and critiqued.

One such idea was his notion of projection. Jung relied on this concept as basic for his understanding of the relationship between psychology and alchemy. For a number of analysts, projection as a theory is problematic and at best a limited concept by which to understand psychological transactions and relationships. Schwartz-Salant (1995) noted that going beyond the theory of projection would seem to require a fundamental shift in metapsychology if not ontology. In explicit response to projection theory, Schwartz-Salant (1998) has emphasised a shift in focus to the idea of a 'psychic field' that extends beyond the analytical assumptions that form the basis of the idea of projection. In so doing, he echoes a contemporary ethos that imagines psychic life from outside a traditional Cartesian and Kantian paradigm.

Hillman's innovations, noted earlier, propose a radical revision of 'classical' and 'clinical' paradigms. For him, these approaches are filled with presuppositions that lead to reductive and literalised renderings of alchemy's powerful imagistic potential. The interpretation of alchemy in this reductive way leads to what he calls a 'psychology of alchemy'. The problem is that our current notions of psychology are far too limited to do justice to the import of alchemical images and processes. Hillman calls for a total revisioning of psychology and the development of an alchemical psychology, placing the non-reducible language of alchemy first, as a marker to note its irreducible quality as a realm of language, imagination and soul.

Kugler (1983) likewise emphasised the contribution of language for a paradigm shift, but while Hillman might be said to emphasise a phenomenological attitude towards the place of soul, Kugler also emphasises the formal structures of linguistics and phonetic patterns. Samuels (1989) also moves towards a new vision of the plural psyche, and Odajnyk (1993) contributes the notion of the meditation complex as an energetic field. Marlan (1997a) describes the field as an 'alchemy of desire' and calls attention to Jacques Derrida's idea of *différance*, which Derrida states is 'neither a word nor a concept' but a playful way to imagine a field of indeterminacy. Giegerich (1998) brings to bear philosophical and psychological criticism and inspired by Hegel introduces a new understanding of the 'logical life of the soul'. Tanaka (personal communication, 2000) followed Giegerich in pushing us towards the importance of theory to dispel our theoretical confusion. Focusing on a 'field approach' and linking all these thinkers to this notion in no way is an attempt to suggest that they are all saying the same thing. It is rather to note that in their own way, and from within their own frames of reference, they all are responding to the limitations of a Cartesian/Kantian paradigm and are struggling with a new way of seeing and imagining a path beyond the classical paradigms.

In addition to a critique of the metaphysical remnants that remain in Jung's thought, the issue of Jung's relationship and perhaps dependence on Christianity is a current issue. While classical analysts are critical of the limitation of the present-day Christian model, for many it is something that needs to be developed to achieve a more adequate reflection of psychic reality. Others have turned to Egyptian (Abt, Zabriskie), Greek and pagan (Hillman) or oriental (Odajnyk, Kawai) and Sufi (Hillman, Raff) traditions to understand alchemy.

Finally, an issue for current reflection is the further development of ideas about the goal of alchemy and analysis. As noted, Odajnyk (1993) and Raff (2000) both see the potential of going beyond what Jung felt to be the possible goals of the individuation process as Jung imagined it. Odajnyk speaks of the actual experience of self-realisation and enlightenment, and Raff of the third *coniunctio* and the inclusion of a transpsychic union of self and ally. Hillman would still see these extensions and possibilities as not going far enough. What Hillman calls for is a reimagining of the idea of the goal itself. For him, all of the above would fall into a spiritual literalism and his way of thinking breaks with the tradition of the spiritualisation of alchemy and with heroic notions of attainment. For him, the goal is the psychological cure of 'me' which means going beyond the desire for improvement. This critique resonates (differences aside) with the work of Giegerich, who sees the negation of the 'me' as essential for the soul. To what extent and in what ways these critiques differ from the surpassing of the ego implied in the more spiritualised approaches is a matter for continued debate and reflection.

As can be seen from the above, there are many who extend, apply and/or revise Jung's work. There are many complementarities and differences, but, in all, the vitality of Jung's work on alchemy remains an essential inspiration to contemporary analysts. Many issues remain to be developed, deepened and dialogued. In the end, perhaps the 'true' meaning of alchemy will remain as elusive as the philosopher's stone itself.

Notes

1 Psychoanalytic scholar Sonu Shamdasani has pointed out the limitations of relying on *Memories, Dreams, Reflections*, because of its editorial liberties, but he still suggests that individual paragraphs are accurate though thoroughly recast (personal communication, 25 September 2000).
2 For a bibliography of Edinger's work, see *Psychological Perspectives*, 39: 58–59.
3 *Quadrant* (summer, 1978) 2(1): Introduction and *Calcinatio*; (winter, 1978) 3(1): *Solutio*; (summer, 1979) 4: *Coagulatio*; (spring, 1980) 5: *Sublimatio*; (spring, 1982) 8: *Coniunctio*; (spring, 1981) 6: *Mortificatio*; (fall, 1981) 7: *Separatio*; (spring, 1982) 8: *Coniunctio*.
4 The introduction to the *Salt* book is published in this book as Chapter 4.
5 Published in this book as Chapter 3.

6 In Jung's original understanding of the Otherness of the Self to the ego, he also anticipated the vision of Lacan.
7 Published in this book as Chapter 5.
8 Published in this book as Chapter 6.
9 Published in this book as part of Chapter 8.

References

Cleary, T. (1991) *The Secret of the Golden Flower*. San Francisco, CA: Harper.
Coward, H. (1985) *Jung and Eastern Thought*. Albany: State University of New York Press.
Edinger, E.F. (1978a) 'Psychotherapy and alchemy 1. Iintroduction'. *Quadrant*, 2(1): 4–16.
—— (1978b) 'Psychotherapy and alchemy II. Calcinatio'. *Quadrant*, 11(1): 17–37.
—— (1978c) 'Psychotherapy and alchemy III. Solutio'. *Quadrant*, 11(2): 63–85.
—— (1979) 'Psychotherapy and alchemy IV. Coagulatio'. *Quadrant*, 12(1): 25–46.
—— (1980) 'Psychotherapy and alchemy V. Sublimatio'. *Quadrant*, 13(1): 57–75.
—— (1981a) 'Psychotherapy and alchemy VI. Mortificatio'. *Quadrant*, 14(1): 23–45.
—— (1981b) 'Psychotherapy and alchemy VII. Separatio'. *Quadrant*, 14(2): 41–61.
—— (1982) 'Psychotherapy and alchemy VIII. Coniunctio'. *Quadrant*, 15(1): 5–23.
—— (1985) *Anatomy of the Psyche: Alchemical Symbolism in Psychotherapy*. LaSalle, IL: Open Court.
—— (1994) *The Mystery of the Coniunctio: Alchemical Image of Individuation*. Toronto: Inner City.
—— (1995) *The Mysterium Lectures: A Journey through C.G. Jung's Mysterium Coniunctionis*, ed. J. Dexter Blackmer. Toronto: Inner City.
—— (1996a) *The Aion Lectures: Exploring the Self in C.G. Jung's Aion*, ed. D.A. Wesley. Toronto: Inner City.
—— (1996b) *The New God-Image: A Study of Jung's Key Letters Concerning the Evolution of the Western God-Image*. Wilmette, IL: Chiron.
Fordham, M. (1960) 'The relevance of analytical theory to alchemy, mysticism and theology'. *Journal of Analytical Psychology*, 5(2): 113–128.
Gad, I. (1999) 'Alchemy: the language of the soul'. *Psychological Perspectives*, 39: 92–101.
Giegerich, W. (1998/2001) *The Soul's Logical Life*. Frankfurt: Peter Lang.
Grinnel, R. (1973) *Alchemy in a Modern Woman*. Zurich: Spring.
Henderson, J.L. (1978) 'Practical application of alchemical theory'. *Journal of Analytical Psychology*, 23(3): 248.
—— (1987) *The Splendor Solis* (video). San Francisco, CA: C.G. Jung Institute of San Francisco.
Henderson, J.L. and Sherwood, D.N. (2003) *Transformation of the Psyche: The Symbolic Alchemy of the Splendor Solis*. Hove: Brunner-Routledge.
Hillman, J. (1970) 'On senex consciousness [Lead and Saturn]'. *Spring*: 146–165.
—— (1978) 'The therapeutic value of alchemical language', in R. Sardello (ed.) *Dragonflies: Studies of Imaginal Psychology*. Irving, TX: University of Dallas.

—— (1979) *The Dream and the Underworld*. New York: Harper and Row.
—— (1980) 'Silver and the white earth, Part I'. *Spring*: 21–48.
—— (1981a) 'Silver and the white earth, Part II'. *Spring*: 21–66.
—— (1981b) 'Alchemical blue and the *unio mentalis*'. *Sulfur*, 1: 33–50.
—— (1981c) 'The imagination of air and the collapse of alchemy'. *Eranos Yearbook 50*. Asona, CH: Eranos Foundation, 273–333.
—— (1981d) 'Salt: a chapter in alchemical psychology', in J. Stroud and G. Thomas (eds.) *Images of the Untouched*. Dallas, TX: Dallas Institute of Humanities, pp. 111–123. Also in S. Marlan (ed.) (1995) *Salt and the Alchemical Soul*. Dallas, TX: Spring, 145–179.
—— (1983) *Healing Fictions*. Barrytown, NY: Station Hill.
—— (1986) 'Notes on white supremacy: the alchemy of racism'. *Spring*, 46: 29–58.
—— (1989a) 'The yellowing of the work', in M.A. Matoon (ed.) *Proceedings of the Eleventh International Congress of Analytical Psychology, Paris*. Zurich: Daimon Verlag.
—— (1989b) *A Blue Fire*, introduced and edited by T. Moore. New York: Harper and Row.
—— (1993) "Concerning the Stone: Alchemical Images of the Gold," *Sphinx*, Vol. 5, 1993, 234–265.
—— (1997) 'The seduction of black', in S. Marlan (ed.) *Fire in the Stone*. Wilmette, IL: Chiron, 42–53.
—— (2003) 'A note for Stanton Marlan'. *Journal of Jungian Theory and Practice*, 5(2): 102–103.
—— (2004) 'The azure vault: the caelum as experience'. Keynote address at the Sixteenth International Congress for Analytical Psychology, Barcelona.
Holt, D. (1973) 'Jung and Marx'. *Spring*: 52–66.
—— (1987–1988) 'Alchemy: Jung and the historians of science'. *Harvest*, 33: 40–61.
Jacoby, M. (1984) *The Analytic Encounter: Transference and Human Relationships*. Toronto: Inner City.
Jaffé, A. (1967) 'The influence of alchemy on the work of C.G. Jung'. *Spring*: 7–26.
Jung, C.G. (1928) 'The relations between the ego and the unconscious', in *CW* 7: pars. 202–406.
—— (1942) 'Paracelsus as a spiritual phenomenon', in *CW* 13: 189.
—— (1946) 'Psychology of the transference', in *CW* 16: pars. 353–539.
—— (1951) *Aion*. *CW* 9ii.
—— (1953) *Psychology and Alchemy*. *CW* 12.
—— (1955–1956) *Mysterium Coniunctionis*. *CW* 14.
—— (1958) *Psychology and Religion: West and East*. *CW* 11.
—— (1963) *Memories, Dreams, Reflections*. New York: Pantheon.
—— (1979a) *General Bibliography*. *CW* 19.
—— (1979b) *General Index*. *CW* 20.
Kawai, H. (1996) *Buddhism and the Art of Psychotherapy*. College Station: Texas A&M University Press.
Kirsch, J. (1995) 'Transference', in M. Stein (ed.) *Jungian Analysis*, 2nd edn. La Salle, IL: Open Court, 170–209.
Kirsch, T.B. (2000) *The Jungians: A Comparative and Historical Perspective*. London and Philadelphia, PA: Routledge.

Kugler, P. (1983) *The Alchemy of Discourse: An Archetypal Approach to Language*. Lewisburg, PA: Bucknell University Press.

McGoveran, P. (1981) 'An application of an alchemical model for milieu functioning'. *Journal of Analytical Psychology*, 26(3): 249–267.

McGuire, W. and Hull, R.F.C. (eds.) (1977) *C.G. Jung Speaking: Interviews and Encounters*, Bollingen Series XCVII. Princeton, NJ: Princeton University Press.

Marlan, S. (1995) 'Introduction to salt and the alchemical soul', in S. Marlan (ed.) *Salt and the Alchemical Soul*. Woodstock, CT: Spring, XV–XLV.

—— (1997a) 'Fire in the stone: an inquiry into the alchemy of soul-making', in S. Marlan (ed.) *Fire in the Stone*. Wilmette, IL: Chiron, 7–41.

—— (1997b) *Fire in the Stone: The Alchemy of Desire*. Wilmette, IL: Chiron.

—— (2000a) 'The metaphor of light and its deconstruction in Jung's alchemical vision', in R. Brooke (ed.) *Pathways into the Jungian World*. London and New York: Routledge, 181–196.

—— (2000b) 'The black sun: archetypal image of the non-self', unpublished paper presented at the International Symposium of Archetypal Psychology.

—— (2001) 'The metaphor of light and renewal in Taoist alchemy and Jungian analysis'. *Quadrant* XXXI(2), 33–53.

—— (2005) *The Black Sun: The Alchemy and Art of Darkness*. College Station: Texas A&M University Press.

Newman, K.D. (1981) 'The riddle of the Vas Bene Clausum'. *Journal of Analytical Psychology*, 16(3): 229–243.

Odajnyk, V.W. (1993) *Gathering the Light: A Psychology of Meditation*. Boston, MA and London: Shambhala.

Raff, J. (2000) *Jung and the Alchemical Imagination*. York Beach, ME: Nicolas-Hays.

Robertson, R. (1999) 'A guide to the writings of Edward F. Edinger'. *Psychological Perspective*, 39(summer): 47–62.

Samuels, A. (1989) *The Plural Psyche: Personality, Morality and the Father*. London and New York: Routledge.

Schwartz-Salant, N. (1995) 'Introduction to Jung on alchemy', in N. Schwartz-Salant (ed.) *Jung on Alchemy*. London: Routledge.

Schwartz-Salant, N. (1998) *The Mystery of the Human Relationship: Alchemy and the Transformation of Self*. London and New York: Routledge.

Sharp, D. (1999) 'Tribute for E. Edinger'. *Psychological Perspectives*, 39(summer): 17–18.

Spiegelman, J.M. and Miyuki, M. (1985) *Buddhism and Jungian Psychology*. Phoenix, AZ: Falcon Press.

Stein, M. (1985) *Jung's Treatment of Christianity: The Psychotherapy of a Religious Tradition*. Wilmette, IL: Chiron.

—— (1992) *Understanding the Meaning of Alchemy: Jung's Metaphor of Transformative Process* (audiotape). Chicago, IL: C.G. Jung Institute of Chicago.

Sullivan, B.S. (1989) *Psychotherapy Grounded in the Feminine Principle*. Wilmette, IL: Chiron.

Tanaka, Y. (2001) 'The alchemical images and logic in analytical psychology,' *Harvest* 47 (1), 7–30.

Von Franz, M-L. (1966) *Aurora Consurgens*. New York: Pantheon.

—— (1979) *Alchemical Active Imagination*. Dallas, TX: Spring.

—— (1980) *Alchemy: An Introduction to the Symbolism and the Psychology.* Toronto: Inner City.

—— (1992) *Psyche and Matter.* Boston, MA: Shambhala.

Von Franz, M.-L. (2006). 'Psychological commentary', in Muhammad Ibn Umail & T. Abt (eds.) *Corpus alchemicum arabicum: Book of the explanation of the symbols, kitāb hall ar-rumūz.* Zurich: Living Human Heritage Publications,

Wagner, S. (1998) 'A conversation with Marie-Louise von Franz'. *Psychological Perspectives*, 38(winter): 12–42.

Wilhelm, R. (1931/1962) *The Secret of the Golden Flower: A Chinese Book of Life*, trans. and explained by R. Wilhelm with a foreword and Commentary by C.G. Jung. New York: Harcourt, Brace and World.

Zabriskie, B.D. (1995a) 'Jung and Pauli: a subtle asymmetry'. *Journal of Analytical Psychology*, 40, 531–553.

—— (1995b) 'Exiles and orphans: Jung, Paracelsus, and the healing images of alchemy'. *Quadrant*, 26(1 and 2), 9–32.

—— (1996) 'The matter of psyche'. *San Francisco Library Journal*, 14(4), 5–32.

—— (1997) 'Fermentation in Jung's alchemy', in M.A. Mattoon (ed.) *Proceedings of the Thirteenth International Congress for Analytical Psychology, Zurich 1995.* Einsiedeln, Switzerland: Daimon Verlag, 542–555.

—— (2001) 'Jung and Pauli: a meeting of rare minds', in C.A. Meier (ed.) *Atom and Archetype: The Pauli/Jung Letters, 1932–1958.* Princeton, NJ: Princeton University Press, xxvii-l.

Chapter 2

Jung and alchemy
A daimonic reading

I am grateful to the editors, Jean Kirsch and Murray Stein, for the invitation to reflect on my reading of Jung's alchemy and, particularly, for the opportunity to do so in a personal and subjective way as opposed to a strictly academic one. For me, this is not an easy distinction. I find it difficult to separate personal and academic work in any absolute way. Jung once wrote, "My life is what I have done, my scientific work; the one is inseparable from the other".[1] Again, in his "Late Thoughts", he elaborated: "making 'theory' ... is as much a part of me, as vital a function of mine, as eating and drinking".[2] Likewise, I find that to whatever extent my academic work has become meaningful and integrated into my life, the apparent categories of personal and academic no longer sit strictly outside one another.

The editors have posed a few questions to guide contributors, which aim to consider why we still read Jung and how, as well as how to do so deeply and well. Reading Jung's alchemical work is no easy task, and alchemical texts are themselves even more difficult. Von Franz has noted:

> As soon as we get into the [alchemical] texts you will understand ... how alchemy came to be forgotten, and why still, even in Jungian circles ... when it comes to alchemy, they give up, and either do not read, or grumble while reading his books on the subject.[3]

She goes on to say that "[t]his is because alchemy, in itself, is tremendously dark and complex".[4] Likewise, Edward Edinger recognized how difficult alchemy was to understand: "We encounter a wild, luxuriant, tangled mass of overlapping images that is maddening to the order-seeking conscious mind".[5] Hillman, too, has commented that "the phenomena of alchemy present a chaos".[6] He quotes Bonus of Ferrara:

> [T]he only method that prevails is that of chaos ... all the writers seem to begin ... with that which is quite strange and unknown ... The consequence is that one seems to flounder along through these works, with only here and there a glimmering of light.[7]

Jung had a similar first reaction. His early attempt to understand alchemy left him with the feeling that "[t]his stuff is impossible to understand ... blatant non-sense".[8] And yet, it continued to intrigue and fascinate him and eventually became a major part of his life's work. In fact, as Hanegraaff describes, Jung's interpretation of alchemy came

> as a breath of fresh air ... while historians had been struggling against a sense of futility, Jung seemed to have found the key that could 'make sense' of alchemy, and even endow it with meaning and significance for modern man.[9]

Jung read and meditated on alchemy with great care. One might imagine his reading to be not unlike that expressed in the *Mutus Liber*, a seventeenth-century alchemical text known as a silent book: "Pray. Read, Read, Read. Read Again. Work and you shall find".[10] An unfolding of this idea is carried by the Persian alchemist/philosopher Rhazes: "One book opens another".[11]

Some of Jung's closest followers were aware that Jung's writings on alchemy were difficult to read, and so it is not surprising that some of them dedicated themselves to helping readers gain access to his primary works. A number of these analysts and scholars have been essential to my own reading, especially Marie-Louise von Franz, Edward Edinger, James Hillman, and Wolfgang Giegerich.

For von Franz and Edinger, Jung's works were authoritative, so they did not criticize Jung or offer any fundamentally different approach. They tended to see their own work basically as a bridge to Jung's, but this evaluation does not represent the extent to which their own contributions have extended both our understanding of Jung and alchemy, and the field of analytical psychology as a whole.

For me, von Franz's uncanny symbolic sensitivity, her appreciation of the "dark feminine", her works on alchemical history and active imagination, and her exploration of psyche and matter—to say nothing of her work on the *Aurora consurgens*—have been important companions to my reading. The work of Edinger has also affected me deeply. His book, *Anatomy of the Psyche*, organizes the typical operations and stages of the alchemical process and, in so doing, brings order to the chaos of alchemy. Perhaps even more directly than von Franz, Edinger lays out guiding principles for how to read Jung.[12] Like von Franz, he held Jung in the highest esteem, if not in a profound idealization. His first principle for how to read Jung is to recognize Jung's magnitude:

> [R]ealize that Jung's consciousness vastly surpasses your own.... If you make the assumption that you know better than he does and you start out with a critical attitude, don't bother. The book isn't for you. Jung's depth and breadth are absolutely awesome. We're all Lilliputians by comparison.[13]

I read such statements with ambivalence and draw back from what appears to be Edinger's god-like projection onto Jung. Yet, I too hold Jung's work in the highest esteem, and I deeply respect Edinger's integrity. Nevertheless, Edinger's seeming foreclosure of a critical attitude appears to my taste as too literal. For me, the best way to read Edinger is to accept the importance of approaching Jung with an open mind and initially suspend judgment in order to remain open to what we do not understand. Edinger is keenly aware of the temptation to criticize as a defense against the anxiety of not knowing. In Zen Buddhism, only the empty vessel can receive, and by being empty, we become teachable. In the face of the difficult challenge of Jung's alchemical work and with respect for the laborious process he went through to gain insight into this field, an initial bracketing of one's criticism is a reasonable approach. For me, it is not hard to idealize Jung's work in alchemy. Perhaps it is the case, as Harold Bloom has noted, that "[w]e read, frequently if unknowingly, in quest of a mind much more original than our own".[14]

Edinger's second principle for how to read Jung is to appreciate that Jung presents "psychic facts", rather than "theories about facts". From my perspective, however, the separation between theories and facts is a bit problematic in that it takes for granted a vision of *reality* based on a clear subject–object perspective that may not do justice to the complexity of the relationship between thought and reality. Still, my critical reading of Edinger may not do justice to his vision since, by "psychic fact", I believe he means something beyond psyche as a literal "object" of consciousness. Based on Jung's views of amplification, he developed a method of *cluster thinking* that is more like a phenomenology of images that gives one a variegated, dynamic, and mosaic-like view of the psyche.

The third principle is what Edinger calls "the 'fruit cake' principle".[15] By this, he means that "you must read Jung the way you eat fruit cake – very slowly. The reading is exceedingly rich, exceedingly delicious, because it is the richness of psyche itself".[16] Jung gives us "kernels ... rich pieces of nut and heavy fruit which have to be masticated and digested slowly in order to be appreciated".[17] For Edinger, you cannot read Jung's alchemical work the way you read an ordinary book. Each kernel, each image, has to be unpacked "the way one works on a dream".[18] One has to have the capacity to enter into the unknown and to stay open, to "disidentify from the ego sufficiently" in order to go on in the work. For me, Edinger's recommendations about keeping an open mind, thinking in images, "cluster thinking", reading slowly, patiently, diligently, while disidentifying from the ego are all good advice when reading Jung's alchemy. Edinger's personal depth and profound introversion, as well as the integrity of his order-seeking mind, make him a compelling reader of Jung.

Nevertheless, in spite of my positive regard for both von Franz and Edinger, they, at times, too easily translate alchemy into a conceptually taken-for-granted framework of Jung's psychology, and such a reading sets the stage for the criticism and alternate readings of James Hillman and Wolfgang Giegerich. Hillman's approach to reading alchemy resists translating its images and language into the structures of any conceptual rationalism that leaves the image behind. He gives these examples:

> White Queen and Red King have become feminine and masculine principles; their incestuous sexual intercourse has become the union of opposites; the freakish hermaphrodite and uniped, the golden head ... have all become paradoxical representations of the goal, examples of androgyny symbols of the Self.[19]

For him, these are moves from "precision into generality".[20] Hillman challenges us to imagine the process of reading alchemy differently. For him, sticking to the image recovers the point of the ancient Greek maxim "save the phenomena", and allows us to speak imaginatively and to dream the dream onward. He is not simply suggesting that we replace our concepts with "the archaic neologisms of alchemy"[21] or take alchemical language literally as substitutions for our own concepts. It is not the literal return to alchemy that he proposes, but rather a "restoration of the alchemical mode of imagining".[22] For Hillman, this means the move from a psychology of alchemy to an alchemical psychology rooted in the fundamental principle of the imagination and not in reified fixed structures of theoretical abstractions.

If Hillman moves from conceptual rationalism to image and imagination, and from a psychology of alchemy to an alchemical psychology, Giegerich moves from image and imagination to a radically revised notion of "the concept". For Giegerich, the conceptual is something not to move beyond, but to arrive at, as a furthering of dialectical thinking beyond imagination. One might characterize this move as one from an imaginal and alchemical psychology to an animus psychology not interested in "saving the phenomena", but rather in following the path of thinking out of the imaginal to the logical life of the soul. Reading alchemy from this perspective leads Giegerich to note that while for Jung "medieval alchemy was the historical link between the ancient past (mythology, Gnosticism, Neoplatonism) and the present", for Giegerich "it is also the link between the imagination and dialectical logic",[23] as well as a link to his revisioned notion of psychology.

In addition to these analysts, a number of historians also have influenced my reading: Sonu Shamdasani, Adam McLean, Lawrence Principe, William Newman, Hereward Tilton, Wouter Hanegraaff, Hayden White, Ruth Meyer, and others—all have contributed perspectives on how I read Jung and his alchemy. Within the limits of this paper, I cannot elaborate the complexity of all these positions. In general, many of them share a conviction that there are problems in our reading of Jung due to a tendency to project speculative theories onto Jung's life and his reading of alchemy.

Shamdasani has demonstrated the value of historical criticism through his correction and revisioning of what he has called the "Jungian legend".[24] In a similar way, McLean has criticized interpreters of alchemy for projecting their theoretical fantasies onto what alchemists *actually said*. For him, both psychological and esoteric interpretations of alchemy, including Jung's, have fallen prey to this problem. Like Shamdasani, he has worked diligently to make unknown texts available to modern readers and has taught courses on how to read alchemy. He describes his way of approaching alchemical texts as a forensic reading.[25] Like McLean, Principe and Newman have been highly critical of Jung for what they consider his a-historical and overgeneralized reading and "for effectively writing laboratory alchemy out of the picture".[26] They reject the idea of a psychological or spiritual interpretation of alchemy. On the other hand, other historians such as Tilton and Hanegraaff have shown the limitations and problems with Principe's and Newman's readings, including their not well-researched criticisms of Jung.[27]

If there is any shadow to the historical readings of Jung and alchemy, it is a tendency to view historical reading as getting it "right", getting to the "real" Jung or "real" alchemy. Nevertheless, setting criticisms aside, classical amplification and active imagination (von Franz), cluster thinking (Edinger), sticking with the image (Hillman), following the logical life of the soul (Giegerich), historical rectification of the Jung legend (Shamdasani), and the forensic reading (McLean) continue to influence me. These are all strong and persuasive readings, and I read with them, through them, as well as against them—stepping back and reading Jung again and again, trying to find my own perspective. Harold Bloom has noted: "Reading well is best pursued as an implicit discipline; finally there is no method but yourself, when your self has been fully molded".[28] In a resonant voice, Giegerich has written: "every potential reader has to try for himself to lift Jung's work and see what happens. No other person can do it for him".[29] Reading Jung's alchemy is heavy lifting.

If I step back from Jung in my academic reading, it is less a stepping back from Jung than from the shadow of certain essentialist readings. By this, I mean readings that place emphasis on fixed and unchanging structures and static views of the archetypes that have minimized individual, cultural, and historical differences and that reify a centralizing tendency and concept of the center. The latter is an understandable temptation since the process of centering became, for Jung, the touchstone for the recognition of the self and for the individuation process. He represented the center and centering process in mandala-like forms such as the "Window on Eternity", the golden castle mandala, and in an impressive geometric rendering of the Philosophers' Stone. Although I find such images beautiful and profound, they can easily become encrusted, rock-hard representations of a dynamic psychic reality difficult to describe in abstract form. These images came to Jung as a compensation to the chaos of the unconscious, and he created them in his effort to gain stability in the midst of this turmoil. Thus, Jung was able to see the potency of the self and the healing value of the centering process. Images representing this stabilizing function capture the "archetype of orientation and meaning",[30] but it is important to remember that the self is also a destabilizing power that continues to deconstruct the ego's effort to represent reality in any kind of static hypostasis that obscures the self's reality. I have attempted to read Jung with this concern in mind and have valued a postmodern sensibility, perhaps best characterized by Jacques Derrida, who has been credited "with the achievement of finding a solution to the fundamental logical task of the postmodern situation: switching from stability through centering and solid foundations to stability through greater flexibility and decentering".[31]

In many places, Jung likewise resists Cartesian clarity and values a dynamic reading. In "Paracelsus as a Spiritual Phenomenon", he writes about our "understandable desire" for unambiguous clarity:

> but we are apt to forget that in psychic matters we are dealing with processes of experience, that is, with transformations which should never be given hard and fast names if their living movement is not to petrify into something static. The protean mythologem and the shimmering symbol express the process of the psyche far more trenchantly and, in the end, far more clearly than the clearest concept; for the symbol not only conveys a visualization of the process but – and this is perhaps just as important – it also brings a re-experiencing of it, of that twilight which we can learn to understand only through inoffensive empathy, but which too much clarity only dispels.[32]

Reading Jung in a way that conjures up that twilight draws the reader closer to what lies within it. This twilight is a softer light and, by it, the ego's brightness is diminished. This reading gives room to the unconscious, to dreams and visions, and allows for the unknown to play an important role. I call such a reading a daimonic one.

I have been reading Jung and his alchemical work for most of my adult life and continue to do so. There is something about the arcane and impenetrable quality of alchemy and Jung's passionate reading of it that continues to draw me back into its mad obscurities, its dark matter, and its fantastic images. My basic laboratory is the analyst's consulting room and the library, with its old texts and tomes. "Pray, Read, Read, Read. Read again. Work and you shall find", says the *Mutus Liber*, an old alchemical text aimed at the production of the Philosophers' Stone.[33] And yet, my love of alchemy draws me down to the basement, from library to lab, from texts to textures, from weighty tomes to the weight of lead—to the al-chemistry of the soul, to its fire and heat, to anthor and alembic, holding and cooking, combustion, distillation, cooling, sublimating, transformation, multiplication, and refinement—to what comes alive in the work.

I remain passionate about alchemy and am deeply drawn to its images and objects, to its smells and colors, to its aesthetics, art, and artistry, to its graphics and symbolic designs, and to its hermetic vision of the transformation of matter—to what matters to the soul and to Jung's reading of it. For me, alchemy is a madness, a journey into the unknown and unimagined. Its *nigredo* is poisonous, a "blacker than black" darkness. But if one has the skill, good luck, or divine favor, it may be a *pharmacon*, a poison that also heals, and in the healing, one can find a light that shines in the midst of darkness and is said to reveal a miracle that Jung called the Self and the alchemists, the Stone.

Jung found such an image in his now famous Liverpool dream. At the core of the dream is the following:

> While everything round about was obscured by rain, fog, smoke, and dimly lit darkness, the little island blazed with sunlight. On it stood a single tree, a magnolia, in a shower of reddish blossoms. It was as though the tree stood in the sunlight and were at the same time the source of light.[34]

Jung commented that the "dream represented my situation at the time.... Everything was extremely unpleasant, black and opaque – just as I felt then. But I had had a vision of unearthly beauty, and that was why I was able to live at all".[35] In the midst of darkness, Jung experienced a self-generating source of light and noted, "This dream brought with it a sense of finality"[36] and a vision of the goal. "Through this dream", Jung wrote, he "understood that the self is the principle and archetype of orientation and meaning ... its healing function".[37]

Later, in *Alchemical Studies*, Jung wrote about the relationship between the lapis and the tree. In the "Consilium coniugii", Senior said:

> Thus the stone is perfected of and in itself. For it is the tree whose branches, leaves, flowers, and fruits come from it and through it and for it, and it is itself whole or the whole [*tota vel totum*] and nothing else.[38]

The stone refers to taking "wisdom with all thy power, for from it thou shalt drink eternal life, until thy [stone] is congealed and thy sluggishness depart, for thence cometh life".[39] These alchemical comments could well be understood as an amplification of Jung's Liverpool dream.

Between 1918 and 1920, Jung wrote that he began to understand the individuation process and the Self as the goal of psychological development and to represent it in mandala-like form. One of the beautiful mandalas he drew around this time he identified as a representation of the Philosophers' Stone. Shamdasani has noted that "[i]n a manner of speaking, Jung had found the philosopher's stone before he had come to his psychological understanding of alchemy".[40]

The Ariadne-like thread that led to Jung's serious reading of alchemy is dramatically portrayed in *Memories, Dreams, Reflections*, a text I consider to be one of the best descriptions of Jung's encounter with alchemy and the subsequent unfolding of his ideas. *MDR* is a rich weave of events, inner and outer, that reads like a complex mystery story, a page turner that I return to again and again. I continue to do so with the knowledge that *MDR* is a complex text that contains many omissions and other problems noted in Jungian scholarship over the years.[41] I will refrain from reiterating the now well-known issues that make *MDR* a less than historically accurate "autobiography" or "biography". Clearly, the Jung portrayed in *MDR* is at least in part a "fiction", but I would claim that these fictional elements are just as important for reading Jung's biography as they are for the psychological reading of his alchemy.

On the other hand, Shamdasani has pointed out the dangers of the divide between fantasies of Jung and his historical actuality. He is alarmed by the fact that even "professional Jungians are not immune to this":[42]

> Jung's dreams and fantasies, all too often, have functioned like Rorschach ink blots, and attracted all manner of fantasies, and … the boundary line between novels and plays about Jung and non-fictional works has not always been as sharp as it could be.[43]

Yet, I remain skeptical that any absolute line can be drawn between the fictional Jung and the historical figure. Although historical scholarship can help correct the worst biases, the fantasy that we can or should completely purge the fictive elements of our reading and arrive at the "correct" perception of the way things really are adds another fiction to our misreadings of Jung.

The master words "interpretation" and "reading" are themselves debatable.[44] Hayden White, a historian by training and an important figure in debates about practices of historical and literary interpretation, argues that there is always a fictional dimension to what some perceive as a historical fact. For him, historical narratives are always also fictions that "have more in common with their counterparts in literature than they have with those in the sciences".[45] In this way, White links mythic and historical consciousness and challenges the radical oppositions between history, fiction, fact, and fantasy. He insists on the fictive elements in all historical narrative. For White, "history as a discipline is in bad shape today because it has lost sight of its origins in the literary imagination … [i]n the interest of *appearing* scientific and objective".[46] For White, this does

> not mean the degradation of historiography to the status of ideology or propaganda. In fact, this recognition [of "the fictive element"] would serve as a potent antidote to the tendency of historians to become captive of ideological preconceptions which they do not recognize as such but honor as the "correct" perception of "the way things *really* are".[47]

For him, "history has served as a kind of archetype of the 'realist' pole of representation",[48] but historical realism should never be read "as unambiguous signs of the events they report, but rather as symbolic structures, extended metaphors".[49] A good professional historian consistently "reminds his readers of the purely provisional nature of his characterizations of events, agents, and agencies found in the always incomplete historical record".[50] Just what is meant by the "fictive element", "symbolic structures", and "extended metaphors" needs continued reflection and refinement. If one way of reading Jung reflects the "realist" pole of representation, perhaps White's insight gives room for a "fictive" pole, leaning toward the contributions of a psychological, subjective, and daimonic element in all readings?

This perspective has been richly elaborated by Ruth Meyer in her book *Cleo's Circle: Entering the Imaginal World of Historians*,[51] where she shows that "being an historian is in part an imaginal activity"[52] and "that dreams, visions, and altered states form an unacknowledged and misunderstood part of the historian's creative process".[53] Perhaps a mysterious intertwining of the fictive and real is the ideal goal of any historian, psychologist, or general reader, but it is easy to err in either direction, subjective or objective, and perhaps a one-sided reading may be impossible to avoid. I have no doubt that my reading is an errant one, and while I applaud and remain excited about the ongoing scholarship that will no doubt give us a more comprehensive and perhaps more "accurate" picture of Jung, I think it is also important to realize that our understanding of Jung is always dependent on interpretation. No matter what materials we have before us, interpretation is the key factor; that is, the Jung we come to know personally and collectively is never simply the real or literal Jung, but a figure known through individual and collective fantasies and transferences as well as historical "evidence". Perhaps it is even the case, as literary critic Harold Bloom has argued, that every reading is also a misreading.

As noted, Shamdasani has demonstrated the value of his approach to historical criticism. However, I would hold with White and Meyer that history must always be interpreted and that we live in a historical and psychological world in which imagination and fiction both play an essential role. To believe that we will ever get to the "real" Jung is a limiting fantasy since the "real" Jung is always a Jung-for-us. He is always a figure immersed in a fabric of relationships and contexts of psyche and world. He is an inner figure and a collective one—a figure that has, and will continue to have, many faces.

Shamdasani begins his book *Jung and the Making of Modern Psychology* by noting that Jung has been seen as an "Occultist, Scientist, Prophet, Charlatan, Philosopher, Racist, Guru, Anti-Semite ... Polygamist, Healer, Poet, Con-Artist, Psychiatrist, and Anti-Psychiatrist".[54] As he notes, "what has Jung not been called?" and "the very proliferation of 'Jungs'" drive Shamdasani to wonder "whether everyone could possibly be talking about the same figure" and to recognize that Jung "has become a figure upon whom an endless succession of myths, legends, fantasies, and fictions continues to be draped. Travesties, distortions, and caricatures have become the norm. The process shows no signs of abating".[55] After decades of myth making, Shamdasani notes, "one question becomes more insistent: who was C. G. Jung?"[56] He quotes Jung's remark, "Don't make a legend of me".[57] While careful scholarship can help us correct the worst biases of the Jungian legend, I do not think we can ever escape the truth of mythos, and we must, by necessity, "dream the dream onward". Perhaps it is the case that Jung is all of this and more.

Even prior to current scholarship, both Jung and Jaffé had acknowledged the many problems with *MDR* that make it less than an accurate, scientific, or objective account of Jung's life and work. In Jung's own words, what he has written uses an "improvisation ... born of the moment",[58] a passionate retrospective and brief sketch. Jaffé notes that it was "written in response to a special occasion" and, therefore, one should "not expect it to be comprehensive".[59] For Jung, accurate, literal, and historical events were of little importance. They had, in his words, become "phantasms ... barely recollect[ed]".[60] They were events that he had "no desire to reconstruct" since they no longer "stirred his imagination".[61] What was important to Jung were his inner experiences. They were what remained vibrant and alive and which over the years had "grown all the more vivid and colorful".[62] It is precisely these experiences that continue to draw me to this text and make *MDR* not simply less, but also more, than an ordinary autobiography or biography. I do not read *MDR* for a factual account of Jung's life, but rather because his description of his inner world opens onto a larger view of psychic reality. I consider *MDR* a document of the soul that recounts important *fictions*—archetypal moments that reach out beyond Jung's personal life and toward a vision of the objective psyche. *MDR* is replete with such moments, which include fantasies, dreams, visions, and synchronistic experiences.

Jung's openness to the power of the unconscious is vividly described in *MDR* as "hitting upon a stream of lava", a fiery magma that burst forth from the unconscious and provided "the *prima materia* for a lifetime's work".[63] It was "like fiery liquid basalt; out of [which] crystallized the stone that I could work".[64] For Jung, these experiences were the heated fires that reshaped his life. Like the figure of Faust in Goethe's classic epic, Jung opened himself to the unconscious out of which a new way of seeing emerged. With Goethe's words, he proclaims: "Now let me dare to open wide the gate / Past which men's steps have ever flinching trod".[65]

The visions that came did not always come benignly, and his descent into the unconscious initiated Jung into a period of great uncertainty and isolation. At one point, he regarded his work on alchemy as a sign of his inner relationship to Goethe. Jung felt that Goethe's secret was that he was in the grip of a process of archetypal transformation that has continued through the centuries. If Jung's engagement with the unconscious was a kind of madness, as some have claimed, it was also the beginning of his *opus magnum* or *divinum*[66]—a divine madness and, at the same time, a growing sense of archetypal reality.

I imagine the "madness" Jung experienced to be the kind described by Plato and Aristotle. For Plato, poetic inspiration was a form of divine madness, and Aristotle likewise noted that great genius was always mixed with insanity. Plato and Aristotle, both champions of the rational, show a deep ambivalence about insanity, an ambivalence that Plato helps to differentiate in the *Phaedrus*, one of his great dialogues on love. Socrates comments on two kinds of madness, "one produced by human infirmity, the other a divine release of the soul from the yoke of custom and convention".[67] If Jung at times came close to the first kind, his strength of character brought him forward to a liberating vision. Ultimately, Jung experienced his "inner madness" as "a suprapersonal process of the mundus archetypus (archetypal world)" that "was alive and active ... a living substance"[68] in both Goethe's creative process and his own. He confesses that these experiences haunted him and, in Goethe's case, led to the production of a classic work of literature, whereas Jung was single-mindedly driven to the mysteries of the personality and to the development of a new vision of psychology. The struggle to work his way through this difficult process and come to terms with the unconscious required that Jung abandon the idea of the ego's superordinate position. He felt compelled to let himself be carried along by the current of his experiences without knowing where it would lead.

Like Jung, I find myself gripped by Jung's story of his descent into the unconscious and his fateful encounter with alchemy. I find something infectious about this story. I read it over and over again, and identify with Jung's experience as a symbolic "as if", an inflation—part transference, part fetish, part *participation mystique*, and part poetic inspiration. What feels like an autonomous process draws me into a phantasmagoria of alchemical fiction, one that has become an important part of my life and study.

In the preface to James Hillman's book *Healing Fiction*, the poet George Quasha quotes Wallace Stevens as saying, "The final belief is to believe in a fiction, which you know to be a fiction, there being nothing else. The exquisite truth is to know that it is a fiction and that you believe in it willingly".[69] Quasha contends that our reality is created through our fictions; to be conscious of these fictions is to gain creative access to and participate in the poetics of soul making. My own reading of Jung is filled with such "fictions" in Quasha's sense. Harold Bloom quotes Virginia Woolf's advice about reading, that "there is always a demon in us who whispers, 'I hate. I love', and we cannot silence him".[70] Like Bloom, "I cannot silence my demon" who loves alchemy and identifies with Jung's mad passion. According to Shoshana Felman, Gérard de Nerval also hints at the daimonic quality of this passion:

Every reading, says Nerval, is a kind of madness since it is based on illusion and induces us to identify with imaginary heroes. Madness is nothing other than an intoxicating reading: a madman is one who is drawn into the dizzying whirl of his own reading.[71]

I do not read Jung for history, but for his-story. While I am interested in Jung's history, I am not a historian and have little to contribute to the objective facts of Jung's life. Jung once wrote, "You read as much into a book as out of it",[72] and my reading of Jung is an errant one insofar as his-story has also become a my-story. For me, reading Jung daimonically has meant a bracketing of my academic ego and letting myself be carried by fictions and gripped by an archetypal passion, a kind of madness that opens onto the scene of a magical adventure requiring an engagement not only with Jung and alchemy, but also with my own psychic depths.

One captivating moment of my identification with Jung's story was his report of a series of dreams that he felt prefigured his discovery of alchemy:

Beside my house stood another, that is to say, another wing or annex, which was strange to me. Each time I would wonder in my dream why I did not know this house, although it had apparently always been there. Finally came a dream in which I reached the other wing. I discovered there a wonderful library, dating largely from the sixteenth and seventeenth centuries. Large, fat folio volumes, bound in pigskin, stood along the walls. Among them were a number of books embellished with copper engravings of a strange character, and illustrations containing curious symbols such as I had never seen before.[73]

At the time, Jung reports, he did not realize that the images in these dreams represented alchemical symbols. He was only aware that these images fascinated him. He thought the unknown wing of the house represented something unconscious in himself and that the dream referred to alchemy, which at the time he knew little about, but which he "was soon to study".[74] Many years later, he had acquired a collection of alchemical books very much like the library in his dreams.

One of the most compelling parts of his story is the idea that somehow behind such dreams is the working of the objective psyche, leading the way to Jung's discoveries as if following a teleological thread or seeing a fate prefigured and meant to be. The images of Jung's library and of ancient alchemical books activated in me a passion to see Jung's library, as if it were possible to enter his dream and to make it my own, to hold in my hands the texts that he found so essential for his work and that were progressively becoming important for my own. One summer while I was teaching in Zurich, my wife Jan and I had the good fortune to visit Jung's library and to examine and study his alchemical books. I was able to hold in my hands Jung's copy of the *Artis Auriferae* and the *Rosarium Philosophorum*, an experience as real as it was dreamlike.

The story of a dream leading to alchemical books and their mysteries is not unique to Jung. One example is from a story about the famous alchemist Nicolas Flamel (1330–1418). (The extraordinary events of his life have been popularized in J. K. Rowling's *Harry Potter and the Philosopher's Stone*.) According to legend, Flamel had a vision of a mysterious book. Later, in a Paris bookstall, he discovered what he imagined to be the book from his dream. It was entitled *The Book of Abraham the Jew*.[75] It was replete with mysterious images, and legend has it that it contained the secret of the Philosophers' Stone. I had often fantasized about this book, although I could never find it. After visiting Jung's library, I was in Basel at an old bookshop and asked the dealer if he had any old alchemical books. He said he had a very rare one, which turned out to be a copy of *The Book of Abraham the Jew* (see Figure 2.1). Such experiences stir my imagination.

Another strange coincidence concerned John Dee (1527–1608), an English magus and alchemist. I have felt a special connection to Dee because of a powerful dream I had earlier in my life.

> I am in some kind of underground cavern; I think Egyptian. I feel something in my chest start to fly up and out of my body to an opening. It is a cat being resurrected. It is a numinous feeling, powerful and real. Organ music is starting to play deep and resonant, and a voice says, "Who is John Dee?"

At the time, I had never heard of John Dee and puzzled over my dream. When I discovered who Dee was, it gave me the chills and the dream has stayed with me throughout my life. Is it possible that such a dream has any relationship to John Dee, the Elizabethan alchemist who collected one of Europe's great alchemical libraries? During his lifetime, Dee was also noted for his ability to converse with spirits. Is it possible that his spirit and my dream truly reach beyond the subjectivity of time and place—and reflect a connection to the archetypal world? Is it possible that my dream was already connecting me to a transpersonal reality that was to become important in my future? Perhaps this is another mad fantasy, a wild inflation, but dreams have convinced me that they speak to a world beyond the ego.

Many years after the John Dee dream, another dream experience reawakened such questions. I dreamt that two small rabbits had fallen into a window well in front of my house. When I awoke, the dream bothered me, and I began to think of it subjectively: What had fallen into a hole or trap? Was I stuck somewhere or depressed? Nothing I worked on seemed to reveal the dream's meaning. A few days later, while out in the garden, the memory of the dream returned. I suddenly decided to look in the window well—and there I found two small dead rabbits. I was deeply saddened and wondered: If I had looked right after I had the dream, perhaps I could have saved them?

Figure 2.1 The unification of air and earth, from Eleazar's *Uraltes Chymisches Werck*, 1735. (Photo courtesy of the author and Jan Marlan.)

Is it possible that the souls of these rabbits were calling out for help? Is it possible that my dream was connecting me to the objective psyche? Whatever the case, the existential impact of this experience led me to recognize the importance of not simply and automatically reducing dreams to a personal level.

I am aware that such "fictions" are a slippery slope: illusion, intoxication, inflation, and daimonic passion. Such a state destabilizes our sense of the factual, the real, and the line between fiction and truth. It is a challenge to our everyday sensibilities. Perhaps it is the madness of the daimon that says "I love". A daimonic reading can be perilous, but I believe that opening the gates to the unconscious is important, and I have come to see that the corrections to these inflations can be found within the fictions themselves. An example of this is found in the following story.

On my first trip to Zurich many years ago, I saw Jung's house for the first time. I walked up the driveway, very excited to be close to Jung's spirit. I wanted to carry home some of this feeling, something more substantial than a memory I knew would fade. I wanted an object, a material thing associated with Jung—even a stone to put on my desk to hold this spirit firm.

I collected a few rocks from the ground and took them with me. I placed one on my desk and the others in a glass vessel. At times, I would give one to a good friend on a special occasion. Through the stones, I felt I had a special connection to Jung, a *participation mystique*, a rock-hard alchemy. When I touched these stones and looked at them, the feeling of connection was reinforced—Jung and I were one in stone, a gift from psyche. Eric Neumann would call this oneness an ego-Self identity that calls for an ego-Self separation.[76] This deflation came in the form of a dream:

> I am at the side door of Jung's house. I desperately want something of Jung's to take home with me. I knock and Emma Jung comes to the door. I explain who I am and tell her how important her husband is to me and ask her if there is anything of his she could give me. She says "I'll be right back" and goes into the house. She returns and on the ground before me she places a pair of Jung's shoes. With excitement, I step into them – only to discover they are far too big.

My first reaction to this humorous dream was the deflation it brought in its wake, but as time went on, the gift I took home with me was that Jung's shoes were not for me. This recognition led me to understand the problem of the *imitatio* of Jung: that simply identifying with Jung was not the way to follow what his spirit opened in my soul. With this recognition, I was able to relate to Jung's work in a more differentiated way. There was movement in my archetypal transference and a response to it, and my small feet were a catalyst to a further development of my soul.

Through experiences like the ones I have recorded here, it became clear to me that dreams, synchronicities, and living in an archetypal fiction have sustained my lifelong interest in reading Jung and alchemy. For me, it was and is important to live in the fire of imagination, to find the lava flow that participates in shaping one's life journey. Such "fictions" are essential components in my reading of Jung, and I believe this is the way Jung read his own life. It requires following the promptings of the unconscious "as if" they contain a meaningful *telos* that can shape one's life.

But living in such fantasies and so close to the fire can lead to getting burnt. Opening to the unconscious is only part of the story, though I would claim that it is an essential one. One must also turn toward the unconscious and engage it. Alchemical texts are filled with descriptions of how to work with this fire, and Hillman has noted: "The alchemist must be able to fight fire with fire, using his own fire to operate upon the fires with which he is operating. Working the fire by means of fire".[77] I believe this is the passion Jung brought to his lava, and it is what prepared him to study alchemy and sustained him in the process of doing so.

I have allowed myself for the purpose of this reflection to draw apart the personal and academic to a greater extent than has been my custom. When I reflect upon what draws me to read Jung, it is a passion that continues to stir my imagination, to follow a mythos that carries me along in a fictional "as if" that suggests a mysterious *telos*. I have called this way of reading Jung a daimonic one because it is open to the unconscious and to enacting its promptings in a way that gives them substance in daily life. I consider this a living extension of active imagination and a gesture of respect to Jung's work and to the psychic reality it invokes. Like every responsible active imagination, it also requires an ongoing engagement with one's fictions, and a living dialogue with otherness and with our reading. "Reading well", says Bloom, "is one of the great pleasures that solitude can afford you, because it is, at least in my experience, the most healing of pleasures. It returns you to otherness".[78] Such a process often draws me down into my depths and out beyond them and to the limits of my understanding. It relativizes my point of view and, in so doing, continues to open new horizons and to broaden my vision. It gives meaning to what originally appeared as nonsense and helps to deconstruct the fixity of stale meanings. It opens a fertile abyss and connects me with the larger world. Reading Jung's alchemy is ponderous and difficult, but ultimately it enlivens me with a sense of richness and substance. It is both inflating and deflating. Following Jung's insights into alchemy is by no means a benign quest. It is a *massa confusa* filled with impasses and dead ends, with shadows and suffering. But, for me, it is also an entrance to the treasure house of the soul.

Notes

1 C. G. Jung, *Memories, Dreams, Reflections*, recorded and edited by Aniela Jaffé, trans. Richard and Clara Winston, New York, Pantheon, 1963, p. 222 (*MDR*).
2 Ibid., p. 327.
3 M.-L. von Franz, *Alchemy: An Introduction to the Symbolism and the Psychology*, Toronto, Inner City, 1980, p. 13.
4 Ibid.
5 E. F. Edinger, *Anatomy of the Psyche: Alchemical Symbolism in Psychotherapy*, LaSalle, IL, Open Court, 1985, p. 14.
6 J. Hillman, *Alchemical Psychology*, Uniform Edition, vol. 5, Putnam, CT, Spring Publications, 2010, p. 7.
7 Ibid., p. 8.
8 Jung, *MDR*, p. 204.
9 W. J. Hanegraaff, *Esotericism and the Academy: Rejected Knowledge in Western Culture*, Cambridge, Cambridge University Press, 2012, pp. 293–294. (Quoting Walter Pagel, "Jung's views on alchemy", *Isis*, 1948, vol. 39, nos. 1–2, pp. 44–48, quote from p. 48.)
10 A. McLean, *A Commentary on the* Mutus Liber, Edinburgh, Magnum Opus Hermetic Sourceworks, p. 59.
11 C. G. Jung, *Psychology and Alchemy, The Collected Works of C. G. Jung*, vol. 12, Princeton, NJ, Princeton University Press, 1953/1968, p. 315.
12 See "Pretace", in Edward Edinger, *The Aion Lectures: Exploring the Self in C. G. Jung's Aion*, ed. Deborah A. Wesley, pp. 11–13, Toronto, Inner City Books, 1996; and Edward Edinger, *The Mysterium Lectures: A Journey through C. G. Jung's* Mysterium Coniunctionis, ed. and trans. J. Dexter Blackmer, pp. 17–21, Toronto, Inner City Books, 1995.

13 Edinger, *Aion Lectures*, p. 11.
14 H. Bloom, *How to Read and Why*, New York, Simon and Schuster, 2000, p. 25.
15 Edinger, *Aion Lectures*, p. 12.
16 Ibid.
17 Ibid.
18 Edinger, *Mysterium Lectures*, p. 18.
19 Hillman, *Alchemical Psychology*, p. 15.
20 Ibid.
21 Ibid., p. 18.
22 Ibid.
23 W. Giegerich, *The Soul's Logical Life: Towards a Rigorous Notion of Psychology*, Berlin, Peter Lang Publishing, 1998, p. 134.
24 S. Shamdasani, *Jung Stripped Rare by His Biographers. Eren*, London, Karnac, 2005, p. 3.
25 A. McLean, *Adam McLean's Study Course on Reading Alchemical Texts*, published privately, 2005–2006, Lesson 24, p. 4.
26 Hanegraaff, *Esotericism*, p. 289.
27 Ibid., pp. 290–291.
28 Bloom, *How to Read and Why*, p. 19.
29 Giegerich, *The Soul's Logical Life*, p. 60.
30 Jung, *MDR*, p. 199.
31 P. Sloterdijk, *Derrida. An Egyptian: On the Problem of the Jewish Pyramid*, Cambridge, Polity Press, 2006, pp. 7–8.
32 C. G. Jung, *Alchemical Studies, The Collected Works of C. G. Jung*, vol. 13, Princeton, NJ, Princeton University Press, 1953/1968, p. 199.
33 See A. McLean, *A Commentary on the Mutus Liber*, Edinburgh, Magnum Opus Hermetic Sourceworks, 1982, p. 59.
34 Jung, *MDR*, p. 198.
35 Ibid.
36 Ibid.
37 Ibid., p. 199.
38 Jung, *Alchemical Studies, CW 13*, p. 423.
39 Ibid., p. 421.
40 S. Shamdasani, *C. G. Jung: A Biography in Books*, New York, W. W. Norton, p. 169.
41 See S. Shamdasani, "Memories, dreams, omissions", *Spring*, 1995, vol. 57, pp. 115–137; and *Jung Stripped Bare*.
42 Shamdasani, *Jung Stripped Bare*, pp. 2–3.
43 Ibid., p. 118.
44 Vincent B. Leitch (ed.), "Introduction", in *The Norton Anthology of Theory and Criticism*, New York, W. W. Norton, 2001, p. 3.
45 H. White, "The historical text as literary artifact", in Vincent B. Leitch (ed.), *The Norton Anthology of Theory and Criticism*, pp. 1712–1729, New York, W. W. Norton, 2001, p. 1713.
46 Ibid., p. 1729.
47 Ibid., p. 1728.
48 Ibid., p. 1719.
49 Ibid., p. 1721.
50 Ibid., p. 1713.
51 Ruth Meyer, *Clio's Circle Entering she Imaginal World of Historians*, New Orleans, Spring Journal Books, 2012.
52 M. Watkins, "Praise for *Clio's Circle*", Spring Journal & Spring Journal Books, www.springjournalandbooks.com/cgi-bin/ecommerce/ac/agora.cgi?cart_id=7095785.18039*le6YC4&p_id=03293&xm=on&ppinc=search2 (accessed 15 April 2012).

53 Ibid.
54 S. Shamdasani, *Jung and the Making of Modern Psychology: The Dream of a Science*, Cambridge, Cambridge University Press, 2003, p. 1.
55 Ibid.
56 Ibid., p. 2.
57 Ibid., p. 1.
58 Jung, *MDR*, p. 222.
59 A. Jaffé, "Introduction" in *MDR*, p. xiii.
60 Jung, *MDR*, p. ix.
61 Ibid.
62 Ibid.
63 Ibid., p. 199.
64 This is from an additional sentence in the German edition of *MDR*, as translated by Giegerich. Jung quoted in Giegerich, *The Soul's Logical Lift*, p. 61.
65 *Faust*, Part 1; Goethe quoted by Jung in *MDR*, pp. 188–189.
66 Jung, *MDR*, p. 206.
67 B. Jowett, *The Dialogues of Plato: Phaedrus*, New York, Random House, 1937.
68 Jung, *MDR*, p. 206.
69 George Quasha, "Preface", in J. Hillman, *Healing Fiction*, pp. ix–xii, Barrytown, NY, Station Hill Press, 1983, p. ix.
70 Bloom, *How to Read and Why*, p. 20.
71 S. Felman, *Writing and Madness: Literature/Philosophy/Psychoanalysis*, Ithaca, NY, Cornell University Press, 1985, p. 64.
72 C. G. Jung, *The Red Book: Liber Novus*, ed. Sonu Shamdasani, London, W. W. Norton, 2009, "Liber Primus", p. 244, n. 145.
73 Jung, *MDR*, p. 202.
74 Jung, *MDR*, p. 202.
75 R. Patai. *The Jewish Alchemists*, Princeton, NJ, Princeton University Press, 1994, pp. 218–233.
76 E. Neumann, *The Origins and History of Consciousness*, London, Routledge & Kegan Paul, 1949.
77 Hillman, *Alchemical Psychology*, p. 22.
78 Bloom, *How to Read and Why*, p. 19.

Chapter 3

Fire in the stone
An inquiry into the alchemy of soul-making

James Hillman writes: "Soul making has as its goal a resurrection in beauty and pleasure…. In a curious way, you and I crown matter, have been crowning matter, many times, perhaps since childhood. Recall the stones…" (Hillman 1993, 261, 265). This reflection on what the soul wants begins and ends with stones, and in an elementary sensate engagement with matter. As a child, the discovery of stones filled me with an odd pleasure. I loved to play in the dirt and saw the dark earth as a cosmos teaming with life. And there were the stones—alive and yet dead; they were precious to me, and I reveled in their beauty and in their variety of shapes, sizes, colors, and textures.

I collected them and returned to this play daily. There was something enigmatic—foreign—about them; yet in some way, they were more intimate than the world of human discourse. With the stones, I was alone, yet not alone. They held a secret, and my secret was with them. As I grew up and this experience began to fade, I continued to have moments of reconnection with the place in my soul that was touched by them. I remember one night having a vision of being an anthropologist from another world in the future. I had landed on earth and was walking around; everything seemed new and interesting, particularly the stones scattered on the ground. They had a numinous aura, as if they were jewels lying there free for all to enjoy, an open treasure.

Over the years, I have continued to take pleasure in, and wonder about, stones. I would occasionally bring them home to set on a shelf or desk and enjoy their natural beauty that contained many memories from childhood and extended into a mystery that seemed to stand on a threshold between myself and some other, between life and the beyond, between ego and the unknown. In later years, as I developed an interest in alchemy, I was naturally intrigued by the fact that one of the most pervasive images of its goal was the lapis or philosopher's stone, an image as compelling as the original stones of childhood and whose meaning remains elusive.

In his essay, "Concerning the Stone: Alchemical Images of the Goal," James Hillman asks: "Why the stone? What, in particular, does this image of the goal say to the soul?" (1993, 249). In this work, he sets out again to respond to the question: "what does the soul want?" He explicitly asked this question in his earlier work, *Healing Fiction* (1983, 83). The direction of my essay was inspired and given focus by Hillman's work, which seem naturally linked and also bring the question of the soul's desire to yet another level of articulation. Together, they form a matrix for the following reflection on psyche's purpose.

Psyche's purpose: what does the soul want?

That psyche has a purpose and exhibits an intentionality beyond ego consciousness was one of C.G. Jung's assumptions and contributions to libido theory, as well as to a vision of a creative unconscious (Jung 1956, 137). The question "what does the soul want?" (Hillman 1983, 185; 1993; Jung 1956, 137) is a way of posing this question of intentionality, and it is a question at the heart of a Jungian psychology. The notion of a creative process at the core of human existence is a way of imagining the question of intentionality, and it predates analytic theory in our earliest attempts to visualize life's energies. From mythology and philosophy, Jung gives examples of such numinous images, citing the cosmogonic significance of Eros in Hesiod; the Orphic figure of Phanes, the shining one and first created father of Eros; and the Indian god of love Kama, who is, as well, a cosmogonic principal. From the pre-Socratics through Plato and Aristotle, and from the Neoplatonists down through modern and contemporary philosophers, images that suggest that life has a creative purpose have permeated the thoughts of mankind (Jung 1956, 137).

In all the above, life's creative desire is never simply equated with what a person consciously wants. Creative desire is beyond the ego and, at times, demands a complex play between a personal and a cosmogonic force, and this complexity is likewise found in Jung's vision. Jung demonstrated that psyche's intention was not identical with the conscious will. This problematized any simple understanding of subjectivity and lies at the core of Jungian theorizing. At the simplest level, with Freud and Jung, respectively, we learn that we are not masters in our own house and that the desires of the soul seem to have a mind of their own and can often master us. The architecture of Jungian thought is rooted in this paradoxical awareness, and it has led over time to an enlarged vision of psyche with the development of personified notions such as the shadow, anima, and other archetypal structures that seem to exhibit relatively autonomous aims, often departing from conscious intention. Discovering more than one autonomous center of desire reveals a field of tensions fundamental to Jung's view of psyche's dynamics.

The theme of Jung's last major work, *Mysterium Coniunctionis*, was the tension of opposites that animates the individuation process and constellates a larger center of personality capable of embracing divergences of the Soul. Jung calls this larger structure the Self. It is as if this Self has a purpose that exceeds our competing desires, and/or opposes or complements varying desires which can be glimpsed only from a perspective not totally identified with the ego or any other complex. One may then begin to differentiate the desire of the ego from the desire of other figures of psyche and from what Jung ultimately felt was the larger architect of the Soul.

How then to know what the soul wants: the turn to classical alchemy

For Jung, classical alchemy was an important source of information for understanding psychic processes and for gaining a widened perspective on psychological transformation. Alchemy served him, in part, as a paradigmatic model of the individuation process and, as Edward Edinger (1985) has noted, as a model that expresses a basic phenomenology of the objective psyche, an objective paradigm against which it is possible to orient our understanding of psyche's intentions. The use of such a model was important for Jung because the alchemical corpus was seen to exceed, in richness and in scope, any individual understanding derived from case material.

On the basis of individual cases, Jung noted that one or another aspect of the individuation process tends to predominate and that the material of each case necessarily reflects different moments of a larger view of psychic possibility. For Jung, any attempt to understand the individuation process on the basis of an individual's material alone would have to remain content with "a mosaic of bits and pieces without beginning or end" (1963, 14: 555–556). In short, alchemy for Jung helped to describe the individuation process in its "essential aspects."

Jung and essentialism

While it is debatable whether it is at all accurate to characterize alchemy or Jung's approach as "essentialist," there has been a tendency to understand his use of archetypal material as an essentialist paradigm, insofar as he places an emphasis on a universal, fixed, and unchanging (essential) meaning. Insofar as Jung's work stresses this, its purpose is the identification of patterns which serve to emphasize the continuities of human life from the earliest times to the present, and the structures of similarities across cultures as well. Jungians have, time and again, documented the value of such an approach, and this has become one of the identifying marks of a Jungian psychology and the import of the term "archetypal" in the classical sense. The limitation and shadow side of this emphasis is a tendency to minimize individual, cultural, and historical differences.

This shadow has brought the Jungian approach into disfavor in some quarters of our contemporary intellectual climate, and essentialism in general has been critiqued from a variety of philosophical orientations, particularly from within feminist and poststructuralist positions. It has been argued that since meaning is never completely known (a position Jung also takes), a dependence on concepts of universal and unchanging structures rather than on a plurality of individual meanings can radically miss, alter, and limit our understanding, as well as distort the subtle nuances of experience. Today's emphasis on the particulars challenges the concept of an essential human nature in general. It has become abundantly clear that the shadow side of essentialist thinking has led to issues of race, gender, and class oppression (Childers and Hentzi 1995, 20). This recognition has led in the direction of abandoning essentialist assumptions with a certain gain, but also with a felt loss of foundations which have served as paradigmatic. One result of this philosophical and cultural perspective is to raise the specter of relativism with all its inherent difficulties (Edwards 1972, 3–4: 76).[1]

Subtler readings of Jung can avoid the inherent problems implicit in both a rigid essentialism and relativism. It is possible to see these positions as archetypal poles which, when split off, represent a fixation of thought. Ideally, from a Jungian point of view, these polarities represent a dynamic play in the alchemy of desire, an interplay that the analyst takes account of in the work of theory and analysis. The analyst must pay careful attention to the most personal and particular dimensions of an individual's life, gender, culture, and history, as well as how these particulars reflect and take part in the larger structural dimensions of human existence. Jungians hold a vision in which individual and archetype are interdependent and interpenetrative. When this integrated view breaks down, it can lead to splits which tend to privilege one or the other side of a false division. These splits can become metaphysical positions, and Jung never intended his thoughts to be read in that manner. David Miller comments that to see the Jungian archetype as an essentialist structure is unsophisticated and that it is by no means a metaphysical postulate. An authentically Jungian hermeneutic precisely de-essentializes meaning, rather than locating an essentialist meaning or a psychological essence (Miller 1995, 196–208).[2] Still, this essentialist perception of Jung's work remains, casting a shadow that has motivated psychological revision.

Archetypal psychology, the post-modern voice, and the alchemy of desire

Archetypal psychology has been particularly sensitive to the essentialist shadow of Jungian psychology and how it, as well as other depth psychologies, can rigidify their metapsychological positions and become "official" statements, which, by virtue of these theories, already declare to know what the soul wants (Hillman 1983, 94). This thrust of archetypal psychology is in line with the contemporary ethos against the essentialist tendency but seemingly unlike it, approaching the question of the soul's desire by turning directly to it through a dialogue revivifying an ancient tradition of speaking directly with the soul. Like the sacred dialogue of the Egyptian with his Ba, or Socrates with Diatoma, Hillman (1983, 86) re-engages the soul's voice following Jung's example of active imagination, privileging the alterity of voices from the background of psyche in order to hear the silence beyond the ego's speech. For Hillman, what the patient consciously says and desires is always "entangled in another factor like a thread pulling back, a reflective hesitancy which keeps assertions about what one really wants from ever finding direct speech" (1983, 85).

Hillman's reflective hesitancy, like Jacques Derrida's "gesture that hesitates between the assertive and the interrogative" (Rabaté 1994, 197), refuses the logocentrism of literal answers and refers to an unspeakable "third." For Derrida, this third is attributed to *différance*, while for Hillman, it refers to soul. *Différance* is a term coined by Derrida, indicating a condition for the possibility of meaning and is therefore presupposed by every pair of binary oppositions (Faulconer 1990, 120–121).[3] The term itself like a true symbol in Jung's sense resists hypostatization and remains a playful undecidable. This unspeakable third for Hillman, while never identifiable with what the ego is able to say it wants, is nevertheless "expressed" by the subtle voices of the silent speech of the unconscious. They are the subtle voices of subtle bodies, imagined voices that mark the space of consciousness with traces even as they are usually distanced, repressed, and deferred; they haunt our imagination and our dreams.

An example for me emerged when I was asked to give a lecture on psychiatry and religion. My host mentioned to me that the group would be interested in the personal experience of a Jungian analyst. When I began to write, I did so in a kind of intellectual, impersonal way and from an ego-oriented position, a kind of writing that did not particularly grip me. The writing had little soul, no images or dreams, and little of what gave dimension and value to my work. This soulless writing had no humor, no root metaphors of the kind that drive the soul toward a deepened life. That night I had a dream:

> I was invited to give a talk, it turns out to be with children.... When I started to speak I was very intellectual, abstract, and factual. As I looked out at my audience, I noticed a young boy who looked bored and pained....

As I imagined my way into the dream, I felt the little boy's response of pain and boredom to the kind of talk ego was doing. I began to pay more attention to the image of this child and wondered about what he wanted. This was a starting place that allowed me to change both my relation to him and the style and quality of my talk. It became simpler and more communicative. It was well received, and I felt a sense of gratification.

An interesting amplification and reflection on this kind of experience comes from the work of play therapy. Linney Wix notes that psychotherapy today is so progressive and heady and that "all the wordy head stuff does not impress the child. They merely want you to be present, not absent somewhere in your head" (1993, 58). This is true not only for the literal child, says Wix, but for the archetypal child as well. It demands that we take off our logical, rational hats and put on the sandals of Hermes (Sullwood 1982). This means a move from the "head place to the place of ground and matter" (Wix 1993, 58). Wix states that in order to do this, we would do well to retrograde to some degree, to "walk backwards," to delay our ego selves, to allow a pathway to our own unconscious. "If we do not learn this backward walk of Hermes, then we are denying the place of the child, the place of soul" (1993, 60). For Wix, this movement toward the more "primitive" and "natural" is not simply regressive, but also points toward the future. The child soul in its role as a mediating symbol can unite and differentiate.

In this brief example, what the soul seemed to want differed from the ego attitude which needed to be changed to allow a fresh voice into the space of psyche. The change required less intellectual distance and a making of room for the voice of a young boy, perhaps for the voice of soul. One should be careful here not to literalize these moments in the soul's dialectic as what the soul wants in some hypostasized way, for at other moments, the soul may call for intellect or other voices, the point being simply the importance of the dialectic play of desire, the engagement with the voices on the margin of consciousness. Hillman distills and articulates the desire of some of these other voices from his work of active imagination, including the "desire to be loved ... to be heard ... to be named and seen ... and to be let out of the fiction of interiority" (1983, 127). Often, these voices of soul are the voices of those dimensions of psyche that are kept down and below, the inferiors, the voices of "the child, the woman, the ancestor and the dead, the animal, the weak and hurt, the revolting and ugly, the shadows judged and imprisoned" (Hillman 1983, 113).

What seems important in all the above is to recognize that there are others, subtle voices on the fringe of consciousness, that we are called to account for and that can lead to further levels of differentiation and depth. We then speak meaningfully of a multiplicity of intentions in the play of desire, of a dialectic of desire in which these complex intentionalities encounter one another, where the desire of the ego meets the desire of the shadow, anima, animus, and other voices of the psyche. The field of desire is one in which these differing vectors of the soul engage, rub up against one another, collide, mesh, melt, vaporize, coagulate, differentiate, and articulate themselves in forms, patterns, dramas, stories, finding direction, and perhaps dissolving again in a cycle of the soul's transformative experience. It is these processes that I refer to as "the alchemy of desire."

These voices do not provide us with an overall metapsychological answer or denote a general conclusion, nor do they simply make empirical points.

Rather, they engage us in a subtle field of traces, exchanges, and fictional enactments so that we can develop an ear to the soul's desire.

These voices, unlike the privileged speech of logocentrism, are not simply present to themselves in an unmediated way, but are part of the play of signification. They belong to a wider field of psyche (Hillman), or of signs (Derrida). What this suggests both psychologically and linguistically is that the voice of ego or consciousness (the voice of presence) always already intends another echo or trace tacitly implied as an aspect of the interdependence of voices in a larger dialogue. The priority of ego's speech present to itself, thinking itself an unmediated and direct expression, is itself an effect in a larger context and does not simply speak, but is spoken. Derrida's deconstructive approach, like Hillman's psychology of soul, relativizes the ego, so that the traditional historical privileging of conscious over the unconscious, ego speech over the voice of the imaginal, is thrown into radical questioning and paradoxical play.

In this alchemical play, the hard fast boundary of the ego is progressively loosened and coagulated so that the clarity of binary opposition, important at one moment, is led to a recognition of other possibilities and to the imaginal, out of which the opposites may diacritically engender each other in the many shades of psyche's potential. The imaginal play of psyche itself is inarticulate yet spoken, inaudible yet heard, latent yet manifest, absent yet present, and more subtly, it is out of the space between these metaphysical opposites that the voice of desire articulates itself in the medium where silence and expression meet. If one reads Hillman's understanding of the imaginal voice and the image in this way, then the voices of archetypal psychology and post-modern philosophy can be seen to share a medium.

The shared medium of post-modernism and archetypal psychology: fictional space

For Derrida, diacritical awareness of *différance* helps to move insight more subtly into and beyond the binary vision of metaphysical opposites, while Hillman "sees through" opposites and reevaluates the antithetical mode of thinking:

> One is always never-only-one, but bound in a *syzygy,* a tandem from which ... we become able to reflect insight itself, to regard our own regard.... Each insight presupposes a perspective from which it is seen ... so when we meet the opposites our question will no longer be how to conjunct, transcend, find a synthetic third. For such moves take antithesis literally ... instead our question will be, what have we already done to lose our twin who was given with the soul.
>
> (1983, 103)

This perspective shifts awareness to a field beyond opposites to the play of the imaginal and to the realm of fictions. The psychological space opened by post-modernism and archetypal psychology is one that might mutually be called fiction, not in the traditional sense of imaginary, but rather in the drawing of its meaning from the Latin etymology of the word "fictive," indicating the capacity to shape or mold. In this space, consciousness comes to be, and with it, a sense of movement or purpose, not in the sense of known goals, but rather as guiding fictions that "show the way" (Hillman 1983, 105). Jungian and archetypal psychology speak of this directedness, "that for the sake of which" (Hillman 1993, 226) as telos, a notion that speaks directly to the question of what the soul wants, and which gets revisioned in archetypal psychology. With regard to the direction of the soul, archetypal psychology is in some respects closer to Heidegger than to Derrida: "... for Heidegger, there is something like a direction, what he calls destiny and perdurance" (Faulconer 1990, 125). According to Faulconer, "It is this 'direction' or 'destination' that is the most important difference between Heidegger's and Derrida's thought":

> According to Heidegger, as a temporal being, as futural, Dasein is "the original outside-itself." In other words, because Dasein is essentially temporal, coming from the past and directed toward the future, it is always already beyond the moment. Or, more accurately, the moment itself is transcendental, stretching out beyond the point of the now, both backward and forward.
> (Faulconer 1990, 125)

This odd philosophical construction, "always already beyond the moment," strange to the analyst's ear, breaks down a literal conception of temporality and opens up a new psychological space which we might relate to fictive space. It is not simply the space of being-in-time in the Heideggerian sense, but the space of soul's temporality. This would mean that time and telos can no longer simply be taken literally, but require a new understanding of the soul's way of movement and its goal.

The revisioning of telos and goal

The notion of telos is revisioned in Hillman's essay on the stone. In psychological language, Hillman, like Heidegger, emphasizes circularity, repetition, and reflexivity. Hillman notes that *circulatio* and *rotatio* are among the last operations of the opus (1993, 259). The *rotatio*, like a turning wheel, announces that no position can remain fixed, no statement finally true, no end place achieved. "The *rotatio* also returns telos to itself to its root meaning. *Telos* does not simply mean end, aim, goal, purpose, finis" (Hillman 1993, 259). Rather, following Onians (1973), Hillman suggests that the root meaning is a "turning around," *telos* as circling or circle (Hillman 1993, 260).

Psyche's own motion is not going literally somewhere else; there is no journey outside the soul:

> The libidinal compulsion, the organic towardness of hope and desire that would always go further for a far away grail, turns around on itself and dissolves itself.… The snake eats its own tail, a goal image of deconstructive subversion.
>
> (Hillman 1983, 260)

What is accomplished in the alchemical work, according to Hillman, is a moment, "when you *awaken within the idea of the goal*, the goal is not somewhere else out there calling for attainment, but you are within the idea…" (1983, 261). Hillman's description, like a hermetic circle or Zen Satori, returns psyche to itself, to its own waters. This return sets the stage for a new understanding of the motion of the soul and of renewal.

An example of this occurred to me at a time when a dreamer was obsessed with the idea of spending time in a Tibetan monastery. He had been working on some images in the midst of his analysis, and he heard a voice from a dream the night before, which said: "you are already in a Tibetan monastery." Listening to the voice both relieved the obsession and helped him to enjoy the pleasure of working within the immediacy of his own psychic reality. This movement was not a movement away from the world and its possibilities, but rather a movement more fully into the space of the world in which he was living. It freed his imagination to see life in a larger context and left him with feelings of mystery and vitalization not unlike the feelings I described earlier in relation to the stones. It then seemed to me that his energy had been drained off by imagining life's fullness elsewhere and in the future, to a place he could go to out there. The awakening within his psyche allowed him to feel an intimacy with that to which he was already connected. The bodily pleasure of this recognition was renewing a sense of archetypal *jouissance*.

Separation and return to instinct and archetypal ground: the process of revivification

In our Western world, the fixation of the process of separation from our instinctual/archetypal lives has been pronounced, resulting in overly intellectualized, sublimated, and devitalized removal from ourselves and our depths. We become out of touch with our instincts, flying out into the future, into the clouds vaporizing into a split-off mentalism. Our goals are outstretched in time ahead of us, and we become specters of ourselves in the rapid paced pursuit of progress and development in an attempt to revitalize our disembodied existence. While in the West this condition has been exaggerated, it also seems to represent a larger structural possibility of the soul.

Jung was aware of the importance of psyche's autonomy and the separation of consciousness from instinct (without which there would be no consciousness of the kind we know). He also emphasized the dangers of isolation, desolation, and unbearable alienation which the separation from instinct can cause. All these can lead to endless error and confusion (Jung 1953, 12: 131), and thus the need for rites of renewal which attempt to abolish the separation between the conscious mind and the unconscious and to bring about a reunion of the individual with his or her instinctual/archetypal make-up.

Many of Jung's cases document the soul's struggle to reconstruct a relationship to this instinctual/archetypal ground. In 1935, Jung presented one such case at Eranos and again at the Terry lectures at Yale in 1937. This case is of a man whose religious orientation was in irreconcilable conflict with what Jung called a pagan anti-ascetic tendency. The patient's attempts at spiritualization and sublimation were essentially ineffective in coming to any deep resolve. His instinctual personality had been neglected in favor of an intellectual/spiritual attitude, and his instincts were demanding his attention by attacking him in the form of uncontrollable outbursts. Jung noted that the patient was naturally afraid of these tendencies of the unconscious and that his attempts at sublimation were ineffective. Jung then suggested that what was needed was "real transformation," by which he seemed to mean something quite different than sublimation. A sublimated solution to the conflict between the man's "Catholicism" and "pagan joie de vivre" was far too superficial, and the relationship between his spiritual and worldly attitudes was set up in a way that dulled the sharpness of his moral conflict, obscuring his deep pain and distress. This, according to Jung, resulted in a religious sentimentality instead of the *numinosum* of divine experience (1958, 11: 32).

Jung then reported his patient's now well-known dream in which there is a gathering of people, a peculiar ceremony taking place, apparently of a magical character for the purpose of reconstructing a "gibbon." Jung states that the gibbon or monkey refers to the dreamer's instinctual personality which needs to be reconstructed, a prospect frightening to the dreamer, but necessary in order to undergo an important reintegration of split-off instinctuality and to bring about the transformation into a new man. Jung amplifies the gibbon image, pointing to man's archaic, bestial foundations and to the importance of the archetypal Dionysian mysteries which play an important part in rites of renewal. For Jung (1953, 129), these rites point beyond Freudian notions of regression to the archaic and infantile and rather to man's fundamental psychic disposition, and have been lost in our times and come closest to us in dreams. Johnson notes that this loss "is the great tragedy of contemporary western society... we have virtually lost the ability to experience the transformative power of ecstasy and joy" (1987, vi). It is the importance of the Dionysian energy that Johnson emphasizes.

These rites are often connected to the animal, and in these or such dreams, the ego must be displaced from its central role, while the center is reserved for the reconstructed gibbon, a symbol for that part of the psyche which goes down into the subhuman and yet reaches above and beyond everyday consciousness to the animal god. Jung (1953, 131) amplifies the image with the cynocephalus or dog-headed baboon associated with Thoth-Hermes, the highest among the apes known to the Egyptians.

In Jung's experience, the conscious mind, as we know it, can only claim a relatively central position and must put up with the fact that the unconscious psyche transcends and, as it were, surrounds it on all sides, connecting it backward with physiological states, on the one hand, and the archetypal dimension, on the other (1953, 132). Hillman (1979, 43) forwards Jung's examination of the monkey and its archetypal relevance, noting both the importance of the restoration of the beast and yet the incredible danger in doing so. He warns of the importance of "how the assimilation takes place: whether it be for the sake of humanity or for bestiality" (Hillman 1979, 43). With the monkey comes an ambivalence of madness and the wisdom of nature, the deepest shadow of prehistoric man, and his highest potential.

For Jung and Hillman, the assimilation takes us deeply into the ambivalences of the shadow, a return which is necessary if fallen man is to restore his divine likeness. For both, our period of history calls up the ape as a compensation to the ego-centricity of our time, requiring the return of the monkey into the foreground. Hillman observes the importance of this figure in its archetypal form in the work of the alchemist Robert Fludd, who also placed the ape in the center of his cosmic mandala, showing the relationship between man, nature, and heaven. Picasso, in his late paintings, also depicted the return of the monkey as a chthonic force of the psyche, which Jung saw in terms of the journey through the psychic history of mankind and which had as its object the restoration of the whole man (Hillman 1979, 43).[4]

The dream as access to the soul's desire—a mosaic of bits and pieces without beginning or end: clinical vignettes

The appearance of the monkey in our time continues in the dreams of contemporary patients expressing the soul's desire for wholeness in order to reconnect with their instinctual and archetypal ground. Dreams as the soul's mirror offer us a unique view into the alchemy of desire, into its particular complexity. While for Jung, individual examples drawn from case material are limited to a "mosaic of bits and pieces" and cannot demonstrate the "essential nature" of the individuation process, he and other clinicians nonetheless offer us, through an individual example, the precise way in which our essential human possibilities are actualized and inscribed in their particular uniqueness. The gathering of these examples constitutes an analytic lore and reference, demonstrating our healing fictions. As a whole, these particular stories of the soul's desire mark with poetic precision a range of metaphors of transformation, from the more common to the margins of our analytic experience.

Gene Monick, a Jungian colleague, related an interesting monkey dream to me. The following dream took place at the closure of his analytic training in Zurich. This dream seemed to me a compelling image of the "crowning of matter" and instinct:

> I am a medical student present at a pathology demonstration in medical school. The male cadaver, with an open abdomen, is on an operating table and we students. probably twenty of us, are standing behind a rope barrier watching the professor demonstrate how one ascertains the cause of death.
>
> He reaches behind himself and pulls out a one thousand pound gorilla, placing it next to the body. The gorilla begins to eat the viscera from the body. The professor says that he knows the cause of death when the gorilla gets ill from eating a diseased organ. I push to the front of the students to see better. I am fascinated.
>
> The gorilla then reaches up into the thoracic cavity of the cadaver and pulls out a tiny baby monkey, perhaps eight to ten inches long, as though he were delivering it at birth. Then a flight of golden steps descends over the table, and the gorilla ascends the steps, holding the baby monkey in its palm, places the monkey on a throne at the top of the steps, and places a crown upon its head. I am spellbound.

Monick presented the dream to his supervisors in the final session with them. They are reported to have said to the candidate: "Monick, your god is a monkey. Forget everything you learned here. Go back and practice with your instinct and intuition."[5] While this example of the emergence of the animal into the foreground is anecdotal and not meant to exemplify an analysis of the dream or even the full context of exchange, it does resonate with the significant recognition of the monkey as an important archetypal figure for our time.

The next clinical vignette echoes this story, as well as Jung's example of the gibbon image, while offering a contemporary variation on the theme. It is from the analysis of a successful businessman who, while having wide-ranging creative and spiritual energies, was struggling to make room for them in his everyday life. He had been losing his energy for pursuing the same professional demands that had made him successful. He had a strong moral conscience, but had difficulty with some shadow issues and with integrating both his sexual and spiritual needs. He had felt for some time that there was something else his soul desired, but was not sure what it was. He was having a hard time making room for what he thought could help him reorient and renew his life. He had fantasized about allowing four hours each morning to read, meditate, and work on his dreams, feeling that these activities would be a good balance. Even though his financial situation would allow for this and he consciously wanted it, something stood in the way of making a significant enough adjustment in his situation. He then had the following dream:

> He is with a small group of three or four men. They went to the edge of a pond where a monster was supposedly living. They played music for four hours in an attempt to awaken the monster. He remembers either telling them or thinking to himself "this was not a good idea." They started to return to the city, leaving the woods behind where the pond was located. They had not stirred the monster. Apparently, as they got closer to the edge of town, a distance from the woods where the pond was, a huge King Kong-like creature was stalking. Everyone in the city started to flee as the creature approached. Musicians, who were friends of his, started to head underground to hide. He thought they would be better off hiding above ground, where they could avoid being cornered, although at the risk of being more visible. He thought, but was not sure, that he jumped down into the crowd going underground. King Kong roamed through the city, crushing buildings. He remembers coming out from hiding after days had passed. People were in mass confusion (*massa confusa*), with little law and order. [The patient is a person who always follows the rules.]
>
> He then found food at a sandwich vendor's stand. Everyone with him just took sandwiches without paying, even though the vendor was there. Later, at the end of the dream, he and his friends realized that King Kong had not hurt anyone even though he had been roaming the area for many days. He then realized that perhaps the ape was good and was actually there to befriend and help them. He also discovered that a very small white bird moved in advance of him at a given distance. He saw the bird outside and tried to communicate with it. He thought that perhaps it was an advance messenger, some sort of intermediary with whom he could communicate and through it learn about King Kong. As he approached the bird and King Kong, he feared that King Kong would be roused, but if he stayed on the other side of the bird, such that the bird was between them, King Kong could not be roused. He tested this by stepping back and forth over the place where the bird was. He

then realized that he was dancing with the bird and that it was an intermediary, and also that Kind Kong was a very sensitive, huge force that was there to help.

The final image of the monster was of an extremely large, colorful creature sitting in a sphinx-like posture.

While an exhaustive analysis of this dream is not possible in this context, I would like to make a few observations.

The dreamer feels himself to be somewhat alienated from his instinctual life, at times feeling that he is not in his life vitally, but instead observing it from behind a glass shield. His soul seems to desire a reconnection with his depths and a vitalization of his life. The dream begins with a constellation of the masculine psyche and a going to the edge of a certain depth, under which something felt to be monstrous, is living. Yet, there seems to be an ambivalent desire to awaken it, calling it forth in a time frame (four hours), concordant with the dreamer's waking fantasy of the time he needs, but is having difficulty taking. In the dream, the call of music at first seems to bear no results, and the dream ego is feeling some concern about awakening this force. Suddenly, the big ape-like energy awakens and causes panic, fear for his life, and the desire to hide. Certain structures are crushed, and *massa confusa* results with the breakdown of law and order. After that, the dream ego finds itself breaking rules, taking nourishment without paying (something the waking ego would never do). Consciously, the patient is a very moral, law-abiding man to a fault. After this breakdown and breakout, the dream ego has a new observation—that although this powerful energy has been released for some time, it really has not hurt anyone—and the idea dawns that it may not be a bad force, but instead be a good one which is there to befriend.

The possibility of communicating with this energy emerges by virtue of a certain spirit which flies out in advance, as an intermediary between the dream ego and the ape-like entity. The dreamer then begins to experiment with how close he can get to it, seeking to find a proper relationship, moving closer and retreating, in a dance-like fashion. As he moves in relation to this energy, he begins to feel that the ape is a very sensitive creature and may have even come to help. This, then, seems to open the way for a new appearance of this huge energy as a multicolored, highly differentiated mystery, a riddle of the soul which presents itself as if to ask an important question. What began as a terrible fear of being overwhelmed by the Dionysian psyche threatening an enantiodromia emerges as something which, while crushing old structures, also allows a new relationship to the mysterious, highly differentiated mysteries of psyche with which the ego can have a relationship.

It is not surprising that the patient had a good deal of resistance to this archetypal energy, fearing that given a little room, it could destroy everything. This is the danger and the promise of the wild man archetype.

It is interesting to notice the parallels not only with Jung's patient, but also with Robert Bly's (1990) elaboration of the *Iron John* story, in which there is a large man covered with hair from head to foot. For Bly, this wild man lies at the bottom of the psyche of every modern man. Making contact with him is the step that every modern man has to make, according to Bly. For the man who has the courage to go down to the bottom of the pond, it is a step surrounded with fear even more so now that "corporations do so much work to produce the sanitized, hairless, shallow man.... For generations now, the industrial community has warned young businessmen to keep away from *Iron John* and the Christian Church is not fond of him either" (Bly 1990, 6).

Whatever one thinks of Bly's scathing critique, it seems to follow, psychologically, that the more removed we become from our primitive and instinctual nature, the more frightening it becomes, and the more it is desired and needed by the soul. Welcoming the hairy man is risky and requires a willingness to descend into the depths of the male psyche and "accept what's dark down there" (Bly 1990, 6). This is the kind of activation that occurred in my patient, and his approaching the depths enlivened his primitive energies. His dream laid out the potential for descending and accepting this deeper mystery.

In the following dream, the patient was back at college and walking along the sidewalk when he heard music, a fast-paced ethnic jig. He decided to dance in an almost involuntary way with joy and excitement. His feet moved quickly back and forth (like his dance with the bird). Then, he approached some steps and went down. This archetypal step is amplified by Hillman who, quoting Jung, says that, "the journey through the psychic history of mankind has as its object, the restoration of the whole man — [and that] it is upon the 'essentially primitive creature' that the *kairos* depends" (Hillman 1979, 43). Hillman, like Jung, sees this primitive creature as having a divine quality which is always based upon an animal. For Hillman (1979, 47), to remain human requires maintaining a connection with this animal, with the subhuman, remaining true to one's shadow and to the madness which is, as well, the wisdom of nature, that is, the unconscious itself. Ape as *familiaris*, guide, and companion means reintegrating some of what has been split off by the nineteenth-century religious view of man (Hillman 1979, 48). It is a return to the all too human, which has been buried or cast behind us in our climb to the light. From our rarified position, what is left behind looks too much like a monkey, "too hairy, too embarrassing, too tricky and [oddly] too wise" (Hillman 1979, 44).

To live with our central axis represented by the ape's folly, anarchy, and vice is always to be hearing his music, to have our ear to the shadow/angel. This is to remain in contact with the subhuman, yet divine, center (Hillman 1979, 47). A return to this archetypal energy is not a transcendence of good and evil, but a staying within these opposites and an integrating of them from below (Hillman 1979, 48). For Hillman, quoting Jung, this means remaining within the tension of ambivalence, "where the gods are symbolized by animals, where the holy ghost is a bird, and the wise old man is a big ape" (quoted in Hillman 1979, 44). At the end of the dream described earlier, we leave our patient with the animal (the higher ape?) seen in a new light, in a multicolored mystery, and with the bird messenger as a link to what does seem to be a carrier of instinctual wisdom.

The relationship with this emerging energy and descent to its depths can be seen in an alchemical image taken from the *Rosarium* (Figure 3.1). This descent, which depicts the soul's return to the material body, is also a vitalization and revivification. It is a way of imagining what the soul wants and is a relinking with the body and the world. It is a relinking to the instinctual/archetypal lived body—animal, erotic, and sacred. It is the moment where the soul descends from heaven "beautiful and glad" (Hillman 1993, 264). The soul yearns to enjoy this world and "has as its goal a resurrection in beauty and pleasure" (Hillman 1993, 261). For Hillman, resurrection of the ape is likewise a resurrection of the libido, an erotic power which heralds the alchemical *rubedo*, the vital reddening of life. With the reddening comes

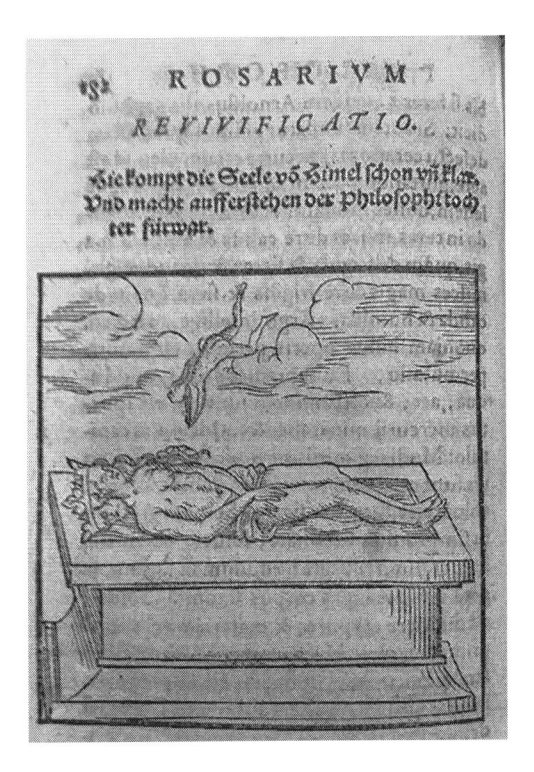

Figure 3.1 The return of the soul. Revivification, from the *Rosarium philosophorum*. (Photo courtesy of the author.)

the enlivening that earlier was missing and which now began to show itself as his world began to be colored. The image of the red stone was one of the important images of the goal for alchemy, a vision of the perfection of the stone and a crowning and exultation of matter (Hillman 1993, 264–265).

Fire in the stone: a ruby dream

The final dream and clinical vignette centers on an image of the red stone and is from a young man at the beginning of his third year in analysis. He grew up in a fundamentalist religious family and, although he was consciously separated from their values, unconscious connections continued to bind him. He was in a position below his level of talent and creativity, and his soul yearned for something more. Yet, he had trouble seeking a fuller life and a position more commensurate with his potential. He involved himself in a number of relationships with women, but often felt unappreciated and undervalued; in addition, he undervalued himself in spite of some considerable gifts. He was able, in the course of our work, to have a productive relationship with the unconscious which roared below the surface of his conscious adaptation, and at the time of this dream, he was feeling the need to make a move in his life. He was bored with work and drawn to new possibilities about which he was ambivalent, yet very excited.

> He is at work in his office, and all the furniture has been removed from it. The carpet on the floor is different. He thinks it is a new rug: it is loosened at the ends and is blowing up. He hears a deep roar from down below from the ventilation system. Then an Indian woman appears to him; he is not sure why she is there. He doesn't know whether she is an employee, but doesn't think so. She has a wide face and large, deep black eyes. She is beautiful in an exotic way. He starts to approach her, fearing he may be moving too fast or being too forward. He lays her down on the carpet and realizes that below the carpet is a grate, and he hears a low roar coming from underneath. It is the main ventilation duct, which has been thinly veiled by the carpet. He begins to run his hand up her thigh to find she has a gold clip covering her clitoris. The clip is ornate, and at her vaginal opening, there is a large ruby rock so she cannot have intercourse. He is freaked out by this, but remembers she is from a different culture. He wonders about her being clean because the clip on her clitoris reminds him of bondage and prostitution.

Again, while a more complete analysis is not possible here, there are a number of useful elaborations of this dream that forward our reflection on what the soul appears to want. Taking up the dream with this question in mind leads us to recall the patient's feeling of boredom with his work and the need to move on. One might imagine his soul as feeling empty in the place of work. What made him feel comfortable there is gone—the furniture has been removed. Something new is on the ground and there is a loosening; a spirit is blowing up. He hears something down below: it is a ventilation system—a system that carries the flow of air or spirit. One gets a sense at the beginning of this dream of the inner vision of the outer situation—of the soul's emptying out, of its new covering, of its loosening, and of the flow of its spirit.

As the patient considers leaving his current job, he is under-going a movement which seems to lay the ground for the appearance of this exotic woman (anima). He is not sure why she is there, but whatever she represents, he is interested. In his analytic exploration of this image, he reflected on his sense that she was not an employee, and he realizes that he doesn't want to be an employee either. She is broader, deeper, and different than this ego identification. He lays her down on new ground, only to discover that something is blocking both her pleasure and his entering her as well. What blocks his entry is a large red ruby.

This situation sets up a certain complexity of the soul. The dreamer seems to want to enter into her directly, but he is confronted with an impasse, and so begins the alchemy of desire. The desire to enter in rubs up against a stone. A first exploration of this stone revealed an interesting and rather startling association: that the ruby is his birth stone. Why, we wondered, would his birth stone stand in the way of entering into this new, exotic possibility? A first level of exploration revealed a number of associations to his past, to his birth "rite." Coming from a fundamentalist religious background on his mother's side made it clear that seeking money and material success, as well as pleasure, was not only frowned upon, but was in the worst case scenario, "working with the devil." In this way, the patient's unconscious connection to his mother inhibited his soul's desire to seek out new possibilities since to do so would be dirty and resemble prostitution. However, the dream ego had enough differentiation to hold such negative judgment in relative suspension. This woman might be more than a prostitute because she is from another culture and has a more mysterious sense about her. Nevertheless, the issue of money was a block to him, both desired and tabooed, and it created a sado-masochistic position in which it blocked and promised pleasure at the same time. A gold clip (money holder) covered and marked the place of pleasure.

All of our piecing together of historical material made sense to the dreamer. He even remembered that before his mother had joined her religious sect, things were different. He felt that she was then very sensitive to him, and he recalled a time when she had given him a small bag of polished stones, one of which was a small ruby. This was very important to him, marking the time before his mother transformed her life by entering into a fundamentalist religious sect. The patient felt some nostalgia and grief for the mother he had lost. This memory made sense of the patient's desire to return to the experience of his mother before her change—to enter into her and re-experience the pleasure of her "bejeweled body"—but this experience was blocked. This interpretation, while ringing true to the dreamer, also felt limited. He felt that the stone and the woman of his dream had a more mysterious meaning and he wasn't satisfied. He stated that the dream ruby was not the one his mother had given him and, as much as he could identify the maternal longings, they were qualitatively different from what this mysterious woman seemed to hold out.

We returned once again to the stone, drawing forth further possibilities that seemed to complement, amplify, and deepen what we had arrived at to this point. In describing the stone, he stated:

> A ruby comes out of the earth, and when it does, it's nothing special. It comes out of a very rough, dirty mine or something. It takes somebody with knowledge about what they are really looking for to bring it into its fullness.

He reflected: "In some way, I guess I come from a dirty, rough place and through others and myself, I was able to form into what I was meant to be." I stated to him that he had, indeed, come through a lot and that now he had a many-faceted nature and was cut beautifully, and that others valued him. This released a good bit of sadness.

One could say that I was mirroring the patient in a way that recaptured a maternal mirroring that he was longing for and felt blocked from. In a sense, this seems right; yet, I have come to feel with the patient that what is getting mirrored is more mysterious, and that the deeper "mirroring" is accomplished by the specificity of the image and the dream. It is through reflection on the image that the patient was able to arrive at the experience of what the soul wanted—a sense of recognition of his difficult journey, of what he had been through and what he was meant to be. The more positive sense of self which he may have experienced and anticipated as a child was now carried in the soul in a stone of many facets, in the reddening of this desire, in his buried potential held by the feminine. In the stone was a more exalted sense of being. By further imagining himself into the stone, the patient stated that it felt elemental, and that he, as stone, felt polished, centered, more powerful, attractive, and coveted. In reflecting this, he realized how he never allowed himself to think or feel these thoughts, could not enter them. In this way, his soul's desire was blocked, but through the image, he was now moving toward his buried potential.[6]

If Jung is correct that the Self is not an introject, but is itself projected onto our earliest experiences of the parental imagos, then the stone as a mirror reflects not simply the mother, but what the mother originally carried that belonged to the patient that is his stone. His birthstone was the carrier of the inextinguishable flame that was there at the beginning, and which for a while was promised to him through his relationship with his mother. The differentiation distinguishes the personal from the archetypal transference and suggests that the mirror of transference is carried not simply in the analyst, but in the image—image as mirror transference to the archetypal potentials of the soul. In my patient's dream, this potential is carried by an exotic woman whose reddened stone is held in the genitals, keeping the image of the self from appearing simply as a sublimated spiritual value.

Interestingly, as well, the red stone was one of the important images of the goal of western and eastern alchemy. Katon Shual (1995, 45) has linked the notion of the philosopher's stone as first matter to the eastern concept of Rasa, noting that *Rasaratnakara* means making a jewel of Rasa.[7] While referring to the stone, Rasa also refers to the essence of bodily fluids, especially to those secreted by the body when sexually aroused, as well as to the emotional and aesthetic sentiments that are part of the act of love. In this image, sexuality and divinity are intimately intertwined. Shual notes that in magical practices, partners make a dedication in the sacred space of the circle, and the genitals are seen as visible representation of the divine. One of the tasks of this initiation is the discovery of the esoteric doctrine of the body.

In light of this amplification, it is interesting to consider the notion that the "esoteric body" is also a libidinized body that, according to Hillman, maintains an Aphroditic quality, which serves to maintain a sensate attraction to the goal, "as a pleasurable pull toward beauty."[8] Voluptas, according to Apuleius, "lies curled in the womb of Psyche" (Hillman 1993, 262–263) and, like our red stone, is contained by the exotic otherness of the self, a reddened mirror of the soul.

Hillman makes an imaginal correlation that connects our last two dream examples, linking the libidinized stone with the resurrection of the ape, seeing in both a material "generative erotic power which reddens into life" (1993, 164, 263). Both images lead to an exaltation, which Martin Ruland's (1964) alchemical dictionary defines as an operation by which a matter is altered in its inclinations and is elevated to a higher dignity of substance and virtue (Hillman 1993, 265). My patient certainly felt an elevated sense of dignity and substance as he felt mirrored in the stone. His reddening had not changed his story, but revealed it to him in a way he could not see without the stone. His story was what it was, but could now be seen in a larger perspective, and he could appreciate having made the journey. At the end of the analysis, he shared the following from his diary:

> In the three years that I was in analysis, I worked on my externally formative problems such as my alcoholic father, passively controlling mother, a cataclysmic religion, and the shame of growing up in a poor

neighborhood, only as a backdrop to the much bigger internal world. The analysis was really not about solving problems as much as it was an opportunity to value and appreciate a much larger and diverse sense of the self. It was a discovery which made the suffering of the past somehow just part of the bigger picture, rather than the focus. The unwitting benefit of hardship is that it builds character and soul. I didn't particularly want to be building character as a twelve-year-old forced into stepping into my father's absent shoes with the weight of God's damnation upon me, but beyond the pathology of that role lies someone who withstood the storms and invariably came out a better and wiser sailor.

Hillman, describing the reddening, states that it does not mean that something is transcended and spiritualized, but rather that a nobler notion of matter prevails. Matter is crowned, and thereby its virtues are revealed and its inclinations alter from being the "lodestone of dumb, concrete daily obstruction to the ruby rocks that provide our life with daily pleasure" (Hillman 1993, 265).

Conclusion

This exploration of the alchemy of desire was not intended to prove or demonstrate any particular conclusion, but rather to inquire into the questions of psyche's intention. Through reflection and examples, the hope is that these bits and pieces amplify our analytic lore and show how the soul seems to exhibit a creative direction. In this regard, our inquiry followed post-modern and archetypal sensibilities which suggest some revisioning of our traditional concepts of telos and goal and, together, open the notion of a fictional space in which an alchemy of desire is enacted, emphasizing particular images of the soul's intention. Images such as the monkey and the stone, while having archetypal significance, function in a very particular way in each context and are best read with a non-essentialist eye.

Notes

1 Relativism as a general philosophical idea that is understood in a variety of ways can refer to the relativity of knowledge as functionalism, historicism, skepticism, or ethical relativism. Not all relativistic theories are simply equatable with subjectivism. What is implied here is the experience of a loss of foundations, of absolutes, of universals, and of basic structures—the struggles that ensue with this breakdown (Edwards 1972, 3–4: 76).
2 The developmental perspective in Jungian psychology also shares with archetypal psychology a sensitivity to the shadow of essentialism in Jungian thought. I have chosen to emphasize the archetypalist approach since I think it is more radical and in tune with the ethos of the contemporary intellectual trends. The developmental approach, while also less subject to the shadow of essentialism, often loses the archetypal perspective and remains rooted in a traditional subject-object dichotomy and in an ego psychology.

3 Faulconer explains:

> The point of Derrida's discussion of *différance* (a neologism and one among several names he uses for what he is talking about), is to show the origin of systems in difference (the "space" between the elements or threads of any system), and deferral (the deferral of any "last word," of any metaphysical resolution in the transcendent, of any final re-presentation) — in play, if play is conceived not as arbitrariness, but as give and take.
>
> Classically philosophy has dealt with binary differences—being and nothingness, space and time, plenitude and emptiness, true and false, sameness and otherness, male and female. However, one or another member of these sets of dyads has always held the upper hand, has always been the origin in terms of which the other was discussed: being has been taken to be a more fundamental concept than nothingness, space more than time, plenitude more than emptiness, true more than false, sameness more than otherness, and male more than female. In each case, one of the elements of these pairs has been made fundamental, has been privileged, and while the other has been explained in terms of it. In each case, one of these elements is the presence (the transcendent) we make manifest in expression and explanation, and the other element is supposedly made absent.
>
> Such privileging of one element of a pair idealizes closure, bringing explanation (and, indeed, all discourse) to a halt if the privileged element succeeds in taking on the ontological status of the medieval God, the unchanging source of all being. Any adequate explanation would re-present the unchanging source fully; it would no longer need to be spoken. Nothing more could be said once the adequate explanation was given; continued explanation would merely mark a previous failure to explain adequately.
>
> Thus, on this traditional, privileging view, the end of thinking and explanation is absolute silence, the silence of a god who needs no longer to speak, for everything has been said.
>
> (1990, 120–21)

Faulconer goes on to define *différance* as,

> the space between the pairs of the metaphysical tradition, and deferral, the deferral of the final presencing promised by privileging one element of those pairs—[différance] accounts for the necessity of continued speaking. The space between the pairs is the space from which any presence springs, the space from which any privileging of one thing over another is possible. Presence is not a result only of the privileged term itself. It is a result of the play of the elements, a play that makes the elements, as elements of metaphysical pairs, possible. Because the elements of the pairs exist only in play with one another, the privileging of one element always carries with it the denied member of the pair; the denied member insinuates itself in every re-presentation of the privileged member.
>
> (1990, 121)

4 A number of Picasso's monkey drawings are contained in Cox and Povey (1995, 163–171).
5 Personal letter from Gene Monick, Jungian analyst.
6 It is an interesting amplification to note that the ruby has many names in Sanskrit, some of them clearly showing that the Hindus valued it more than any other gem. For instance, it is called *ratnaraj*, "king of precious stones." The glowing hue of the ruby suggested the idea that an inextinguishable flame burned in this stone. From this fantasy comes the assertion that the inner fire

could not be hidden as it would shine through the clothing or through any material that might be wrapped around the stone. See Kunz (1913, 101).
7   Shual links the Indian alchemical and Tantrik traditions together.
8   Hillman emphasizes the importance of sensuous content, noting that the word libido belongs to a word cluster, including libation, as pouring of liquid, *deliquore* (to make liquid, meet), *laetus* (moist, fat, fruitful, glad), and the German *lieben* or love, as well as *liaber* (free), related to the God liber, the procreative fertility figure.

References

Bly, Robert. 1990. *Iron John.* Woburn, MA: Addison-Wesley Publishing Co., Inc.
Childers, Joseph and Gary Hentzi, ed. 1995. *Dictionary of Modern Literary and Cultural Criticism.* New York: Columbia University Press.
Cox, Neil and Deborah Povey. 1995. *A Picasso Bestiary.* London: Academy Edition.
Edinger, Edward. 1985. *The Anatomy of the Psyche.* La Salle, IL: Open Court.
Edwards, Paul, ed. 1972. *Encyclopedia of Philosophy*, 3–4. New York: Macmillan/Collier.
Faulconer, James. 1990. "Heidegger and Psychological Explanation: Taking Account of Derrida." In *Reconsidering Psychology: Perspectives from Continental Philosophy*, edited by J.E. Faulconer and R.N. Williams, 116–135. Pittsburgh, PA: Duquesne University Press.
Hillman, James. 1979. "Senex and Puer." In *Puer Papers.* Section 8. Irving, TX: Spring Publication.
———. 1983. *Healing Fiction.* Barrytown, NY: Station Hill Press.
———. 1993. "Concerning the Stone: Alchemical Images of the Goal." *Sphinx* 5, 234–265.
Johnson, H. Robert. 1987. *Ecstasy.* San Francisco, CA: Harper and Row.
Jung, Carl Gustav. 1953. *Psychology and Alchemy. Collected Works* 12. Princeton, NJ: Pantheon Books.
———. 1958. *Psychology and Religion: West and East. Collected Works* 11. Princeton, NJ: Pantheon Books.
———. 1963. *Mysterium Coniunctionis. Collected Works* 14. Princeton, NJ: Pantheon Books.
Kunz, George Frederick. 1913. *The Curious Lore of Precious Stones.* Philadelphia, PA and London: Lippincott.
Miller, David, ed. 1995. *Jung and the Interpretation of the Bible.* New York: Continium.
Onians, Richard Broxton. 1973. *The Origins of European Thought.* New York: Arno Press.
Rabaté, Jean Michal. 1994. *The Johns Hopkins Guide to Literary Theory and Criticism*, edited by M. Groden and M. Kreiswirth. Baltimore, MD and London: John Hopkins University Press.
Shual, Katon. 1995. *Sexual Magick.* Oxford: Mandrake Press.
Sullwood, Edith. 1982. "Treatment of Children in Analytical Psychology." In *Jungian Analysis,* edited by Murray Stein, 235–255. Boston, MA: Shambhala.
Wix, Linney. 1993. "Hermes and His Tricks in the Child Therapy Relationship." *International Journal of Play Therapy* vol. 2, no. 1: 49–62.

Chapter 4

Salt and the alchemical soul
Freudian, Jungian, and archetypal perspectives

The inspiration for these reflections on the alchemical meaning of salt emerged while reading an essay by James Hillman entitled "Salt: a Chapter in Alchemical Psychology."[1] In it, Hillman cited two major essays indispensable to alchemical psychology: Ernest Jones' paper "The Symbolic Significance of Salt in Folklore and Superstition," first published in Imago, 1912, and C. G. Jung's "Sal, Salt as an Arcane Substance," a section of his Mysterium Coniunctionis, first published in 1955. These three essays form a cohesive background for reflection on the image of salt, the alchemical soul, and psychology. My goal is to provide an opportunity to reflect on the image of salt as well as on differing genres of depth psychology, the psychology of alchemy, and the emergence of an alchemical psychology.

While a historical curing and maturing is implied, the intent of this essay is not aimed at a developmental judgment. While seasoning implies ripening, it is also the recognition and appreciation of flavoring, each approach yielding a certain relish, taste, zest, and interest to the matter at hand. Each genre of depth psychology tinctures the material, and the material tinges the approach: "The stuff of which we write becomes the stuff with which we write."[2]

This is a reflection about the imagination and images. Particularly, it is about the image of salt as an essential principle of the alchemical soul. We will follow salt as it draws forth ideas and essences from the history of human expression and discover a ubiquitous and mysterious substance which has been pursued down through the ages and across cultures. Throughout this essay, salt is revealed as a carrier of excessive significance in the notion of the male fertilizing power (Ernest Jones), through the erotics of lunar symbolism (C.G. Jung), to the activation of the image as a psychological substance initiatory of an alchemical mode of psychology (James Hillman).

Each of these approaches to depth psychology reflects a way of seeing both the substance and psyche of salt. Salt seems to have become not only a subject, but the seasoning of depth psychology *par excellence*, and each way it is imagined, in Freudian, Jungian, and archetypal psychology, has its own unique flavor. Each thinker invites reflection not only on salt, but on a genre of depth psychology. The way an image is understood, developed, and deepened depends on the approach, on the style of the imaginal reality that reflects it. Through each approach, a particular understanding emerges. Through each lens, we are invited to read a development of analytic perspective: psychoanalysis applied (Jones), expanded (Jung), and brought alive (Hillman).

There are reasons why these writers consider the image of salt so important. Homer called salt a divine substance, and Plato described it "as especially dear to the Gods..."[3] It has played a significant role in religious, ceremonial, and magical practices, from baptism to a charm against the devil. It has played a role in medieval Christianity in the Latin Church as *sal sapientiae*, in mystical writings, and in alchemical images of heavenly Sophia as sodium.[4] The history of salt has "cast light in unexpected directions, as on the medieval foundations of monasteries, the causes of the French revolution and on the environmental crisis in the twentieth century."[5]

The ceremonial use of salt has touched a wide range of human behavior, feeling, and expression, from marriage rites and customs to economics, from fertility to friendship, from superstition to the fundamental stuff of human life. Not surprisingly, salt has become a focus for depth psychologists. "Freud has shown that a by-way in psychology may lead to a country that yields an unexpectedly rich harvest," wrote Ernest Jones,[6] and Jung has extracted a revolutionary psychology from the most arcane of subjects. One of salt's compelling metaphoric features is its continued appearance in various cultures, across time and distance. To rewrite Blake, we can see the world in a grain of salt.

Logos and the patriarchy: semination

Ernest Jones, full of youthful enthusiasm and filial devotion to Freud, desired to contribute to Freud's developing science and extend its application toward an understanding of the psychological roots of superstition. Armed with the metaphors and methods of natural science and associationism, he set out to apply the light of psychoanalysis to the darkness of superstition, particularly the superstitions surrounding salt. Scientific method provides the infrastructure of Jones' essay, and absorbed in the conflict between science and supernaturalism,[7] he follows the rational architecture of inductive methods, hypotheses, and inferences from "definitely ascertained facts and then ... test[ing] them in their capacity to resume the whole range of accessible evidence."[8] Jones attempts to prove the value of psychoanalysis as a scientific procedure so that he may use its heuristic power to cut below the external point of view and discover what salt has essentially stood for in the human mind.[9]

No superficial investigation explains what Jones defines as the "excessive significance"[10] given to the superstitions of salt. Jones realizes that salt begins as a fundamental datum of reality, as part of the external world, *res extensa*, with an objective meaning inherent in its properties as a literal object. It is thus deprived of a fundamental, metaphoric nature. Soul is separated from the world,[11] and so salt's excessive significance must be derived from an external source, from a more primary idea in the unconscious. For Jones, this more fundamental idea is "overcharged with psychical significance,"[12] and the secondary idea may be said to represent or symbolize the primary one.[13] He arrives at this more primary idea by summing up his observations about salt:

> Salt is a pure, white, immaculate, and incorruptible substance, apparently irreducible into any further constituent elements, and indispensable to living beings. It has correspondingly been regarded as the essence of things in general, the quintessence of life, and the very soul of the body. It has been invested with the highest general significance – far more than that of any other article of diet... The durability of salt, and its immunity against decay, made it an emblem of immortality. It was believed to have an importance in favoring fertility and fecundity, and in preventing barrenness. ....[14]

Having described the popular conception of the qualities he discovered, he goes on to say:

> If the word salt had not been mentioned in the preceding description anyone accustomed to hidden symbolism, and many without the experience, would regard it a circumlocutory and rather grandiloquent account of a still more familiar idea – that of human semen.[15]

Semen then lends itself well to such associations and for Jones the idea of salt had acquired much of its significance from its being "unconsciously associated with that of semen."[16] This "fulfills at least one postulate of all symbolic thinking – namely that the idea from which the excessive significance is derived is more important psychically than the idea to which this is transferred ..."[17]

Thus far, Jones views his findings as a hypothesis which must now be proven by the "ordinary rules of science,"[18] and he uses anthropological material and folklore to confirm his hypothesis. Jones carefully enumerates his evidence, including mice becoming impregnated through eating salt and wedding customs in the Pyrenees, in which salt is put in the left pocket to guard against the man becoming impotent. He moves easily from Shakespeare to Frobenius, where he finds that salt is a direct equivalent of semen.[19]

The demands of scientific demonstration then press him to turn his attention to ontogenetically deeper roots, where he finds the idea of urine as an infantile equivalent to semen. Jones demonstrates that many of the customs and ideas he found associated with salt are duplicated with urine, including magical powers, healing and initiation ceremonies, and significant analogies to religious performances. One striking example is in regard to baptismal symbolism:

> All the evidence, from comparative religions, from history, anthropology, and folklore, converges to the conclusion, not only that Christian and other rites of baptism symbolize the bestowment of a vital fluid (semen or urine) on the initiate, but that the holy water there used is a lineal descendent of urine, the use of which it gradually displaced.[20]

Following his "scientific method" and understanding of symbolism, Jones concludes that "the ideas of ... urine and semen are interchangeable equivalents in the unconscious."[21]

Questioning whether or not natural scientific methodology is or should be a criterion of psychoanalytic findings, Charles Taylor composed a thesis offering an interesting critique of Jones, employing Jones' rules. While appreciating the formidable extent of Jones' scholarship, Taylor suggests that he fails to live up to scientific method and follows a characteristically Freudian approach to the significance of an archetypal image.[22] It is a tendency of early Freudian interpretation "to pick out some partial congruence an image has with what it is said to represent ..."[23] and not to take seriously "those associations which deny his hypothesis."[24] Taylor points to the painful and darker associations absent in Jones' essay, such as "bitterness, the morah of the sea, its sting in wounds, the saltiness of tears, or its sterilizing power."[25]

Following a Jungian approach, Taylor analyzes the way the many associations to salt link it to different qualities depending on the context in which it appears and chastises Jones for lumping them all together, "forcing all interpretation into a pre-determined conclusion."[26] For Taylor, like for Jung, salt is more feminine than masculine,[27] and it is the "patriarchal bias" of the early Freudians which forced all interpretation into a single mode and influenced Jones' "selection of semen as the hidden reference behind the ... association to salt."[28]

It is ironic that Jones was suppressing feminine, sea-related imagery of salt. He subjected himself to Freud in much the same way he subjected the image of salt to a patriarchal bias. Freud praised Jones for his willingness to subordinate his personal ambition to "the interests of the cause,"[29] and Jones replied "therefore my work will be to try to work out in detail and to find new demonstrations for the truth of ideas that others have suggested. To me, work is like a woman bearing a child; to men like you, I suppose it is more like the male fertilization."[30] The semen that Jones unconsciously discovers might be said to be Freud's, the seed that originally inseminated him. Semen then has an excess, a more polyvalent potential that may include

Jones' observations, but in the end exceeds his reductive attempt to master the image.

While semen has a definite sexual connotation, it also possesses many other meanings. For Jung:

> ... Freud's idea of sexuality is incredibly elastic and so vague that it can be made to include almost anything. The word sounds familiar enough, but what it denotes is no more than an indeterminable x that ranges from the physiological activity of the glands at one extreme to the sublime reaches of the spirit at the other. Instead of yielding to the dogmatic conviction based on the illusion that we know something because we have a familiar word for it [e.g. semen], I prefer to regard the symbol as an unknown quantity, hard to recognize and, in the last resort, never quite determinable.[31]

Jones' one-to-one pairing of salt and semen ignored the breadth of covert and archetypal associations that a powerful emblem like semen contains. If Jones in the name of science tried to be ambiguous, Jung in the name of empiricism capitalized on ambiguity.

Jung's comments throw light on the use Jones makes of Paracelsus' *De Origine Morborum Invisibilium* to substantiate his own thesis and demonstrate the connection between salt and semen. Paracelsus teaches, "Incubi and Succubi emanate from the sperma found in the imagination of those who commit the unnatural sin of onan, but that this is no true sperma, only corrupted salt."[32] Jones uses this example to deftly link the idea of salt with that of semen.

However, to Paracelsus, like Jung, the image of sperma is much more complex and filled with ambiguity. Franz Hartmann, in his book on the life and teachings of Paracelsus, cites him saying:

> Imagination is the cause of Incubi and Succubi and fluid Larvae. The sperma coming from the imagination is born in Amor Hereos. This means a man may imagine a woman, or a woman a man, to perform the connubial act with the image created in the sphere of mind. From this act results the expulsion of an ethereal fluid, impotent to generate a child but capable of bringing Larvae into existence.[33]

Commenting on the meaning of sperma, Hartmann notes the distinction from its common meaning. He states: "This semen, however, is not the sperma of the visible seminal fluid of man, but rather a semi material principle contained in the sperma, or the aura seminalis, to which the sperma serves as a vehicle,"[34] and further "the physical sperma is a secretion of the physical organs, but the aura seminalis is a product (or emanation) of the liquorvie."[35]

But Jones characteristically uses Paracelsus and others as materials to corroborate, confirm, and amplify his hypothesis.[36] The meaning of "semen" remains that of a repressed sexual image. Although he devotes himself to the feminine—folklore, anthropology, history, and myth—it is his commitment to the male fertilizing principle and the myth of patriarchy that gives his text its precarious tension.

Jones' text is overrun with examples which, if often fascinating, are excessive and far outweigh the purpose of demonstrating his stated goals. His relish for detail exhibits an almost fetishistic passion, "the pleasure lying in making the subject as complete as possible."[37] Yet, his filial devotion to Freud and science seems to hold an upper hand. From another perspective, if Jones thought of himself as a son/lover in relation to Freud, then his anima possession reveals itself in his love for myth and symbol, for the unique and odd, for the customs and rites of the world's cultures. It is their presence as passionate obsession, though subjugated to logocentric ends, that expresses itself like the furies from the unspoken beneath the darkness of superstition. The Dionysian tumult of their exotic images is an objection to the repression of the scientific method. Any reader will be seduced and lured by these intriguing examples, but the senses are soon dulled by the extent to which they are used. In a sense, Jones' essay is like all alchemical monstrum—a premature, unholy marriage of domination, a beautifully grotesque antique of early psychoanalysis, but like the monsters of ancient myth, fascinating and compelling, as if the unfulfilled promise of imaginal revelation is waiting to be born.

Salt as the arcane substance: *aura seminalis* and the erotics of lunar symbolism

While Freud and Jones privileged logos over Eros, in Jung, submerged Eros returns with scholarly and imaginative force.[38] His reflection on the image of salt begins with a fundamentally different approach from Jones. For Jung, the image of salt, as all images, requires a fundamental respect for its context to be properly understood, and it is to this context that the meaning of the image is initially referred, and, perhaps fundamentally, deferred. While both Jung and Jones place the image of salt in a variety of contexts, Jung lingers over the lessons inherent in each example rather than using the collective examples to reach unifying conclusions. For Jones, contextual meaning is an instrumental proof of a general theory that suggests a latent meaning for the metaphor of salt. For Jung, contextual citations serve as amplifications of the image of salt. This is part of his method, necessary "in order to do justice to the various aspects of the unconscious that are expressed by salt ..."[39]

Beginning with his theory of *correspondentia* axiomatic in the Middle Ages, Jung begins by placing salt in alchemical contexts. "The method of alchemy," he says, "is one of boundless amplification." The amplification or "*amplificatio* is always appropriate when dealing with some dark experience which is so vaguely adumbrated that it must be enlarged and expanded by being set in a psychological context in order to be understood at all."[40]

For him, the image is initially dark and ambiguous, a mystery which, when placed in context, enlarges and differentiates itself so it can be seen in a more variegated way. Common similarities of form give relief to the psychological structure in which the mystery is embedded. The result is a metaphoric, symbolic, and psychological sense of what is revealed by the unconscious. For Jung, the symbol is not a word or concept, a clear and distinct idea, but rather an image pointing to other images, a range of images that cannot yet be formulated in any other or better way.

Jung argues that various aspects of the unconscious are expressed by salt.[41] His reflections begin in a chapter concerned with the notion of opposites and their union, and follow a section devoted to lunar symbolism in which salt is a special instance.[42] Jung places salt in the alchemical triad of *Sulfur-Mercurius-Sal*, where it is found that *Mercurius* partakes of both masculine (red, sulfur) and feminine (lunar, *sal*). If Jones finds his "seminal substance" confined to the masculine, Jung finds it beyond gender, an arcane substance closer to the understanding of Paracelsus. Jung states that "*Mercurius* is not just the medium of conjunction but also that which is to be united, since he is the essence or 'seminal matter' of both man and woman."[43] Jung explains that *Mercurius* "usually stands for the arcane substance, whose synonyms are the panacea and the 'spagyric medicine.'... The latter [is identified] with the balsam of Paracelsus ... [which] is to be found in the human body and is a kind of aetheric substance,"[44] or, we might say, an imaginal substance.

Sal is ultimately traced by Jung to both masculine and feminine identifications and eventually found in all things. He quotes Hermes: "Our salt is found in a certain precious salt, and in all things. On this account the ancient philosophers called it the common moon."[45] While primarily related to lunar psychology, philosophical alchemy employed salt as a cosmic principle. Yet due to its radically paradoxical nature, Jung traced it as one of the designations for the "Arcane Substance."[46] Jung amplifies his supposition by noting salt's appearance in the early Middle Ages, where under Arabic influence salt water is a synonym for the *aqua permanens*. Jung quotes Seniors' unequivocal statement: "*Mercurius* is made from salt."[47] In Latin alchemy, *Sal Alkali* plays the role of the arcane substance,[48] and in *Allegoriae Sapientum*, the lapis is described as *salsus* (salty).[49] Jung finds even clearer associations among later alchemists, such as Mylius, in whose writing salt is synonymous with the tincture, the earth dragon who eats his own tail and the "ash ... the diadem of the heart."[50] Basilius Valentinus speaks of *sal spirituale* and defines it as "the seat of virtue which makes the art possible ... it is the quintessence, above all things and in all creatures. The whole magistery lies in the salt and its solution ... and is altogether a mystery to be concealed."[51] "As the arcane substance it is identified with various synonyms ... [but] above all it is an *ens centrale*."[52]

Toward the end of *Mysterium Coniunctionis*, Jung asks: "What then, do the statements of the alchemists concerning their arcanum mean, looked at psychologically?"[53] In order to answer this question, he returns to his method for understanding dreams and his definition of a symbol as "the best possible formulation for still unknown or unconscious facts...."[54] Thus for Jung, the image of salt, while continuing to be differentiated, remains a symbolic mystery deferred, an arcanum of imagination, which he traces and amplifies in alchemy, classical mythology, Egyptian and Chinese religion, folk ideas, superstitions, and magical papyri, finding it to be an expression of male and female, light and dark, good and evil, black and white, typical of the bipolarity of an archetype.

The bipolarity of white and black belongs to salt, though the blackened aspect linking salt with the nigredo is rarely mentioned.[55] Jung traces the dark nature of salt in its "fetid smell," its relation to "malefic Saturn," and its "murderous quality."[56] For Jung, whiteness, associated only with semen in Jones' essay, is seen symbolically in the images of the "white stone," "the white sun," "the full moon," "the fruitful white earth cleaned and calcined." As a white substance, it is also the "white woman," "the salt of our magnesia and the spark of the *anima mundi*" or world soul.[57]

Linking the archetype with the imagination and the soul, Jung throws some light on the overlapping significations of salt. "The obscurity begins to clear up when we are informed, further, that one of its principle meanings is soul."[58] As soul, Jung equates salt with the "spark of the *anima mundi*" and "daughter of the *spiritus vegetativus* of creation."[59] As a soul image, salt is associated with the anima and the feminine principle of "Eros, which brings everything into relationship."[60] Jung sees the work of Eros as necessary to bring the opposite dimensions of the arcanum into connection, and he focuses on two of the most outstanding properties that are brought together in the image of salt—bitterness and wisdom.[61] The factor common to both is the functioning of feeling:

> Tears, sorrow, and disappointment are bitter, but wisdom is the comforter in all psychic suffering. Indeed bitterness and wisdom form a pair of alternatives: where there is bitterness wisdom is lacking, and where wisdom is there can be no bitterness. Salt, as the carrier of this fateful alternative, is coordinated with the nature of women.[62]

For Jung, the patriarchal mind split off from Eros can never achieve insight without the participation of feeling. Wisdom can come from bitterness only as a differentiation of feeling and it is differentiated feeling which begins to unify the opposites.[63]

The work of unifying opposites requires a fundamental transformation, not simply an intellectual synthesis. It is a work of emotional engagement, of working in the dark and with the dark side of the psyche, with what Jung calls the shadow. According to Jung, Freud underestimated the difficulty of this type of transformation, for it takes far more than the ego as a rational mediator. "What [Freud] did not see was that the confrontation with the shadow is not just a harmless affair that can be settled by reason."[64]

Jung sees the shadow as exerting "a dangerous fascination which can be countered only by another *fascinosum*."[65] This *fascinosum* is found by Jung in the inner life of man like a "spark of light" and "those laboring in the darkness must try to accomplish an opus that will cause the 'fishes' eyes' to shine...."[66] He distinguishes this possibility of illumination from that of revelation, and suggests that this potent revelation can "yield a bitter water by no means acceptable to our human judgment."[67]

Jung connects this alchemical insight to the process of analysis and to the process of making the unconscious conscious:

> It is bitter indeed to discover behind one's lofty ideals narrow, fanatical convictions, all the more cherished for that, and behind one's heroic pretensions nothing but crude egotism, infantile greed, and complacency. This painful corrective is an unavoidable stage in every psychotherapeutic process.[68]

While Freud halted the process at the "reduction to the inferior half of the personality," Jung's notion of transformation included a vision of the Self.[69] The idea of wholeness held the tension of the radical opposites and produced a transcendent possibility not unlike the alchemist's idea of the lapis, philosopher's stone, or arcane substance. Quoting Khunrath, Jung notes that salt is seen to have the "paradoxical double nature of the arcane substance," an image containing the "most potent opposites imaginable" for which reason it was also called the *rebis*.[70]

Jung found that the meaning of salt is not found in common salt. By following its multiple contexts, the image is enlarged, amplified, polyvalent, and radically deferred, reflecting various aspects of the unconscious. It is a symbolic, psychological, and imaginal substance, an instance of lunar symbolism, an aetheric and cosmic principle. As such, it is far more than a mental, rational principle, but constitutes an *ens centrale*, an embodiment of the alchemical soul, a principle of Eros and the Self. In moving from Jones to Jung, we go from salt as an image of "semen" to the *aura seminalis* whose potency is in the spark of the *anima mundi* creating not only literal life, but a transcendent possibility. By viewing all these meanings together, Jung felt that he approached a clarified vision of the whole. He noted that "the sum of all these statements is seldom or never ... formulated in any

Salt: the dissemination and fervor of the alchemical soul

one author...."[71] In the end, Jung considered his method a circular art and follows Olympidorus who stated: "Thus the key to the meaning of circular art is the synopsis thereof."[72]

If Jung's approach to salt emphasized a scholarly method of amplification, and Jones relied on association, Hillman executes a stylistic shift. His intention is less to extend Jung's psychology of alchemy than to develop an alchemical way of psychologizing and restoring an alchemical mode of imagining.[73] In this not untypical turn of phrase, Hillman twists psychology in such a way that it activates the image and the imagined use of analogy, giving depth to daily experiences.[74] While Jung and Jones have examined salt "in a scholarly manner in order to give an objective meaning," Hillman attempts to "bring over the reader to the image of salt as a personally recognizable experience."[75] This shift in pedagogy, while bearing similarities to both the phenomenological and post-modern traditions, does not fall easily into any category and is best understood in the context of his position on alchemical language.

Hillman's approach contributes to and departs from the Jungian tradition. On the one hand, Hillman wants to deliteralize our abstract "concepts, distinguishing between words and things," while on the other to "re-materialize our concepts giving them body, sense, and weight."[76] For Hillman, alchemy's beauty lies in its "materialized language which can never be taken literally."[77] The point here is not to simply restore the "neologisms" of alchemical language as literal, but rather to restore a way of imagining and returning matter to our speech.[78]

Salt for Hillman "matters," and he begins with it as a psychological, metaphorical substance and archetypal principle. He activates the image and, like Jung, traces it in alchemical texts, finding those "qualities of human life that belong to the very substance of personality."[79] His model is a microcosmic/macrocosmic approach which asks that we enter the world of matter using our senses to find qualitative differences, and that we find metaphors or analogies of physical processes in our experience.[80]

> The work of soul-making requires corrosive acids, heavy earths, ascending birds; there are sweating kings, dogs and bitches, stenches, urine and blood....[81] I know that I am not composed of sulphur and salt, buried in horse dung, putrefying or congealing, turning white, green or yellow, encircled by a tail biting serpent, rising on wings. And yet I am! I cannot take any of this literally, even if it is all accurate, descriptively true.[82]

Thus, "salts belong to the very stuff of the psyche. [Salt] describes one of our matters...."[83] and this matter is formed by descent into the experiential component of the body in its "blood, sweat, tears, and urine."[84] Developing Jung's idea that salt refers to Eros, Hillman says that salt is the "objective ground of personal experience, making experience possible."[85] That is, salt makes events sensed and felt, giving taste and flavor, underlining that these events are both common and yet mine. In other words, salt acts like the "ground of subjectivity,"[86] and as subjects we are always subjected to our experiences.

When subjected to pain and suffering, our subjectivity can become initiatory. Alchemy for Hillman helps to differentiate kinds of suffering. Salt refers to those experiences which are sharp, stinging, and acute, and burn with wit and bite. They can be corrosive, acrimonious, and make sense through self-accusation and self-purification. Salt is purgative. Lead, by contrast, is chronic and dense, heavy and oppressive, a gloomy kind of suffering without a specified focus, senseless and constipated.[87] "Where salt tastes the details of its pain by remembering precisely and with piercing agony, lead cannot see."[88] Hillman notes that the curing of these conditions also differs, "where salt requires a pinch, often feeling the pinch of the events that sting, lead seems to require time...."[89]

Going beyond our traditional understanding of healing, Hillman points to the fact that, in the light of alchemy, felt experience takes on a different meaning. Through it, we can imagine our deep hurts not only as "wounds to be healed but as salt mines from which we gain a precious essence and without which the soul cannot live."[90] Hillman asserts: "We make salt in our suffering and, by working through our sufferings, we gain salt, healing the soul of its salt-deficiency."[91] This seems to be why we fixate on our wounds and why we are drawn back again and again to our childhood hurts. Pain brings us both to our body and to the body psyche. We have a need to look back, says Hillman, and it is in this looking back that we create salt and soul.

One paradigmatic story of looking back, Hillman notes, is that of Lot's wife (*Gen.* 19:26). Though there are a number of interpretations, Jewish and Christian commentators have referred to looking back as an act of searching for those who have been left behind. It is the resulting bitterness of separation and loss which can overwhelmingly turn one to salt. In lesser ways, "family fixations are also salt mines. The disappointments, worries, smarts ... the evening with photo albums and keepsakes are ways the psyche produces salt."[92] The danger here lies in fixation. The stuff that creates a sense of subjectivity and the life of the soul can also be that by which our lives are stuck and even destroyed. Too much or too little salt is problematic for the soul.[93]

The fixative quality of salt is not simply negative. Hillman gives a number of striking examples from dreams and situations dealing with themes of youthful impulsivity: carelessness, young love, lovers' fights, and even studying for exams. These examples enact stages of the salt/sulfur conjunction, where salt is said to wound or slay impulsivity (sulfur). This action on sulfur in right proportion helps to preserve relationships and build structure.

"We need salt in microcosmic ecology for fixing, keeping, preserving."[94] Salt acts to integrate the personality, to coagulate our alienated driftings, to vitalize our flatness, and to ground our "winged speculations" in tangibility. These psychological movements take place not only in the conscious application of wisdom, but in autonomous psychic movement. "The soul forces its tangibility upon us and brings home our common and base susceptibility to human pain."[95]

Hillman has activated the image of salt, following its analogies in metaphor and archetypal principle in the materiality of psyche and in psyche's personal and common experiences. He has found it an alchemical substance that gives flavor and taste to experience. It is through salt that we experience our pain and suffering. It is a substance that requires the right dosage, and in proper relation to other elementals, it can build structure, integrate, ground, and vitalize our lives. From the wisdom of Paracelsian medicine to the literature of D. H. Lawrence, Hillman pursues the fervor of salt, and it is this fervor which becomes the focus of the last section of his paper.

Jones' fervor led him to semen and Jung's to the *aura seminalis*; Hillman finds fervor in dissemination. Although Hillman does not use the word dissemination, the term characterizes an aspect of his style which flavors his work. As defined by Barbara Johnson, dissemination "is what subverts all ... recuperative gestures of mastery. It is what fails the attempt to progress in an orderly way toward meaning or knowledge, what breaks the circuit of intentions of expectations through some ungovernable excess...."[96]

If Jones' passion is for cutting below and Jung's is for finding unification of opposites, then Hillman's is for differentiation and particularization: "Salt requires particularization, it forces one to take note of the specific taste of each event, tangibility means recognition and discrimination of specific natures."[97] It would seem that this move toward particularization is precisely what works against the inherent tendency of salt "to clot, cement, coagulate, and congeal."[98] For Hillman, it is "the very nature of salt to literalize and conserve itself into a crystal body."[99] This aspect of salt affects the way it is discussed. Writings about salt tend to "conclude with a clotted thought, a reduction to a basic idea,"[100] such as semen or Eros. While both Jones and Jung spill salt out into multiple contexts, their approaches tend to congeal. Even in Jung's approach of highly polysemic amplification, Hillman finds a tendency to press toward a master trope leading to an overvalued idea (Eros) symbolically representing the overcoming of opposites.

Hillman's discussion of this tendency in Jung bears a resemblance to the work of Jacques Derrida. Both critique the move from highly particularized multiplicity toward any teleological and transcendent function and unitary resumption of meaning. For Hillman as well as Derrida, the

> *polysema* or polythematism doubtlessly represents progress in relationship to the linearity of the monothematic writings or reading that is

always anxious to anchor itself to the tutelary meaning, the principle signified of a text. That is its major reference. Nevertheless, *polysema*, as such is organized within the implicit horizon of a unitary resumption of meaning that is within the horizon of a dialectics ... that at a given moment, however far off, must permit reassemblage of the totality of a text into the truth of its meaning...[101]

If that polythematism or polytheism remains within a dialectical movement toward wholeness or unity, it loses its generative multiplicity. Thus for Hillman, any insight or experience presented as truth or faith closes in on itself and becomes "virginal."[102] Even the "salt of wisdom (*sal sapiantia*) ... [can] become crystallized and destructive when taken alone...."[103]

Hillman believes that this destructive aspect of salt takes place when salt is *in extremis*, when by its own "lethal and volatile" nature, it crystallizes into its own "inherent virginity"[104] and thus fixates and moves toward an even purer essence. He notes that we can recognize this when "the principle of fixation has become a fixation of principle. Then salt is unable to be combusted ... by sulphur ... [and] neither life nor insight [is] possible, only dedication, barren and pure."[105]

It is in Hillman's refusal to nominalize and to depart from particularization, in his call to an irreducible generative multiplicity, that one can find the heaviest concentration of salt. If there is any place one feels the fervor of salt, it is in this aspect of his approach. He aims at both theoretical concerns and, perhaps even more poignantly, at the larger cultural, political, and doctrinal affairs, where an overdose of salt shows itself in "puritanism, fanaticism, [and] terrorism."[106]

For Hillman, "society is always in danger of the fervor of salt"[107] and it is his passion to subvert the destructive aspects of fixation wherever they occur. While there are strong resonances with post-modernism, the acid of Hillman's iconoclastic enthusiasm is mediated by an equally strong fundamental valuing of the concrete image and psychic need for substantiality. He is acutely aware of the hyperactivation of salt. Hillman warns us that "the dosage of salt is an art: it must be taken *cum granosalis*, not corrosive, bitter irony and biting sarcasm or fixed, immortal dogma, but the deft touch which brings out the flavor."[108] If at times its saltiness overwhelms the reader, the insights into this essay never homogenize and congeal. Hillman's text continually self-deconstructs. His iconoclasm turns on itself so that the result, while never without substance, does not harden into a dogma, but serves as a vessel of soul making.[109]

In reflecting on these three thinkers, it is interesting to consider the perspective of Richard Rorty who characterized scientific thinking as a successive development of new languages, metaphors, and vocabularies.[110] Using Rorty's perspective, we might see that these three authors are using different metaphors and languages to approach the nature of the human soul. In each, there are different understandings of salt, as well as multiple approaches for reaching that understanding. In soul making and the making of depth psychology, literal "truth" has been de-emphasized and displaced by a perspectival approach. Salt serves as a Nietzschean example of truth perceived in terms of a multiplicity of metaphors.[111]

Rorty likewise has come to see the "human self as created by the use of a vocabulary, rather than being adequately or inadequately expressed in a vocabulary ..." and, for the most part, "truth is made rather than found."[112] In this spirit, one might read the work of these three thinkers as "metaphoric redescriptions rather than insight into nature."[113] Mary Hesse described such redescriptions as the stuff of scientific revolutions. Rorty also notes the Kuhnian point that "even in the sciences, metaphoric redescriptions are the mark of genius and of revolutionary leaps forward."[114]

If this orientation is credible in the natural sciences, it is that much more so for the genres of depth psychology. It is interesting to consider depth psychology less in terms of a development toward truth than as a field of archetypal perspectives. Nietzsche said, "The whole idea of representing reality by means of language, thus the idea of finding a single context for all human lives, should be abandoned...."[115]

It is not my intention to juxtapose these thinkers in order to decipher the true meaning of salt, nor to favor any depth psychological approach, but rather to recognize and appreciate a particular genius. Derrida has noted that as long as criticism attempts to decide on the truth or meaning of a text, it is operating within the horizon of metaphysical thought.[116]

For Rorty, it "somehow became possible, toward the end of the nineteenth century, to take the activity of redescription more lightly than it had ever been taken before. It became possible to juggle several descriptions of the same event [and image] without asking which one was right – to see redescription as a tool rather than a claim to have discovered essence."[117] This requires a spirit of playfulness that allows for alternative descriptions and overrides the demand for one "right description."[118] This playfulness is essential if we are not to fall prey to the fervor of salt to congeal into a single-mindedness. Hillman states:

> Unless we are trained in the nature and power of salt, as were the alchemists, we may become unwitting terrorists of the night, bending iron through fanatical devotion to singleness ...[119]

Both Jones and Jung have been critiqued for the tendency of each of their approaches to congeal into a fixed narrative. But we have seen that this tendency is inherent in the fervor of salt. This fervor was also evident in Hillman's passion for deconstruction.

Above and beyond these critiques, one cannot help but appreciate these authors for the richness of their contribution. Jones' particular appeal lies in his youthful enthusiasm, his dedication to Freud and the psychoanalytic charter, and his fervent commitment to science. He is passionate in his love of myth and symbol, and his devotion to collecting the odd customs and rites of antiquity is remarkable. These customs and rites are themselves part of a psychological gold mine, and his use of them as anthropological proofs marks his work as a fundamental example of applied psychoanalysis.

Jung impresses us by going against the tide of its time. He open-mindedly investigates the most arcane of subjects with a sustained and mature scholarly force. One cannot help but admire his patience, his capacity to tolerate ambiguity, and his willingness to enter into the dark side of psyche and labor there until the "fish eyes shine." Jung's vision is transformative and revolutionary, and the enormity of his scholarship has created an impressive school of depth psychology. The *Mysterium Coniunctionis* is a difficult but fundamental work, and his essay on salt is an intrinsic piece of that vision.

Finally, Hillman's essay on salt and the alchemical soul is an exemplary rendering of archetypal (and alchemical) psychologizing. It is representative of a new start, style, and genre of psychology. His insights mark a non-reductive imagining which forces a reconsideration of one's stance and makes one take note of the particulars of each image and situation. Hillman's work is admirable for its refusal of staleness in thought and its astute psychological and cultural criticism. His work opens a new chapter in cultural *and* depth psychology and is remarkable for its simultaneous iconoclasm and expression of a substantive psychology.

The grouping of these ideas has not been to affirm some hierarchy or to impose any kind of order on them. From an archetypal point of view, sensitivity to a variety of perspectives tends to produce psychological insights and "to restore psychology to the widest, richest, and deepest volume, so that it resonates with soul."[120] In such an approach, we find "vitality in tension, learn from paradox, gather wisdom by straddling ambivalence, and gain confidence in trusting the confusion that naturally arises from multiplicity."[121]

In the end, the seasons and seasoning of depth psychology are preserved in the salt. Each thinker's work is meant to be read slowly and savored, to be enjoyed for the richness of its imagery as well as for insight into the styles of the imagination that have structured the different genres of depth psychology. Hopefully, these reflections will enrich and reward the reader and give range to the way psychological work is imagined.

Notes

1 James Hillman, "Salt: A Chapter in Alchemical Psychology," *Images of the Untouched*, ed. Joanne Stroud and Gail Thomas (Dallas, TX: Spring, 1982), 111–137.
2 Ibid., 130.
3 Ernest Jones, "The Symbolic Significance of Salt in Folklore and Superstition," *Essays in Applied Psychoanalysis*, vol. II (1912, rpt. London: Hogarth, 1951), 23.

4 Ibid., 24.
5 Robert Multhauf, *Neptune's Gift* (Baltimore, MD: Johns Hopkins UP, 1928), xiii.
6 Jones, 109.
7 Andrew R. Paskauskas (ed.), *The Complete Correspondence of Sigmund Freud and Ernest Jones 1908–1939* (Cambridge, MA: Harvard UP, 1993), 115. From a letter dated August 31, 1911.
8 Jones, 23.
9 Jones' scientific orientation preceded his psychoanalytic work. In 1909, he published 18 scientific articles in the field of neurology. In an early exchange of letters with Freud, he suggested that Pearsons' *Grammar of Science* "is the grandest exposition of the fundamental principles of science" and that as a student, it inspired him "with clear and high scientific ideals." See Paskauskas, 49. Letter dated March 30, 1910.
10 From the very beginning, psychoanalysis was concerned with explaining the nature and function of "excessively intense ideas." This phrase is found in the inaugural paragraphs of Freud's 1895 manuscript, "Project for a Scientific Psychology," (Sigmund Freud, *SE Vol. V*, 295). The above is noted by Richard Boothby in "Dynamics of Presence and Absence in Psychoanalysis."
11 Jones' scientific approach here can be contrasted with Hillman's, which begins: "Alchemical salt, like any other alchemical substance, is a metaphoric or 'philosophical' salt. We are warned in various alchemical texts not to assume that this mineral is 'common' salt ..." See Hillman, 111.
12 Jones, 41.
13 Ibid., 41. Jones elaborates his notion of symbolism in his now classic paper, "The Theory of Symbolism," which was published in 1916, four years after he published his paper on salt. His work on symbolism is considered by some to be the most remarkable work of the Freudian School. An evaluation and explication of this work is summarized and critiqued in an important lengthy footnote in Paul Ricoeur's *Freud and Philosophy*, 502–505. In this note, Ricoeur shows how Jones places symbolism in the general class of indirect representations. The symbols represent hidden or secret ideas. True symbolism, says Jones, (1) represents repressed unconscious themes; (2) has a constant meaning or very limited scope for variation in meaning; (3) betrays the limited and uniform character of the primordial interests of mankind—not in the sense of Jungian archetypes, but more as stereotypes; (4) is archaic; (5) has linguistic connections, strikingly revealed by etymology; and (6) has parallels in the fields of myth, folklore, and poetry. Thus, the range of symbolism is restricted to substitute figures that arise from compromise between the unconscious and censorship. All symbols represent themes relating to the bodily self and sexuality is a recurrent theme. Jones claims that this view of symbolism is scientific and critiques other approaches to symbolism. Ricoeur's critique here is relevant to the legitimization of other perspectives. He states,

> Psychoanalysis has no way of proving that repressed impulses are the only sources of what can be symbolized. Thus, the view that in Eastern religions the phallus becomes the symbol of a creative power can not be dismissed for psychoanalytic reasons, but for philosophical reasons which must be debated on other grounds.

Ricoeur points out that Jones is disdainful of the view that symbols may have an "anagogic" meaning (Silberer), a "programmatic meaning" (Adler), or a "prospective meaning" (Jung). According to Jones, these authors abandon the methods and canons of science, particularly the conceptions of causality and determinism. Again for Ricoeur, the argument is not psychoanalytic but philosophical. For Ricoeur, such a position does not account for the symbolic domain in Western tradition since Plato and Origin, but only for the pale metaphors of ordinary language and its rhetoric.

14 Ibid., 42–43.
15 Ibid., 43–44.
16 Ibid., 44.
17 Ibid., 44.
18 Ibid., 44.
19 Ibid., 46.
20 Ibid., 71.
21 Ibid., 85. It is of interest to find validation for Jones' equation in June's early study of "a case of neurosis in a child" in *CW 4*, *Freud and Psychoanalysis*. In the tenth interview with the child, Jung describes infantile theories about fertilization and birth:

> The child had always thought that the urine of a man went into the body of a woman, and that from this the embryo would grow. Hence the child was in the water, i.e. urine, from the beginning. Another version was that when the urine was drunk with the doctor's syrup, the child grew in the head ...
> (221–22)

Compare this with Jung's later understanding in *CW 12*, *Psychology and Alchemy* (227, Figure 121). The figure depicts the transformation of Mercurius in the Hermetic vessel. The homunculus shown as a "pissing manikin" is an allusion to the *urina puerorum* (*aqua permanens*) – from the *Cabala Mineralis* (227). Also side by side with the idea of the *prima materia*, that of water (*aqua permanens*) ... plays an important part ... Like the *prima materia*, the water has a thousand names; it is even said to be the original material of the stone (*Psychology and Alchemy*, 223).

And in Hillman,

> among the sources of salt, urine holds a special place. According to the model of the macrocosm/microcosm, urine is the human brine. It is the microscopic sea within or the 'waters below.' ... Urinary salts are residual traces afloat in the lower person ... there is psychic life in the lower person independent of what goes on above, and this life is an *intense, burning, personal necessity which no one else can tend for you and for which time and place and privacy must be found* ...
> (120, italics mine)

Here, one can see Hillman's emphasis in bringing the image into a psychologically near-experiential understanding.

22 Charles H. Taylor, Jr., *Salt in Dreams and Psychotherapy: Images of Differentiations*, (unpublished thesis presented to the C.G. Jung Training Center of New York, 1979), 5. Taylor's thesis adds to the psychoanalytic understanding of the image of salt as well as contributes to the methodology for studying it. His study is aimed at both an exposition of the symbolic meaning of salt, and to my knowledge is the only study based primarily on clinical cases. Beyond his critique of Freudian methodology in Jones and his support and critique of Jung, he offers a creative insight into what makes salt life supporting or life denying which he suggests has to do with the quantity. Thus for Taylor, salt is an important image of differentiation. His study also integrates modem studies on the

physiology of taste as an empirically based starting point for an examination of salt in a way which attempts to stay close to its natural properties.
23 Ibid., 7.
24 Ibid., 12.
25 Ibid., 3.
26 Ibid., 12.
27 Ibid., 12.
28 Ibid., 7.
29 Paskauskas, 59. Letter dated May 22, 1910.
30 Ibid., 61. Letter dated June 19, 1910.
31 Carl Jung, "The Practical Use of Dream Analysis," *CW 16* (Princeton, NJ: Princeton UP, 1954), 156–157. (*addition mine).
32 Jones, 46.
33 Franz Hartmann, *The Life of Paracelsus and the Substance of his Teachings* (London: Kegan, Paul, 1896), 63–110.
34 Ibid., 72, fn. 1.
35 Ibid., 71–72. "The *liquor vie* is related to *Prana* in which is contained the nature, quality, character, and essence of beings and which ethereal life fluid in man may be looked at as invisible or hidden man...."
36 Jones, 106.
37 Paskauskaus, 62. Also on March 15, 1912, Jones writes, "The type of work I like doing is that of taking a small subject that can be covered completely such as Salt Symbolism and dealing with it fully...." (136).
38 Jung's reflections on salt are contained in his last work, *Mysterium Coniunctionis*, originally published in German in 1955–1956. It contains Jung's reflections on the alchemical soul and was completed in his eightieth year. It has been considered by many to be his most arcane and complex contribution to a psychological understanding of alchemy and to a comprehensive understanding of his vision and work. His reflections on salt are contained in Chapter III, "The Personification of Opposites," and follows his discussion of lunar symbolism. A very helpful discussion of the above is contained in Edward Edinger's *The Mysterium Lectures, A Journey through C.G. Jung's Mysterium Coniunctionis* (Toronto: Inner City Books, 1995).
39 Jung, *Mysterium Coniunctionis*, 184.
40 Jung, *Psychology and Alchemy, CW12* (Princeton, NJ: Princeton UP, 1953), 277. Also see *CW 3*, 187:

> Even the most individual systems are not absolutely unique, but offer striking and unquestionable analysis within these systems. From the comparative analysis of many systems the typical formulations can be discovered. If one can speak of reduction at all, it is simply a reduction to general types but not to some general principle arrived at inductively or deductively, such as sexuality or striving for power. This paralleling with other typical formulations serves only to widen the basis on which the constriction is to rest.

The editor points out that the above are early, tentative formulations of the archetypal theory as well as of the method of amplification.

See also R. Hobsan, "Imagination and Amplification in Psychotherapy," *Journal of Analytical Psychology*, Vol. 16, No. 1, Jan., 1971, 79–105:

> As subjective and objective analogies accumulate, the meaning of the symbol is extended and enriched. Apparently disconnected images become intelligible and there is a disclosure of psychic content. The final outcome is an infinitely varied picture in which certain lines of psychological development stand out as possibilities.

Salt and the alchemical soul 99

For Jung, "the deeper you go, the broader the base becomes..." (*CW 5*, 93). Amplification widens the foundation upon which the construction of an interpretation rests.
41 Jung, *CW 14*, 184.
42 Ibid.
43 Ibid., 462.
44 Ibid., 465.
45 Ibid., 184, fn. 383. The quotation from Hermes Jung notes is in the Rosarium Philosophorum (Art, aurif. II, 244).
46 Ibid., 188.
47 Ibid., 189. Recall also the relation of *aqua permanens* and *aqua pontica* (dirty water) as symbolic enlargements of the notion of urine in Jones. See Figures 121 and 223 of Jung's *Psychology and Alchemy*.
48 Ibid., 189.
49 Ibid., 77.
50 Ibid., 189–190.
51 Ibid., 190.
52 Ibid., 198.
53 Ibid., 540.
54 Ibid., 540. Jung goes on to speak about his theory of compensation and the importance of the arcanum for a dissociated consciousness.
55 Ibid., 191.
56 Ibid., 251–252.
57 Ibid., 240. Jung notes that for the alchemists, *magnesia* was as a rule of the arcane substance and not a specific chemical one. See note 629.
58 Ibid., 240.
59 Ibid., 241.
60 Ibid., 241.
61 Ibid., 246.
62 Ibid., 246.
63 Ibid., 245–249. Charles Taylor critiques Jung for equating Eros with differentiated feeling, pointing out that Eros shoots the arrow that connects one person with another, but that he is masculine (not feminine), the assertive counterpart to the allure of Aphrodite. Eros has less to do with understanding and wisdom than has salt. "The suffering brought about by Eros connections may well lead to (if worked on) differentiated feeling but there is no assurance that it will" (Taylor, 29).
64 Ibid., 253.
65 Ibid., 254.
66 Ibid., 255.
67 Ibid., 255–256.
68 Ibid., 256.
69 Ibid., 256.
70 Ibid., 250.
71 Ibid., 249. Jung does not use the term *aura seminalis*, but it is another image of the arcane substance and shows how an expanding and symbolic notion of semen can be seen from a Jungian point of view.
72 Ibid., 249, fn. 661.
73 James Hillman, "Salt: A Chapter in Alchemical Psychology," *Images of the Untouched*, ed. L Joanne Stroud and Gail Thomas (Dallas, TX: Spring, 1982), 112.
74 Hillman notes that "Freud's method of associating all through memory, or Jung's method of amplifying all through history and culture ... each have the effect of losing the image." See *Spring*, "An Inquiry into Image," (1977), 86–87.

Hillman's preference is for analogy which refers to a relation where there is a likeness in *function* but not in *origin*. Analogy like amplification can adumbrate an image and give it weight and extension, but unlike interpretation, it does not posit a common origin of the similarities, such as semen, Eros, etc. Hillman feels that in Jung there is at times a tendency to press for an underlying structure, while his emphasis is to keep the image alive and well by returning to it each time for a fresh sense of it. See Hillman's *A Blue Fire*, ed. Thomas Moore (New York: Harper Collins, 1989), 86–87, for a discussion of analogy.
75 James Hillman, "Salt: A Chapter in Alchemical Psychology," *Images of the Untouched*, ed. Joanne Stroud and Gail Thomas (Dallas, TX: Spring, 1982), 112.
76 James Hillman, "The Therapeutic Value of Alchemical Language," *Dragonflies, Studies in Imaginal Psychology*, ed. Robert Sordello, (Irving, TX: University of Dallas, 1978), 39.
77 Ibid., 39.
78 Ibid., 40.
79 Ibid., 112.
80 Ibid., 113.
81 Hillman, "Salt": 37.
82 Ibid., 39.
83 Ibid., 113–114.
84 Ibid., 117.
85 Ibid.
86 Ibid.
87 Ibid., 118.
88 Ibid.
89 Ibid.
90 Ibid.
91 Ibid., 117–118.
92 Ibid., 120.
93 Both Hillman and Taylor note the importance of the right amount of salt being a critical factor.
94 Ibid., 125.
95 Ibid., 128. Hillman reflects that perhaps Jung is writing about Eros.
96 Barbara Johnson in Jacques Derrida's *Dissemination* (Chicago, IL: University of Chicago Press, 1981), xxxii.
97 Hillman, 127.
98 Ibid., 130.
99 Ibid.
100 Ibid.
101 Jaques Derrida, *op. cit.*, 44.
102 Hillman, *op. cit*, 132.
103 Ibid. To what extent Derrida's critique can be applied to Jung's dialectics requires further demonstration. Hillman has stated that we no longer practice Jung's theory of symbols nor did Jung himself always practice it. In fact, symbols in Jung's theoretical sense when put into practice often become signs. For Hillman, one of the reasons we no longer practice Jung's approach to symbols is that they are no longer unknown to us. In a sense, they became dead metaphors (Derrida) worn away by our familiarity and our tendency to assimilate living psychic reality to conceptualizations. Archetypes then become reified theoretical concepts. (See "Archetypal Psychology, Post-Modernism and the Symbolic Function," in *Methods*, Western Human Science Archives, Dallas, TX: University of Dallas, 1996.) With regard to the aforementioned critique, it

Salt and the alchemical soul 101

is also of interest to look at Derrida's reading of the dialectics of classical idealism. While Derrida does not aim his critique at Jung, he does focus on Hegel's dialectic which aims at the overcoming of binary oppositions in a third term which is *aufhaben* lifted up. What, if any, the relationship might be to Jung's transcendent function is an open question. Some Hegel scholars refuse the idea that the dialectic simply leads to any ontotheological synthesis, and that the third term of the dialectic is another generative negation. However, in Hegel's logic, he does determine difference as contradiction not unlike what Jung calls the opposites, and this move draws critique of Hegel from Derrida and of Jung from Hillman. While at first glance it seems easy to imagine that Hegel and Jung are not at all comparable, Sean Kelly makes an argument to the contrary in his book *Individuation and the Absolute, Hegel, Jung and the Path Toward Wholeness* (Mahwah, NJ: Paulist Press, 1993).

104 Ibid., 131.
105 Ibid., 132.
106 Hillman, *op. cit.*, 132.
107 Ibid.
108 Ibid., 132.
109 The clearest statement of Hillman's seft-deconstructive style is from *Re-visioning Psychology* (New York: Harper and Row, 1975) 229:

> A Processional Exit: Though this has been a groundwork of irreplaceable insights, they are to be taken neither as foundations for a systematic theory nor even as a prolegomenon for any future archetypal psychology. Soul-making needs adequate ideational vessels, and it equally needs to let go of them. In this sense all that is written in the foregoing pages is confessed to with passionate conviction, to be defended as articles of faith, and at the same time disavowed, broken, and left behind. By holding to nothing, nothing holds back the movement of soul-making from its ongoing process, which now like a long Renaissance processional slips away from us into memory, off-stage and out of sight .... and when the last image vanishes, all icons gone, the soul begins again to populate the stilled realms with figures and fantasies born of the imaginative heart.

See also William Kerrigan speaking of Derrida, who states: "Because of the new demands of his peculiar (and I think, unusually scrupulous) intellectual integrity require him to occupy and vacate positions, simultaneously ..." in *Taking Chances: Derrida, Psychoanalysis and Literature*, ed. J. H. Smith and W. Kerrigan (Baltimore, MD: Johns Hopkins UP, 1984), 86.

110 Richard Rorty, *Contingency, Irony and Solidarity* (New York: Cambridge UP, 1989).
111 Ibid., 27.
112 Ibid., 7.
113 Ibid., 16. In the above, Rorty is following the thought of Mary Hesse.
114 Ibid., 28.
115 Ibid., 27.
116 Alan Bass notes that for Derrida, criticism derives from the Greek, Krinein, to "decide." All criticism, thus far, has been programmed by the metaphysical "decision" to value truth, presence, meaning ... Speculative dialectics aims to master, to unify, and to reappropriate contradiction. Truth is reached by negation and reconciliation. For Derrida, the "illogic" that leaves the opposites unresolved represents a profound challenge to metaphysical thinking, that construes contradiction only in terms of resolution, in terms of "deciding" in

the name of truth. (See pp. 72–74 of "The Double Game: An Introduction," in *Taking Chances: Derrida, Psychoanalysis, and Literature*, pp. 66–85. Baltimore, MD: The Johns Hopkins University Press, 1984.)
117 Ibid., 39 [my insertion].
118 Ibid., 39–40.
119 James Hillman, *Salt: A Chapter in Alchemical Psychology*, 136.
120 James Hillman, *A Blue Fire* (New York: Harper and Row, 1989), from commentary by Thomas Moore, pp. 37–38.
121 Ibid., 26.

Chapter 5

The metaphor of light and renewal in Taoist alchemy and Jungian analysis

The metaphor of light is fundamentally intertwined with the history of Eastern and Western consciousness. It is nearly inconceivable to "envision" a way of thinking that doesn't rely on this metaphor. As a result, from the most common jargon of communication to the most rarified intellectual pursuits, the metaphors of light and vision appear to be essential factors of consciousness. In many of the world's languages, myths, sciences, philosophies and religions, we find abundant confirmation of this view (Jay 1994, pp. 11–12).

In both Taoist alchemy and Jungian analysis, the ideas of light and renewal are also important if not fundamental metaphors. This is particularly true in the classical alchemical work, *The Secret of the Golden Flower*, the first text of its kind to have been translated into Western languages (Cleary 1991, p. 3). Richard Wilhelm first published it in German in 1929, and it was quickly followed by an English translation. Both German and English versions include an extensive commentary by C. G. Jung, who was sent a copy of the text by Wilhelm in 1928 (Jung 1961, p. 204). It was this text that Jung felt served to confirm and parallel his own work and which gave him access to his later alchemical studies.

For Jung, Taoist alchemy and his approach to depth psychology both sought renewal of psychic life through a reconciliation of opposites, leading to a sense of Self as a harmonious whole in intimate relations with the Cosmos. In such a broad generalization, one can easily see the parallels between these traditions, but many scholars have raised questions about an easy equation. James Hillman (1979a), Joseph Needham (1976), Thomas Cleary (1991), Walter Odajnyk (1993) and others have all in their own way reopened the question with regard to the relationship between analysis and spiritual discipline.

It is my intent to continue this dialogue by focusing on the metaphor of light and renewal in both traditions and to give some parallel examples for consideration. The Taoist images chosen for this purpose are drawn from *The Secret of the Golden Flower*. The first is the image of the *circulation of light* (Wilhelm 1929) or *the turning the light around* as the process is translated by Cleary (1991). The second is the emergence of the spiritual embryo as an image of new birth and renewal. Both images are essential elements in the process of Taoist alchemy. In this context, I will present analytic parallels to these images; that is, moments in analysis where what appear to be archetypally related concerns emerge in a patient's dream life. This then can serve to compare the work of Taoist alchemy as a spiritual discipline with the individuation process of Jungian analysis.

Taoist alchemy

The movement from the light of ego consciousness to the light of the larger vision of the Self in psychological terms is the work of Taoist alchemy. In *The Secret of the Golden Flower*, this transformation is achieved by the method of "turning the light around" in order to restore direct contact with the essence and source of awareness, that is, with the Original Mind. In Taoist alchemy, there are two minds or two lights, called Original Spirit and personality. The Original Spirit is the formless essence of awareness distinct from what is called conscious spirit and sometimes simply personality. The essence of inner alchemy is the work of bringing these two lights together. It is important for our task of understanding the relationship of Taoist alchemy and depth psychology to ask how we imagine this conjunction. For the way in which we imagine bringing these two lights together is one of the most interesting mysteries of psychological and alchemical work. In this conjunction, have the two lights become one? Does the conscious spirit or personality integrate with or become subservient to the Original Spirit? In what ways do we want the two to inform or change each other? *The Secret of the Golden Flower* attempts to answer these questions.

Before going on to consider this issue, I'd like to take a moment to notice that the two minds or lights of Taoist alchemy seem to be an archetypal theme. Roob has noted:

> It is said of the philosopher ... Empedocles that he claimed the existence of two suns. The hermetic doctrines also include a double sun, and distinguish between a bright spirit sun, the philosophical gold, and the dark natural sun, corresponding to material gold. The former consists of the essential fire that is conjoined with the ether or the glowing air. The idea of the vivifying fire—Heraclitus (6th century, BCE) calls it the 'artistic' fire running through all things—is the legacy of Persian magic. Its invisible effect supposedly distinguishes the Work of the alchemists from that of the profane chemists. The natural sun, however, consists of the known, consuming fire, whose precisely dosed use also determines the success of the enterprise.
>
> (Roob 1997, p. 25)

Likewise for the Islamic scholar Henri Corbin (1978), light has a double nature, an innerness that is also an outerness. This dual vision is characteristic of the Primordial Man whose light is ultimately the *mundus imaginalis* (Corbin 1978, p. 6). Jung, too, mentions two images of light, the great light and the inner light of nature hidden and invisible, "a little spark without which the darkness would not be darkness" (Jung 1967, p. 160).

The relationship between these two lights varies from tradition to tradition and it is not possible here to elaborate further upon these amplifications but in all of them with which I am familiar, the conjunction of lights is a complex issue that is not adequately understood as a simple unity, and as such would lose the differentiations between the two modes of awareness. *The Secret of the Golden Flower* describes the relationship of conscious spirit and Original Mind as a relationship between host and guest in which there is a progressive movement from a focus on mental objects to the essence and source of the mind. The movement is seen as a developing one of going beyond fluctuating emotions and vacillation from state to state or subpersonality to subpersonality (Cleary 1991, p. 145).

As the relationship with the Original Mind continues to mature, one is said to arrive at a turning point where the process of return to the essence and source of awareness becomes spontaneous and stabilizes. This crystallization produces a subtle body sometimes called the spiritual embryo. This embryo might be said to parallel what Jung called the *filius*, for which Taoist alchemists have many names and images. In alchemy, light and dark, male and female, are joined together in the idea of the chemical marriage, and from this marriage, the *filius philosophorum* emerges and a new light is born (Jung 1967, p. 126). In Taoist alchemy, this is considered the real light, not simply the perceptual light of the eyes, but also the fire of spirit. This fire is both the result of and that which emerges from the refining of the opposites and unfolds beyond them as the "Golden Flower." Just how this flower is experienced and understood is of the utmost importance. Is it singular or dual, one or many? Can our rational categories capture its significance, or is it that the flower that can be named is not the eternal flower? Is this the flowering of the Tao so well described by Lao Tzu?

Whatever our conclusion, the movement in the metaphor of light as pictured in *The Secret of the Golden Flower* might be said to be a movement from a one-sided privileging of light over darkness and consciousness over the unconscious to a new vision of light mysteriously described as inner, invisible and as vivifying fire, *mundus imaginalis filius*, Primordial Man or Golden Flower.

While all of these images are different and should be differentiated, they can all be seen as referring to the ineffable result of the work of alchemy. It is a process that produces a sense of "inner light" that is neither simply subjective or objective, nor one or dual, but a light that results in a new sense of being and of Cosmos. Robert Romanyshyn put it this way:

> Alchemy is a style of consciousness, a way of knowing and being, which in holding together the tension of spirit and matter, releases the imaginal

domain of experience and reality. The imaginal is an autonomous landscape which is neither a material fact nor a mental idea. As such it requires a way of thinking which is neither empirical nor rational. As Jung put it—the alchemists did not think in either/or categories.

(Romanyshyn 1998)

One might then say that this light is an archetypal expression of awakening, an awakening to a new vision perhaps best described symbolically and imagistically. *The Secret of the Golden Flower* differentiates this vision in images such as the yellow bird, the mysterious pearl, the diamond body, the sun wheel, the Golden Pill, the great emptiness, the inner copulation and the holy embryo. It is not adequate to translate these alchemical mysteries into rational idioms. Too much is lost in literal expression. Yet, on the other hand, it is dangerous to see them as mere idealizations.

In a letter to Chang Chung Yuan in July 1950, Jung communicated his appreciation for Taoist thought. He considered it to be one of the most perfect formulations of a universal truth he had ever encountered; yet because of its universal character, he feared that for Westerners Taoism would remain only an ideology that carried with it the possibility of being practiced in only the most superficial and imitative fashion, further splitting practitioners off from their own depths. For this reason, he emphasized the importance of retranslation, that is, of approaching the truths of Taoism from within the context of one's own culture. Jung felt that he already inadvertently was doing just this in his analytic explorations. He emphasized that the images of the alchemical process could become only words and ideals masking a hidden mystery that remained out of reach. For this reason, he felt it essential that the individual discover a way to those "indispensable psychological experiences that open the eyes to the underlying truth". Jung was aware that his sentiment was shared by the Eastern disciplines, and one might even say that these traditions made direct experience a central concern, since many of them emphasize the techniques and skillful means by which one can go beyond nominalism and abstraction. Still, Jung feared that Westerners would fall into the trap of strengthening the conscious ego and intensifying the split with the unconscious, and that this would aggravate the already chronic Western ailment of the over-determination of the will.

Jungian analyst Walter Odajnyk suggests that this is the case even for such sophisticated scholars as Thomas Cleary who retranslated and offered a new commentary on *The Secret of the Golden Flower*. Cleary has made valuable contributions to our continuing understanding of the text and to Taoist alchemy. Yet for most Jungians, his commentary remains thin, in that it is based on an understanding of "consciousness" and "spirit" that appear to be split off from contact with the unconscious as Jungians have come to understand it. This leads Cleary to a number of naive assumptions about the analytic process and its similarities and differences from Taoist alchemy. Odajnyk feels that a major problem of Cleary's is his identification with a transcendental perspective which throws the lower person and the evocative cultural and indigenous symbolism of the earth soul into the shadow (Odajnyk 1993, p. 201).

This split between spirit and soul has been richly elaborated by archetypal psychologist James Hillman in an essay entitled "Peaks and Vales." In this paper, Hillman draws apart spirit and soul in order to point to the differences between spiritual disciplines and analysis, suggesting that the former—particularly in the West—relies on the metaphor of the spirit, while the latter emphasizes soul. If we are going to find parallels and differences between analysis and Taoist alchemy, and attempt to bridge the understanding between East and West (a goal of Jung's), it may first be necessary to differentiate these two practices (Hillman 1979a, p. 57).

For Hillman, the spiritual perspective always posits itself as superior and operates well in a fantasy of transcendence among ultimares and absolutes. The world of spirit and its images blaze with "light, fire, wind and sperm" (Hillman 1975, pp. 68–69). "Its direction is vertical and ascending," it is masculine, active and carried by the Appollonic archetype with its high level sublimations, abstractions, refinements and purifications. Spirit separates high and low and chooses the high within which to make all One within it. Spirit is up at the peaks, which wipes out history. Time as well as our particular ethnic roots are seen as illusion. For Hillman, history has become the great repressed. Soul, on the other hand, sticks to the realm of experience. It moves indirectly in circular movements where retreats are as important as advances, preferring labyrinths and corners, giving a metaphorical sense of life through words like close, near, slow, deep (*ibid.*, p. 69). It is the patient part of us, vulnerable, suffering, passive and remembering. The soul, says Hillman, is like "a mermaid who beckons the heroic spirit into the depths of passion to extinguish its certainty (*ibid.*)."

Now when we look at Taoist alchemy, and particularly *The Secret of the Golden Flower*, we find elements of both spirit and soul and their subtle intermingling. When Hillman draws these "opposites" apart in order to make us feel the difference, this attunes us to what happens when a complex text is seen from the narrowed perspective of one who can only find the spiritual element in the text. It is this spiritualized perspective that Odajnyk sees as Cleary's bias.

For Cleary, the practice of Taoist alchemy seems to lead to the peaks, to a going beyond images, thoughts and feelings to a clarity of mind beyond the "quirks of personality" (Cleary 1991, p. 141). He emphasizes the capacity for deliberated thought, and the ability to think and observe with detached clarity. This clear thinking allows us to put down useless thoughts and take up useful ones by means of an independent discernment of the will.

To accomplish this level of spiritual awareness, says Cleary, we must remove the psychological seed from the temporal husk (*ibid.*, pp. 150–153). It is this view of the psychological that leads Cleary to a Western spiritualized psychological perception so different from the depth psychological perspective of Jung and Hillman, which is deeply involved in the earth, soul, history, the depths of psyche, its images and symbols.

While the above is only a small sampling of Cleary's comments, I believe that they represent a perspective which permeates his interpretations. It is not even that such a perspective is entirely wrong or that it does not reflect some aspects of Taoist alchemy, but that the spirit of these interpretations leaves too much behind. It loses the metaphoric and difficult alchemical dimension of the text, or translates this into a more rationalized psychology. It leaves out the unconscious, and in its clear light, it purges the text of mystery and soul, leaving us with a *Secret of the Golden Flower* without a secret. In its place, we find emphasis on detached spirit, transcendence, conscious clarity and will, all of which fall prey to the dangers Jung and Hillman have noted—splitting off the historical person and strengthening the conscious ego, which imagines itself as a transpersonal center yet is devoid of earth and shadow.

Through meditation practices, it is possible to experience the transpersonal core of the psyche, but this experience alone does not necessarily indicate a fully developed and mature personality (Jung 1967, p. 8). A

> danger with spiritually inclined people is that they can pursue Self-realization at the expense of personal development, producing people with a highly evolved spiritual perspective who are essentially infantile, socially unadapted, full of instinctual impulses and egoistic concerns. This observation is not meant to cast any personal aspersions on Cleary but only to point to a phenomena in order to reveal a spiritual shadow often overlooked.

If we are to have a better understanding of Taoist alchemy and analysis, of East and West, it is important to see that both traditions share the importance of going beyond this spirit/soul split and recognize that their interrelationship is fundamental in a fuller development of the person. Without this development, our spiritual sight may be blind. The Greek philosopher Heraclitus made a similar point when he said, "The eyes and ears are bad witness for me if they have barbarian souls" (Freeman 1962, pp. 32, 107). It is an important insight of Jung's that he recognized a person may hold the highest spiritual ideals and remain a barbarian if his or her shadow is split off or unintegrated. That is why Jung and many Jungians remain cautious about notions of transcendence that don't begin in a fuller development of personality, starting with the ordinary concerns of daily life, with our neuroses and pathologies and our social, political, philosophical and religious delusions, which Western alchemists call the *prima materia*.

For Jung, the process of turning the light around must be more than a technical procedure of the will. It requires a profound movement of the soul. The process of inward turning is truly possible in its deepest sense only when the instinctual and personal life has been adequately developed; "Our eyes are open to the spirit only where the laws of earth are obeyed" (Jung 1967, p. 8). Jung also noted that the striving for spiritual heights can obscure the dark earth, whose emotionality and instinctuality reach back into the depths of time and history, and that this turning must constitute an initiatory death and transformation if it is to be a genuine movement of soul.

Jungian-analytic parallels

In the following clinical examples, the processes of inward turning, instinctual response and personal development are seen in the analytic work with dreams.

A short time after the beginning of an analysis, a woman asked a not atypical question about how long her treatment would take. One might attempt to answer this question externally on the basis of a fixed idea, diagnosis or clinical experience. But it is my conviction that such answers are neither precise nor truly analytical or phenomenological. It is the work of the analyst to refer the subject more deeply to their own resources, out of which an answer may be forged, or more typically to the unconscious concern which, when seen, may allow the question to deepen or change form. Such revisioning sometimes occurs as a patient engages his or her dream life. In this case, the following dream was reported directly after my patient asked me about the length of treatment and I deferred the question.

First dream

> I have been looking for my car for some time and then I realized I am in it. I want to get back on the highway. I discover that I have turned off on a detour. I have to go down and around, since the road back to the highway is blocked. I am now walking and there are some old men and women in the clearing. An old woman comes toward me. She looks like a bag lady. She is picking up bits of paper and other scraps and putting them into her bag. I am helping her. The old woman looks me in the eye and says, "It's going to be a long winter."

In this dream, we find the dreamer seeking for her vehicle, for a way to continue on her path. She is no longer on the "highway" she has been traveling on.

She wants to get back on her way but she has turned off onto a detour. The path she has been on is blocked and she has to descend and go another way. Before paying attention to the new scene that occurs in the clearing, I'd like to stop for a moment with the dreamer in her situation of impasse, detour and descent.

This situation is a characteristic one reflecting the frustration of not being able to simply go on as before. One might imagine this as the kind of situation that could lead into analysis: the old direction is not working, and a symptom of illness blocks our typical paths which no longer bring the same gratifications, or we are simply not able to go on. Yet, we often persist in trying to go about things in the same way, passing over the fact that we have been moved into a different position in different circumstances. Sometimes, we discover that we are off the road and we find ourselves turning around, descending and going in a different direction. Fairy tales sometimes reflect such situations and require their characters to change direction, which shifts the center of gravity and opens a new scene. In this way, the logos-oriented ego is decentered, which is a condition for the possibility of any transformation or continued journey.

The French philosopher, Paul Ricoeur, sees such a decentering as paradigmatic for psychoanalysis. Psychoanalysis displaces the center in order to gain a different perspective. The ego is decentered and humiliated, but this humiliation is precisely what is needed to correct or supplement its logocentric position. For Ricoeur, it is impossible that man may know himself directly. Only by a series of detours does he learn about the fullness and complexity of his own being and relationship to being (Ricoeur 1970, pp. 422–427).

In Ricoeur's case, the emphasis on indirectness becomes a philosophical methodology, while for the analyst, clinical symptomatology and expressions of the "instinctual unconscious" serve to decenter our egos and alter its narrative force which carries us along. In her article, "Stopping As Mode of Animation," Pat Berry shows how impasse and even imprisonment can be crucial to a new kind of movement that opens up imaginal space (Berry 1982, p. 147). This notion has been popularized by Joseph Campbell as a "call to adventure," which he describes by way of some typifying images such as "the dark forest, ... and the loathly, underestimated appearance of the carrier of the power of destiny" (Campbell 1949, pp. 52–53). For Campbell, as for Berry, this happening signifies a mythical event: that destiny has summoned the individual and transferred the center of gravity from within the pole of his society to a zone unknown. Campbell sees this as an archetypal and universal situation. For the analyst, each patient's entrance into such a space is a unique variation on this theme.

For the above-mentioned patient, the clearing expressed an opening in which she encounters a lowly, and in some ways loathsome, figure who also seems to speak with the voice of destiny. Here in the "clearing," a new scene opens itself, in which she encounters an old woman whom she describes as resourceful, making use of every little bit to survive. The woman was collecting little bits of paper and placing them in her bag along with the help of my patient, who, it should be noted, had been writing her dreams down on similar scraps of paper. It was literally fall and the dreamer had the feeling that this old woman was preparing to endure the "coming winter and cold weather." If one chose to take this dream scene in part as a beginning response to the patient's ego concern about the length of treatment, one might suggest that from the perspective of an old, weathered and resourceful part of the soul, there was already a sense of preparation for enduring a "long cold period of time." One might imagine that "she" already knew that the analysis would last longer than the dreamers ego might want it to, and that some part of her psyche was already turning and preparing for it. One might say that the old woman prepared for such a "time" is aware of the *via longissima*; in her look, she conveys the sentiments Jung discovered in the alchemical text, *The Rosarium Philosophorum*, which states that it is a very long road, and therefore patience and deliberation are needed. From this perspective, one might view this image as a response to the ego's questioning, giving information to and for the ego, a map for its journey along the highway of life. It is in this sense that Jung states that the dream compensates for the limited view of the ego, filling it out and correcting its hurried, impatient vision. Yet from a more archetypal perspective, one might also suggest that what the old woman prepares for is not necessarily the literal time of analysis, which is the ego's concern, but more a readying for a coming coldness of being that must be endured. The "winter" did in fact come to express the misery, barrenness and inner frigidity of cold rage that had burned in her since childhood. As the analysis continued, the history of her bare survival and the tortures she endured were imaged in a series of dreams where armies had ravaged and brutally beaten women, leaving them bloody and broken on the ground, helplessly dying and massacred.

My patient did remain in analysis, as if compelled by the knowledge of the old woman, and seemed to know—as Hillman has stated—"[A]nalysis remains incomplete if" it has not ventured "into the frozen depths ... that in depth psychology are areas of our archetypal crystallizations, the immovable depressions and mutisms of catatonia" (Hillman 1979b, pp. 168–169). Often, my patient could not express feelings that were obviously very powerful and she remained frozen and unable to speak or express herself for long periods of time. Below the surface, there seemed to be a place that remained utterly inaccessible except for a distant stare and a death-like pallor on her face.

Dream four years later

> I see a Chinese family sitting around in a circle cooking a frog in an odd shaped primitive double boiler. When the whole thing is done it would weigh one pound. The idea was that the frog was being boiled down.

We do not have time to do justice to the dream but some relevant elaborations include that the frog is a cold-blooded creature. My patient felt close to the frog and describes how it sits removed, still and lifeless in a cold frozen position. In her identification with the image, she described how, growing up, she had felt ugly and toad-like and had memories of how her father ridiculed her and her mother's femininity, of how she had withdrawn and watched in a somewhat schizoid manner. The "frog complex" was now in the vessel being heated up, activated and boiled down to a smaller size. She comments on how the small size reminds her of a child. It is interesting that Jung has noted that the frog, more than any other cold-blooded animal, anticipates man. In this regard, it is not without interest that in my patient's next dream, she was pregnant. She was looking into her womb; she reached in and took out what looked like a pyramid in the center of which was a tiny child. She decided that it was not ready and put it back in for further incubation (Marlan 1994, pp. 39–48). I want to point to the long and difficult process of reversal, from the path she was on and what was required before the birth of the embryo could even begin to be prepared and ready. It is an example that for the analyst must be held alongside descriptions of the emergence of the spiritual embryo or new life in Taoist alchemy for the sake of comparison.

Dream many years later[1]

Many years later, after this patient had terminated her analysis, she asked to meet with me for a discussion of another dream:

> I'm in Artic water, waist deep. A section of a glacier has dropped off and there are chunks of ice floating about. There are also swaddling babies (wrapped tightly in white cloth—they look like cocoons) bobbing up from the water. I am grabbing them and handing them to outstretched arms of people on an ice floe (some sort of organized rescue team) who are receiving them and wrapping them in heated blankets. I can hear them talking in hushed tones. I am working urgently to catch these bundles as they rise and before they start to sink again. Activity is continuing as I wake.

My patient had returned to let me know that the long period of frozenness was beginning to melt. New life was emerging from the icy depths and she was receiving it with outstretched arms, keeping her new potentials from sinking back into the unconscious. Psyche was holding and wrapping this life in a warm embrace. She is now rescuing and finding support for this new potential and she continues to work to put them in firm hands.

In this next clinical example, we will return to the alchemical theme of two lights, of turning the light around and the dreamer's development.

Again, a deep, instinctual reaction seems to be an essential turning point for this woman who was struggling with her Christian God image. For some alchemists, the light of the Christian deity could stand in the way of the light of nature or *lumen naturae*, a kind of light that became obscured as the development of Christianity split off from the pagan power of nature. The split was a cultural and religious divide in Western culture, which is paralleled by splits in individuals.

The dreamer was brought up in a strict Catholic tradition, and had been struggling with her desire for a warmer, more sensual life, desiring to be in better touch with her sexuality, eros and bodily sense of self. She experienced her needs as in conflict with her religious training and felt a strong tension with what seemed to be a patriarchal and removed sense of God. Her dreams opened up a heroic and unthinkable reaction to her God image and drew her down into the flower of her femininity and toward a chthonic light at the core of her inner life. This dream came at a time after her analyst had moved away and she felt abandoned, and she had not yet started analysis with me.

Dream

> I am simultaneously an observer and a small naked infant crawling on a white Easter lily. I am crawling around the flower; it is white, no color, and I am craving to feel its texture and to feel something more, more sensuality. The flower is floating in a dark sky with lots of little lights, like stars in the night. Then I feel a beam of sunlight: it warms my body and gives me a good feeling of being grounded and embodied and a feeling of sensuality. Just as this feeling begins, Jesus Christ on the cross emerges from below and is positioned between me and the sun and, in so doing, casts a shadow over me. I then feel cut off from the light and the warm feelings I was beginning to have. I feel panic that I will freeze to death and won't be able to get any nourishment. Then I feel myself growing very large and, in a burst of rage, I punch Christ in the face, knocking him off the cross, and he and the cross fall down below me. I feel some guilt but then also notice another kind of light coming from deep within the core of the flower; it has a silvery quality.

Again, it is not my purpose here to go into a full analysis of the dream but only to point out how the instinctual and spontaneous psychic reaction of the dream ego leads the way to an important inward turning from a patriarchal God image that overshadows her connection to a warmer and embodied sensuality. Here, the old conflict between spirit and instinct, religion and sensuality, male and female, places the dreamer in the cold shadow of the deity.

Jung has shown how in our complexes the ancient gods reside and how they return at the archetypal core of our symptoms. Greek myth placed

Pan as a God of nature. The ancient mythological religion was essentially a nature religion, the transcendence of which by Christianity therefore suppressed the kind of nature expressed in such figures as Pan. Hillman placed Pan in a cluster of meanings interestingly associated with the abandonment of the child (echoing the dreamer's abandonment), and that is the Pan which appears in the symptom of panic as a protective instinctual/archetypal reaction in a time of crisis.

This dream supports what many commentators on Pan have stated—that Pan never really died; he was repressed and still lives in our symptoms, and returns when our instincts assert themselves. In our dreamer, Pan does return in her panic and rebellion, and, filled with fear and rage, she strikes down her God image. This destructive/creative act inflates the dreamer who breaks a taboo, which seems to allow her then to turn toward a new light and flowering of her soul. This instinctual act of rebellion seems to be an essential component of both spiritual development and individuation. *The Secret of the Golden Flower* states, "If people can kill the mind the original comes alive" (Cleary 1991, p. 25), an idea reminiscent of the Buddhist saying, "If you meet the Buddha on the road, kill him," and the alchemical idea that the old king must die for regeneration to take place.

If these vignettes are at all suggestive, they will demonstrate Jung's statement that the process of inward turning is truly possible only to the extent that the instinctive and personal life has been adequately developed, and that the old dominant images that hold psyche in thrall—whether an ugly old frog or a divine Christ—undergo a mortification or death. In our first vignette, we can see the deep inner movements necessary to overcome early images of ugliness or wounding to the feminine, and what was required to boil down the complex deeply frozen in cold repressed rage. In this kind of cooking, one can see potential for the emergence of the embryo—a sign of the potential for new life. Likewise in our second dreamer, without her instinctive movement of striking down the God image, any attempt to free herself from the cold shadow of the divinity would seem impossible. It took the action of the dream ego expressing panic, rage and inflation to clear the way for a process of turning around, an inward turning necessary for the psyche's unfolding.

In both cases, the required "turning" presupposes an encounter of impasse, an intervention from the autonomous psyche that sets the stage for a deeper movement of the soul. It is a process imaged here by boiling or striking down an old image, but it is more fully imagined in the complexity of our dreams. I would suggest that these experiences are not simply linked to the particular pathology of the dreamers, but that in both healthy and neurotic individuals, the work of change is complex and arduous, and requires not simply transcendence but transformation. What is archetypal is not the particulars of each individual's psyche, but the alchemical process itself, which seems to engender a movement toward renewal of psychic life through a *nigredo* experience and in a reconciliation of opposites, a process that can be seen in both Taoist alchemy and Jungian analysis.

While one can trace this process in these examples, it is not the case that the transformations depicted earlier represent the subtlest stages of personal development. It is interesting, however, that the images used to designate high levels of development, such as the turning around of the light and the birth of the embryo in Taoist alchemy, appear in the above at moments of important change. The images, while not the same, are parallel in suggesting the possibility that their presence both in meditative experience and in analysis could express an archetypal process of transformation, manifested in different ways and at different levels of psychic development.

Jung's final statement of the higher levels of the *coniunctio* is described in his work, *Mysterium Coniunctionis*. In the last chapter of this text, he describes what he calls the "greater *coniunctio*," the union of opposites through which the philosopher's stone is produced. The *coniunctio* or alchemical marriage was the last procedure of the alchemists who hoped to unite previously purified substances that existed in complementary but opposed positions. In psychological terms, the opposites that need to be united are the conscious and unconscious aspects of the psyche. The final goal was the reconstitution of the Self. This alchemical conjunction was nothing less than a restoration of the original state of the Cosmos and is the Western equivalent of the fundamental principle of classical Chinese philosophy, namely the union of *yin* and *yang* in the Tao.

The unification of "opposites" in Taoist alchemy and Jungian analysis

The tradition of inner alchemy also expresses this unification in phenomenological and poetic descriptions, which move the heart and soul as well as the mind. For example, the *coniunctio* is described as follows:

> Once the two things meet, they join inextricably, the living movement of creative energy now coming, now going, now floating, now sinking. In the basic chamber in oneself there is an ungraspable sense of vast space, beyond measure; and the whole body feels wondrously light and buoyant. This is what is called "clouds filling the thousand mountains ..." (Cleary 1991, p. 41) "... the coming and going is traceless, the floating and sinking are indiscernible. The channels are stilled, energy stops: this is the true intercourse. This is what is called "the moon steeped in myriad waters.
>
> (*ibid.*, p. 42)

Another example is given by Chang Po-Tuan in his *Introduction to Alchemy*:

> The pores are like after a bath, the bones and circulatory system are like when fast asleep, the vitality and spirit are like husband and wife

in blissful embrace, the earthly and heavenly souls are like child and mother remembering their love.

(*ibid.*, p. 101)

An even more enigmatic description is given by a female adept of the Complete Reality School (CRS) of Tao, Sun Bu-er in her poem.

> At the right time, just out of the valley,
> You rise lightly into the spiritual firmament.
> The jade girl rides a blue phoenix,
> The gold boy offers a scarlet peach.
> One strums a brocade lute amidst the flowers,
> One plays jewel pipes under the moon.
> One day immortal and mortal are separated,
> And you coolly cross the ocean.

(Cleary, p. 103)[2]

In a story entitled *Chi Po & the Sorcerer: A Chinese Tale for Children and Philosophers*, Oscar Mandel creates a scene in which the young Chi Po approaches his teacher, the sorcerer Bu Fu, for his first lesson. The fictional character of Chi Po was based on that of one of China's great painters, Ch'i Pai-shih. The account goes as follows:

> "Tell me, sproutling," said Bu Fu at the beginning of an important lesson, "if your mother and father could give you anything you desired, what would you ask of them?"
>
> That was a question Chi Po had often dreamed of himself, and had answered, too, in his dreams. So he replied without hesitation: "A new hoop and a pair of blue silken trousers for myself, a rocking-chair for father, and jade earrings for mother."
>
> "Excellent!" Bu Fu exclaimed; "I love, support and admire that hoop, those trousers, that rocking-chair and those earrings. Excellent! What would happen to philosophy without them? But now, go sit at the door of my cave, watch the sky and the trees, take note of the inquisitive wind and the dignity of the clouds, observe how the squirrels and the rabbits live their lives without us, and dream of the brush and of your hand sweeping over the silk of your next painting."
>
> With this Bu Fu pronounced several frightful gutturals, and abandoning Chi Po at the mouth of the cave, he went gathering acorns. Only the bulbul remained with Chi Po. He sat on a branch where he could watch the newcomer, and you could see by the tilt of his head and the angle of his beak that he doubted whether Chi Po could *do* it.
>
> And it wasn't easy. Now that Bu Fu had reminded him of the good things he liked to dream about (and I haven't mentioned them all), Chi Po found it hard to send his thoughts into the trees and to keep his eye

on the changing moods of the clouds. But the afternoon was warm, and Chi Po settled drowsily with his back to the cave, chewing on a pine needle as he sat. He watched a cloud leave the top of a cedar and edge cautiously over to the top of another cedar—"like a tightrope walker," thought Chi Po. And then he heard the wind: it ooooed against the rocks, frushled among the leaves, tickled in the pines, and then went loose above the earth. And on top of the wind went the snitting of the sparrows, the plak-plak of wild geese, the kris-kris of magpies, and above all, the strange lilling of the scarlet-throated winterwinch that one sees only when one is asleep.

All of a sudden Chi Po noticed an ant, a tiny ant, a baby ant, strolling on the ground. It strolled out of the shadow of a huge inch of a pebble and climbed onto a splinter of a twig. On the splinter it basked awhile in the sun like Chi Po, then it nosed a larger ant with which it exchanged a friendly how-do-you-do. When this was done it wormed its way down a hole, stumbled out again, and traversed a thousandth part of an old sandal Bu Fu had thrown out of his cave. Thereupon—

"Young one," said Bu Fu, returning with a basket full of acorns, "what is on your mind?"

"Oh," said Chi Po, a little ashamed, "nothing."

"Perfect," cried Bu Fu, his beard quivering. "You have understood my lesson. Now go home, because I have witchcraft in hand. Come back tomorrow. If your mind is still free of that clutter of hoops and rocking-chairs—admirable clutter, don't misunderstand me, child!—I may allow you to paint a single dragonfly on a lonely lotus flower."

....

"So," said Bu Fu the next day, when Chi Po came puffing up to the cave, "what of the clutter?"

"I hope I have left it behind, sir," answered Chi Po.

"For the time being?"

"For the time being. And my fingers are wide awake. Are they allowed to try the dragonfly?"

"Sitting on the lotus blossom. Have at it, lad!"

And Bu Fu told Chi Po why a dragonfly needs a flower, and why a flower needs a dragonfly, for the one stays in the ground and rises from the ground upward, while the other moves about and descends from the sky downward.

"Therefore," said Chi Po, "I must paint them where they meet, where down flows into up and up flows into down."

(Mandel 2014, pp. 105–107)[3]

If these poetic images and descriptions reflect the subtlest levels of the *coniunctio* as a traceless union referring to a seamless oneness, it is also vital that we do not fall into the idealisms we've been discussing by interpreting this "union" as a simple oneness. According to Jung and Hillman, this can lead to an error that results in what the alchemists called a *monstrum* or premature unity, which is any union which does not differentiate itself into distinct realities. This premature quality of vision can hold true even for those ratified spiritual states described in the images of "pure light, or the void, ... or merging bliss," etc. (Hillman 1979a, p. 57). In his paper, the "Silver and White Earth," Hillman further elaborates his position:

> ... to go through the world seeing its one underlying truth in synchronistic revelations, its pre-established harmony, that God is man and man becoming God, inner and outer are one, puer is senex, senex puer. That nature and spirit, body and mind are two aspects of the same invisible energy or implicate order thereby neglects the acute distinctions joined by these conjunctions so that our consciousness no matter how wise and wondrous is therefore premature and monstrous. And by monstrous alchemy means fruitless, barren without issue.
>
> (Hillman 1981, pp. 56–57)

To have a productive conjunction requires that each figure of the pairing remains stubbornly different. Hillman thus describes what a conjunction is not. It is not a balanced mixture, or a composite adding this to that. Nor is it a blending of substantial differences into an arrangement or a symbolic putting together of two halves or two things into a third. Seeing as fundamental the stubborn resistance of differences and incommensurabilities means that paradox, absurdity and overt enormity are more characteristic of a union than are androgynous wholeness or harmony of the *unus mundus*. The alchemical conjunction beyond simple *monstrums* is more like an absurd pun or the joy of a joke than the bliss of opposites transcended. As a psychological event, it takes place in the soul as a recognition, an insight, an astonishment! It is not the reconciliation of two differences but the realization that differences are each images which do not deny each other, oppose each other or even require each other.

The quality of the conjunction that Hillman describes is captured in the following poems, the first of which is said to summarize the operations of inner alchemy:

> Jadelike purity has left a secret of freedom
> In the lower world:
> Congeal the spirit in the lair of energy,
> And you'll suddenly see
> White snow flying in midsummer,
> The sun blazing in the water at midnight.
> Going along harmoniously,
> You roam in the heavens

> Then return to absorb
> The virtues of *the receptive*.

(Cleary 1991, p. 39)[4]

The second is an obscure Haiku, which humorously captures the subtlety of "the conjunction":

> On how to sing
> the frog school and the skylark school
> are arguing.[5]

In the above, the so-called problem of opposites dissolves into metaphor, which is to say that the kind of consciousness that imagines "opposites" as contradiction or problematic has itself dissolved into a metaphoric mode of hearing (Hillman 1981, p. 58). It is this kind of metaphoric sensibility of hearing and receptivity that is important in both Taoist alchemy and Jungian analysis.

In this paper, I have raised the question of a relationship between spiritual discipline and Jungian analysis, and have argued that spiritual states and experience can be split off from the depths of the unconscious and personal life. Seen in this way, there are significant differences of direction in the two approaches. However, it has also been the case that, as Jung suggested, there are important parallels between his approach and *The Secret of the Golden Flower*. Both traditions seek to reconcile "opposites" that lead to a larger sense of the unity of life in relation to the Cosmos. For both, this unity is not a simple oneness described by a highly rationalized and ego-oriented spiritualized psychology, but rather a metaphoric complexity. It is this complexity, which brings us as Westerners closer to understanding the goal of Taoist alchemy, the circulation of light and renewal in the birth of the spiritual embryo.

Notes

1. This dream occurred after this article was originally published and has been added here to illustrate the psyche's continued telos.
2. From *The Secret of the Golden Flower: The Classic Chinese Book of Life* by Thomas Cleary. Copyright © 1991 by Thomas Cleary. Used by permission of HarperCollins Publishers.
3. Reprinted here with the permission of the author.
4. From *The Secret of the Golden Flower: The Classic Chinese Book of Life* by Thomas Cleary. Copyright © 1991 by Thomas Cleary. Used by permission of HarperCollins Publishers.
5. "On How To Sing (Haiku)" from INTRODUCTION TO HAIKU by Harold Gould Henderson, copyright © 1958 by Harold G. Henderson. Used by permission of Doubleday, an imprint of the Knopf Doubleday Publishing Group, a division of Penguin Random House LLC. All rights reserved.

References

Berry, Pat. (1982). "Stopping as a Mode of Animation," in *Echo's Subtle Body*. Dallas, TX: Spring Publications, 147–161.
Campbell, Joseph. (1949). *The Hero with a Thousand Faces*. Princeton, NJ: Princeton University Press.
Cleary, Thomas (trans.) (1991). *The Secret of the Golden Flower: The Classic Chinese Book of Life*. San Francisco, CA: Harper.
Corbin, Henri. (1978). *The Man of Light in Iranian Sufism*. Boulder, CO: Shambhala Press.
Freeman, Kathleen. (1962). *Ancilla to the Pre-Socratic Philosophers*. Oxford: Basil Blackwell Oxford.
Hillman, James. (1975). *Revisioning Psychology*. New York: Harper & Row Publishers.
———. (1979a). "Peaks and Vales," in *Puer Papers*. Spring Publications, Irving, TX: University of Dallas, 54–74.
———. (1979b). *The Dream and the Underworld*. New York: Harper & Row Publishers.
———. (1981). "Silver and the White Earth, Part II," in *Spring*. Dallas, TX: Spring Publications, 21–66.
Jay, Martin. (1994). *Downcast Eyes*. Berkeley, CA: University of California Press.
Jung, C. G. (1961). *Memories, Dreams, Reflections*. Anelia Jaffé, ed. New York: Pantheon Books.
———. (1967). "Commentary on The Secret of Golden Flower," in *Alchemical Studies*. Princeton, NJ: Bollingen Foundation, Princeton University Press, 1–56.
Mandel, Oscar. (2014). "Chi Po and the Sorcerer," in *Otherwise Fables*. Pasadena, CA: Prospect Park Books, 89–174.
Marlan, Stanton. (1994). "Dream Maps as an Articulation of the Multiple Intentionalities of Psyche." *Methods—A Journal for Human Science*. Dallas, TX: University of Dallas, 39–48.
Needham, J. (1976). *Science & Civilisation in China*, Volume V: 3. London, UK: Cambridge University Press.
Odajnyk, Walter V. (1993). *The Gathering of Light: A Psychology of Meditation*. Boston, MA: Shambhala Press.
Ricoeur, Paul. (1970). *Freud and Philosophy*. New Haven, CT: Yale University Press.
Romanyshyn, Robert. (1998). Personal communication.
Roob, Alexander. (1997). *Hermetic Museum, Alchemy & Mysticism*. New York: Taschen.

Chapter 6

The metaphor of light and its deconstruction in Jung's alchemical vision

Eyes and ears are bad witnesses for humans who have barbarian souls.
—Heraclitus, Fragment 107[1]

Introduction

The metaphor of light is fundamentally intertwined with the history of western consciousness. Our very language demonstrates the pervasiveness of this metaphor and its intimately connected twin metaphor of vision and enlightenment; it is nearly inconceivable to *envision* a way of thinking that doesn't rely on one or the other of these metaphors. As a result, in the most common means of communication, light and vision appear to be an essential factor of western imagination and our view of consciousness. In language and myth, in science, philosophy and religion, we find abundant confirmation of this view:

> From the primitive importance of the sacred fire to the frequency of sun-worship in more developed religions – such as the Chaldean and Egyptian – and the sophisticated metaphysics of light in the most advanced theologies [and philosophies], the ocular presence in a wide variety of religious practices has been striking. Some faiths, like Manichaean Gnosticism, have fashioned themselves "religions of light"; others, like the often polytheistic Greek religion, assigned a special role to sun gods like Apollo. Unearthly, astral light surrounding the godhead, the divine illumination sought by the mystic, the omniscience of a god always watching his flock, the symbolic primacy of the candle's flames – all of these have found their way into countless religious systems.
> (Jay 1994: 11–12)

It is not surprising then to see that Jung also relied on light's metaphorical depths in the way he imagined his own self-understanding and in the theories he constructed. For him, "darkness has its own peculiar intellect and its own logic, which should be taken very seriously" (Jung 1955: para. 345). "One does not become enlightened by imagining figures of light, but by making the darkness conscious" (Jung 1967: para. 335). Even in his late alchemical writing, he states that the soul is "an eye destined to behold the light" (Jung 1953: para. 14). Light and vision as fundamental to our western consciousness are the inheritance of modern man and the tradition of modernity, but it is also a tradition that has brought suspicion and even aroused hostile reaction. Its privileged role has always been challenged, and today's challenge is at the center of current debate (Jay 1994: 13). Jung was a modern man and was both a shaper and participant in the culture of modernity, a central metaphor of which is light and vision. In postmodern times, the tradition of modernity has come under deconstructive scrutiny, revealing its dark shadow. The light the eye was "destined to behold" displayed a blind spot with regard to vision itself.

The shadow of vision

For the postmodern mind, the hegemony of vision and the entire western intellectual canon has become defined as a privileged view of "a more or less exclusively white male European elite" (Tarnas 1991: 400). Jung belonged to this elite, informed as he was by his European language and historically rooted in a Christian and Cartesian world view. It was an elitism that brought with it charges of racism and colonialism (Ortiz-Hill 1997: 125–133). Ortiz-Hill, while not wanting simply to point at Jung's "clay feet," raised many important questions about his Eurocentrism. Here, he joins others within and outside the Jungian community whose critiques have helped both to de-idealize Jung as well as to make us painfully aware of the cultural biases and presuppositions of our own time. A critical eye to Jung's personal and collective shadow is an important part of our current consciousness, but this should not blind us, as sometimes it has, to his important contributions and to the development of his ideas beyond his biases as he and his work developed and matured.

What I find of particular value in Jung was his capacity for continual self-reflection. He had the desire and ability to stand outside himself with critical insight. If in our time we have come to see Jung as Eurocentric, it was also an awareness he had of himself, an awareness that ultimately brought him to the very edge of his modernity and perhaps beyond it. One might imagine the seeds for this awareness developing as he prepared for his trip to Africa in 1925–1926.

Jung's travel in Africa

As Jung contemplated his journey, he expressed his desire to be "in a non-European country where no European language was spoken and no

Christian concepts prevailed" (Jung 1963: 238). In short, he wanted "to see the European from outside, his image reflected back to him by an altogether foreign milieu" (ibid.) and "to find a psychic observation post outside the sphere" (ibid.: 244) of his own culture. Jung "wanted to find that part of [his] personality which had become invisible under the influence and pressure of being European" (ibid.). Jung was aware of the limitations of his conscious situation: and in his travels, the invisible "other" which he sought looked back at him, reflecting his whiteness as if from a dark mirror, primordial, terrifying and numinous. He identified with the light of consciousness and, like the Elgonyi of East Africa, whose solar mythology he studied but perhaps did not fully understand, he feared the darkness into which the sun passed at night. This fear of the blackness of Africa emerged most poignantly as he struggled with a dream of an "American Negro" (Jung's expression) whom he identified as his barber, and who

> [i]n the dream ... was holding a tremendous, red-hot curling iron to my head, intending to make my hair kinky – that is, to give me Negro hair. I could already feel the painful heat, and awoke with a sense of terror.
> (ibid.: 272)

Jung took this dream as "a warning from the unconscious" (ibid.: 272) and he concluded that his "European personality must under all circumstances be preserved intact" (ibid.: 273). One might say that what the dark light of the dream threw into relief was Jung's modernity, his identification with the light of consciousness and its underlying myth of "the continuous 'Chain of Being' that stratifies and holds in order a hierarchical cosmos ... with Europeans being at the pinnacle of evolutionary development" (Ortiz-Hill 1997: 127). What was revealed to Jung was his desperate clinging to his identity as a white male psychiatrist, for whom "going black" and "kinky" meant a deep regression and the danger of being overrun by instinct.

For Jung, becoming Negro was also a *Nigredo*, a terrifying blackness (Gr: *melanosis*) from which he could, for the moment, only retreat. One might however imagine that he was on the brink of what he had hoped for at the beginning of his travels, which was to find that part of himself that had become invisible under the pressure of being European. To engage this Other required a *Mortificano,* a terrifying descent or *Nekyia* into the blackness of the *Nigredo*, which is synonymous with the experience of death (Edinger 1985: 169). To retreat before this death anxiety seems quite natural, but some have raised the question as to whether Jung perhaps more than most was threatened with concerns about the disintegration of the Self (Brooke 1991: 60–61, following Papadopoulos 1984, and Winnicott 1964). It is interesting to note that it was not until after he had assimilated this experience that a deeper theoretical distinction between ego and Self was made (Brooke 1991: 61). Still, as Ortiz-Hill notes, in Jungian theory, there is a persistent concern about "being overwhelmed by the psyche, by instinct, by the anima, by the shadow, by the female, or ethnic 'other'" (Ortiz-Hill 1997: 133), such that he felt the need to ask what he considers to be an unavoidable "Freudian question": i.e. "what was the moment of being engulfed that led Jung to see himself a potential victim of being overwhelmed by 'otherness' within and outside himself?" (Ortiz-Hill 1997: 133).

Whatever import there may be in evaluating Jung's personal dynamics, it is also important to note that the archetypal terror of the *Nigredo* experience is by definition fundamentally threatening and wounding to the ego. Alongside the question of personal dynamics, we must ask: "Could there be an archetypal aspect to darkness that might account for our disdain, as well as the fear, the physiological shudder it can release?" (Hillman 1997: 45). For Hillman, the essence of this fear lies in the black radix itself, and Edinger provides an archetypal, if compensatory understanding as well, when he comments that the ego, "by daring to exist as an autonomous center of being, takes on substantial reality but also becomes subject to corruption and death. The ego is eventually eclipsed – falls into the blackness of mortificatio" (Edinger 1985: 163). Thus simply to psychologize or analyze these fears into personality dynamics and/or "race relations" (Hillman 1997: 52) does not get at the archetypal imagination of these fears. Hillman undoes the equation Negro is *Nigredo* (an identification unconsciously made by Jung), placing it back from its cultural projection into the heart of our archetypal dynamics (ibid.: 50). While this analysis does not preclude the evaluation of personal dynamics against this archetypal background, personal analysis alone is inadequate to represent the full range of both structural and archetypal levels of meaning.

Returning to Jung's dream, it is of interest to follow Adams (1996) who suggests that, rather than expressing a warning, "the unconscious is attempting to compensate his ego's too-civilized white European attitudes" (Adams 1996: 79). From this perspective, the dream may not be warning Jung to avoid "going black" but "inviting, encouraging or challenging him to do so" (ibid.: 79). Or, as Edinger comments, "dreams that emphasize blackness usually occur when the conscious ego is one-sidedly identified with the light" (Edinger 1985: 150).

From both Adams and Edinger, one gets a sense of the compensatory possibilities of Jung's encounter with the darkness of his invisible other and how his dream might have served psyche's attempt toward decentering, deepening and darkening Jung's Eurocentric ego, attempting to him into touch with his and the culture's archetypal shadow. In terms of archetypal dynamics, Hillman goes beyond the theory of compensation and notes that blackness, the "subtle dissolver," when mixed with other hues brings about their darkening and deepening, or—in alchemical psychology's language—their suffering (Hillman 1997: 48). For Hillman: "black steers all varieties of brightness into the shade" (ibid.), but its deeper purpose is not simply that

of compensating the ego—to shade its natural innocence a necessary step—
but also to introduce

> the deeper invisible realm of shades, the Kingdom of Hades, which is
> the ultimate 'subtle dissolver' of the luminous world…. Like a black
> hole [this pull of the underworld] sucks into it[self] and makes vanish
> the fundamental security structures of western consciousness.
>
> (ibid.)

If we consider the archetypal meaning of blackness, this places Jung's anxiety less in his neurosis, historically or structurally seen, but more at the existential core of his Being. For it is this blackness that "breaks the paradigm [and] dissolves whatever we rely upon as real and dear" (ibid.). Jung's existential anxiety then might be seen not only personally, but also as an underlying archetypal dimension of the angst at the root of western metaphysics and modernism, and perhaps as a fundamental dynamic of the human condition. It is the anxiety of every man standing before the dissolution of foundations and which has a particular coloring in Jung and in the visionary tradition and its hegemonic role in the modern era.

The hegemony of vision

Whatever personal anxieties Jung may have felt returning from his fear of "going black," he also echoed the collective anxiety of a culture standing at the edge of modernity. In this paradigm-breaking blackness lay the deconstructive counter-vision of postmodernity ready to translate "the great phenomenal world into the inked abstractions of letters, numbers and lines, replacing the palpable and visual given[s of phenomenology and presence] with the [postmodern] data of marks and traces" (ibid.), or as Hartman was to put it, "the blackness of ink or print suggests that écriture is a hymn to the Spirit of the Night" (Jay 1994: 510, quoting Geoffrey Hartman). Could we then call the semantic insights of Derrida, Lacan and others a "black art"? By deconstructing presence into absence, the *Nigredo* makes possible psychological, if not cultural, change. Is it any wonder, then why so many find postmodernism so threatening and complain of not being able to grasp it? For Hillman, "each moment of blackening is a harbinger of alteration, of invisible discovery, and of dissolution of attachments to whatever has been taken as truth and reality, solid fact, or dogmatic virtue" (Hillman 1997: 49). One such truth and dogmatic conviction that needed to be unsettled has been the "founding trope of western metaphysics, the privileging of whiteness over blackness, light over darkness" (Jay 1994: 509, quoting Derrida).

Influenced by Heidegger, Derrida has likewise seen a certain ocularcentrism concealing itself behind the history of metaphysics. What he adds is that in modern times, this perspective has extended itself beyond the margins of philosophy into the politics of culture, into power relations and the sociology of racism. Derrida notes that behind our western visionary tradition is the shadow of phallocentrism, egocentrism, ethnocentrism and a heliopolitics "driven by the 'violence of light' and threatening to impose the ontological order of presence wherever its mastery can reach" (Levin 1993: 7, quoting Derrida). Derrida put it this way: "the white man takes his own mythology, Indo-European mythology, his own logos, that is the mythos of his idiom, for the universal form of that he must still wish to call Reason" (Jay 1994: 509, quoting Derrida). This not only privileges one race over another, but it also derives from the time-honored privileging of the sun as the dominant locus of signification: "value, gold, the eye, the sun, etc." (ibid.: 509). In Jungian language, one might say that Derrida is pointing to the cultural power shadow of western thought and the dominance of one archetypal form literalized in the Eurocentric logos. One might imagine that it was this shadow which looked back at Jung in his identification with western man and his terror of blackness, a shadow Jung was attempting to transform.

Movement toward an alchemical vision

As Jung and his theory matured, the shadow of his Cartesian/Eurocentric bias began to give way, and he developed a fuller, deeper understanding of consciousness. One place this can be seen is in his alchemical work (Brooke 1991: 61). Brooke notes the contrast between Jung's earlier heroic Faustian consciousness and a developing "reverent hospitality" exemplified by the figures Philemon and Baucis. As Jung's consciousness grew more hospitable, the uncertainty and neurotic European anxiety lessened, and his ego began a deeper relationship with the Self. Here, the idea of the Self is not viewed as an enclosed entity, and Brooke's reading helps to bring Jungian psychology and existential phenomenology into closer proximity with each other.

The value and interface of these traditions have produced fruits for each and for depth psychology in general. One example is the manner in which Brooke uses Heideggerian insights to describe Jung's later and more mature vision of "consciousness as the illuminating realm within which the being of the world can shine forth" (ibid.: 58). In the poetics of this image, Brooke tries to point to a way of understanding consciousness from beyond the Cartesian separation of subject and world. Here, Brooke too inevitably relies upon metaphors of light, yet tries to point beyond light versus dark to the primordial structures that found psychological life. This is a vision more appropriate to Jung, whose explorations into the shadow and the darkness of the unconscious have rendered him anything but a figure who can adequately be described as avoiding the dark side of the psyche. But:

what would be a productive way of addressing the kind of consciousness that Jung's explorations open up? Following Brooke's lead into existential phenomenology demands that one also enter into the complexity and development of this field as well as into the developments in Jungian psychology radicalized in archetypal and alchemical psychology.

Tension and development in existential phenomenology

It is of no small consequence to note the critical interface of existential phenomenology with its postmodern challenges. Derrida, for instance, has critiqued Heideggerian thought as a photology and heliocentric metaphysics with its implications for heliopolitics. In fact, Derrida suggests that the entire movement of most Western thought from Parmenides to phenomenology, including Heidegger, falls under this critique.

He cites Heidegger's notion of "bringing to light" and others' use of this metaphor as problematic. Here, Derrida is in a long line of French intellectuals for whom the reliance on light and vision is denigrated. This denigration has been richly documented by Jay (1994) in his book *Downcast Eyes*. In this work, the intricacy of the metaphor of vision and light is explored in complex reflections from phenomenology to postmodernism in France with important implications for our understanding of consciousness. Jay's work documents the attempt of French intellectuals to undermine western ocularcentrism, an attempt to free consciousness from its power shadow. The history of this critique has also led to a crisis of Enlightenment described by Habermas as a "new unsurveyability" (Jay 1994: 592), an image pointing to the ironic consequences of the French critique.

While negative skepticism is not always the fault of the best French critics and philosophers, their work has often led some to speculate if their cynicism might be rooted in the possibility that most postmodern thinking is itself an obsessional exercise of the Cogito that never really cuts through the very paradigms it wishes to deconstruct. Hillman (1997), for example, suggests that deconstructionism, in its "playing with the ambiguity of the 'trace,' troping, displacing, and insisting upon difference and, as well, the absenting of all certitudes from positive propositions" (the French mode of decapitating the cogito), ultimately "becomes one more habitual concretism of Western thought" (Hillman 1997: 13). Hillman suggests that while the French effort may in many ways mimic alchemy in its arcane obstructionism and its deconstructive talk which sounds like the language of alchemy, it does not affect an in-depth alchemical transformation. While it attempts to free the mind from singleness and literalism, "[i]t stops short before the nigredo turns blue" (ibid.: 13). Here, Hillman uses the color imagery of alchemy to point to the importance of transformation, to move the soul beyond intellectual ideation alone. In the alchemical imagination, after blackness comes blueness,

> not cynical, but sad; not hard and smart, but slow. The blues bring the body back with a revisioned feeling, head and body rejoined. .... blue gives voice to the nigredo .... Darkness imagined as an invisible light, like a blue shadow, behind and within all things.
> (Hillman 1997: 13)

While Hillman points to the importance of feeling, recognizes the shadow and pastiche of postmodernism, and offers important observations, it is too global a condemnation. The work of deconstruction is also a slow and careful reading of texts, playful at times, capturing important moments of soul and a sensitivity to the human condition. Derrida, for instance, following Freud's insight into the link between castration and blindness, notes that "only man knows how to go beyond seeing and knowing, because only he knows how to cry .... Only he knows that tears are the essence of the eye – and not sight" (Jay 1994: 523, quoting Derrida). Jay continues: "Eyes that cry implore rather than see: they invite the question from the other: whence the pain?" (ibid.: 523). In this moment, Derrida's thoughts reveal a soulful awareness that glows with a vision of blueness.

Similarly, Nye (1993) in her critique of patriarchal vision sees it as dying, as a dead vision and a vision of death, but she states that the only way to prepare for the birth of another vision is from the depths of our suffering. Paraphrasing Nye, Levin (1993) asks:

> What would have happened, she wonders, if those Greek men had turned back, after learning from their vision of the Forms, to look at one another, their gazes engaged by the interactions of friendly conversation? And what would have happened if they had turned and looked at women, looked with eyes moved by feelings of friendship, admiration, and respect?
> (Levin 1993: 26, citing Nye)

In the above, I propose we find the blue quality of soul, of slowness, the feeling and imaginative revisioning characteristic of alchemical transformation. It is this kind of revisioning of vision that can directly be found not only by looking again at myth, but by turning again to the light of alchemy.

The alchemical *lumen naturae*: the light of nature

The *lumen naturae* was image of light at the core of ancient alchemical ideas. The aim of alchemy was to beget this light hidden in nature, a light very different from the western association of vision as separate from darkness.

It was a light Jung came to see in his alchemical studies. In an Arabic treatise attributed to Hermes, the *Tractatus Aureus*, Mercurius says: "I beget light but the darkness too is of my nature" (Jung 1942: 125). In alchemy, light and dark, male and female, are joined together in the idea of the chymical marriage; and from the marriage (of light and dark), the *filius philosophorum* emerges and a new light is born: "They embrace and a new light is begotten of them, which is like no other light in the whole world" (Jung 1942: 126, citing Mylius). This light is a central mystery of alchemy. It is of interest to imagine this alchemical marriage as a continuation of Nye's fantasy about what would have happened if the masculine psyche had embraced not only women, but also the "feminine" dimension of psyche with friendship and respect. Might we speculate that perhaps a filius could have been born, a new consciousness which might have changed the whole development of western culture?

Jung traces the idea of the *filius* to the archetypal image of the Primordial Man of Light, a vision of the Self that is both light and dark, male and female, and for which Jung finds amplification in Prajâpati or Purusha in India, Gayomort ("mortal life") in Persia—a youth of dazzling whiteness like Mercurius—and in Metatron, who in the Zohar was created together with light. The Man of Light was also described by Paracelsus as identical with the "astral" man: "The true man is the star in us. The star desires to drive men towards great wisdom" (ibid.: 131). It is of interest to see Jung's insight resonating with Derrida's reading of solar mythology, which suggests that the light of the sun should not simply be linked to the light of Enlightenment.

> The sun is also a star... like all the other stars that appear only at night and are invisible during the day. As such it suggests a source of truth or properness that was not available to the eye, at least at certain times.
> (Jay 1994: 510, citing Derrida)

Jung, like Derrida, mentions two images of light: the great light and the inner light of nature, hidden and invisible, a little spark without which the darkness would not be darkness.

Likewise, for Corbin (1978), light has a double nature, an innerness that is also an outerness. This dual vision is characteristic of the Primordial Man whose light is ultimately the *mundus imaginalis* and which, according to Corbin, must not be confused with the "imaginary" in our current understanding of the term.

The double nature of light is itself an archetypal theme along with the invisibility of the so-called "inner light." It is a light which is neither simply subjective nor simply found in the outer world, in phenomena or in our speech, but it "buildeth shapes in sleep from the power of the word" (Jung 1947/1954: 195, quoting *Liber de Caducis*) and can be found in dreams.

The attainment of this light was for Paracelsus—who, according to Jung, was a well-intentioned, humble Christian—his most secret and deepest passion. His whole creative yearning belonged to the *lumen naturae,* the divine spark buried in the darkness "whose sleep of death could not be vanquished even by the revelation of God's son" (Jung 1942: 160). For some alchemists, the light of the Christian deity could even stand in the way of the light of nature which was obscured as the development of Christianity split off from the pagan power of nature.

Light and lumen: a contemporary dream

This split between the light of the God-man and light of nature can be seen in the dream of a contemporary woman who was brought up in a strict Catholic tradition, and who had been struggling with her desire for a warmer, more sensual life and desiring to be in better touch with her sexuality, eros and bodily sense of self. She experienced her needs as in conflict with her religious training and felt a strong tension with what seemed to be a patriarchal and removed sense of God. Her dream opened up a heroic and unthinkable reaction to her god-image and drew her down into the flower of her femininity and toward a chthonic light at the core of her inner life. The dream came at a time when her analyst had moved away, and she had not yet found another analyst. It went as follows:

> I am simultaneously an observer and a small naked infant crawling on a white Easter lily. I am crawling around the flower; it is so white, no color, and I am craving to feel its texture and to feel something more, more sensuality. The flower is floating in a dark sky with lots of little lights, like stars in the night. Then, I feel a beam of sunlight: it warms my body and gives me a good feeling of being grounded and embodied and a feeling of sensuality. Just as this feeling begins, Jesus Christ on the cross emerges from below and is positioned between me and the sun and, in so doing, casts a shadow over me. I then feel cut off from the light and the warm feelings I was beginning to have. I feel panic that I will freeze to death and won't be able to get any nourishment. Then, I feel myself growing very large and, in a burst of rage, I punch Christ in the face, knocking him off the cross, and he and the cross fall down below me. I feel some guilt but then also notice another kind of light coming from deep within the core of the flower; it has a silvery quality.

A clinically satisfactory interpretation of this dream is not the purpose, nor a possibility, in the context of this chapter, but I would like to offer a few reflections on its archetypal nature. The context of the dream is important, in that it took place after the dreamer's analyst had moved to a new city and her analysis was interrupted. She felt abandoned and in some ways like an infant deprived of mother's breast. The psyche images the dreamer both as observing ego and as infant out in space on a lily-white Easter flower. I will not follow, for our purpose here, the transferential and/or genetic implications of the image, but rather stick with the metaphoric and amplificatory dimensions of the dream.

Whatever the flower may come to express, it is the current ground of the infant, and it is floating in space. She is crawling around on it and feeling it is too white, too pure, no color, no redness or texture, and she is attempting to find a more sensual connection. It is of interest that the Easter lily is symbolically related to purity, the Virgin Mary and the promise of renewal in Christ. As she seeks a more sensual connection, two things occur: she begins to feel the warmth of the sun, a ray of light, and this gives her a feeling of being grounded and embodied, but as soon as this occurs, her god-image, Jesus on the cross, emerges placing her in the cold shadow of the deity, as Christ stands in the way of the energy which began to inform her. Here, the old conflict between instinct and spirit, religion and sexuality, re-emerges, amplifying the cut off feeling of the infant Self, whether from her mother's breast, analyst, lost god-image or feeling of embodiment.

At this juncture, the dreamer panics and in her symptom of panic, the dream begins to move archetypally toward a telos. Jung has shown how in our symptoms, the ancient gods reside, and Hillman has noted that the repressed god returns at the archetypal core of our symptom complexes and can be found in the analyst's consulting room. Greek myth placed Pan as a god of nature. The ancient mythological religion was essentially a nature religion, the transcendence of which by Christianity therefore meant the suppression of the kind of nature expressed in gods such as Pan. It is of interest to note that Hillman (1972) placed Pan in a cluster of meanings associated with the abandoned child (echoing the dreamer's abandonment), and that Pan appears in the symptom of panic as a protective, instinctual/archetypal reaction in times of crisis, the only way he can appear in our time. Plutarch reports the famous cry that went through late antiquity: "Great Pan is dead!" (Hillman 1972: xxii, quoting *de def. or.* 17). Hillman notes that this saying has become oracular, one meaning of which is that nature has become deprived of its creative voice. We have lost psychic connection with nature, except perhaps through dreams. The voice of nature has lost its light and "[has fallen] easily to asceticism, following sheepishly without instinctual rebellion [the] new Shepherd. Christ, with his new means of management" (ibid.: xxii). If our dream is of any proof, it supports what many commentators on Pan have stated: that Pan never died, he was just repressed and still lives, not merely in the literary imagination but in the repressed, which returns when our instincts assert themselves. In our dreamer, Pan does return in panic and rebellion: filled with rage, she strikes down the god-image.

This destructive/creative act inflates the dreamer who breaks a taboo which then allows her to notice a new light coming from within the flower. This light might be seen as the *lumen naturae* or light of nature, the light that Hillman eluded to as repressed with the fall of Pan. Here, the dreamer reverses this situation, striking down the patriarchal god-image that blocked the way to her light, as she moves toward it in the womb of the flower. This flower might truly then prove to be an Easter flower, a flower of rebirth. Neumann (1955) reminds us that the ancient Goddess Sophia achieves her supreme visible form as a flower. She does not vanish in the nirvana-like abstraction of a masculine spirit, but rather like the scent of a blossom, her spirit always remains attached to the earthy foundation of reality (Neumann 1955: 325).

Irigaray (Jay 1994) identifies and amplifies the split that seems to have required the appearance of Pan and Sophia, a scene in which the masculine spirit had split off from the earthy ground. She links this to the vision of Platonic truth aimed at the sun and the Forms, in which the role of the mother was eclipsed in favor of the father, the solar origin of ideas. In this way, says Irigaray, the powerful birth process is forgotten and repressed in the service of a male myth of autogenesis, a move to the intelligible rather than the sensual world. With this move, she says that there is a loss of mediation, of path and trail, and the need for further opening of a kind of diaphragm. Such a visually grounded philosophy forgets the materiality of the eye socket, the cave, the womb, and one might add the unfolding of the flower. With regard to the flower of our dream, it is interesting to see Irigaray conceded that the only kind of sight that might escape this phallocentric economy was the Buddha's gaze at a flower (Jay 1994: 537–538, citing Irigaray).

This flowering toward a greater sense of wholeness seems to require a change in the main god-image and a diminution of direct light. For Hillman, this means a "prolonged acceptance of a twilight state, an *abaissement* and rededication of ego-light, softening it by sacrificing each day some of its brightness, giving back to the gods what it has stolen" (Hillman 1979: 49). This new light implies an increased "interiority" with each new hot idea, first being drawn through the labyrinthine ways of soul or, as Irigaray might put it, the diaphragmatic pathway. It is precisely this soft blue reflective light that our western penchant for immediate and direct vision obscures.

Hillman's sensibility has been echoed by thinkers as wide-ranging as philosopher Walter Benjamin, who formulated a critical theory of modernity, and Japanese novelist Jun ichirō Tanizaki, whose aesthetics amplify this vision in another context.

The ego brightness of western consciousness was foreseen and feared by Benjamin who critiqued "a world enchanted and dazzled by shining objects, the fetishized commodities of late capitalism" (Levin 1993: 23). According to Levin, Benjamin anticipated Foucault's analysis of panopticism with an observation about the early days of electricity in which he already saw the potential danger in nineteenth-century projects for city lighting bused on the idea of a universal illumination, an idea so appealing to the Enlightenment mentality (ibid.).

Benjamin's anxiety about dazzling and shining objects mirrors the sensibility of Tanizaki who found it so hard to be at home in the west with things that glitter and shine. Tanizaki described the westerner as progressive, always determined to better his lot, "from candle to oil lamp, oil lamp to gaslight, gaslight to electric light – his quest for a brighter light never ceases, he spares no pains to eradicate even the minutest shadow" (Tanizaki 1977: 31). In contrast, he describes the Japanese aesthetic which loves the light of nature, soft light, darkness and shadows, giving examples of the love of dark patina on silver, to the love of jade—"that strange stone with its faint muddy light"—and smoky crystals, "the impure variety ... with opaque veins crossine their depth" (ibid.: 10–11). In Tanizaki, we find a strong aesthetic critique of modernism with a romantic longing for a past and a diminishing aesthetic itself falling into the shadow of contemporary life.

In the above, we note the separation between light and lumen, modemist vision and the light of nature, the light of the sun and that of the flower, and the tension between Christian and Pagan visions. The dual aspect of light is an archetypal concern and its mysteries continue into contemporary times.

Conclusion

If in the west we cannot simply rely on a romantic reversion to an ancient Oriental aesthetic way of seeing (Tanizaki) or return to a literal alchemy, a point Hillman (2010) makes, or if the downcast eyes of French intellectualism are insufficient (Jay), still it has become clear that all of the above have made us more conscious of the shadow of western religion, metaphysics and modernism, but beyond their critiques, these responses to our condition have offered many insights toward the revisioning of contemporary consciousness. Jung, too, has been taken as an exemplary modern man with both personal and cultural shadows, but he is also a man whose arduous journey into darkness has taught us, echoing Heraclitus' insight, that vision is not to be trusted in those who have barbarian souls. Jung's journey from a heroic patriarch to a man of receptivity was that of a traveler who learned that darkness has its own logos. If, as Jung said, the soul is destined to behold the light, it must be seen as the soft light of the *lumen naturae*.

This is not the light of the heroic white European, Christian, Cartesian, racist, colonialist, phallocentric, logocentric, politically heliotropic vision. Nor is it the light of its critics with its skeptical, negative, cynical, smart, hard judgments that led to a new "unsurveyability." If we have any hints of the seeds for the future, it is in a slow, sometimes sad, bodily light, connected with shadows and shades, male and female, in the depths of our suffering with relatedness to others and the invisible otherness of ourselves. It is a connection with our strangeness—with friendly respect, and through attention to our dreams—in imaginative revisionary and alchemical transformation, and thus perhaps in a change in or deeper understanding of our god-image. In all of the above, we are left not with a single vision but with multiple possibilities. It is of interest to notice that here Jung, archetypal psychology and postmodernism share a resonance. It is a resonance also in accord with Jay for whom it is "precisely the proliferation of models of visuality that the antiocularcentric discourse, for all its fury against the ones it distrusts, tacitly encourages" (Jay 1994: 591). What Jay means as postmodern criticism might be seen to argue that the antidote to privileging any one visual order is a multiplicity of seeing, a dialectics of seeing: "it is better to encourage the multiplication of a thousand eyes, which, like Nietzsche's thousand suns, suggests the openness of a human possibilities" (Jay 1994: 591).

Bal (1993) and Flynn (1993), respectively, suggest the importance of many different ways of seeing and many different practices of reason, multiplying perspectives and proliferating points of view. In particular, Flynn asks if we do not need a gaze of reciprocity, generosity and friendship. Warnke (1993) adds the importance of an aesthetic education which likewise could multiply our perceptions, expand our horizons and deepen our moral vision (Levin 1993: 22). To these sentiments, I would suggest that we add the late work of Jung and archetypal psychology, for Jung at the end of his work envisioned the light of consciousness as having multiple intensities, composed of scintilla or sparks, like the stars in a night sky. For him, the Self as an expression of the Primordial Man is not a vision of fixed essences, but of multiple illuminations, radiating both as single monad but at the same time with many faces and many eyes (Jung 1947/1954).

The multiplicity is radicalized in archetypal psychology in Hillman's polytheistic view. Both these and the postmodern ideas resonate with the end phase of the alchemical work imaged in the display of the *cauda pavonis*, an exquisite display of colors in the peacock's tail which heralds the illuminatory multiplicity of psyche.

The image indicates the restoration of the whole person not seen as a synthesis or sublation, or Hegelian uplifting, but as Hillman put it, as a prolonged acceptance of a twilight state, a hesitancy that does not subsume all into a fixed position. This is echoed by Jung in his *Alchemical Studies* when he states:

> deeper insight into problems of psychic development soon teaches us how much better it is to reserve judgment .... Of course we all have an understandable desire for crystal clarity, but we are apt to forget that in psychic matters we are dealing with a process of experience, that is, with transformations which should never be given hard and fast names

if their living names if their living movement is not to petrify into something static, The protean mythologem and the shimmering symbol express the process of the psyche far more ... clearly than the clearest concept: for the symbol not only conveys a visualization of the process ... it also brings a re-experiencing of it, of that twilight which we can learn to understand through inoffensive empathy, but which too much clarity dispels.

(Jung 1942: 162–163)

A similar sentiment was also expressed by Bion, who stated:

Instead of trying to bring a brilliant, intelligent, knowledgeable light to bear on obscure problems, I suggest we bring to bear a diminution of the light – a penetrating beam of darkness; a reciprocal of the searchlight.... The darkness would be so absolute that it would achieve a luminous, absolute vacuum. So that, if any object existed, however faint, it would show up very clearly. Thus, a very faint light would become visible in maximum conditions of darkness.

(Bion 1974: 37)

The complexity of our times demands that we transcend simple one-sided judgments and enter into a broader vision, as well as entertain many ways of imagining. From critics and debunkers Stern and Noll to classical analysts Edinger and von Franz, Jung has been as devil and saint, Eurocentric racist and compassionate wise man. The sheer range of evaluation testifies to the sense that Jung carries a multiplicity of mythical projections and perhaps for this reason is an exemplary modern man, a man at the crossroads of cultural transformation. He deserves to be seen with no fewer sensibilities than those he gave to us with which to see.

Note

1 Many thanks to Aaron Higgins-Brake for his translation.

References

Adams, M.V. (1996) *The Multicultural Imagination*, London: Routledge.
Bal, M. (1993) "His master's eye," in D. Levin (ed.) *Modernity and Hegemony of Vision*, Berkeley: University of California Press, 379–404.
Bion, W. (1974) *Brazilian Lectures*, Rio de Janiero: Imago Edition.
Brooke, R. (1991) *Jung and Phenomenology*, London: Routledge.
Corbin, H. (1978) *The Man of Light in Iranian Sufism*, Boulder, CO: Shamhala.
Edinger, E. (1985) *Anatomy of the Psyche,* LaSalle, IL: Open Court.
Flynn, T. (1993) "Foucault and the eclipse of vision," in D. Levin (ed.) *Modernity and the Hegemony of Vision,* Berkeley: University of California Press, 273–286.

Hillman, J. (1972) "An essay on pan," in J. Hillman and W. Roscher (eds.) *Pan and the Nightmare*, Zurich: Spring Publications.
—— (1979) *Puer Papers*, Dallas, TX: Spring Publications.
—— (1997) "The seduction of black," in S. Marlan (ed.) *Fire in the Stone*, Wilmette, IL: Chiron Publications.
—— (2010) "The Therapeutic value of alchemical language: A heated introduction," in J. Hillman (ed.) *Alchemical Psychology*, Putnam, CT: Spring Publications, 9–19.
Jay, M. (1994) *Downcast Eyes*, Berkeley: University of California Press.
Jung, C.G. (1942) "Paracelsus as a spiritual phenomenon," *CW* 13.
—— (1953) *Psychology and Alchemy*, *CW* 12.
—— (1955/1956) *Mysterium Coniunctionis*, *CW* 14.
—— (1963) *Memories, Dreams, Reflections*, New York: Pantheon Books.
—— (1967) *Alchemical Studies*, *CW* 13.
—— (1960) "On the nature of the psyche," *CW* 8, 159–234.
Levin, D.M. (ed.) (1993) *Modernity and the Hegemony of Vision*, Berkeley: University of California Press.
—— (1997) *Sites of Vision*, Cambridge, MA: The MIT Press.
Neumann, E. (1955) *The Great Mother*, Princeton, NJ: Pantheon Books.
Nye, A. (1993) "Assisting at the birth and death of philosophic vision," in D. Levin (ed.) *Modernity and the Hegemony of Vision*, Berkeley: University of California Press.
Ortiz-Hill, M. (1997) "C.G. Jung in the heart of darkness," *Spring* 61, 125–133.
Papadopoulos, R. (1984) "Jung and the concept of the other," in R. Papadopoulos and G. Saayman (eds.) *Jung in Modern Perspective*, Craighall: A. D. Donker.
Tanizaki, J. (1977) *In Praise of Shadows*, Stoney Creek, CT: Leete's Island Books.
Tarnas, R. (1991) *The Passion of the Western Mind*, New York: Ballantine Books.
Warnke, G. (1993) "Ocular criticism and social criticism," in D. Levin (ed.) *Modernity and Hegemony of Vision*, Berkeley: University of California Press.
Winnicott, D. (1964) "Book review of *Memories, Dreams, Reflections*, by C. G. Jung," *The International Journal Psycho-Analysis*, 45, 450–455.

Chapter 7

Facing the shadow
Turning toward the darkness of the nigredo

Jung's notion of the shadow is an important contribution to the theory and practice of depth psychology and psychoanalysis. This notion was developed early on by Jung and he later found further support for it through his study of alchemy—for example, this quote from Michael Maier captures the archetypal essence of Jung's idea: "The Sun and its shadow complete the work" (*Atalanta Fugiens*, Emblem 45). The way the shadow has been understood has naturally developed in the context of each writer's orientation within the field, sometimes emphasizing its classical, developmental, and/or archetypal place and meaning within an overall conception of psychic life and view of analysis. As older categories begin to blur, thinking within the field continues to differentiate and thought deepens.

In this essay, I will not precisely trace the history of the concept in Jung's work or within the field in general beyond what is necessary for my reflections, nor provide a summary of the Jungian literature on the shadow. Such information is widely available from many sources. My intention here is to look at the shadow as a living psychological phenomenon that continues to have more to teach us about the psyche.

Facing the shadow is one of the more important goals of Jungian psychoanalysis. In earlier editions of his book, *Jungian Analysis*, Murray Stein described the aims and goals of Jungian analysis as "coming to terms with the unconscious" (Stein 1995, 38). Facing the shadow is a key aspect of this overall work. Stein notes that coming to terms with the shadow means "calling into question the illusions one clings to most dearly about oneself, which have been used to shore up self-esteem and to maintain a sense of personal identity" (Stein 1995, 40). Facing the shadow and confronting one's illusions are understandably painful moments in analysis.

In the most general sense, one might define the shadow as referring to the darkness of the unconscious, to what is rejected by consciousness, both positive and negative contents as well as to that which has not yet or perhaps will never become conscious. Turning toward this darkness means facing the unacceptable, undesirable, and underdeveloped parts of ourselves, the crippled, blind, cruel, ugly, inferior, inflated, and sometimes vile, as well as discovering the potentials for further development of which we are unaware. For Jung, our attempt to fit in with our families and with historical and cultural values results in the personality developing what he called a persona, a mask through which adaptation is facilitated, but a nevertheless necessary structure of relationship.

In order to adapt, those aspects of the larger personality deemed unacceptable are often denied, repressed, and split off from the developing personality. As a result, they can become tortured, wounded, maimed, and can recede into the dark where ultimately they may be killed and buried. Other potentials of the self that have been conscious may likewise be resisted and never come into conscious relationship with the personality. This dynamic process helps to form that part of the psyche Jung called the shadow. In spite of its banishment to a nether world, the shadow continues to play a dynamic role in our psychological life.

Jung explored the way in which the shadow emerges into awareness, often through irrational eruptions that impede consciousness. The shadow's trickster-like behavior acts as if it had a mind of its own, sending conscious life into a retrograde movement, where something other than the personal will seems to hold sway. The shadow appears as well in dreams, projections, transferences, and counter-transferences and, while on the one hand resisting consciousness, on the other it seems to be pursuing it by seeking confrontation and challenges, often leaving the person terrified and retreating from contact. Angst about the shadow is not surprising. Some current dream images of patients reveal the shadow emerging in the form of primitive disembodied voices and spirits, wounded animals, impervious cold-blooded prehistoric and mythical beasts, stalkers, murderers, and sexual perverts. In addition, patients' dreams have presented images of disgusting beer-drinking alcoholics, down-and-out gamblers, heavily made-up unattractive women, men with outrageously bad taste, dull-witted jerks, and paralyzed figures locked into frozen rages. Deep emotion has often accompanied images such as those of severe and at times incurable illness, as well as scarred, disfigured, and sometimes dead infants and children haunting graves and burial grounds.

Jacques Lacan once noted that "psychoanalysis involves allowing the analysand to elaborate the unconscious knowledge that is in him not in the form of depth, but in the form of a cancer" (Lacan, in Fink 2007, 74). Facing such horrific images is indeed like facing a cancer not necessarily manifested physically but psychically, proliferating and often leading to narcissistic mortification, humiliation, despair, and depression. In the face of such images, rational order can be shaken. Opening our psychic life to such images can be wounding and destabilizing, and there is a natural and understandable resistance to doing so.

I wrote about the most difficult and darkest images of the shadow in *The Black Sun* (Marlan 2005). *Sol niger* is the quintessential image of the primordial shadow, and in its blacker-than-black dimension, it resists assimilation. Facing it is one of the most difficult tasks for analysis and is often not possible. Descriptions about the Tantric goddess Kali, for example, attempt to capture this overwhelming dimension of psychic life. She is powerfully destructive, brutal, bloody, and death-dealing. She stands in the way of an enlarged vision of the Self, a terrifying shadow goddess hard to allow into consciousness. She's often repressed, too frightening to face, but her illuminating dance is essential to the wholeness of psychic life. It is hard to imagine facing such a potent goddess, but important to allow this horrific vision and to call her forth into full awareness.

These powerful descriptions give us a hint about facing this aspect of the primordial shadow. It is difficult to translate this into analytic principles, but clearly the hard work of facing the shadow and of analysis is in part learning to turn toward the painful, unpleasant, and at times horrifying figures of the psyche, and thus toward the unacceptable aspects of the self. The deepest recesses of the archetypal shadow may be unredeemable, and we may need to let go of Salvationist hopes or be driven to do so, but not all shadow figures are as horrifying as *Sol niger* and Kali. These images remind us that life can be tragic and that the unconscious is not invariably benevolent.

There are limits to what analysis can accomplish, and this is sobering to our overzealous expectations. In such instances, the analyst may be called upon to sit with the analysand in and through loss, grief, despair, and the tragic experiences of life, and be company on the ship of death and in silence be witness to the limits of analysis and to the hopes and dreams of the human soul. And yet, there will be moments when the "death" we face may turn out to be a symbolic one, heralding an alchemical process of *mortificatio* and *putrefactio,* which can lead to renewal and the opening to a deepened symbolic life.

Stein has noted that "persons in analysis are asked explicitly or implicitly to stay receptive to the unconscious—to the less rational, more ambiguous, and often mysterious side of the personality" (Stein 1995, 39). It is important that the analyst as well is prepared to venture into the darkest recesses of the shadow as a participant and guide with the capacity to sit still, stay present, accompany, and facilitate facing the darkest aspects of psychic life. In so doing, the shadow figures may show themselves to compensate or complement a one-sided conscious position, and facing them can lead to a more integrated personality. Still, the question remains: how to face such figures.

Not all shadow images are horrific, but nevertheless they remain difficult to face. Hillman speaks of the broken, ruined, weak, sick, inferior, and socially unacceptable parts of ourselves (Hillman 1991). For him, curing these shadow images requires love. He asks:

> How far can our love extend to the broken and ruined parts of ourselves, the disgusting and perverse? How much charity and compassion

have we for our own weakness and sickness? How far can we ... allow a place for everyone?

(Hillman 1991, 242)

Because the shadow can be socially unacceptable and even *evil*, it is important that it is carried by us, which means that we do not project our unacceptable parts on to others and/or act them out. This is an ethical responsibility.

The importance of refraining from creating scapegoats loaded down with our own evils is particularly urgent in today's world situation. This was one of the main concerns of Erich Neumann, who considered the shadow a moral and ethical issue of prime importance (Neumann 1969). For *Neumann*, facing the shadow and integrating the psychic opposites can lead to the development of a supra-ordinate unity. Carrying Jung's ideas further into the ethical dimension, Neumann found a basic tendency in the psyche that he called centroversion—a dynamic aspect of the self that can enlarge and balance the personality. For Hillman as well, a moral stance toward the shadow is essential and cannot be abandoned, but this is not enough: "At one moment something else must break through" (Hillman 1991, 242–243). Facing the shadow and its cure requires a conjunction of seeming opposites, a confrontation, and a paradoxical union of two incommensurables: "the moral recognition that these parts of me are burdensome and intolerable and must change, and the loving laughing acceptance which takes them just as they are. ... [One] both judges harshly and joins gladly." Each position holds "one side of the truth" (Hillman 1991, 243). Hillman gives an example from the Jewish mystical tradition of the Chassidim, where "deep moral piety is coupled with astounding delight in life" (Hillman 1991, 243).

To achieve such an attitude requires considerable psychological development, but it still seems almost impossible to imagine taking delight in the deeply heinous and virulent aspects of the shadow. How can we participate in the implications of perversity, with Nazi images of the Holocaust, and with the terrorist shadow? Could Job join gladly with the dark side of God, which according to Jung required a moral transformation and Job's personal outrage? Yet, while feeling judgments are essential to ethical life, moral outrage can also be inflated, so rational and one-sided, that one can miss seeing into the paradoxical and transformational aspects of such horrific images. Therefore, without more fully understanding the psychological implication of such images, we are left with only black or white possibilities.

For Hillman, the traditional psychoanalytic position of the Freudian school was too rational and did not do justice to the psyche. According to him, Freud

did not see fully enough that each image and each experience had a prospective as well as a reductive aspect, a positive as well as a negative side ... [or] see clearly enough the paradox that rotten garbage is also fertilizer, that childishness is also childlikeness, that polymorphous perversity is also joy and physical liberty ...

(Hillman 1991, 243)

These paradoxical images require the positions of both Freudian and Jungian psychoanalyses and, according to him, are not two specific and conflicting positions; rather, the reductive and prospective aspects of the shadow must be seen together in the paradoxes of symbolic life.

Jungian psychoanalysis carries both reductive and prospective vectors within itself. Jung took for granted the psychoanalytic view, which relies on a series of energetic and developmental notions, including adaptation, resistance, denial, suppression, repression, conflict formation, splitting, projection, the return of the repressed, and so on. In addition to those, he contributed a series of his own conceptual perspectives, mythopoetic and archetypal insights that emerged from his experience of himself and his patients. His choice of the experience-near term "shadow" reflects this contribution and was based on the notion that the unconscious tends to personify itself, as in dreams. Such personifications "show the most striking connections with the poetic, religious, or mythological formulations" (Jung 1959, para. 516). Later in life, Jung deepened this notion in his alchemical work. These personifications, when faced, can point in the most surprising directions.

One difficulty in thinking about Jung's idea of the shadow is that he relied on both modes of discourse, and the two styles of thought are often imagined as diametrically opposed. Yet, they engender a complexity of personal and archetypal, scientific and mythical, causal-reductive and teleological perspectives. Lambert has described these opposites linguistically in terms of the distinction between the language of the intellect and the language of imagination (Lambert 1981). Samuels has noted that "the goal of having a model in which both languages play a part may be difficult to achieve" (Samuels 1985, 6). And yet, I believe, this is the aim of Jungian analysis. It is most often the case that these two orientations, directed thinking and imagining, play a role in all Jungian orientations, but that one of them becomes privileged and reduces the other to a secondary position, consciously or unconsciously. In short, these two languages may be said to shadow one another, perhaps by necessity.

The philosopher Paul Ricoeur addressed a similar concern with regard to Freudian analysis. In his book *Freud and Philosophy,* Ricoeur speaks of the possibility of carrying and engendering opposed interpretations, each of which is self-consistent, into relation with one another. He describes these orientations as hermeneutic strategies: one turned toward the "revival of archaic meanings belonging to the infancy of mankind, the other toward the emergence of figures that anticipate our spiritual adventure" (Ricoeur 1970, 496). For Ricoeur, what psychoanalysis "calls overdetermination cannot be understood apart from a dialectic between [these] two functions, which are thought to be opposed to one another but which symbols coordinate into a concrete unity" (ibid., 490). I believe that Jung was seeking this same unity in his understanding of a symbolic life.

For Ricoeur and Jung, concrete symbols carry both functions and link these orientations which oppose and yet ground one another. "Such symbols both disguise and reveal. While they conceal the aims of our instincts, they disclose the process of self consciousness" (Ricoeur 1970, 497). Living in relation to such symbols and images requires a continuing dialectic between thought and imagination, between what Jung called fantasy and directed thinking (Jung 1956, para. 39) and between what is conscious and unconscious. Ultimately, for Ricoeur, it is philosophical and conceptual thought that is able to rise above the shadow to a privileged position. However, from a Jungian perspective, there is a danger in theories becoming too removed from their unconscious base and from life. Theories, too, cast a shadow, and Jung struggled with this issue:

> Conscious and unconscious do not make a whole when one of them is suppressed and injured by the other. If they must contend, let it be a fair fight with equal rights on both sides. Both are aspects of life. Consciousness should defend its reason and protect itself, and the chaotic life of the unconscious should be given the chance of having its way too—as much of it as we can stand. This means open conflict and open collaboration at once.... It is the old game of hammer and anvil: between them the patient iron is forged into an indestructible whole, an "individual."
> (Jung 1959, para. 522)

For Jung, the prospect of rising above images and symbols into the conceptual abstractions of science, philosophy, and religion was questionable. He sought instead to bind together and maintain the tensions of psyche life in a way that produced a paradoxical and transcendent but still concrete possibility. This meant staying closely connected to the shadow and imaginal life and not leaving the unconscious or shadow behind. For Jung, it was important to think and theorize, but also to "dream the dream onward" while at the same time not believing naively in the literalism of the unconscious.

According to Jung, the technical languages of philosophy, science, and theology could easily turn one-sided, pressing other modes of discourse into the shadow. This is a position taken up and elaborated by Hillman, who argues for the importance of a language not unlike that of the alchemists in which images do not disappear into concepts (Hillman 1978). To be clear, Hillman is not proposing that we abandon our concepts, just that we do not use them one-sidedly in a way that always translates fantasy thinking into directed thinking. When this happens, "our concepts extend their grasp over concretely vivid images by abstracting (literally, 'drawing away') their matter" (ibid., 125).

One of Jung's main, and perhaps most important, contributions is his use of personification, in which he retains the imagistic quality of thought. As a result, emphasis on the concrete imagery of the shadow has been an important contribution of the Jungian and Archetypal approach. For Hillman, as for Jung, the founding of the psyche upon images and personification "rather than upon concepts borrowed from the sciences or philosophy [means that] even Jung's metapsychology remains psychology" (Hillman 1975, 22). According to Hillman, Jung never deserts the psyche in search of explanatory principles outside of its own imaginal world. I believe this is what Edinger also meant when he noted, "As Jung studied alchemy he found that this luxuriant network of images was, indeed, the psyche's 'own water' which could be used to understand the complex contents of the psyche" (Edinger 1985, 1).

For Jung, Edinger, and Hillman, the fundamental facts of psyche's existence are fantasy images; for them, image *is* psyche. In the pursuit of privileging this aspect of Jung's heritage, Hillman deconstructs Jung's famous distinction between archetypes per se and archetypal images. Archetype per se is disregarded. For some analysts, this casts a theoretical shadow of its own.

Kenneth Newman is representative of the latter position. He argues that privileging the image, as is the case to some extent with Jung and even more so with Hillman, neglects an important aspect of the scientific imagination. For Newman, there is a psychic hole within the image, "a shadow of the shadow," where the a-imaginal is found, and "psyche has the capacity to access ... that which eludes any image because it is outside the sensorium of man" (Newman 1993, 38), but not outside of his imagination. For Newman, "the imagination can see through and beyond what the eye sees ..." (ibid.). Giving recognition to the realm of the a-imaginal is important and is the reason why the scientific imagination comes into being. He notes that science is "not an instance where nominalism and rational explanation are squeezing out soul, but a realm outside of soul" (ibid., 41). Rather, the reverse is the case:

> Anima-zation or feminine soulizing creates its own lacuna, which eclipses other worlds. And in that umbra, which we have called the shadow of the shadow, we find the animus and masculine soulizing. Scientific thinking is a manifestation of masculine eros relating to the a-sensorial and a-imaginal, by virtue of no longer being image bound, for not all things imaginary are imaginal.
>
> (ibid.)

Neil Micklem is likewise concerned about knowledge of what is beyond sense and image. However, instead of imagining access to this a-imaginal world through science, he turns to religion, and particularly to the paradoxical teachings of Meister Eckhart. Opening oneself to the a-imaginal is opening to a transpersonal world of divinity, which requires detachment, emptiness, and "switching off from the senses and ridding ourselves of images in order to gain not the image, but the real thing" (Micklem 1993, 120).

Newman's "science" and Micklem's "religion" find resonance with the masculine eros of Wolfgang Giegerich (1998), who has also critiqued Jung and Hillman for granting fundamental priority to images. In his book *The Soul's Logical Life*, Giegerich turns to philosophy, particularly the philosophy of Hegel, for inspiration. Like Newman, Giegerich argues that thinking has been undervalued and underdeveloped under the weight of images in Jung's and Hillman's psychologies. Giegerich's work turns from the imaginal to the logical.

While Newman, Micklem, and Giegerich see a shadow side to privileging images as the basis for psychic life, each of them thinks about the a-imaginal in his own way. Nevertheless, they agree that a theoretical or metaphysical shadow is cast when the primary focus is on images. Jung's Kantian influence led him to be more cautious about making what he considered to be metaphysical statements about the real, at least within the realms of philosophy and religion. His orientation remained psychological, and this was why his focus on images was fundamental.

From my perspective, it is important to continue to struggle with the relationship of concept and image without subjugating one to the other, without letting one or the other fall into the shadow. Newman's focus on the a-imaginal as a hole in the images might be seen as part of the dynamic property of images themselves, as a place where thought can reach out beyond psyche. But if thinking becomes disconnected from the subtle body of the image, masculine eros can degenerate into its animus-laden shadow. For me, the hole in the image can also be imagined as an access point to the unimaginable void, the place where images are both deconstructed and reanimated, and where the subtle body announces a mysterious and paradoxical view of images beyond pictures or representations. In this sense, the shadow of the image intimately belongs to it. What most critics of archetypal psychology have failed to note is that for Hillman, too, not everything archetypal can be contained by the psyche "since they manifest as well in physical, social, linguistic, aesthetic and spiritual modes" (Hillman 1983/2004, 13).

Jung ultimately saw in alchemy that the work of facing the shadow was a paradoxical union of opposites at the core of psychological and alchemical work. In the chapter, "The Paradoxa," in his late work, *Mysterium Coniunctionis*, Jung speaks of the importance of the opposites to the alchemists and how they attempted "to visualize the opposites together but to express them in the same breath" (Jung 1963, para. 36). In this vision, the sun and its shadow are intimately linked and reflect the archetypal and cosmic structures in which consciousness and shadow are eternally at play. This great conjunction suggests the alchemical lapis and the Philosopher's Stone, where the *prima materia of the shadow and the illuminated goal of the opus are mysteriously bound together.* For the alchemically oriented analyst, the shadow is not only the beginning of the work, it is the end as well.

References

Edinger, Edward. 1985. *Anatomy of the psyche.* La Salle, IL: Open Court.
Fink, Bruce. 2007. *Fundamentals of psychoanalytic technique: A Lacanian approach for practitioners.* New York: W. W. Norton and Co.
Giegerich, Wolfgang. 1998. *The soul's logical life.* Frankfurt: Peter Lang.
Hillman, James. 1975. *Revisioning psychology.* New York: Harper & Row.
———. 1978. The therapeutic value of alchemical language. *Dragonflies* 1: 118–126.
———. 1983/2004. *Archetypal psychology.* Putnam, CT: Spring Publications, Inc.
———. 1991. The cure of the shadow. In *Meeting the shadow: The hidden power of the dark side of human nature*, ed. Connie Zweig and Jeremiah Abrams, 242–243. New York: G. P. Putnam's Sons.
Jung, Carl Gustav. 1959. Conscious, unconscious, and individuation. In *The Archetypes and the collective unconscious. The collected works of C.G. Jung,* Vol. 9i, Gerhard Adler (ed.) and R.F.C. Hull (trans) 275–289. Princeton: Princeton University Press.
———. 1963. *Mysterium Coniunctionis. The Collected Works of C.G. Jung,* Vol. 14, edited by Gerhard Adler and translated by R.F.C. Hull. Princeton: Princeton University Press.
———. 1956. *Symbols of transformation. The collected works of C.G. Jung,* Vol. 5, Gerhard Adler (ed.) and R.F.C. Hull (trans.). Princeton: Princeton University Press.
Lambert, Kenneth. 1981. *Analysis, repair and individuation.* London: Academic Press.
Marlan, Stanton. 2005. *The black sun: The alchemy and art of darkness.* College Station: Texas A&M Press.
Micklem, Neil. 1993. The shadow of wholeness. *Harvest: Journal for Jungian Studies* 39: 114–124.
Neumann, Erich. 1969. *Depth psychology and a new ethic.* New York: G. P. Putnam & Sons.
Newman, Kenneth D. 1993. Science: The shadow of the shadow. *Harvest: Journal for Jungian Studies* 39: 37–42.
Ricoeur, Paul. 1970. *Freud and philosophy: An essay on interpretation.* New Haven, CT and London: Yale University Press.
Samuels, Andrew. 1985. *Jung and the post-Jungians.* London and New York: Tavistock/Routledge.
Stein, Murray, ed. 1995. *Jungian analysis.* La Salle, IL: Open Court.

Chapter 8

The black sun

Part A. Archetypal image of the non-self

Jung states in *Memories, Dreams, Reflections* (1963) that he regards his work on alchemy as a sign of his inner relationship to Goethe, whom he imagines as in the grip of an archetypal process—a process also alive and active within him as a living substance, the great dream of the *Mundus Archetypus*, the archetypal world. It was his main business and essential to his goal of penetrating the dark secrets of the personality.

Jung notes that the alchemist Mylius refers to the ancient philosophers as the source of our knowledge about *Sol niger*, the black sun, but the phenomenon remains relatively unexplored. In several places in his collected works, Jung writes of *Sol niger* as a powerful and important image of the unconscious. To consider the image in this light is both to recognize its vastness and unknown quality as well as to place it in the historical context of depth psychology and of psyche's attempt to represent the unrepresentable. This way of imagining *Sol niger* is to see it in its most general sense, but Jung has also extracted from the alchemical literature a rich and complex if scattered phenomenology of the image. *Sol niger*, the black sun, blackness, putrefactio, mortificatio, the nigredo, poisoning, torture, killing, decomposition, rotting and death all form a complex web of interrelationships that describe a terrifying, if most often provisional, eclipse of consciousness or of our conscious standpoint. This nigredo process has been considered the most negative and difficult operation in alchemy. It is also one of the most numinous, but very few authors other than Jung have explored the theme in its many facets. In addition to the aspects just described, Jung also finds in this image of blackness a non-manifest latency, a shadow of the sun, as well as an Other Sun, linked to both Saturn and Yahweh, the Primus Anthropos.

For the most part, *Sol niger* is equated with and understood only in its nigredo aspect, while its more sublime dimension—its shine, its dark illumination, its Eros and wisdom—is imagined elsewhere in different operations, images, and colors—in white, yellow, red, or gold. So one way of imagining alchemical and psychological work is to move out of and away from blackness, as a development from black to white, from nigredo to albedo, the classic alchemical formula. But to focus on movement and transition from one stage or color to another, as useful as this might be, runs the risk of not seeing with that dark eye which sees into blackness for itself and not simply as a passage to whiteness, to change and new generation. There is a temptation to read alchemy in this way. Consider the following:

> O happy gate of blackness, cries the sage, which art the passage to this so glorious change. .... For putrefaction precedes the generation of every new form into existence.
> (Edinger, p. 149)

Also:

> That which does not make black cannot make white, because blackness is the beginning of whiteness.
> (Edinger, p. 148)

and, finally, from Paracelsus:

> Putrefaction is of so great efficacy that it blots out the old nature and ... bears another new fruit. .... Putrefaction takes away the acridity from all corrosive spirits of salt, renders them soft and sweet.
> (Edinger, p. 148)

Classical passages such as these may lead one to focus on whiteness, the albedo of new form, and the soft sweetness of renewal. But this developmental view is often a defense against the radicality of black, the harshness of the raven's call, drawing attention to the "blacker than black" aspect of the soul.

Robert Bosnak (1986) describes this nigredo aspect of blackness as a "dark, often repugnant underworld," a place of "stench, disintegration, repulsion, and depression," of "dissolution" and "decay." "[T]hings rot ... like garbage, before they can be reduced to ... rubble." "The future is dark and confused." "[F]eelings of emptiness and isolation" are pervasive and seem as if they "will last forever." It is "a bottomless pit," "the heart is heavy," it is "pitch dark," death is "the only reality," and at bottom "there are no images" (pp. 60–68).

It is this radical blackness that resists any Salvationist perspective emphasized in allegorical readings of alchemy. James Hillman has been an important voice critiquing any such literal reading of steps and stages, emphasizing instead a way of seeing that regards each "phase" for itself, not just as a part of a sequence or process, but rather as a mythical idea, a place or better, a topos. In this way, he tries to see through the linear progression of unidirectional models simply progressing in time.

One of the dangers in placing blackness into a process of development or individuation is the tendency to move too quickly away from its radicality, its depth, severity, and suffering; and this can miss the rich differentiations that exist within blackness itself. At the risk of falling prey to the pitch of blackness, I would like to slow down our passage through *Sol niger* and attempt to move further into it.

Jung states: "Right at the beginning you meet the 'dragon,' the chthonic spirit, the 'devil,' or, as the alchemists called it, the 'blackness,' the *nigredo*, and this encounter produces suffering" (McGuire & Hull 1977, *Jung Speaking*, p. 228). Edinger notes that this work is dangerous and requires torture, killing, and the experience of death. His elaboration of *mortificatio* is elaborately laid out (forgive the pun) in his *Anatomy of the Psyche*.

Perhaps the darkest dimension of *Sol niger* is its most materialized aspect when psyche is seen to co-mix with physis at what Jung speculated was the psychoid dimension of the infra-red end of the spectrum of psychological life. Jung followed the alchemist Gerard Dorn in noting that this aspect of *Sol niger* is a place of physiological destructive actions, which turn the salts in the body into chalk. He also observed that "[t]he sun [and its shadow are] evidently an instrument in the physiological and psychological drama of return to the prima materia, the death that must be undergone if man is to get back to the original condition ..." (Jung, 1954, para. 118).

One of the most profound descriptions of this state of affairs has been written by the Romanian philosopher, Emil Cioran [Sir-ran] (1911–1995), in his book *On the Heights of Despair*. Cioran has been called the connoisseur of apocalypse and theoretician of despair. "No modern writer twists the knife with Cioran's dexterity. . . . His writing . . . is informed with the bitterness of genuine compassion" (Bill Marx, *Boston Phoenix*, from back cover of Cioran, 1992).

I would like to quote a passage from Cioran's reflection on death:

> Why don't we want to accept that one can entertain lively meditations on death ... the most dangerous issue existing? Death is not something from outside, ontologically different from life, because there is no *death* independent of life.... (23)
>
> To see how death spreads over this world, how it kills a tree and how it penetrates dreams, how it withers a flower or a civilization, how it gnaws on the individual and on culture like a destructive blight, means to be beyond tears and regrets, beyond system and form. Whoever has not experienced the awful agony of death, rising and spreading like a surge of blood, like the choking grasp of a snake which provokes terrifying hallucinations, does not know the demonic character of life and the state of inner effervescence from which great transfigurations arise. ... It's not the luminous drunkenness of ecstasy, in which paradisal visions

conquer you with their splendor and you rise to a purity that sublimates into immateriality, but a mad, dangerous, ruinous, and tormented black drunkenness, in which death appears with the awful seduction of nightmarish snake eyes. To experience such sensations and images means to be so close to the essence of reality that both life and death shed their illusions and attain within you their most dramatic form. An exalted agony combines life and death in a horrible maelstrom: a beastly satanism borrows tears from voluptuousness. Life as a long agony on the road to death is nothing but another manifestation of life's demoniacal dialectics, in which forms are given birth only to be destroyed. …. (24)

The feeling of the irrevocable, which appears as an ineluctable necessity going against the grain of our innermost tendencies, is conceivable only because of time's demonism. The conviction that you cannot escape an implacable fate and that time will do nothing but unfold the dramatic process of destruction is an expression of irrevocable agony. Isn't nothingness, then, salvation? But how can there be salvation in nothingness? If salvation is nearly impossible through existence, how can it be possible through the complete absence of existence? (28)

Since there is no salvation either in existence or in nothingness, let this world with its eternal laws be smashed to pieces! (28)

Cioran, like Hillman, attempts to see beyond Salvationist fantasies. His description wounds our narcissism and affronts our egos, and is a violence to our complacent identities.

For Giegerich, such a hurtful cut is necessary; the soul must be torn away, or turned around, and as we shall see in a moment, turned inside out in a violent reversal of orientation. For him, the mortificatio and putrefactio are logical operations in material and chemical imagery but if they are so, it is important not to lose sight of the fact that these operations are excruciatingly personal and painful, and resist any uplifting dialectic. Hillman describes the psyche in a process of *mortificatio* as trapped, nailed down in inertia and in the extension of matter. It is a time, he says, of symptoms and "the grinding sadistic mortifications of shame" (2010, p. 90). This process involves a flaying, having one's skin stripped off and/or, metaphorically, to be assaulted with stinging criticism. While this may at times be self-imposed, the experience of it from the point of view of the ego is that it is something one painfully undergoes.

The following dream is of an analytic candidate after one of his yearly reviews in which he felt attacked and treated sadistically. He felt terrible pain and a great deal of shame. The dream is as follows:

I am in a room with two women, one of whom may be Joan A. (she is a candidate who was wounded when not admitted to training).

A television is on covering a gruesome story; it may be a news item. A woman is on an operating table. She looks like she is being tortured or having an operation which is extremely painful (By now I am in the operating room and no longer seeing this on a TV screen.). She is lying there naked and various parts of her skin have been surgically removed. There are some disturbing surgical instruments on the table beside her (it is a cold metal table).

Two parts of the operation have occurred. A large square of her skin has been pulled back from her solar plexus and fastened to the operating table. As well, the skin of her left hand has been removed. She is now waiting to have the skin on her face removed. She is terrified. The moment comes and the skin is peeled off. It is a horrifying experience. Her face changes with the removal of the skin, as though her looks have changed. It is blackened and almost statue-like. Then another procedure starts and I realize that another face is going to be grafted back on to her face. The people doing this have decided to give her a disfigured face. It's almost as though it's her original skin turned inside out. They start applying the new face. It is horribly distorted.

The scene changes and the woman who was on the table is now a tall man with dark hair. He is a wayfarer and he is heading towards a pathway, like a suspended boardwalk, suspended from a series of buildings. He says, "Christ says I should take my journey using the back road."

Here, one can see psyche's experience of narcissistic offense and mortification, being pinned down and tortured, painfully exposed, stripped naked, flayed, turned inside out, and blackened to the point where one feels disfigured. One could easily imagine the dreamer crying out with Jeremiah, who had a profound experience of being afflicted, of being worn down, pierced, humiliated, ridiculed, and tainted (Edinger 1985, pp. 159–160).[1]

In these instances, the vindictiveness of *Sol niger* is vividly apparent. In its most literal and destructive forms, it can be seen to accompany blindness, cancer, psychosis, murder, suicide, death, narcissistic mortification—it is a general spoiler of life. These experiences represent the nigredo, putrefaction, and mortificatio—all aspects of *Sol niger* (Figure 8.1).

Given the devastating impact of this dimension of blackness, it is not surprising that there is a desire to escape its consequences, to move away, out of its grip.

Hillman recognizes the importance of not turning away from this nigredo. He is one of the few who stays with the image long enough to begin the process of seeing through it to the intention of blackness itself. In "The Seduction of Black" (2010), he begins to point beyond the *nigredo* aspect without leaving it behind. Blackness too has a purpose. It warns, teaches endurance, dissolves attachments, and sophisticates the eye, so that we may not only see blackness, but by means of it. To see through blackness is to

Figure 8.1 The black sun, *sol niger, nigredo, putrefactio.* From Mylius, *Philosophia reformata*, 1622. (Public domain.)

understand its continuous deconstructive activity necessary for psychological change. But while Hillman does not abandon us to blackness, he doesn't rescue us from it either. One must be careful not to simply expect a return to the beauty of the colored world. Ironically, a danger in reading Hillman is precisely a literal return to this colored world, as we follow him from black to blue, from blue to white, from white to yellow, to the reddening of the rubedo.

Psychologically, it is easy to be seduced as we follow Hillman's moves from the blackest mortifications of despair to the achievement of depression and melancholy where, in blue beginnings, Venus collaborates with Saturn and imagination leads to the sweetness and harmony of albedo whitening. This perfection rots, but only to yellow, making a way for the rubedo (the reddening libidinal activity of the soul). This movement resurrects and revivifies matter, crowning it in beauty and pleasure, truly a garden of earthly delights. Such a reading, however, is not Hillman's intent and literalizes the linear pull of his work into a banal cliché and catechism. It is always too easy to collapse complexity into facile formulations. A careful reading of his texts, in spite of pointing beyond the nigredo, resists any easy exit from blackness.

As on moves from color to color, the traces of black remain like a subtle body which imbues the soul with its ongoing essence. Consider the following. In "Alchemical Blue and the *Unio Mentalis*" (2010), Hillman writes: "The transit from black to white via blue implies that blue always brings black with it. Blue bears traces of the *mortificatio* into the whitening" (p. 102).[2] Like black, blue brings traces of darkness into the albedo. In "Silver and the White Earth" (2010), Hillman elaborates on this: "'Putrefaction extends and continues even unto whiteness,' says Figulus.... We must therefore amend our notions of the white earth ..." (2010, p. 168). Likewise, in the transit from white to yellow, the process is marked by putrefaction, rotting, decay, and death: "Yellow signifies a particular kind of change usually for the worse" (1991, p. 78), in other words, the work of blackening. Even in the "final stage" of the rubedo, in the reddening, we witness the final dissolution of sun lit consciousness. So even while Hillman indicates the soul's movement through the color matrices of alchemy, in each move the subtle essence of blackness itself works within, in such a way that the essence of blackness is never left behind.

I have attempted to extract black back from the array of colors in order to give full acknowledgment to its subtle presence. While blackness appears somewhat different when seen through blue, white, yellow, and red, its essence remains. Here, blackness need not be understood only as a literal color but, as Hillman notes, as a "qualitative differentiation of intensities and hues which is essential to the *unio mentalis*" and the act of imagination (2010, p. 112). In this way, black remains as a subtle body embracing psyche with its ongoing essence, repeating, deconstructing, tincturing, making itself felt in the very pigment of our soul. It is an essence of multiple differentiations and layers of meaning.

Writers and painters have long known about the many qualities of blackness. The following is a remark by the famous Japanese painter and printmaker, Hokusai:

> There is a black which is old and a black which is fresh. Lustrous [*brilliant*] black and matte black, black in sunlight and black in shadow. For the old black, one must use an admixture of blue, for the matte black an admixture of white; for the lustrous black gum [*colle*] must be added. Black in sunlight must have grey reflections
>
> (Gage 1999, quoting Hokusai, p. 229)

In her book, *The Song of Solomon*, Toni Morrison (1977) states:

> There're five or six kinds of black. Some silky, some wooly, some just empty. Some like fingers. And it don't stay still. It moves and changes from one kind of black to another. Saying something is pitch black is

like saying something is green. What kind of green? ... Well, night black is the same way. May as well be a rainbow

(p. 40)

Hillman, too, echoes the above: there are "blacks that recede and absorb, those that dampen and soften, those that etch and sharpen, and others that shine almost with the effulgence — a *sol niger*" (2010, p. 91).

In this moment, black begins to shine, no longer simply confined in the nigredo, and joy is oddly linked to blackening, to deconstruction, or as Lacan might have said, the lack is linked to *jouissance*. This black joy is also recognized in the sublime beauty of Hades where Hillman tells us that everything becomes deeper, moving from visible connection to invisible one, and the invisible glows with the presence of the void.

The link between bliss and blackness is also made by Stanislov Grof and is captured in a series of paintings described in his work, *LSD Psychotherapy*. In this figure, the black sun is "depicted as the ultimate source of creative energy in the cosmos" (Grof 1980, p. 284). Grof states that through suffering, one reaches the black sun, the manifestation of the innermost core of the human being, the Divine Self, which he associates with transcendental bliss, not unlike the descriptions of the Tantric tradition.

In relation to another painting depicting the fire of an erupting volcano, Grof describes a patient who had experienced its destructive power, but was now appreciating the creative aspect of the glowing magma. It is this creative fire which was at the core of Jung's work, a fire that also contained the volcanic metaphor of the stream of lava, the incandescent matter. It was an image important to Jung in his vision of the psyche. Grof is clearly and deeply aware of both the destructive and creative dimensions of this primordial process; yet, he separates *Sol niger*, the "destructive" part, from the transcendent black sun, which I believe runs the risk of splitting the archetype apart. As I see it, both experiences are intimately intertwined and present in the blackness of *Sol niger* as an archetypal image. It is only through such an image that the soul shows itself as both the dark underworld and its fruitful and shining possibilities. Hillman notes that from one perspective, the blackness of night is the source of all evil, but from the viewpoint of the Orphics, night was the depth of love. This mystical love is well described by George Scheper (1992) in his study, "Illumination and Darkness in the Song of Songs." Though Hillman resists proponents of religious darkness and their mystical language, for Scheper, these mystics become our most reliable phenomenologists of a dazzling darkness, of Eros and self-forgetting. In the *Song of Songs*, the Shulamite's night quest for her lover reads like a mystic *desendu ad inferno* and in terms of the poetics of love, the mystic descent into darkness, whether in the story of Orpheus and Euridyce, Demeter and Persephone, Ishtar and Dumuzi, all symbolize the overwhelming redemptive power of passion and darkness. In this spirit, the Hebrew *Song of Songs* resonates with the work of St. John of the Cross, who also speaks about the sweetness of darkness and ecstatic love.

The passion of ecstatic love is also prominent in Sufi mysticism. Henri Corbin (1978) links such esoteric passion with what the Sufis call black light, considered the highest spiritual stage and the most perilous initiatory step. The black light is an attribute of a majesty that sets the mystic's being on fire shattering the apertures of the human organism. It is a light that is not contemplated; it attacks, invades, annihilates, and then annihilates the annihilation. For Corbin, this light requires an unknowing which as such is knowing. This luminous night is finally identified with a state of mystical poverty in the sense in which the Sufi is considered as poor in spirit. The mystic is so totally absorbed that he no longer has an existence of his own. He returns, like the Taoist alchemist, to his original condition called the luminous night or dark midday.

For the Sufi, this absolute subject can hardly be called a subject at all since it is truly found in its own negation. Negation is its essence, and, as Giegerich (1998) has said, to enter the land of soul is death to the self. It is a land of no-self. The person who would do psychology would no longer exist. Death is always now and, as with the mystic's self-annihilation, to enter this state means to bathe in negation: the psychologist as truly psychological has to speak as one who has died as an ego personality. The art of psychological discourse is to speak as someone already deceased. In his paper, "Concerning the Stone: Alchemical Images of the Goal" (2010), Hillman speaks just this way when he talks about "the psychotherapeutic cure of 'me'" (p. 255). When we see through to this level, the work is over, we no longer work at consciousness, developing ourselves, nor possess a distinct grid by means of which we recognize where we are, how we are, maybe even who we are, and I would add in the light of *Sol niger*, *if* we are. Our lives are not our lives, and for Hillman's Archetypal Psychology, the libido moves to a cosmic erotic dynamic that permeates the world because it loves the world. While matter is exalted, the subjective self disappears. Here, says Hillman, the material base of me-ness has been dissolved, calcined, tortured, putrefied, and distilled to a clarity that can be completely seen through as if it were not there at all. Not a speck of literalism remains not even spiritual literalism. I think it is important to understand that this ideal of the non-self should not itself be understood literally. There is a misunderstanding in freezing the notion into a positive entity of non-being, and I don't think this is what Hillman intends. This move would see the stone as hard rather than soft, as the alchemist imagines it.

It is only with continuing reflection that we might ask whether or how much such a statement corresponds to what Giegerich means by the logical life of the soul. Is the non-self a sublated self? How might such ideas be related to the psychology of the Buddhist idea of non-self, the kabbalistic *en sof* as nothing, the Sufi's spiritual intoxication (*fana*) as a relief from self, or even Lacan's idea of a subject or Jung's notion of the Self? It's not possible here to address these questions, but an interesting reflection on some of this can be found in David Miller's paper, "Nothing Almost Sees Miracles" (1995–1996). While there are important differences between these ideas, there is considerable consensus in perceiving the need to describe something like a non-self.

It appears to me now that *Sol niger* might be considered an archetypal phenomenon having two integrated poles and multiple differentiations. At one end, the non-self can be seen in its most literal form locked into the *nigredo* and mortification of the flesh. The non-self leans toward physical annihilation and literal death. But at its other pole, the archetype is no longer confined in the *nigredo* and reflects itself in a different light, where annihilation is linked to the presence of the void understood as absence, Eros, and self-forgetting, to the majesty that sets the soul on fire.

For Derrida, the violence of annihilation is reflected in the replacement of Ra, the sun, by *his* son, Thoth. Thoth, like Hades, is a dangerous supplement, as he says—ready to replace Ra by violence if need be, altering the sun's ordinary light with the dark light and infernal glow of the *lumen naturae*. This light is the light of his son, of *Sol niger*—a light which shines more subtlety in the différance *between* them, in the invisible body of love (1981, p. 93).

Experientially, these two poles of the archetype are in eternal embrace, crossing one another in a dance that might look like the structure of DNA or the way Merleau-Ponty (1969) describes the crossing in the chiasm in his *The Visible and the Invisible*. In this chiasm, there is a strange reversal in the order of time. Giegerich notes something similar: negation is not a simple, unidirectional subversion, but also *an already being* on the other side in the land of soul. In this translocation, there is a being in two places at once; literal space and time are suspended. "Things like to happen together," Chinese philosophers say.

For Hillman and his alchemical psychology, in what might be called an integrated archetype, things do happen together, "The pain [and suffering are] not prior to the goal, like crucifixion before resurrection." Rather, with every "gilding [there is] also a poisoning." "The pearl is also always grit, an irritation as well as a luster" (2010, p. 240).

The same could be said for Hillman himself who is just such an irritant to any psychology that would imagine itself free from blackness. His vision darkens every bright eye, poisons every well, and befouls every cradle, but this irritant also shines with the luster of *Sol niger* like an Other Sun whose effulgence has lighted our way into a new millennium of psychology.

In conclusion, and as I sort out the receding from the oncoming, the dying from the living, I can no longer imagine this so literally. As we come into the twenty-first century and see *through* the fantasy of development as simple progress, and *into and beyond* the consulting room, it must be with the dark eye of *Sol niger*. There, death and life are intertwined in both the historical and the archetypal psyche. I believe we never simply rise above or go beyond, but remain always on the threshold.

Part A was an unpublished paper and a precursor to my book The Black Sun (2005) *and what follows was the book's Epilogue.*

Part B. Epilogue to *The Black Sun: The Alchemy and Art of Darkness*

I began my exploration of the black sun as an experiment in alchemical psychology. It begins and ends with an enigma, with a movement from the *nigredo* of light to the mystery of an illuminated darkness. Imagined in juxtaposition to light, darkness casts a shadow and sets the stage for a new Faustian bargain, not with the forces of darkness, but with the forces of light. In so doing, the primacy of light is declared, and the values of science, technology, rational order, patriarchy, and progress lead the way into modernity with its astonishing contributions to the spread of civilization and to consciousness itself. We have noted, however, that if light and the sun have led us into the present, it has also led to a massive repression and devaluation of the dark side of psychic and cultural life and displayed a blind spot with regard to vision itself. In my book *The Black Sun*, I pointed to the shadows of phallocentrism, logocentrism, and heliopolitics, driven by the violence of light, a condition I considered psychologically and which is symbolized by a one-sided identification with King/ego and the tyrannical power of an undifferentiated, unconscious shadow. I noted that the despotic King as *prima materia* must be relativized and I examined the alchemical phenomenology of the *mortificatio* in which this primitive King is tortured, beaten, humiliated, poisoned, drowned, dissolved, calcined, and killed.

These alchemical operations lead to a *nigredo*, or descent into darkness, that ultimately empties the soul and leaves only skeletal remains and the infernal light of *Sol niger*. *Sol niger* has been a difficult image to throw light upon since, like a black hole, it sucks all light into itself. Thus, in alchemy and, following it, in the depth psychology of Jung, the black sun has been associated with darkness almost exclusively.

My strategy was to stick with this image and to resist any Salvationist attempt to reach beyond it. Rather, my thought was to hesitate before the darkness, to pause and enter its realm, following it in alchemy, literature, art, and clinical expressions. Entering this world of darkness, I encountered *Sol niger* in its blacker-than-black aspects and saw its most literal and destructive dimensions associated with narcissistic mortification, humiliation, delusion, despair, depression, physiological and psychological decay, cancer, psychosis, suicide, murder, trauma, and death.

In short, I followed it into the heart of darkness, into the worlds of Hades and Ereshkigal, to Kali's cremation ground and Dante's world of ice, where *puer* visions of light and eternity give way to Saturnian time and the perils of night. Here, rational order breaks down, and traumatogenic defenses come into play to prevent the unthinkable, but the unthinkable itself presents us with a mystery, the mystery of a death that is not simply literal, but also symbolic. Alchemy portrays such mysteries in a strange and paradoxical confluence of images: corpses and coffins with sprouting grains and black suns that shine. It is a mystery that calls for more than defense and constellates a necessity that must be entered. As such, I conceived of it as an ontological pivot point, marking a desubstantiation of the ego that exhibits both death and new life, light and darkness, presence and absence, the paradoxical play intrinsic to *Sol niger* as a black sun.

For the alchemists, the unrepresentable can be perceived only by the inward person and was considered a mystery at the heart of nature itself. Its odd light, the *lumen naturae*, was considered to be a divine spark buried in darkness and could be found in both the prime matter of the alchemist's art and in the *soma pneumatikon* or subtle body. I traced the images of the subtle body in many esoteric traditions as well as in the imagery of contemporary patients.

For all of the traditions I explored, the subtle body was a microcosm of a larger universe and an image of the divine in human form. This form has shown itself in symbols of the primordial human being, who, understood psychologically, is an expression of the Self. For Jung, the Self is an idea that attempts to reflect the wholeness of the human psyche. It was intended to designate a structure that included both consciousness and the unconscious, light and dark, and was considered a central, ordering principle at the core of psychic life. The Self as a transcendental and superordinate structure cannot be made totally conscious. At its core, it is considered to be an unknown mystery that disseminates itself in multiple archetypal images across time and culture. We have seen how these archetypal images more or less adequately represent the wholeness of the archetypal structure that they attempt to express. For Jung, the Self was a psychological lens through which to consider these expressions. These images, perhaps by necessity, always fall short of full expression of the archetype of wholeness.

Concepts and symbols of wholeness as expressions of totality have a tendency to degenerate and move toward abstraction as idealized and rational conceptualizations that seduce us into forgetting that they fundamentally reflect an unknown. With regard to the psyche, Jung writes, "The concept of the unconscious *posits nothing*, it designates only my *unknowing*"

(1973, p. 411). I have noted the importance of preserving this mystery that constitutes the strangeness and miracle of perception at the heart of the *mysterium coniunctionis*. I have concluded that if we speak of unity or wholeness, it is important not to lose sight of stubborn differences and the monstrous complexities that, if true to the phenomenon, lead to humor, astonishment, and at times divine awe. As noted, the idea of the Self is Jung's attempt to capture this complexity, but as his theories became assimilated and familiar, his concept was subject to the same fate as all fundamental ideas—they soon lose their original profundity, mystery, and unknown quality.

In our attempt to speak the unspeakable, we have noticed that the Self, too, casts a shadow, and we have focused on this shadow, recognizing the unnamable, invisible, and unthinkable core of the idea, which some have referred to as a Divine Darkness, while others have called it a non-Self. The non-Self is not another name for the Self, but is founded in the recognition of the problematics involved in any representation of wholeness and a mark for the profound expression of this mystery. All of the attempts to name this mystery might be said to leave traces in the language in which we have attempted to speak it. No signifier proves to be adequate to capture the fullness of human experience. The idea of the Self, like a shooting star of darkness, leaves a metaphor in a variety of images inscribed in the margins of our experience. One might imagine these images as traces of silence at the heart of what we have imagined as the Self.

In an attempt to speak about the Self, I have sought to find innovative ways to preserve its mystery, paradox, and unknown quality. Borrowing from postmodern philosophy, I have imagined the Self as a Self under erasure, as an idea and image that has the *mortificatio* and self-deconstruction at its heart. Such a Self is always a non-Self also. It is a darkness that is light and a light that is darkness, and in this way of imagining it, we have a glimpse of *Sol niger*.

Experientially, these two poles of the archetype, light and dark, are in an eternal embrace, crossing one another in a dance that might look like the structure of DNA. As noted earlier, *Sol niger* might be considered an archetypal image of the non-Self, having two integrated poles and multiple differentiations. At one end, the non-Self can be seen in its most literal form locked into the *nigredo* and the mortification of the flesh. Here, the non-Self leans toward physical annihilation and literal death. At its other pole, however, the archetypal image is no longer confined to the *nigredo* and reflects itself in a different light where annihilation is linked to both the presence of the void understood as absence, Eros, and self-forgetting and a majesty that sets the soul on fire.

In all, there is an alchemy and art in darkness, an invisible design rendering and rending vision, calling it to its sourceless possibility. The light of Western metaphysics has obscured darkness; sedimented reason has thrown it into the shadows, naming it only as its inferior counterpart. But darkness is also the Other that likewise shines; it is illuminated not by light, but by its own intrinsic luminosity. Its glow is that of the *lumen naturae*, the light of nature, whose sun is not the star of heaven, but *Sol niger*, the black sun.

Notes

1 This description was inspired by Edinger's discussion of the suffering of the Biblical figure Jeremiah as portrayed by St. John of the Cross in his poem *Dark Night of the Soul*.
2 Hillman quotes Goethe: "blue still brings a principle of darkness with it" (2010, p. 102).

References

Bosnak, Robert. *A Little Course in Dreams*. Translated from the Dutch by Michael H. Kohn and Robert Bosnak. Boston, MA: Shambhala Publications, 1986.
Cioran, Emil M. *On the Heights of Despair*. Chicago, IL: University of Chicago, 1992.
Corbin, Henry. *The Man of Light in Iranian Sufism*. Boulder, CO: Shambhala, 1978.
Derrida, Jacques. *Dissemination*. Chicago, IL: University of Chicago, 1981.
Edinger, Edward. *Anatomy of the Psyche: Alchemical Symbolism in Psychotherapy*. LaSalle, IL: Open Court, 1985.
Gage, John. *Color and Meaning*. Berkeley: University of California Press, 1999.
Giegerich, Wolfgang. *The Soul's Logical Life*. Frankfurt: Peter Lang, 1998.
Grof, Stanislov. *LSD Psychotherapy*. Pomona: Hunter House, 1980.
Hillman, James. *Alchemical Psychology, Uniform Edition of the Writings of James Hillman, Vol. 5*. Putnam: Spring Publications, 2010.
——. "The Yellowing of the Work." In *Paris '89: Proceedings of the Eleventh Congress for Analytical Psychology*, edited by M.A. Mattoon, 77–102. Einsiedeln: Daimon, 1991.
Jung, C.G. *Memories, Dreams, Reflections*. Recorded and edited by Aniela Jaffé, translated by Richard and Clara Winston. New York: Pantheon, 1963.
——. *Mysterium Coniunctionis. The Collected Works of C.G. Jung, Vol. 14*, edited by Gerhard Adler and translated by R.F.C. Hull. Princeton, NJ: Princeton University Press, 1954/1963/1970.
——. *Letters, vol. 1: 1906–1950*, edited by Gerhard Adler and Aniela Jaffé, translated by R.F.C. Hull. Princeton, NJ: Princeton University Press, 1973.
Marlan, Stanton. *The Black Sun: The Alchemy and Art of Darkness*. College Station: Texas A&M University Press, 2005.
McGuire, William and R.F.C. Hull (Eds.). *C.G. Jung Speaking*. Princeton, NJ: Princeton University Press, 1977.
Merleau-Ponty, Maurice. *The Visible and the Invisible*. Evanston, IL: Northwestern University Press, 1969.
Miller, David. "Nothing Almost Sees Miracles." *The Journal of the Psychology of Religion*, 4–5: 1–26, 1995–1996.
Morrison, Toni. *The Song of Solomon*. New York: Signet/Penguin, 1977.
Scheper, George. "Illumination and Darkness in the Song of Songs." In *Analecta Husserliana: The Yearbook of Phenomenological Research*, vol. 38, edited by Anna-Teresa Tymieniecka, Kluwer: Dordrecht, 1992.

Chapter 9

From the black sun to the Philosophers' Stone

Alchemy is a vast subject, and the Philosophers' Stone is one of its most enigmatic ideas. Historically, alchemists argued with one another about the materials, procedures, and nature of the Philosophers' Stone, and nearly every alchemical treatise proclaimed its own recipe as the correct one for the achievement of alchemy's sought-after goal. Typically, there was very little overlap between the views of the adepts. It was not unusual at the beginning of an alchemical work for the writer to start out by mercilessly denouncing other adepts, calling them fools, charlatans, puffers and the like, and proclaiming that only he had achieved the secret of the "Great Work."

In contrast to this, I would like to begin my reflections on the Philosophers' Stone with words of respect rather than words of derision. I am indebted first of all to the remarkable work of C.G. Jung, who opened up a depth psychological way of understanding the mysterious goal of alchemy, and to his classical followers Marie-Louise von Franz and Edward Edinger, both of whom, with a sense of appreciation, clarified and further developed Jung's work. Many other analysts, too many to name for the purpose of this piece, have continued in this tradition—or have contributed to it by reformulating some of Jung's ideas.[1] Several of them have written for a special edition of *Spring* on alchemy, thanks to the vision of Nancy Cater who created a forum in which many of us had an opportunity to contribute our latest ideas on alchemical themes.

In terms of my focus on the Philosophers' Stone, two contemporary analysts stand out as having opened up new trajectories in alchemical thinking about the Stone: James Hillman and Wolfgang Giegerich. Hillman's work on alchemy is prolific and his influential series of papers on alchemical themes is undoubtedly well known to the readership of *Spring*. His most focused work on the Philosophers' Stone, however, is in his seminal paper "Concerning the Stone: Alchemical Images of the Goal."[2] Giegerich, likewise, has contributed an innovative view of alchemical psychology and the Philosophers' Stone in his challenging book, *The Soul's Logical Life*.[3] Like the traditional alchemists, Jung, Hillman, and Giegerich hold differing views of the Stone, though there is often more overlap among them than might be apparent in a quick reading.

One way to imagine the psychological work on the Stone is to follow in the steps of the old alchemists and claim that each thinker advances over those who came before, each representing a version of the best or truest vision of the goal. While such a perspective may ultimately prove to be true, I must confess that I am not yet ready simply to move past Jung's work. Rather, I am still at work trying to understand Jung's alchemical vision *alongside* those of Hillman, Giegerich, and others. While there are many scholars who have presented a number of valuable contributions to the alchemical work, I will be focusing here on Hillman and Giegerich, both of whom offer astonishing insights into the psychic reality of the Stone. Each of their perspectives can be read independently or as contributing to a larger and subtler vision still being articulated. For me, reading Jung side by side with Hillman and Giegerich evokes an image of the alchemical stove: Jung in one alembic cooking on a back burner over a steady low heat, Hillman and Giegerich in differently shaped vessels, boiling up front, while I attempt to prepare my own concoction utilizing the vapors produced by them and others, and seeking to further distill the essences and elixirs necessary for the difficult production of the Stone. (A more comprehensive outcome of these distillations, however, must await a longer work (on the Stone) still in progress. Here, I can offer only a glimpse at the work emerging from the alembics of my colleagues, each with his own ideas and his own compelling images of the Philosophers' Stone.)

Tinctures of stone

For the moment, I will leave Jung's vessel closed and on the back burner, to be taken up later. Peering into Hillman's alembic reveals a phenomenology of the soul's colors: an imaginal rainbow of black, blue, white/silver, yellow, and red. For Hillman, the Stone is first an "idea" of the goal, since the goal must be deliteralized from the beginning.[4] While the Stone has facticity and objectivity, duration and substantiality, it is too complex to be described simply in *senex* metaphors. The Stone is also sensual, soft, waxy, and wounded. It is tender and flexible, oily, rich, and fat. It is vital and combustible and, though emotional, it has a kind of stability and timelessness. It moves in a circular way, turning like a wheel, returning *telos* to itself—"to the subjective urge that has impelled the entire work from the start....the snake eats its own tail"[5]—and the *rotatio* announcing "that no position can remain fixed, no statement can be finally true."[6] It is ultimately the objectification of our subjectivity; yet, it oozes with libido. It is Freudian, pagan, neo-Platonic, Greek, and Italian—a pleasurable pull toward Beauty, toward Voluptas rather than the "mediocrity of ataraxic rationality."[7]

Hillman's patron saints, Corbin, Ficino, and Valla among others, stimulate a reddened psychology dripping with an Aphroditic language, exalting, revivifying, and crowning matter. The goal is not growth, health, development, or transformation "but the seeking and searching of the awakened mind ... like a burning jewel in the stone."[8]

A look inside the Giegerich vessel suggests the need to refine the Stone further. Its inner essence emphasizes the *logical* rather than the *imaginal*. The work of the adept, for Giegerich, would be to liberate the Stone from the confines of "sensate intuition" and "picture thinking." With the dissolution of the imaginal and of sensate intuition, one might be left imagining the Stone as colorless rather than colorful. If Hillman's tincture leans toward *"coagula,"* Giegerich's move is toward *"solve"*—toward the freeing of Mercurius through sublation, through the dialectics of the Negative, the "NOT" or "ou" (from the alchemical saying *"lithos ou lithos,"* that is, "the not-stone stone").[9] For Giegerich, the highest mystery of the whole work is the physical dissolution into mercury, a movement out of the imaginal into the logical. Here, I imagine Kundalini shedding her skin and Thales remarking that all is water (liquidity). Giegerich also notes that *aqua permanens* is "a solid ground that in itself is not solid, not 'ground' at all, but rather liquidity, pure movement, that ... *is* nevertheless solid ground."[10]

So, if Hillman emphasizes wax (the body of the image), Giegerich thinks water (the *solutio* of its body). If Hillman finds soul in the valley, Giegerich points to the peaks. If Hillman critiques sublation,[11] Giegerich considers it to be the *elixir vital.* If Hillman draws inspiration from the Italians, Giegerich finds his in the German Hegel. However, if one has read Hillman and Giegerich carefully, one soon begins to see that all of these caricatures are at best misreadings. Both thinkers are far more complex than such sketches suggest and, while there are crucial differences between them, there are also considerable overlapping themes that call for further study. Placing these ideas into a double pelican and reheating the entire mixture will allow us to see their similar essences circulating and rising up. Both thinkers emphasize the importance of "ideas," and both see that it is essential to go beyond the physical and the literal. Both emphasize the intrinsic link between idea and image, peak and vale, *solve* and *coagula*, and both officiate at the puer/psyche marriage, although the way each tinctures his syzygy differs. And, most importantly for me, both emphasize some version of the "death of the ego." While both might be seen as privileging one side of the syzygy over the other, neither can be accused of disregarding the importance of that which is not given priority.

In order to understand their respective positions, it may be useful also to compare some of their mutual misunderstandings. For example, when Hillman critiques Hegel's notion of *Aufhebung*, what he seems to have in mind is spirit detached from soul, the puer drawn apart from psyche, or anima separated from animus—a procedure that he uses as a heuristic device in his essay "Peaks and Vales."[12] However, to read Hegel's or Giegerich's notion of sublation in this way does not do justice to the complexity of their ideas. Nor does it recognize that for both of them, sublation should never be understood as an either/or. Giegerich clarifies his position on this by noting: "What I offer instead [of an either/or interpretation] is a psychology of interiority. There are not two, but only one, and this 'one' contains its own 'other' within itself."[13] In other words, for Giegerich, thought is not an external other to the image, but the very soul of the image itself. Put in this way, Hillman's critique of sublation, if it is understood as a "climb into the thin air of mountain peaks,"[14] does not hold. Giegerich's notion of sublation already assumes a puer-psyche, anima-animus syzygy. If his thought can be said to lean toward the animus, it is because Giegerich feels that "thought" has been underdeveloped under the weight of the image in imaginal psychology. Giegerich makes it clear that his "pleading for 'thought' [an appeal Hillman makes as well] is not a call to turn our backs on 'image' and on what archetypal theorizing ha[s] accomplished, 'but rather to continue it radically in an attempt to complete it...'."[15]

However, in spite of his desire to develop Hillman's thought, Giegerich actually misconstrues the way Hillman defines image. He believes that Hillman's understanding of image is based on "sensory intuition" and that it is a form of "picture-thinking" in contradistinction to "thought" or thinking proper.[16] But here, just as Hillman's critique falls short of Giegerich's idea of "thought," so Giegerich's critique of Hillman seems to miss Hillman's more radical understanding of "image." After all, in "Image Sense," Hillman writes: "... images are not the same as optical pictures even if they are like pictures. ... We do not literally see images."[17] He adds, giving credit to Edward Casey, that "An image is not what you see but the way you see."[18] That is, we don't see images but see through them. In fact, Giegerich knows that his critique is different from what archetypal psychology actually proposes and that its notion of image has a deeper and more fundamental meaning than he has attributed to it. Seeing images as pictures might be considered to be a remnant of a sensationist psychology that understands images and even the imagination as epiphenomenal to actual things. Although he claims that he does "not want to *reduce*"[19] archetypal psychology's understanding of image to this limited representationalist notion, his critique is primarily aimed at image and the imagination in the narrow sense just described. David Miller also alludes to this issue of "the nonperceptual and nonsensate 'image.'"[20] While Miller's view of image is closer to Hillman's and different from Giegerich's, this difference for Miller is very small and does not diminish his deep appreciation for Giegerich's contribution.

Likewise, Greg Mogenson is aware that Hillman's understanding of image is non-representational and that it functions, in some ways, not unlike the work of negative interiorization as described by Giegerich. This is clear from Mogenson's choice of quotes from Hillman: "The soul's life is not upheld as correct by virtue of exteriority"[21] and "What is reflection then when there is no subject reflected, neither emotion nor external object?"[22] For Hillman, the image is most clearly "a metaphor without a referent."[23] While in many ways I share Miller's sense that in a larger perspective such issues are trivial, and perhaps heuristic on Giegerich's part, they nonetheless point to matters that require further distillation and a "labor of the concept,"[24] as Giegerich might describe it. This is particularly true in the face of the provocative question raised by Mogenson at the end of his chapter "Different Moments in Dialectical Movement."[25] He acknowledges that Hillman, like Giegerich, conveys "the negativity of the image"[26]—but he then calls attention to an even more radical interiorization. Pointing beyond Hillman toward Giegerich's notion of logical form, he asks: "But what of the gold that is to follow?"[27] Here, he alludes to Giegerich's view that "the 'gold' of true psychology is the further negation of the image's silvery negativity into the absolute negativity of a consciousness that can *think* the various moments of each image all at once."[28]

But just what does absolute negativity mean when it comes to Giegerich's "gold," which, like the "stone that is not a stone," is a subtler "gold that is not gold," a gold that is spirit? How is this subtle gold to be differentiated from Hillman's idea? Hillman, too, speaks of gold, not only of silver's imagination of it. What is the difference when we "think" gold in the context of absolute negativity versus when we see it from Hillman's standpoint—particularly when we no longer define the imaginal as simply representing the real? Once we have Giegerich's subtle view of "gold" as totally liquefied Mercurius, can we still distinguish it from lead, silver, or mercury? Are all sublated concepts dissolved in the grand solution of the dialectic? Is "the gold that is not gold" the spirit of gold, the ghost of gold, a tincture of gold, or no gold at all? I suspect that these questions mistake what Giegerich means and that we can distinguish gold's particularity once we have a deeper understanding of the dialectic he proposes. However, just how his gold can be "thought" in comparison to Hillman's "seeing" its sensuous particularity requires further elaboration. When Hillman sees through gold, pushes off from it, he does not go "all the way," according to Giegerich—and for which he faults him. While Hillman's gold is also clearly not the "vulgar gold"[29] but rather the "fantastical gold" of alchemy, his way of speaking about it retains the "golden touch,"[30] the sensate "heart of gold," the "winner's gold," images of gold as "permanently glowing and untarnished," visions of "a consciousness ever shining like dawn, like the sun, without fits of darkening," ever "able to be beaten and beaten yet never crack under the hammer, to be bent, thin as a leaf and so cover mundane things with the shine of glory."[31] Images such as these are ideas of gold released from simple physicality, but they retain a pigment recognizable to the metaphoric ear. While Hillman's move takes him beyond the physical, he stays with the material, the concrete, what I have called here the pigment, a certain impurity that for him saves gold from the "poisonous state of splendid solar isolation."[32]

Therefore, the question about the gold that is to follow (Mogenson's question) is also a question that ultimately applies to the Philosophers' Stone and to the goal of the work. In considering the vision of the Stone in Hillman and Giegerich, it will be important to place Hillman's most radical view of image and of the Stone alongside Giegerich's ideas of "absolute-negative interiority, spirit, thought."[33] For Giegerich, the goal of both alchemy and a "true psychology" is to go *beyond* a psychology rooted in images and the imagination to a psychology rooted in the logical life of the soul. Such a move, for Giegerich, is a true working through of the hierarchical possibilities present in the dialectic and is superior to a psychology that remains rooted in the flesh of images. Since Giegerich does not propose that we eliminate images, the question remains how to understand the similarities and differences between Hillman and Giegerich in a way that moves beyond a side-by-side view of simple difference.[34]

This brings us full circle to my image of the alchemical stove and to my own side-by-side placement of differing views of the Stone. Is it adequate simply to allow different views, perspectives, archetypal stances—or does the "labor of the concept" demand that all views be subject to a dialectic in which "Reason" will produce one position more developed than others? Following Hegel, Giegerich notes that "items that are 'simply different' (*verschienden*) are indifferent to the difference between them."[35] Here, I take Giegerich to be calling for an engagement of ideas versus simply settling for alternative perspectives. He has done much to argue for his well-worked-through positions, and his critiques of imaginal psychology merit careful reading and consideration. Miller and Mogenson have done a masterful job of giving us strong readings of Giegerich's work and of helping us toward a careful consideration of his ideas. What follows is my beginning attempt to work through an interface between Hillman and Giegerich and to raise a number of concerns about any move that relegates images to a status secondary to thought. In opening up the problematic of moving from image to thought, it is not clear whether, or in what way, thought is more fundamental than image, particularly when the image is understood in its most radical way. In addition, a number of philosophers have resisted this move and raised critical questions that must be explored before we can consider abandoning the primary place of image in the work of Jung and Hillman.

Resistance of the remainder

My own hesitation/resistance about a move to spirit/thought is rooted in my belief that Jung and Hillman brought about a major advance in consciousness by revisioning image and imagination, both of which had been in the shadow of Western thought and metaphysics since Plato. Jung's resuscitation of images was a return to soul and began a reversal of the dominant historical process that had depotentiated images and reduced soul to rational intellectual spirit. Hillman's archetypal psychology continued and radicalized Jung's reversal. Hillman has taken note of the hatred for image. The battle between spirit and soul, thought and image, is an old one and even now continues to be fought. The fear of the power of image and of the imagination is very deep in our culture. Giegerich himself has acknowledged that the work of Jung and Hillman was a major step from which "there is no way back."[36] Given that Giegerich's return to the "rational" and to "thought" *is* so powerful, I am concerned that his perspective may be too easily assimilated into the cultural undermining of image, especially since image is still in a fragile revival of its importance, if not its primacy. We must give Giegerich full credit for the complexity of his ideas and for his recognition of the rational. However, although his work does suggest that the rational and the soul are integrated notions, the idea of the rational is so emotionally and psychologically laden with profound cultural implications that Giegerich's perspective, in spite of its sophistication, may serve to continue the repression of the imagination and to turn readers away from the radical innovations of Jung and Hillman. While this in itself is not an argument against Giegerich's position as such, it is an expression of my concern about how his work may be heard and taken up by others.

A move to spirit is an earmark of Hegelian and post-Hegelian Idealism and neo-rationalist philosophies. An example of this, perhaps another misreading, can be seen in the work of Paul Ricoeur, who—in spite of his creative valuing of the symbolic—nevertheless ends up ultimately in a neo-rationalist position in which thought/philosophy transcends mythopoesis. This can be seen in his formulation "the symbol gives rise to thought,"[37] which privileges thinking and tilts the balance away from the primacy of the metaphoric toward the superiority of the rational and the philosophical. My concern here is with the dangers of logocentrism, with what happens when an interpreter, philosophical or psychoanalytic, gives primacy to thought over image, to the rational side of a metaphoric copula, to a formulation in which image and metaphor could be reduced to being simply instrumental, as literary critic Dominick Lacapra has noted.[38] Lacapra's analysis echoes both archetypalist and deconstructivist critiques of the traditional position with its roots in the whole history of thought that gives priority to logos over mythos. It is a position resisted as well by a number of philosophers who take a critical stance toward the Hegelian dialectic and post-Hegelian neo-rationalist thinking and toward Hegel's attempt to sublate the image into the rational. Martin Heidegger, for instance, has commented that the "not" or "negative," referred to earlier as a moment in Hegel's dialectic, cannot be simply overcome or assimilated by reason. The "not" is more than a dialectical alienation on the way to a sublation. In fact, it resists assimilation into the movements of thought. The negation of a negation does not culminate in an unconditional "yes" (i.e. a full assimilation of the "not"). For Heidegger, Hegel's interpretation of negativity is an inauthentic modification of an insurmountable "not"—a "not" that can serve as an access point that transitions from a logical understanding of the soul to a poetic one. For Heidegger, the more important category is not rationality but Being.

Similarly, Edgar Morin, a renowned French thinker, "faults Hegel for considering contradiction a transitory 'moment' of the *Aufhebung*, a moment which is ultimately annulled."[39] Like Heidegger, Morin is arguing, in effect, that the "not" cannot be sublated by any movement of thought and that it represents an unassimilable difference that resists any form of engulfment.

In a spirit similar to Heidegger's and Morin's, Jacques Derrida also recognizes the problem of the unassimilable "not." For him, trying to undo Hegel is like trying to decapitate the hydra. He argues that Hegel's dialectic incorporates all contradiction, and that every attempt to refuse such engulfment is seen as an error to be overcome by the continuing dialectic. He asks: how then to interrupt the operation of *Aufhebung*, how to handle a negative that is more than just a moment in an all-embracing process? How do we escape the perpetual reversal entailed in any oppositional system of thought? What would bring the death knell (*glas*), or laughter (Nietzsche) to bear on Hegel's attempt to achieve absolute spirit without remainder? For Derrida, Hegel's insistence on absolute spirit implies a drift toward rationalism and idealism and requires the creation of a metaphysical edifice, which for Derrida is rooted in a "trembling ground of double entendre."[40]

He describes this trembling ground as a "fabulous scene" which any metaphysics of certainty effaces and yet this scene remains, stirring beneath it.[41] For Derrida, this scene provokes

> an endless confrontation with Hegelian concepts, and the move from a restricted, 'speculative' philosophical economy—in which there is nothing that cannot be made to make sense, in which there is nothing *other* than meaning—to a 'general' economy—which affirms that which exceeds meaning, the excess of meaning from which there can be no speculative profit—involves a reinterpretation of the central Hegelian concept: the *Aufhebung*."[42]

In order to engage Giegerich's particular vision of the Philosophers' Stone, and while realizing that Giegerich's thought is to be distinguished from Hegel's, I find myself agreeing with the critiques which regard the unassimilable "not" as a remainder rather than as a momentary hiatus in the dialectic. In my own work, an expression of the negative that is unassimilable showed itself as the image of *sol niger*, a darkness that refuses conscious assimilation.

The unassimilable darkness was a theme of my book *The Black Sun: The Alchemy and Art of Darkness*. The alchemy and art of this darkness require a further exploration of the light of darkness as an expression of both *sol niger* and the Philosophers' Stone. My work began with the recognition of that which resists conscious assimilation, with a black sun that would not yield or be incorporated by an ego stance. It would not dissolve, go away, or be lifted up, and it challenged my own psychological narcissism to the core. While *sol niger* did not allow itself to be possessed by ego and the ego at times felt more in danger of being possessed by it, a perceptual awareness occurred. The wounded and by now somewhat emaciated ego noticed that what it called darkness had a shine that Jung called the shine of darkness itself, the *lumen naturae*. My book, *The Black Sun*, was the beginning of an exploration of this darkness and of its odd luminosity. This strange lumen was my impetus to explore the Philosophers' Stone as I imagined it, present in a darkness that is no darkness. Could the *lumen* of the Philosophers' Stone be an image in Hillman's sense—something that is not simply an object of consciousness but something we can see through? Could this darkness be called sublated?

My ongoing work on the Stone owes a continuing debt to Jung, Hillman, Giegerich, and others—and, as I have noted, is a work in progress. It began in *The Black Sun* with the blackness of *sol niger*, with the *mortificatio* of brokenness, incision, and wound, castration, cut, negation, with an ultimate "No" to the ego, with what felt unassimilable. As the title of this paper indicates, my attention is now turning from the black sun per se to the Philosophers' Stone. To bring the Stone into focus is not to leave the black sun behind, nor to simply move to an *albedo* psychology. Rather, it is to pursue my suspicion that the Philosophers' Stone has been there all along in the shine of darkness itself and that darkness will be there at the end as well, perhaps as an indispensable *caput mortuum*, the dross or residue that remains in the retort after distillation. In some philosophical and alchemical views, this residue is ultimately eliminated, but my wager and anticipation is that the Stone—whether in the language of revivification and Aphroditic pleasure or in the sublation to pure mercurial liquidity—is always accompanied by a remainder. This remainder, while not best understood as a thing-in-itself, is nonetheless that which resists a consciousness that does not account for its differentiation. At times, to accommodate this difference, the Stone has been described as "the unity of the unity and difference."[43] Such a description attempts to address the complexity of the Stone, but even the idea of "the unity of the unity and difference" privileges unity, although at a higher "logical level." The "unity of the unity and difference" is still a tincture of the syzygy that emphasizes unity as the major trope. The syzygy can also be tinctured to emphasize difference. This would call out for the complementary idea of "the difference of the unity and difference," a difference that resists being lit up by consciousness and which protects the remainder that emits a mysterious light of its own as opposed to a light that consciousness would shine on it. This complementary idea is itself similar to one of the stages of the logical dialectic discussed by the Buddhist sage Nargarjuna. His formulation resists any transcendent unification and reinstates a darkness, a void (*sunyata*) that can also be said to shine.

My exploration here of the shine of darkness begins with two images of *sol niger*. A skeleton stands on a blazing black sun; the image reads "*Putrefactio.*"[44] A black sun burns down on a primarily desolate landscape in the alchemical text *Splendor Solis* (1582). These are images of a place an adept must enter if anything is to be learned about the light of nature and the Philosophers' Stone. Jung writes about this light, the *lumen naturae*, in his *Alchemical Studies*, where he calls it "the light of darkness itself."[45] It is a light "which illuminates its own darkness ... [and] turns blackness into brightness." It is a kind of light that the "darkness comprehends." This light is not the light of our day-world sun, but rather the *lumen naturae* that shines in *sol niger*. It can be seen in the risen black Ethiopian and the reconstituted Kali, and is cultivated in Taoist alchemy. It shines in the Secret of the Golden Flower, and in the *filius philosophorum*, imagined by Paracelsus as a luminous vehicle and referred to by Jung as "the central mystery of philosophical alchemy."[46] It is to this mystery, to this "luminous vehicle," that we turn as we imagine a move from *sol niger* to the Philosophers' Stone. Just as this light is not separate from darkness, so the Philosophers' Stone is not separate from *sol niger* but is intrinsic to it.

Is it then the shining that is problematic? How can darkness shine? In my work on the black sun, it was the shining that seemed most enigmatic. Is it a question then of presence and absence, or of a present absence, or of absence itself? The negation and presence of light is at the heart of the archetypal image/idea of the black sun. The Sun King is mortally wounded by darkness and in the negation of negation, *sol niger* shines; a strange reversal takes place or perhaps is "logically" present from the beginning.

One could say that *sol niger*, the black sun, is already a sublated sun, a philosophical/psychological sun, a sun that is not a sun (as the alchemists say of their stone). It is black and yet, at the same "logical" time, it shines. What is the nature of such a shining, such a consciousness? Is it an image, an idea, or both? Is consciousness too dull a word to express this complexity? Philosophers and psychologists have often found difficulty with words like consciousness, image, and idea, and have struggled to give expression to their meanings in a way not encumbered by the metaphysical and metaphoric prejudices of their times—a seemingly impossible task that on occasion has silenced the best of philosophers. How then to let be manifest what is gathered into the shining?

In our postmodern world, our efforts have often left us with a virtual apophatic orgy of dissemination, of a negation of master tropes (and in their place, sliding signifiers), and of neologisms that require another language to follow the discourse. Yet, our simple common language won't do either. Our best efforts are marked by traces of darkness, perhaps penetrating to the core of language itself, into a darkness that matters—and still there is the shine. How then to speak of it, of what Roger Brooke has called the "fertile and hospitable emptiness within which the things of the world could shine forth"?[47] To speak of the shining is not only to speak in the context of the metaphor of light, but also to speak of the shining in a way that aims at expressing an insight that goes beyond the traditional divide between light and dark, and in a way that approaches a more primordial awareness closer to Jung's more mature vision of the psyche, a vision influenced by the alchemical tradition.

Sparks of reiteration

In my book, *The Black Sun*, I began a consideration of this shining, and wrote of it as an image of light at the core of ancient alchemical ideas. The aim of alchemy, according to Paracelsus, was to discover this light hidden in nature. It is a light very different from notions of light as simply separate from darkness and by extension different from any conception of a consciousness separate from its dark background. My strategy in *The Black Sun* was to hesitate before this darkness, to pause and then to enter its realm of corpses and coffins, of monsters and monstrous complexity, and to engage its most literal and destructive demons: narcissistic mortification, humiliation, delusion, despair, depression, physiological and psychological decay, cancer, psychosis, suicide, murder, and death. Such experiences can traumatize and kill. They can also drive the soul toward the unthinkable, a condition which archetypal defenses seek to avoid. To experience these traumatic moments means to be in the grip of the *mortificatio*, a condition the alchemists knew was essential to reaching the depths of the transformation process. Through illness and/or a shamanic-like initiation, the *mortificatio* drives the psyche to an ontological pivot point, to a desubstantiation of the ego, and to what Theodor Adorno might call an "emaciated" subject,[48] leading to a gateway that is both a dying and a new life.

The black sun is a complexity. Its "blacker than black" dimension shines with a dark luminescence. It can open the way to some of the most numinous aspects of psychic life and can give us a glimpse of the miracle of perception at the heart of what Jung called the *mysterium coniunctionis* and of the Philosophers' Stone. One might imagine such a vision in the Tantric rites of Kali who was worshiped at the cremation grounds where she copulates with her consort Shiva on the body of a corpse burning on a funeral pyre. Kali worshipers enact ceremonials associated symbolically and ritually with the annihilation of the ego. These rituals often depict the death of the ego, out of which, it is said, the "human being arises shining."[49] How is it possible to embrace Kali, the darkness that kills? Who is left to embrace her?

Similarly, for Hegel, "only by looking the negative in the face, and tarrying with it," is it possible that the negative can be "the magical power that converts [darkness] into being."[50] For the Tantrics, if one's worship is successful, if one is able to stay the course open-eyed, to dance Kali's dance, to welcome her, then her blackness is said to shine. This shining can be linked to the alchemical ideas of whitening and silvering, with the proviso that we see this shining *albedo* as part of the complexity of darkness itself and not simply as a literal phase following blackness. From one perspective, the theme of renewal follows from symbolic death, but from another, archetypally and logically, death and renewal are at the core of *sol niger*, and this is expressed in the simultaneity of blackness and luminescence.

Mystical death

How can we further our understanding of this mystical death? How to speak of it? The idea of ego death is a difficult one in the light of the acknowledged importance of the role of the ego in relation to the unconscious in our classical way of thinking. When we think of ego loss, our thoughts immediately go to the problematics of a weak, impaired, or non-functioning ego, to a concern with annihilation anxiety and the defenses of the Self against it, as well as to thoughts of psychosis. Ego psychology has a dominant hold on our everyday psychological culture. Yet, the notion of ego death is and has been in the margins of our tradition: in Jung's idea that "*the experience of the self is always a defeat for the ego*,"[51] in Hillman's "psychotherapeutic cure of me,"[52] in Rosen's "egocide,"[53] in Miller's views about the "no self,"[54] in Giegerich's "death of the ego,"[55] etc. Each has contributed to our understanding of a psychology that relativizes and/or dismembers the ego, and each has a stake in the transformation of our psychological theory.

Giegerich, for example, states that

> the Self is real only to the extent that the ego has been negated, overcome ... one might even say, it exists only as a reality 'over the ego's dead body'[56] ... as one who has long died as ego personality.[57]

"The art of psychological discourse," he continues, "is to speak as someone who is already deceased."[58] Here, Giegerich extends the notion of ego death into the core of psychological discourse itself. For Giegerich, this is a necessary step toward the achievement of a "true psychology" and essential in understanding the goal of both alchemy and a psychological life. For Giegerich, ego death also signifies the death of all positivity and serves as the gateway to a liquification of the subject and thus allows entrance into the logical life of the soul. There is a resonance between Giegerich's reading of Hegel and poststructuralist thought, both of which proceed toward if not a liquification of the ego, at least a displacement of the subject from the center of philosophical, linguistic, and theoretical activities.

Several postmodern philosophers have made this connection between ego death and philosophical activity. For example, philosopher Geoffrey Bennington has remarked that "today taking something philosophically, then, always involves this more or less hidden relationship with death, or, by a slightly violent contraction, whatever I take philosophically is death."[59] Surprisingly, Bennington ends his statement with an enigmatic image, but one which captures his point: "The philosophers' stone is an inscribed head stone." For Marla Morris, another postmodern thinker, what is true of the Philosophers' Stone is also true for the "psychoanalyst's stone."[60] She notes that for Bennington, at the end of the day, it is death that deconstruction is all about.

The philosopher Simon Critchley argues in a similar spirit, noting that "ancient Ciceronian wisdom says that to philosophize [and, in light of Morris' comment, to practice psychoanalysis] is to learn how to die."[61] Critchley's exploration echoes the theme of *sol niger* in that it seeks to "*de-create* narratives of redemption" and to "strip away the resources and comforts of story, fable and narrative."[62] Here, Critchley sounds like Giegerich and, following the work of Samuel Beckett, he seeks to understand "the meaning of ... meaninglessness," what he calls "a redemption from redemption."[63] He notes how Beckett's work "frustrates our desire to ascend from the flatlands of language and ordinary experience into the stratosphere of meaning"[64] and comments:

> As is all too easily seen in both contemporary New Age sophism, crude scientism, and the return to increasingly reactionary forms of religious fundamentalism, there is an almost irresistible desire to stuff the world full of meaning and sign up to one or more salvific narratives of redemption.[65]

Critchley, like Beckett and in the spirit of Giegerich's "birth of Man,"[66] leads us away from the temptation to redemption and toward a Zen-like perception of the ordinary, the "sheer mereness of things."[67] He turns to a number of poets—Wallace Stevens, Rainer Maria Rilke, Ralph Waldo Emerson—to give voice to this perception of the ordinary, a perception not unlike Hillman's whose reading of alchemy seeks to move our understanding and our language outside of redemptive, metaphysical systems and salvationist programs. Like Stevens' expression of particulars, "pond," "leaf," "tree," etc., alchemy, in Hillman's view, speaks more phenomenally and particularly. Its substances stand out, they shine: "metals, planets, minerals, stars, plants, charms, animals, vessels, fires, and specific locales"[68]—and, I would add, stones.

So what kind of "thing" is a stone? For Critchley, like Hillman, perception yields a simplicity of awareness in which the subject/object, person/world dichotomy is altered. In such an awareness, we are like a "thing among things," displaying a shining world of sheer "isness," or, as the Buddhists would say, of "suchness." In such a world, a "stone is not a stone," because stones are part of the alchemical white earth and of matter illuminated from within itself. Ordinarily, we think of matter as illuminated by virtue of an external consciousness separate from its object, but matter, in truth, is better understood as part of the complexity of the materialized soul. Such a soul can alchemically be said to be a stone "cleared of moistures"[69] and objective in the "psychoalchemical" sense as Giegerich has described.[70]

Hillman has noted that depth psychology, including Jung's, has had difficulty in finding a way to express the complex/simplicity of psyche's need to substantiate[71] or likewise of substance's need to speak. For Hillman, the problematic is in part rooted in the way conceptual language splits apart a fundamental unity, "abstracting matter from image."[72] When this occurs, there is a powerful psychic demand to heal the split, to substantiate psyche and to bring it back in touch with something solid. The problem of languaging the soul was present for Jung throughout his life and work. The need to substantiate, to go beyond words and paper, played a role in his desire to personify and in his urge to turn to stone.

Turning to stone

Ultimately for Jung, "words and paper ... did not seem real enough ...; something more was needed."[73] He had "to achieve a kind of representation in stone of [his] innermost thoughts and of the knowledge [he] had acquired." Or, to put it another way, he "had to make a confession of faith in stone." Jung's need to substantiate was responsible for the building of his tower at Bollingen where he felt he was "reborn in stone" and through which he was able to express a concretization of his ideas.[74]

Jung carved his way to self-expression through architecture, sculpture, and his focus on alchemical language and poetry, but even more one might say that he opened himself to the call of stone—to its message, and to the way the world came to him. Jung reports the story of the cornerstone he had ordered for his garden when he was building his tower at Bollingen. When the stone arrived, it was the wrong shape and measurements, and the stone mason, furious, wanted to return it. However, when Jung saw the stone, he claimed it as *his* stone. He felt that he "must have it!"[75] even though, at the moment, he was not sure what he wanted to do with it. In short, Jung welcomed whatever arrived unwanted and unexpected, unlike Faust who murdered Baucis and Philemon. In other words, Jung opened himself up to experiences the ego would often reject, seemingly in good sense. As Jung contemplated the stone, a verse from the thirteenth-century alchemist Arnoldus de Villanova came to him and he chiseled it into the stone:

> Here stands the mean, uncomely stone,
> 'Tis very cheap in price!
> The more it is despised by fools,
> The more loved by the wise.[76]

Jung was aware that this referred to the Philosophers' Stone and, as he contemplated it further, he saw in its "natural structure" a sort of eye[77] that looked back at him, a living other, who appeared to Jung as "the Telesphoros of Asklepios," the healing figure of a child who was seen as roaming through the dark regions of the cosmos and glowing like a star out of the depths, a shining "pointer of the way."[78] In this image and in the stone, Jung captured something in the heart of darkness itself, something that he found in the depths of inorganic matter, something that looked back at him and made a stone a living stone, a Philosophers' Stone that shines. For Jung, stones speak a shining truth and such a truth touches the core of what we have come to call, inadequately, psyche and matter.

Jung's attempt to repair this split in his life and work led not only to stone, but also to innovative formulations in the language of his psychology by which he attempted to embrace both sides of a linguistic divide—subject and object, spirit and matter—using terms such as "psychoid," "synchronicity," and *"unus mundus."*[79] Such terms expressed Jung's urge to go beyond the subjectivity of words and paper in order to express psyche's need to substantiate and the need of substances to speak.

For Hillman, however, such words not only fall short of Jung's goal, but also actually "reinforce the splitting effect inherent" in the neurosis of one-sided abstract language.[80] If this was a problem for Jung, it is also one which is deeply rooted in our collective, historical, cultural, and linguistic consciousness. It is an issue that penetrates into the problematics of perception and language, and into the archetypal psyche itself. How then to express psyche's need to substantiate and substances need to speak?

In his book entitled simply *Stone*, philosopher John Sallis speaks of his desire to substantiate, to find a way to articulate philosophical ideas adequate to the powerful stone monuments he is drawn to investigate, and in and through which he finds a "shining truth."[81] "It will be a matter, then, of attempting to say things in a way that lets the shining of their stone be manifest, that lets be manifest what is gathered into that shining."[82] In his book, he explores the power of stone in "the various guises and settings in which stone appears"[83]—in monuments, the complexity of Gothic cathedrals, Greek temples, and the tombstones of a Jewish cemetery in Prague; in fossils, stone houses, and the power and beauty of wild nature in the mountains of Haute Savoie, France. In his search, he attempts to give voice to the power he discovers in these profound expressions of stone. Sallis writes:

> I would have liked this discourse to be inscribed by a very skillful stonemason, by one who knew just the right slant at which to hold the chisel so as to cut obliquely into the stone and produce well-formed, clearly legible letters, chipping away the stone so as to leave the inscription both in place of stone and yet still in stone, practicing thus a kind of

lithography. I would have liked the well-measured strokes of his hammer to be audible, as he practiced his venerable craft of making stone, in its silence, nonetheless speak.[84]

One might imagine both Jung and Sallis as such stonemasons, adepts who inscribe their *materia* of rock and word such that stone has words and words matter. In both Jung and Sallis, we find stones that speak, living objective stones that shine, modern-day expressions of the alchemists' quest for life in the heart of matter.

Must we turn to stone? The stone that is not a stone

The well-known alchemical saying "Beware of the physical in the material" provides us with a warning not to confuse what the alchemist is after with literal materiality—but it is also important to recognize that a simple psychological or spiritual abstraction misses the mark as well. "The precious goals of alchemy are neither physical achievements ... nor metaphysical truths. ... We are not in the realm of metaphysics or physics,"[85] says Hillman. Sallis makes a similar point, noting that when trying to give expression to what we mean by "stone," it is important to do it in a way that does not split off our subjectivity from the voice of stone itself, nor turn this voice into a projection onto stones.[86] To fall into either one position or another fixes thought into a false subject/object dichotomy. Either the stone that we seek is literally over there in a mind-independent world, or it is simply part of our subjective inner life projected outward. Jung's psychology of alchemy is usually understood in the latter way and, thus, the Philosophers' Stone is seen as a projection of the Self.

I submit that this is one plausible reading of Jung, but it remains unclear exactly what the nature of such a projection entails and just what it is that is projected. Ultimately, the Arcane Substance that Jung often spoke about remained as mysterious as his understanding of the unconscious, and to assume that this projected substance was simply inside our subjectivity misses Jung's deeper understanding of "psychic reality," even if it was not adequately developed. In addition, the problem of projection itself requires a number of philosophical and metapsychological presuppositions that are taken for granted in classical analysis. Going beyond these assumptions requires a fundamental shift in metapsychology if not ontology.[87] Schwartz-Salant deconstructs the notion of "projection" and concludes that using this idea as a framework for understanding what the alchemists are talking about is inadequate. Alchemical "experiences do not always, or even primarily, fit into an inside-outside structure."[88] In its place, Schwartz-Salant constructs a field theory, an intermediate realm between subject and object, mind and matter.

While he applies his field theory primarily to the analytic interaction, it is a move that also has consequences for how we understand both Jung's work with stone and the nature of the Philosophers' Stone.

Although Jung actually worked with literal stone, his more enduring corpus was what he produced through his imagination and with words and paper, that is, his ideas. And likewise, it is with ideas and the imagination that Hillman finds a "rock-hard standpoint from above downward just as firm and solid as literal physical reality."[89] From this perspective, the Philosophers' Stone that is not a stone seems indestructible. It is solid, has objectivity, thing-likeness, facticity, and duration. It is an example of philosophical permanence. Yet, while its hardness wounds, it is also wounded, easily affected. The Stone is complex and resists one-sided descriptions and simple dichotomies. As David Miller has stated, "the course of wisdom consists in deferring one-sided judgment concerning meaning."[90] The *imaginatio* is as much a part of what is imaged as the world is itself the substance of imagination. Robert Romanyshyn makes a similar point:

> Imagining is not something which a subject adds to a merely perceivable world. On the contrary, we imagine and the world is imagine-able. To say one is to say the other. Each is the obverse of the other. In other words, imagining belongs as much to things as it belongs to us. Perception is always less certain than we naively believe it to be, and things are more shadowy than we often dare admit.[91]

In this passage, and throughout his analysis, Romanyshyn cautions us not to collapse the difference between perceiving and imagining. He underlines how the perceivable and the real exhibit a stubborn intractability which mark them as different from the imagination even if we have destabilized their absolute difference. Romanyshyn holds this distinction in place as he continues to subtly refine our understanding of the imaginary and the real. He demonstrates, following Merleau-Ponty and reminiscent of Schwartz-Salant, how perception and imagination are like mirrors "facing each other,"[92] forming "a couple more real than either of them"[93] would be independent of each other. For Romanyshyn, "the imagine-ability of things is their very depth: that is the image of a thing, seen through other things, describes the depth of the real."[94] Romanyshyn's analysis gives amplification to Critchley's insight that things merely are and that we are things too. He sees into the complex materiality of the soul and into a substance's need to speak. For Romanyshyn, the "voice of things" is best served by the language of metaphor and imagination which "inhabits neither the brilliance of the day [spirit] nor the darkness of night [soul], but speaks simultaneously in light and shadow."[95]

If the imagination can be seen to be the voice of things, then one might also understand how "imaginal realities" exhibit a stubborn intractability.

The Philosophers' Stone, as we have noted, exhibits facticity and thingness. It refuses to be altered by the manipulating ego subject, and yet subjectivity is part of its intrinsic reality, a subjectivity that appears as the ego subject dies or is negated and relativized. It is a subjectivity that has been touched by ego death and therefore is no longer subjective. It is a subjectivity that is not subjectivity, a subjectivity in which the me-ness has been "cooked out"—and redeemed from essentialist narratives of meaning.

As Hillman, making reference to Miller, points out, the stone "does not allow itself to be held in meaning"[96] and generality. "It does not yield to understanding." For Hillman, the alchemical process of *ceration* is "designed to obliterate a psychological *episteme* of ... anything that would rigidify the idea of the goal into categories of knowledge."[97] And yet, as Sallis has noted, the stone exhibits a "shining truth,"[98] a truth discovered in a "suspension of the difference that otherwise separates the eidetic from the singular, a *peculiar* suspension in that its very force requires that the difference remain, in the moment of suspension, also intact."[99] If I understand Sallis correctly, such singular yet eidetic moments of "shining truth" recall the sheer "isness of things" discussed earlier, the metals, planets, minerals, diamonds, pearls, stars and stones, the shining particularities that are also oddly universal but which can "never simply be assimilated to the purely eidetic."[100] Such singular moments of perception/imagination are neither inside nor out and must show themselves, be exhibited like pearls so as not to lose their luster, again to use Hillman's metaphor.

The bringing forth of such particulars allows them to shine, and this shine is for Hillman the revelation of Beauty, a term Plato used as well for that "shining truth" which he considered "the most radiant, that which most shines forth amidst the visible, in the singular things that come to be and *pass away*."[101] The Philosophers' Stone is such a radiant truth, but it is a truth that must as well remain in touch with negativity, death, and darkness. It is "not enough," Hillman reminds us, "to shine in the dark."[102] The Philosophers' Stone is linked intrinsically with *sol niger*, "no matter how exalted the stage of any process in life, that stage lives within the context of whatever despair and failure accompanied its creation."[103] Thus, it is not surprising that Schwartz-Salant observes, in relation to the last image of the *Splendor Solis*, that there are "two states—a created self and its purified consciousness ... joined not only with life and body but also with a history of despair and failure."[104]

Likewise, as Hillman notes, in alchemical psychology, "sorrow, solitude and misery can break even the most indomitable spirit."[105] The Philosophers' Stone requires a relationship with the ongoing deconstructive principle of the black sun. Perhaps this recognition of *sol niger* is related to why, for Giegerich, the imaginal requires continuing negative interiorization. But if this is so, just as Giegerich deconstructs the literal residues of the imaginal, so imaginal psychology continues to give flesh to the unseen.

Solve et coagula, say the alchemists. In Hillman and Giegerich, we have two moments of the Stone that not only can live together, but also belong together in the same living mosaic—or do they? Jung has noted: "sometimes Mercurius is a substance like quicksilver [image], sometimes it is a philosophy [thought]."[106] To put it yet another way, if Paul Ricoeur is correct that the symbol gives rise to thought, then perhaps it is also the case that thought gives rise to symbol. What has priority may well be, as Giegerich has noted, a matter of personal and philosophical conviction "of the psychology that one *has*," "that one *is*," "that one lives."[107] Perhaps in the end, thought and image may best be spoken of in a variety of ways: as an alchemical *circulatio*, or in a monstrous *coniunctio*, or as a trembling ground of poetic undecidables (Derrida). Perhaps all of the above might be thought/imagined as metaphors that attempt to speak the unspeakable, an idea perhaps captured in the title of Paul Kugler's book, *Raids on the Unthinkable*.[108] The struggle with these two seemingly irreconcilable moments is well articulated by Alain Badiou who gave expression to the importance of attempting to speak the unspeakable when he stated:

> Let us struggle then, partitioned, split, unreconciled. Let us struggle for the flash of conflict, we philosophers, always torn between the mathematical norm of literal transparency and the poetic norm of singularity and presence. Let us struggle then but having recognized the common task, which is to think what was unthinkable, to say what it is impossible to say. Or, to adopt Mallarme's imperative, which I believe is common to philosophy and poetry: "There, wherever it may be, deny the unsayable—it lies."[109]

In our attempt to express psyche's need to substantiate, we have come to see that the Stone to which we have turned is a "stone that is not a stone." It is rather a Philosophers' Stone. It is a Stone linked to the *lumen naturae* of *sol niger*, a luminous vehicle, a central mystery of alchemy. It is an alchemical achievement involving the death of the ego out of which something emerges shining and yet the shining was already there at the core of darkness. It is a part of the complexity of darkness itself, reflecting the death and shine of a positivity that is perhaps no positivity at all, but rather an image/idea requiring a liquification and/or displacement of the subject. The Stone requires learning how to die, how to decreate narratives of redemption, and thus allowing one to see, with Zen-like astonishment, the perception of the ordinary, the sheer mereness of things. As the poet Theodore Roethke once wrote:

> Near the graves of the great dead,
> Even the stones speak.
>
> (Roethke, 208)[110]

Notes

1 Renos K. Papadopoulos (ed.), Handbook of Jungian Psychology: Theory, Practice and Applications (London: Routledge, 2006).
2 James Hillman, "Concerning the Stone: Alchemical Images of the Gold," *Sphinx*, Vol. 5, 1993, 234–265.
3 Wolfgang Giegerich, The Soul's Logical Life: Towards a Rigorous Notion of Psychology (Frankfurt am Main: Peter Lang, 1998).
4 The description which follows is a condensation of Hillman's ideas drawn from his essay "Concerning the Stone."
5 Hillman, "Concerning the Stone," 260.
6 *Ibid.*, 259.
7 *Ibid.*, 262.
8 *Ibid.*, 253.
9 Giegerich, The Soul's Logical Life, 111.
10 *Ibid.*, 148.
11 For example, Hillman argues that the goal is "not the lifting, the *Aufhebung*, of material worldliness, but the full realization of desire for the world that pulsates in the materials of the elemental psyche, those substances that compose the stone and give its enduring life …." James Hillman, "Concerning the Stone," 261.
12 Hillman, "Peaks and Vales," in *Puer Papers* (Irving, TX: Spring Publications, 1979), 54–74.
13 Giegerich, "Afterword" in Wolfgang Giegerich, David Miller, & Greg Mogenson (eds.), *Dialectics and Analytical Psychology: The El Capitan Canyon Seminar* (New Orleans, LA: Spring Journal Books, 2005), 109.
14 Ibid.
15 *Ibid.*, 108. Portion of quote in single quote marks is attributed to David Miller, "Introduction" in Wolfgang Giegerich, David Miller, & Greg Mogenson, *Dialectics and Analytical Psychology: The El Capitan Canyon Seminar* (New Orleans, LA: Spring Journal Books, 2005).
16 Giegerich, The Soul's Logical Life, 107.
17 Hillman, "Image Sense," *Spring* (1979), 130.
18 *Ibid.*, 134.
19 Giegerich, The Soul's Logical Life, 107.
20 David Miller, "The End of Ending: A Response to Wolfgang Giegerich," *Journal of Jungian Theory and Practice*, Vol. 6, No. 1, 2004, 85.
21 James Hillman, "Silver and the White Earth (Part Two)," *Spring*, 1981, 49; quoted by Greg Mogenson, "Different Moments in Dialectical Movement," in *Dialectics and Analytical Psychology: The El Capitan Canyon Seminar*, 106.
22 Hillman, "Silver and the White Earth, Part Two," *Spring*, 1981, 49; quoted by Greg Mogenson, "Different Moments in Dialectical Movement," in *Dialectics and Analytical Psychology: The El Capitan Canyon Seminar*, 105.
23 Ibid.
24 This is a phrase used by Hegel and borrowed by Giegerich, and here refers simply to the process of working through.
25 Greg Mogenson, "Different Moments in Dialectical Movement," in *Dialectics and Analytical Psychology: The El Capitan Canyon Seminar* (New Orleans, LA: Spring Journal Books, 2005).
26 *Ibid.*, 106.
27 *Ibid.*
28 *Ibid.*
29 Hillman, "Concerning the Stone," 239.

30 *Ibid.*, 240.
31 *Ibid.*, 241.
32 *Ibid.*, 243.
33 Mogenson, "Different Moments in Dialectical Movement," 106.
34 Wolfgang Giegerich, "The End of Meaning and the Birth of Man: An Essay about the State Reached in the History of Consciousness and an Analysis of C.G. Jung's Psychology Project," *Journal of Jungian Theory and Practice*, Vol. 6, No. 1, 2004, 115.
35 *Ibid.*
36 Giegerich, The Soul's Logical Life, 104.
37 Paul Ricoeur, *Freud and Philosophy: An Essay on Interpretation* (New Haven, CT: Yale University Press, 1970), 38.
38 Dominick Lacapra, "Who Rules Metaphor?" in *Dialectics* (Baltimore, MD: John Hopkins University Press, 1980), 15–28.
39 Edgar Morin, *Science avec Conscience* (Paris: Fayard, 1982), 289. Quoted in, and citation provided, by Sean Kelly, "Transpersonal Psychology and the Paradigm of Complexity," retrieved December 26, 2005 from http://www.purify-mind.com/TranspersonalPsy.htm.
40 Quoted in D.T. O'Hara, "The Irony of Being Metaphorical," *Journal of Postmodern Literature*, Vol. 8, No. 2, 324.
41 Jacques Derrida, *Margins of Philosophy* (Chicago, IL: University of Chicago Press, 1982), 213.
42 Alan Bass (translator) in Jacques Derrida, *Margins of Philosophy* (Chicago, IL: University of Chicago Press, 1982), 19–20, n. 23.
43 Giegerich, Dialectics and Analytical Psychology, 3.
44 C.G. Jung, *Collected Works*, Vol. 12: *Psychology and Alchemy*, p. 88, Taken from Mylius, *Philosophia reformata* (1622).
45 C.G. Jung, *Collected Works*, Vol. 13: *Alchemical Studies*, p. 160, § 197.
46 *Ibid.*, p. 126, § 162.
47 Roger Brooks, *Jung and Phenomenology* (London: Routledge, 1991), 99.
48 Donald Kuspit, "Negatively Sublime Identity: Pierre Soulages's Abstract Paintings," retrieved January 23, 2002 from http://www.artnet.com/magazine_pre2000/features/kuspit/kuspit10-7-96.asp.
49 Indra Sinha, *Tantra: The Cult of Ecstasy* (London: Hamlyn, 2000), 52.
50 G.W.F. Hegel, *Phenomenology of the Spirit* (Oxford: Oxford University Press, 1977), 19, quoted in Greg Mogenson, "Different Moments in Dialectical Movement," 97.
51 C.G. Jung, Collected Works, Vol. 14: Mysterium Coniunctionis § *778*.
52 Hillman, *Stone*, 259.
53 David Rosen, Transforming Depression: Healing the Soul through Creativity (York Beach, ME: Nicolas-Hays, 2002).
54 David Miller, "Nothing Almost Sees Miracles! Self & No-Self in Psychology & Religion," *Journal of Psychology and Religion*, Vol. 4–5, 1995, 1–25.
55 Giegerich, The Soul's Logical Life, 18–24.
56 *Ibid.*, 18.
57 *Ibid.*, 24.
58 Ibid.
59 Geoffrey Bennington, "RIP," in R. Rand (ed.), *Futures of Jacques Derrida* (Stanford, CA: Stanford University Press, 2001), 3; quoted in Marla Morris, "Archiving Derrida," in P. Pericles Trifonas and M. A. Peters (eds.), *Derrida, Deconstruction and Education: Ethics of Pedagogy and Research* (Malden, MA: Blackwell Publishing, 2004), 44.

60 Marla Morris, "Archiving Derrida," 44.
61 Simon Critchley, *Very Little: Almost Nothing* (London: Routledge, 2004), xvii.
62 *Ibid.*, xxiii.
63 Ibid.
64 Ibid.
65 *Ibid.*, xxiii–xxiv.
66 Wolfgang Giegerich, "The End of Meaning and the Birth of Man: An Essay about the State Reached in the History of Consciousness and an Analysis of C.G. Jung's Psychology Project," *Journal of Jungian Theory and Practice*, Vol. 6, No. 1, 2004.
67 Simon Critchley, Very Little: Almost Nothing, xxiv.
68 James Hillman, "A Note for Stanton Marlan," *Journal of Jungian Theory and Practice*, Vol. 5, No. 2, 2003, 102.
69 Hillman, "Concerning the Stone," 252.
70 Wolfgang Giegerich, "The Ego-Psychological Fallacy: On 'The Birth of the Meaning Out of the Symbol,'" *Journal of Jungian Theory and Practice*, Vol. 7, No. 2, retrieved from http://www.junginstitute.org/journal/JungV7N2p53-60.pdf.
71 James Hillman, "Therapeutic Value of Alchemical Language," *Dragonflies: Studies in Imaginal Psychology*, Fall 1978, 40.
72 *Ibid.*, 41.
73 C.G. Jung, *Memories, Dreams, Reflections*, recorded and ed. by Aniela Jaffe (New York: Pantheon, 1973), 223.
74 *Ibid.*, 225.
75 *Ibid.*, 226.
76 *Ibid.*, 227. This carved stone became a monument for what his tower meant to him.
77 Ibid.
78 Ibid.
79 Hillman, "Therapeutic Value of Alchemical Language," 41.
80 *Ibid.*
81 Sallis, *Stone*, 2.
82 John Sallis, *Stone* (Bloomington: Indiana University Press, 1994), 4.
83 From back of book jacket.
84 Sallis, *Stone*, 1.
85 Hillman, "Concerning the Stone," 241.
86 Sallis, *Stone*, Chapter 1.
87 Nathan Schwartz-Salant, personal communication, 2000. Quoted in Stanton Marlan, "Alchemy," in *The Handbook of Jungian Psychology*, 280.
88 Nathan Schwartz-Salant, personal communication, 2000. Quoted in Stanton Marlan, "Alchemy," in *The Handbook of Jungian Psychology*, 281.
89 Hillman, "Concerning the Stone," 242.
90 David Miller, "The 'Stone' Which Is Not a Stone," *Spring*, 1989, 116.
91 Robert Romanyshyn, "Voice of Things," *Dragonflies: Studies in Imaginal Psychology*, Fall 1978, 79–80.
92 Robert Romanyshyn, "Voice of Things," *Dragonflies: Studies in Imaginal Psychology*, Spring 1979, 73.
93 Maurice Merleau-Ponty, *The Visible and the Invisible*, 139. Quoted by Robert Romanyshyn, "Voice of Things," *Dragonflies: Studies in Imaginal Psychology*, Spring 1979, 73.
94 Romanyshyn, "Voice of Things," *Dragonflies: Studies in Imaginal Psychology*, Spring 1979, 73.
95 *Ibid.*, 79.

96 Hillman, "Concerning the Stone," 250.
 97 Hillman, "Concerning the Stone," 255.
 98 Sallis, *Stone*, 2.
 99 *Ibid.*, 4.
100 *Ibid.*
101 *Ibid.*, 2–3.
102 Hillman, "Concerning the Stone," 239.
103 Nathan Schwartz-Salant, The Mystery of Human Relationship: Alchemy and the Transformation of Self (London: Routledge, 1998), 216.
104 Ibid.
105 Hillman, "Concerning the Stone," 239.
106 C.G. Jung, *Collected Works*, Vol. 9ii: *Aion*, p. 155, § 240.
107 Giegerich, Dialectics & Analytical Psychology, 108.
108 Paul Kugler, Raids on the Unthinkable: Freudian and Jungian Psychoanalyses (New Orleans, LA: Spring Journal Books, 2005).
109 Alain Badiou, *Theoretical Writings* (New York: Continuum International, 2004).
110 *Print rights:* "Fourth Meditation" from *Words for the Wind: The Collected Verse of Theodore Roethke* by Theodore Roethke, © 1957, 1958, renewed 1985, 1986 by Beatrice Lushington. Used by permission of Doubleday, an imprint of the Knopf Doubleday Publishing Group, a division of Penguin Random House LLC. All rights reserved. *Electronic rights:* Reprinted by the permission of Russell & Volkening as agents for Theodore Roethke, copyright © 1957, 1958, renewed 1985, 1986 by Beatrice Lushington.

Chapter 10

A critique of Wolfgang Giegerich's move from imagination to the logical life of the soul

Part A. The psychologist who is not a psychologist: a deconstructive reading of Wolfgang Giegerich's idea of psychology proper

The work of Wolfgang Giegerich has been an occasion for a great deal of intellectual excitement, struggle, and continuing soul searching, which for me had gone on progressively for over a decade and continues to do so. I consider Giegerich's work to have made an important contribution to our reading of Jung and the Jungian tradition. He is a critical and illuminating thinker who has opened the way for rigorous thinking about fundamental issues of Jungian psychology. Yet, in spite of an appreciative reading of his work, I continue to have a number of significant philosophical and psychological differences with him, both in perspective and emphasis. In this paper, what follows is an archetypal and deconstructive reading of Giegerich's view of 'psychology proper', particularly with reference to his book *What Is Soul?* (2012). By a deconstructive reading, I mean a process by which the author's intention (in this case, to identify the notion of psychology proper) is shown to have internal self-contradiction that does not redeem itself in an adequate dialectical unification.

It is my contention that, in an effort to extend Jung's late view of the objective psyche, Giegerich leans too far in the direction of overcoming and going beyond 'the human, all-too-human' person. In so doing, he defines psychology proper as primarily syntactic rather than semantic, logical rather than empirical, thoughtful rather than imaginative, and so on. What appears as psychology proper is based on a divide in which the human person is no longer a primary focus of psychology.

Insofar as his psychology has moved beyond the human person into the logical life of the soul and has fully attempted to separate itself from all vestiges of the ego, perhaps we can say with him that a radical cut has been made, the Rubicon has been crossed, and we have travelled to a place where no return is possible. We have entered an underworld of the soul's logical life, described by him as 'cold, abstract, formal, irrepresentable' and 'ghostly' (Giegerich 2007, p. 254), totally removed from life, from the human, all-too-human person. This radical cut is difficult because it injures our narcissism, wounds the 'virginal innocence as "natural" consciousness' (ibid.), and dissolves the *unio mentalis*. For Giegerich, the work of alchemy and psychology is precisely aimed at such a dissolution: 'Putrefaction, fermenting corruption, pulverization, dissolution, etc., are all aimed at violently decomposing the imaginal shape of the matter worked with' (ibid., pp. 254–255). For Giegerich, a psychology informed by alchemy has as its goal the task of totally liquefying and freeing the spirit of Mercurius—the spirit that is imprisoned in matter, in nature, in the image, in emotion, and in the body.

On first reflection, it would appear that for Giegerich, philosophically, there is an unbridgeable divide between psychology proper and the everyday life of the human person, and, moreover, to do psychology seems to require keeping them apart. 'Real psychology', in Giegerich's sense, is not an ego psychology and not even a psychology of the person or of people at all. If this characterization is correct, I wonder to what extent or in what way such a psychology is either possible or desirable. To what extent is it possible to pass over to a strictly logical psychology in Giegerich's sense? Can one go over to the other side and not return? Philosophically, is there any such thing as a complete sublation, a complete cut or break that takes us beyond the human ego—beyond life—to a total liquification, even vaporization, in the name of alchemical Mercurius as the goal of psychology? And does such a philosophical vision of psychology absolutize the cut in such a way that the cut becomes cutting—the violence of the kill literalized—and, in so doing, engage in semantic violence? As Giegerich notes, 'No admission for the unqualified' (Giegerich 1998, p. 15). Using caustic language, he goes on to challenge and provoke us by amplifying and extending this idea, all of which I have condensed as follows: 'Only true scholars and seekers enter here. Pay the price. Leave your garments and your ego at the door. Cross the threshold and dive into the abyss you passive, stay-at-home, unscathed pop psychologist!'[1] This would indeed be a cutting view of aspects of personal psychology.

Now, perhaps, this is all just hyperbole and the vitriol of semantic onesidedness in the passion to escape from ego psychology. Giegerich, like Hillman, exhibits such a passion and even a violence, urging separation and strife, *eris* or *polemos*, 'which Heraclitus, the first [philosophical] ancestor of psychology, has said is the father of all' (Hillman 1989, p. 114). One might ask: Can such creative urges at times become insensitive to the virtues of everyday *natural life?* Does it demean the mother-daughter archetype, nature, the sensitivities of the innocent soul? Does it cut right through them in a literal gesture of rape—Hades-like? Does the rage and grief of Demeter go unnoticed or remain ignored? Would she or Persephone be satisfied if Zeus were to tell them their concerns were only semantic? This would indeed be a cold, abstract, formal, and ghostly response to life. Even with Hades a bargain can be struck. Is such a psychology then an absolute psychology of the underworld? Perhaps it is the case that Demeter's perspective, like ours, is so identified with the mother and Persephone, with innocent nature, that they and we see things too much through the eyes of human life and love. We panic in the face of crisis, of going all the way under, of negation, and we are repelled by the marriage of the innocent soul to Hades—to her becoming his wife. If this is the case, perhaps Giegerich's psychology sets the stage for such a wedding. But, even so, the gods are not satisfied with total dominance in the underworld.

Perhaps the cool eye of Hecate's perspective, familiar with the underworld, knows more. Trained in the logical life of the soul, she can see beyond the mother complex, beyond life and love, and has a calm wisdom that exceeds what Hillman derisively calls the 'flap of Persephone' (Hillman 1979, p. 49). Is it the case that both Hillman and Giegerich, in their appreciation of Hecate and the underworld, see psychology as a one-way trip to the shades or to dissolution? Hillman, like Giegerich, reacts against the limitations of ego psychology and to its one-way traffic out of the unconscious toward ego assimilation. Hillman proposes a reversal, another one-way movement into the underworld, 'a vesperal into the dark' (ibid., p. 1), as he calls it, and Giegerich's alchemy articulates the cut that gets us there. But, for Giegerich, even Hillman's psychology remains too linked to the ego and anima.

If it is fair to characterize (though it is too simple) Hillman's contribution as an anima psychology and Giegerich's as an animus one, can or should the two of them be joined in an alchemical marriage, a *circulatio*, with each moment leading in and out of one another? Logical psychology would go beyond all the literal residues of the imaginal, and imaginal psychology would continue to give flesh to the unseen and unseemly—*solve et coagula*, say the alchemists, a dynamic and fundamental syzygy. For me, the telos of Mercurius is not simply aimed at liquification or evaporation. Mercurius is an odd and creative duplex, living on the edge of a trembling ground of poetic undecidables, the site of a monstrous and unstable *coniunctio*, and—as Jung noted—he/she is 'sometimes ... a substance ..., sometimes ... a philosophy' (Jung 1951, para. 240), or sometimes a thought. Panisnick, following Ficino, has commented, '*Eros* impels the spirit out of the corporeal and sensible world, but *Eros* also projects the spirit into that realm and it thereby becomes a dynamic connective between the two worlds' (Panisnick 1975, p. 201).

Giegerich appears ultimately to favour one dimension of Mercurius and one aim of alchemy and psychology, namely, the work of dissolution. When he cites the alchemical operations, he omits *coagulatio* and follows a linear and successionist view of history, pointing out that alchemy properly undergoes a historical dissolution. It remains a question if alchemy and history are so progressive. For me, alchemy also remains active and continues to die and be reborn in an eternal recurrence, still emerging in the present in differing historical forms. Its operations are archetypal, in an eternal play between *solve et coagula*.[2] The dialectic is more circular and requires an ongoing interplay between anima and animus, the positivity of the soul and its ongoing dissolution, a syzygy between anima and animus psychologies. However, to imagine a syzygy between archetypal psychology and the logical life of the soul in this way is also to do both an injustice. Each is more complex than I have as yet indicated. Interior to both theories is an intrinsic relationship between anima and animus, soul and spirit—though overall one might characterize each as leaning in one direction or another and as exhibiting an overarching archetypal pattern.

Giegerich further differentiates and characterizes these fundamentally different patterns, namely, the standpoints of the anima, animus, and syzygy. He observes that both the anima and animus points of view rely on mythical figures or concepts of forces imagined as brought into union by the syzygy above them. But, for Giegerich, psychology can and must rise to the level of the syzygy itself. For him, bringing anima and animus together is a Jungian fantasy based on mythological thinking, in which the anima imagines the syzygical relation in the naturalistic imagery of marriage. Anima and animus are seen from an outside view as images or forces, entities needing to be combined or reconciled. For him, such a relationship needs to be sublated to reveal the subtle structure of the syzygy itself, no longer seen as above or encompassing the anima and animus. As separate figures, they disappear and show themselves as sublated moments, the syzygy. They no longer need to be imagined as yoked together, no need for a yoga to connect them. They are already connected dialectically in the movement of thought as a unity of unity and difference.[3]

In this analysis, Giegerich not only moves beyond an ego and anima psychology but pushes off from an animus psychology as well. In so doing, he appears to follow the phenomenology of spirit beyond the level of force and understanding to an even subtler level.[4] From the logical standpoint of the form of the syzygy itself, there is no longer a concern with the intuition of contents. The work of sublation continues to cut away at the coagulations and remaining positivities of the soul, freeing the spirit for what appears to be a never-ending story, an endless march to Dionysian freedom—but to what extent is such freedom possible? To what extent and how should it be the goal of psychology?

If a true psychology in Giegerich's sense is to be identified with the radical philosophical discipline of interiority and with an ongoing sublation, is something left behind, unaccounted for—a residue that is surpassed, a shadow that lingers and requires our attention if psychology is to be adequate to its calling?[5] Here, I look into the margins of Giegerich's own reflections and into the development of his own concept of the soul. For Giegerich, the goal of his true psychology is virtually identical with his understanding of the alchemical philosopher's achievement of pure gold, which he interprets as the total liquification of Mercurius. But if this is the aim of both alchemical philosophy and his psychology, what should we make of his statement (Giegerich 2008, p. 199) that he has actually never reached true gold in his work? If the master of the discipline of interiority has himself not been able to achieve the radical cut leading to the syzygy itself, to pure thought or true gold, we might ask to what extent is such a goal possible? I suspect that putting this issue this way is not quite fair because it assumes that the gold or goal is some kind of positivity that could be possessed in a moment of literal time and that the radical cut necessary for a true psychology is also a literal event done by the psychologist as a human being. I think such a conception misses the point; it is problematic and needs further elaboration.

Let's recall that, for Jung and Hillman, the goal is important only as an idea and that this de-literalizes the idea of the goal right at the beginning. Goals are not actualized events or psychological accomplishments. They are necessary fictions of the soul-making opus. I think no-one understands this better or has worked more diligently than Giegerich to think through and develop the idea implicit in this view. But it is perplexing that he seems to write about achieving true gold as if it were a literal possibility, rather than clarifying in that moment the misconception of the kind of achievement he indicates he has not attained. Is it the case that in such moments, Giegerich, the human being, falls short of his radical view of psychology and steps into a semantic concern, a moment in which he shows himself to be a 'civil man' and a private individual? Is there a moment of confusion between the practical man and the psychologist? Or, is what we are calling a confusion, an inevitable divide, a shadow that suggests the return of the repressed, of something that fell into a crack in the work of sublation? Does psychology have to remain an activity that leaves the human being behind and separates man from soul?

Near the end of Giegerich's book *What Is Soul?*, he addresses and complicates his position, noting that in clinical work with actual patients, something more may be required than 'true psychology'! He notes:

> As practicing *therapists*, we are not totally identical with the psychologist in ourselves. We must have one leg in psychology and one leg in practical reality, the sphere of the human, all-too-human. We must be able to display a true, unadulterated access to soul as well as a practical knowledge of the world (which includes a realistic insight into human nature) and understand the needs of the patient as human being. And, this is most important, we have to *know when it is a question of one or the other.*
> (Giegerich 2012, pp. 315–16)

This seems to me to be a significant departure from the true psychology Giegerich has been advocating to this point. He continues:

> So while I do not wish to water down in any way the severe requirements presented above for doing psychology, a psychology *with* soul, I also do

> not want to absolutize psychology, as if in the consulting room nothing but psychology was permitted
>
> (ibid., p. 316)

At first glance, it does appear that Giegerich is precisely caught between absolutizing and watering down psychology, as opposed to liquefying it. All of his emphasis on the importance of the radical cut, of crossing the Rubicon to the point of no return, seems contradicted by the return of the practising therapist in the consulting room. Did the stay-at-home psychologist stay, or return home, unscathed? Is it a return of the repressed, of the practical person, the human being who was banished or degraded in the heroic march to a real psychology? Is this the psychology that till now Giegerich claimed is precisely not a psychology of the human person, but a psychology of the soul proper? Is such a divide a regression, concession, or compensation, a semantic falling back into a side-by-side and undialectical view of the psychologist and psychology? Does a true psychology of the soul need the contribution of the common practising therapist to be complete or comprehensive, a magnum opus? Should we now view the psychologist as philosophically divided against him- or herself, against the liberation of thought from its entanglements in the illusions of its ontic identity, or does this divide require a further labour of the concept and sublation to a more integrated view of psychology?

As I noted earlier, Giegerich is aware that this dual, side-by-side view considerably complicates his theory, and he makes an effort to see the divide conceptually in terms of the soul's dual intentionalities, namely, the soul's need for initiation as well as for emancipation: on the one hand, the need for grounding, embeddedness in imagination, myth and metaphysics, and, on the other hand, for emancipation from all the above. For Giegerich, this contradiction needs to be understood in terms of the soul's inner dialectic and self-regulation. The purpose of emancipation from the soul (initiation) is itself a soul purpose, an *opus contra naturam*, a work by and in the spirit of the nature of the soul itself. Even more strongly, Giegerich states: 'Emancipation from soul does not mean absolute defection from soul, because this emancipation from soul conversely occurs only within soul' (ibid., pp. 322–323). So just what is a psychology with soul?

From here, this apparent contradiction/conflict continues to gain complexity. Giegerich goes on to speak both about the individual soul and the condition of soul in modernity, the condition in which we find ourselves already thrown (perhaps in a Heideggerian sense) into the logical condition of psychologically born man. For Giegerich, this is a condition in which myth, metaphysics, gods, and God have become impossible—since modern man is born out of the soul as an autonomous individual, a civil man, an ego. It would appear that the emancipatory intentionality of the soul has been successful in departing from its initiatory needs in the *participation mystique* and anima identification. In fact, the initiatory needs of the soul in modernity are now moving in harmony and support of its emancipatory desires, to be born out of itself and into the world as subjectivity, subjective mind, consciousness, and logical form.

The movement of initiation toward emancipation leads Giegerich to a recognition of the soul's need for historical development. Thus, for Giegerich, modern man's initiation now means the absolute negative interiorization of the phenomenon, deepening into itself and thus releasing itself into spirit and truth. It is in casting off his mythological garments that modern man finds his human dignity. And so, for Giegerich, freedom from soul today is irrevocable and total.

It would appear that the logical life of the soul has been a successful march to freedom and human dignity, but then comes a major caveat and exception—*neurosis*—a most human condition! For Giegerich, neurosis is the soul's stubborn insistence on somehow remaining linked to a mythic or metaphysical identity at a time when the soul knows that such an identity has been historically surpassed. Giegerich submits then that the soul itself 'invented neurosis for itself both as an *incentive* and as a kind of *springboard* to push off from' (ibid., p. 332). But such an emancipation does not come easily or naturally. It requires a struggle against the fascinating pull exerted by myth and metaphysics. Giegerich puts it this way: the soul

> has to actively, systematically, in detail and in full awareness *work off* its own fascination and infatuation with the metaphysical, the mythic, the numinous and suggestive power of the imaginal – *through* pulling itself out of its neurosis, *really* stepping out of it and leaving it behind as the nothing that it is
>
> (ibid.)

Only then has the *full price* been paid for the departure from a previous stage of consciousness, while it is the soul itself that 'emancipates itself from itself' and then becomes 'explicitly and *for itself* a born soul'. It 'is born *as* human consciousness and its infinite *interiority*' (ibid.). This is all the work of the soul, but at the same time, Giegerich notes, it is only the human person who can push off from his or her neurosis and truly be freed of it, and one does go through the utilization of 'strictly analytic, conceptual thought ... [by] uncompromisingly seeing through and critiquing the neuroticness of the soul's pervers[ity] ... in all its practical details' (ibid.).

I'm not sure what to say about what the soul in itself is capable of, but it is hard for me to imagine any human person who has achieved, or could achieve, total freedom from neurosis, from all mythic and metaphysical fascinations, as if there is in fact some other hard-core 'truth' that can be known and that would set one totally free, or be an expression of total freedom. In fact, I would suggest that neurosis is an ongoing tie to myth and metaphysics, and an essentially human characteristic of the soul. Giegerich's definition of this freedom from neurosis is, once again, the repeating refrain: the achievement of infinite interiority, paying the full price, crossing the Rubicon to the point of no return. But here I am reminded of Giegerich's comment about 'true gold', and that he had not achieved it with his work! I wonder if he would claim anything different for the achievement of a total freedom from neurosis? It is for him to answer, but I imagine it would be reasonable for him to tell us that this is a semantic concern and as a 'psychologist', he can think it all the way through. Here again, there is a problematic distinction between the ordinary human, all-too-human being, and the psychologist. At the end of chapter three of his book *What Is Soul?*, Giegerich tells us that as a private individual, as a civil man, he does not confuse himself with the psychologist he 'hopes' he is (2012, p. 316). But what an odd divide this is from the point of view of his psychology. Why hope? Is this the concern of the psychologist who has not made the radical cut, worked this dialectic all the way through? This hope cannot be the hope of the psychologist proper, but only the hope of the human, all-too-human being, and the idea of hoping signifies the divide between them. For Hillman, hope is a fantasy that distracts us from the present and, in this case, from our human reality.[6]

So, does this mean that, as a private individual like the rest of us, Giegerich remains neurotic—attached to myth and metaphysics, and hoping to overcome them? Again, has he fallen back into semantics—or never left it? Either way, there appears to be a continuing and unresolved binary between the private individual and the psychologist—and it is this everyday therapist who is now necessarily invited into the consulting room so that with his instinct and the feeling function, he can help 'the psychologist' discern the actual needs of the soul in each moment, while to the psychologist proper is left only the 'caustic analytic work ... necessary' (ibid., p. 334) to cauterize the patient. It seems to me the case that both the Jungian and the archetypal psychologists, like the rest of us, are always engaged in psychopathology, in mythic entanglements with life and with anima and that this is indeed the price for the flesh of life. From this point of view, both the psychologist proper and the human, all-too-human person are archetypal figures, eternally at play in the quest for the transhuman.

Personally, I would like to think of the psychologist as capable of the full range of clinical responsiveness, using his or her capabilities to discern whatever it is that the soul needs in the eachness of the moment. I would like to imagine such a therapist as an analyst who is not totally identified with being a psychologist proper or with any method or technique, or discipline *per se*, and remembers his or her humanity while offering what's possible in the clinical and human encounter. Giegerich moves in this direction with his idea of the dual intentionalities of the soul, but continues to emphasize one intentionality over the other, running the risk of absolutizing the emancipatory push of our heroic ideals. With regard to this encounter, Giegerich has given the analyst a refined understanding of dialectical and syntactic awareness. The shadow of this contribution is that when it is absolutized and removed from the human, all-too-human, the never-ending quest for liberation and the continuing need to push off from every initiatory connection can be as neurotic as the attachment it tries to cure. As Hillman has noted, it is our pathology which is also our eye to the soul.

In Buddhism, the caustic work of *sunyata*, of the Vajra or diamond cutter, reduces all attachment to nothingness, but nothingness itself needs to logically void itself, which returns the soul to the world in an ever-recurring circle of life. Thus, liberation is not beyond or transcendent to the world of *samsara* image and illusion. It is one with it or, as the Buddhists say, there is not a hair's-breadth difference between them (i.e. yet they remain both *samsara* and *nirvana*). Seen alchemically, this is a hermetic circle embodying the *dual* aspect of Mercurius, which to my mind is not only the liquefying solvent, but the coagulatory agent as well. The liquification of Mercurius is also not a liquification in any literal sense, and the caustic work of analysis need not be literally caustic. As it turns out, the psychologist is also not a psychologist. Another turn of the dialectic reveals the psychologist *both* as a specialist and as a human being. Perhaps this is the case for Giegerich as well, as he hopes to be a good psychologist and yet, in so doing, reveals himself as a psychologist who is not a psychologist and as a human being, human, all-too-human. Is this the failure of psychology proper, of the dialectic, its success, or both? In his work on soul, Giegerich discovers what for me has been a missing remainder in his work, the human being and his feeling function, and it is this that for me exceeds psychology proper, goes beyond, and complicates his work. In so doing, it returns the debt to human feeling, the enigma of the unconscious, albeit not as a static entity, and the mystery that is not vanquished by reason or spirit.

In my criticism of Giegerich, I have pointed to what appears to be a philosophical contradiction or, at least, a tendency to divide a 'true psychology' from the human, all-too-human ego psychology which remains embedded in emotion and images. Yet, for Giegerich, the human person as therapist returns to the consulting room like a return of the repressed (that is, as human, all-too-human) and as a necessary aspect of clinical work. Hence, Giegerich's 'true psychology' must include what he has earlier defined as not psychological at all. Thus, the humanistic subject comes back into play side-by-side with the psychologist, as an Other to all that Giegerich has developed. In this instance, there appears to be a *polarity* or, at least, a *polar* tendency, in which case something does not fully get taken up into his dialectical process, remaining outside as a remainder, but one that remains to be fully acknowledged as the other to the logical life of the soul.

Binary scission or de-emphasis of the personal human subject?

My criticism of Giegerich's view of psychology proper finds resonance and belongs to the recent exchange of ideas in this journal between Mark Saban (Saban 2015) and John Hoedl (Hoedl 2015). Saban finds in Giegerich's work a binary scission in Jung and a 'tendency to exalt one Jung [the esoteric] while disparaging the other [the exoteric]' (2015, p. 679). For Saban, this divide shows a blindness and/or a 'monocular' (ibid., p. 680) perspective towards the complexity of Jung's psychology '*as a whole*' (ibid., p. 679). He argues, as I have, that any attempt by Giegerich to overcome this scission (*coniunctio*) is 'obscured and sidelined by Giegerich's overriding project of dividing ... psychology into two discrete fields, an inferior realm to do with ordinary persons, and a superior realm exclusively concerned with the uroboric communication of "soul" with itself' (ibid., p. 689), i.e. psychology proper.

Saban contends that far from encouraging the tension or play between the two sides of this scission as he considers Jung to do, Giegerich by contrast needs them to be kept in discrete and different hierarchical levels so that he may more easily discard one and embrace the other. Saban attributes this approach by Giegerich to his investment in neo-Hegelian idealism as the last word in theoretical understanding and goes on to cite a number of important other philosophers who have been critical of Hegel's thought: Marx, Nietzsche, Heidegger, Foucault, Levinas, Derrida, Schelling, McGrath, and many others, all of whom, one way or another, reject the absolute idealism at the core of many of Giegerich's working presuppositions. For Saban, the idealist turn as rendered in Giegerich's psychology is inadequate to Jung's complexity and to the more complex conjunction between the two sides of the scission. Jung's psychology does not privilege one side of the divide, but more integrally than Giegerich brings them together in 'simultaneous relation[ship]' (ibid., p. 690). While Saban recognizes that both Jung and Giegerich work toward a unity of opposites, he believes that Giegerich ultimately reduces them to the notion of the soul mediating itself. For Saban, this is a betrayal, not an advance, of Jung's psychology.

In response to Saban's criticism of Giegerich, John Hoedl sets out to address what he considers to be Saban's misunderstandings, arguing that Giegerich has obvious connections to and grounding in Jung's work. This does not mean that Giegerich does not diverge from Jung's ideas. He does. But, for Hoedl, Giegerich is forced to do so as a consequence of his unfolding work. Hoedl then goes on to state his own understanding of what Saban calls the scission, justifying the 'psychological difference' (Hoedl 2015, p. 706) between the *opus parvum* and the *opus magnum*, noting that the divide reflects a different and hierarchical logical status. For Hoedl and Giegerich, the *mundus archetypus* as a superpersonal process has a tendency to be imagined as having nothing to do with the individual as Jung understood it and is a process that takes place beyond personal psychology. While there appears to be a divide, a different logical status, between man and soul, oddly they share the same location, the consciousness of the person. One outcome of this divide or difference in logical status is that psychology proper, the psychologist as psychologist, is focused on the *opus magnum* and as psychologist proper 'must not allow a personal/subjective view into the work' (ibid., p. 706)—and yet, as we have seen, the personal/subjective view is necessary to the clinical work in the consulting room.

For Hoedl, psychology proper allows the archetypal objective psyche to unfold as an expression of its own independently 'logical status' (ibid., p. 704). Quoting Jung, he notes, 'Let *it* have a say now, not you ... who is listening to the *daimonion* ["soul"]?' (ibid., p. 706). For Hoedl as for Giegerich, psychology proper is exclusively focused on allowing the daimon to speak. However, to my mind, it is equally important to speak back to the daimon. In addition, I would claim that the therapist must go beyond the psychologist proper and not limit him/herself to bracketing out emotion, feeling judgements, views, and thoughts, and all other aspects of the human, all-too-human person.

Hoedl at first criticizes Saban for not understanding the 'psychological difference' described earlier, suggesting that the rejection of the personal from psychology proper is not a split in psychological practice and theory. Yet, in the next moment, following Giegerich, he notes the inclusion of what has bracketed out the human person as a necessary part of the clinical situation. Now the clinician's job is back to listening and attending to 'the "soul's" development over time *while* staying ... with the patient' (ibid., p. 707, my emphasis). To achieve this, the analyst must have an eye on both worlds, the psychological (proper) and the personal. While this position is close to Jung's and my own, it appears as an unresolved tension between the two worlds.[7] This perspective seems to me to be a corrective to the overemphasis on the objective psyche and the *mundus archetypus*. It would appear that, in Hoedl's position as well as in Giegerich's, the psychologist as psychologist proper must be seen to be not fully psychological enough and the method of psychology proper does not have the range to treat the human patient as a whole.

Given this acknowledgement of the importance of *both* psychology proper *and* staying with the patient, Hoedl feels free to criticize Saban for emphasizing what appears to him as a scission and ultimately as Giegerich's 'contempt for the ordinary' (Saban, quoted in Hoedl 2015, p. 706). While Hoedl rejects Saban's idea that Giegerich has contempt for the ordinary, he does acknowledge that 'Giegerich regularly *de-emphasizes* the "human" aspect' (ibid., p. 707, my emphasis) and that it takes a '*back seat*' (ibid., my emphasis) to the objective psyche. In this way, Hoedl attempts to minimize what Saban sees as a scission.

Conclusion

It is true that in his writing Giegerich regularly de-emphasizes the 'human' aspect in order to focus on the 'soul' or the 'objective' aspect of consciousness (which, of course, always manifests in the human). From Hoedl's perspective, Giegerich's emphasis is seen as a compensation for 'ego psychology's obsession with the person' (ibid.), personal counselling, and ego-oriented work. If this compensation justifies an 'emphasis' on the purity of psychology proper as a contribution to psychology as a whole, it also must be acknowledged that what gets de-emphasized and/or left out returns to the clinical perspective as necessary and must be included in the work of analysis and in psychological theory, a perspective that goes beyond the limited definition of psychology proper.

It is my sense that Giegerich has included the human, all-too-human as a compensation not simply to emphasize the importance of his differences from ego psychology, but also to compensate for having distanced himself theoretically too far from the ego psychologist and the human, all-too-human in himself. The return of the human, all-too-human is important to work through in both theory and practice, and in the personal psychology of the analyst. I do not want to suggest that the equally important recognition of the heroic intention of Giegerich's emancipatory psychology with its emphasis on the *opus magnum* is not essential, but the 'psychologist proper' must recognize that he is a psychologist who is not a psychologist in the pure sense and dialectically engage the negation of a psychology that is too pure and too separate from our humanity. Whether or not the achievement of a transhuman perspective is, in fact, a viable notion is, for me, a debatable question.[8] In any case, I would contend that there remains an intrinsic and mysterious link between the *opus parvum* and the *opus magnum*, and it is this link that is essential for the practising analyst.

Notes

1 Based on language from Giegerich's discussion of this in Giegerich 1998, pp. 14–20.
2 In all fairness to Giegerich, he responded to this criticism by noting: 'It is true that I did not talk much about coagulation, although it is certainly part of alchemy. But I think it is part of alchemy in a different sense from sublimation, distillation, etc. I make a difference between the particular instantaneous operations and the overall direction of the work. Coagulation is not essential as far as the overall purpose of the work is concerned. Beware of the physical in the matter, the stone that is *not* a stone, *vinum ardens*, the freeing of Mercurius from the imprisonment and Mercurius itself as *quicksilver*. These are a few indications of the goal of alchemy. The end-product is not supposed to be coagulated.

By contrast, in the day-to-day work coagulation may be necessary, for example if the prime matter, as in hysteria, begins so to speak with a prime matter in the status of "diarrhoea". So my point is this distinction between two levels' (personal communication, 3 October 2012).

3 In my paper, 'From the black sun to the philosopher's stone' (Marlan 2006; in this book as Chapter 9), I have complemented this notion of the unity of unity and difference with a balancing idea of the difference of unity and difference.

4 For a discussion of the unfolding of this phenomenological idea, see Hegel's *Phenomenology of Spirit* (1977).

5 See my paper 'From the black sun to the philosopher's stone' (originally published in 2006 and in this book as Chapter 9) and Giegerich's response, 'The unassimilable remnant: what is at stake?: a dispute with Stanton Marlan' (2006) for the beginning of what is an ongoing debate.

6 I would like to include here a response that Giegerich made to my criticism: '[Y]ou contrasted [James Hillman] and me with respect to the topic of hope. I think, however, that there is no difference between his and my view about this. The sentence you used as basis for your comment was one in which 'hope' was used in the trivial everyday sense. But Hillman probably also hoped that when he said something it was sound and not erroneous concerning the deeper psychol. sense of hope, I voiced my criticism of it repeatedly and consistently, e.g., my Coll. *Engl. Papers Vol. III*, p. 12 (or 9–12)' (personal communication, 3 October 2012).

7 This emphasis on the both/and, on the dual rather than unity, can be seen to be an interpretation that aims to go beyond Hegel's idea of the unity of unity and difference, as one can see in Donald Verene's (1998) understanding of twoness, in William Desmond's (1992) idea of metaxological understanding of the dialectic, and in Slavoj Žižek's (2013) idea of the parallax gap.

8 A number of modern philosophers—Hegel, Husserl, Heidegger, and others—have tried to push off from the human subject with the conviction that the meaning and essence of what is called 'human' has changed over time and is a constructed reality. For some, we are in an age of 'posthumanism'. However, Derrida has noted what a difficult task it is and has demonstrated that the above-noted philosophers never quite get beyond humanism and the question of 'man'. With regard to Hegel—and, I would now contend, Giegerich—Derrida insists that although they try to 'think "the end of man" ... it is still *man* whose end preoccupies' them (Derrida, quoted in Howells 1999, p. 133).

References

Desmond, W. (1992). 'Dialectic and evil: on the idiocy of the monstrous'. In *Beyond Hegel and Dialectic: Speculation, Cult, and Comedy.* Albany: State University of New York.

Giegerich, W. (1998). The Soul's Logical Life: Towards a Rigorous Notion of Psychology. *Frankfurt am Main: Peter Lang.*

—— (2007). 'Psychology – the study of the soul's logical life'. In *Who Owns Jung?,* ed. A. Casement. London: Karnac.

—— (2008). 'The unassimilable remnant: what is at stake?: a dispute with Stanton Marlan'. In *Archetypal Psychologies: Reflections in Honor of James Hillman,* ed. Stanton Marlan. New Orleans: Spring Journal Books.

—— (2012). *What Is Soul?* New Orleans: Spring Journal Books.

Hegel, G.W.F. (1977). *Phenomenology of Spirit,* trans. A.V. Miller. Oxford: Oxford University Press.

Hillman, J. (1979). *The Dream and the Underworld.* New York: Harper and Row.
―――― (1989). *A Blue Fire.* New York: Harper and Row.
Hoedl, J. (2015). 'Reflections on the Jungian nature of psychology as the discipline of interiority: a response to Saban's "misunderstandings"'. *Journal of Analytical Psychology,* 60, 5, 698–716.
Howells, C. (1999). Derrida: Deconstruction from Phenomenology to Ethics. Cambridge, UK: Polity Press.
Jung, C.G. (1951/1969). *Aion. CW* 9ii.
Marlan, S. (2006). 'From the black sun to the philosopher's stone'. *Spring: A Journal of Archetype and Culture,* 74, 1–30.
Panisnick, G.D. (1975). 'The philosophical significance of the concept of the philosopher's stone as used in the hermetic and alchemical writings of Paracelsus'. Ph.D. dissertation, University of Hawaii.
Saban, M. (2015). 'Two in one or one in two: pushing off from Jung with Wolfgang Giegerich'. *Journal of Analytical Psychology,* 60, 5, 679–97.
Verene, D.P. (1998). 'Hegel's nature'. In *Hegel and the Philosophy of Nature,* ed. Stephen Houlgate. Albany: State University of New York.
Žižek, S. (2013). Less Than Nothing: Hegel and the Shadow of Dialectical Materialism. *London: Verso.*

Chapter 10

A critique of Wolfgang Giegerich's move from imagination to the logical life of the soul

Part B. The absolute that is not absolute: an alchemical reflection on the *Caput Mortuum*, the dark other of logical light

This paper situates itself as a response to Wolfgang Giegerich's criticism of Carl Jung and in the context of a number of other challenges to Giegerich's revisioning of Jungian psychology. It follows and extends an earlier paper 'A psychologist who is not a psychologist: A deconstructive reading of Wolfgang Giegerich's idea of psychology proper' (Marlan, 2016).[1] While acknowledging Giegerich's work as an important contribution to philosophically thinking through and challenging Jung's ideas, I hold a number of philosophical differences with him in both perspective and emphasis. In my earlier paper, I concluded that in his effort to further develop Jung's late life idea of the objective psyche, Giegerich leans too far in the direction of overcoming and going beyond the 'human, all-too-human' person. In so doing, he defines psychology proper in such a way as to create a divide, a radical cut, that has led to an imbalance between his vision of psychology and the everyday life of our empirical experience.

My criticism of Giegerich is resonated with, and belongs to, a number of recent exchanges, including those between Mark Saban (2015) and John Hoedl (2015), and between Sean McGrath and Giegerich. Saban finds in Giegerich's work a binary scission and a contempt for the ordinary; Hoedl rejects this idea, but nonetheless acknowledges that Giegerich regularly de-emphasizes the human aspect of psychology, which takes a back seat to his view of the objective psyche and of the *opus magnum*. For Hoedl, this emphasis is due to Giegerich's desire to distance himself from ego psychology. Giegerich heroically identifies the 'logical subject' as the real and true subject and object of psychology, a uroboric view of absolute interiority without remainder. This position of Giegerich's is criticized by McGrath (2014) who, following his own reading of Schelling, rejects absolute interiority and sets limits to the incorporation of otherness into any hegemony with absolute consciousness and insists on an unassimilable remainder. While Giegerich (2014a), in response to McGrath, argues for a different interpretation of Schelling, one closer to a Hegelian perspective, this paper argues in resonance with McGrath for the importance of an unassimilable remainder that sets a limit to the idea that all otherness ultimately is for consciousness.

I wrote about this unassimilable remainder in a paper entitled 'From the black sun to the philosophers' stone' (Marlan, 2006).[2] In an appreciative if critical response to that paper, Giegerich (2008) asked, 'What is at stake?' in a notion I had referred to as an 'unassimilable remnant'? It was an idea that emerged for me in my study of *sol niger*. It is in relation to this notion that Giegerich launched his most sustained critique of my idea of an unknown and unassimilable remnant. He continued his 'dispute' in another place asking, 'how then did Jung get to his barrier and Marlan, with all the philosophers he cites behind him, to the unsurmountable "not"?' (2014b, pp. 298–299, fn8). For Giegerich, maintaining such a position in Jung's case—and by extension in mine—is a 'Faustian crime' (p. 296), a betrayal of Jung's truth, an anti-Heraclitian position.

Giegerich goes on to put the notion of an unassimilable/unsurmountable 'not' in the context of the history of philosophy with regard to how one positions oneself 'with respect to Kant and Hegel' (2014b, p. 296). He understands the Kantian position as 'erecting a fundamental, untranscendable barrier across the mental world' (p. 296), a barrier that Psychology as a Discipline of Interiority (PDI) must subvert if it is to arrive at a view of psychology proper. For Giegerich, the task of the psychologist 'is to interiorize ourselves into the phenomena at hand' (p. 298), to take a speculative leap into the 'stone wall' of this barrier as opposed to leaping over it or turning one's back on it as he avers Jung and I do, which he calls a 'sin against the spirit of psychology' (p. 298). Such a crime/sin involves inscribing any impasse or formal limit on consciousness, and maintaining in principle a notion of anything outside or truly 'other' to the logical light of the soul. It is to this dark other that I turn to consider an alternative view of psychology. In so doing, I intend to consider the notion of the unknowable, unassimilable 'not', in terms of the alchemical idea of the *caput mortuum*, understood as residue, residuum, or worthless remains after distillation, and to examine what goes on unconsciously or, as Hegel notes, 'behind the back of consciousness' (1977, p. 56, para. 87).

I would like to begin with Giegerich's question, what is at stake in the notion of an unassimilable remnant? One thing that is at stake is his view of 'psychology proper'. How or to what extent does Giegerich's work surpass Jung's or Hillman's? On the one hand, Giegerich argues vigorously to demonstrate and to prove that his view of psychology is superior, a successionist move beyond Jung and Hillman. On the other hand, he acknowledges, as Jung did, that his psychology is merely a personal confession. He notes that 'psychological positions are not fully accessible to argumentation inasmuch as they express personal vested interests: the "psychology that one *has*", "that one *is*", "that one lives"'. He notes that '[a]ll I can hope to do is to clarify for myself my own position concerning these important issues' (Giegerich, 2005, p. 108).

For the most part, Giegerich argues for his view by well-thought-out arguments and with rigorous philosophical and psychological sophistication. I say for the most part because this sophistication also exhibits a compelling sophistry. His texts are politic, replete with sophistic, hyperbolic, and repetitious rhetorical tropes that cajole, coerce, cut, and cauterize his interlocutors, attempting to establish his views hierarchically, placing himself in a one-up position, Trump-ing his opponents, shaming, ridiculing, and beating them into submission. He rejects other psychologists at the threshold of 'true psychology' as unqualified, unscholarly, passive, and pop—living in fairy tales, Disney worlds, committing Faustian crimes, betraying truth, and sinning against the spirit of 'true psychology'—his 'psychology proper'—and yet he claims that his psychology is nothing special, with only modest aspirations, modest relevance. He does not claim any ontological truth. It is merely methodological, humble, and no one has to agree with his approach—that is, unless one wants to do 'psychology'. Then, one has to approach, treat, and interpret things in the way he specifies (2008, p. 220). While he acknowledges that his psychology cannot prove anything, he sets out to demonstrate what it can do. In 'semantic modesty', he speaks of leaping into stone walls, climbing glass mountains, and finding truth by chasing a naked goddess. All these instances of demonstration presuppose a psychology that leaps beyond Kantian limits.

How then does one position oneself with respect to Kant and Hegel? This is indeed a pivotal question in the history of philosophy, and it remains so for how we understand our psychology today. Asking this question in the context of Giegerich's criticism of Jung and me appears, however, to imply something more and other than simply an open inquiry. On the contrary, it rather expresses a view point and a challenge that places Jung and me with Kant, and Giegerich 'properly' with Hegel. Such an argument relies on a traditional divide between Kant and Hegel, a divide that is essential to the question of the unknowable, unassimilable not. The resolution of this issue is not simply established in favor of Hegel as Giegerich would have it and it is an issue still being debated in philosophical circles. While the movement of Hegelian philosophy considered itself to have overcome the idea of Kant's thing-in-itself, this assumption of victory was in full retreat by 1855 when philosophy was once again chastened by the epistemological and ontological limits set by Kant's critical philosophy. In 1865, Otto Liebman in his book *Kant und die Epigonen* [Kant and his disciples or followers] 'uttered the cry of the neo-Kantians: "Back to Kant"' (Manning, 1993, p. 174) and it is a cry still heard echoing in contemporary debates. But this cry is not enough for a Kantian victory. Hegel's challenge to Kant is still writ large on today's philosophical scene and is a ferment that stirs beneath the surface of our psychological attitudes today. The tension between the ideas of Kant and the ideas of Hegel sets up a debate between two of the most important and complex philosophers of modernity. It can be plausibly argued that all philosophy that has come 'after' Kant and Hegel up to the present day has directly or indirectly pushed off or tried to push off from them. One of the most important issues of contention between the two thinkers has focused on Kant's notion of what he called the thing-in-itself or, more exactly, 'the thing considered as it is in itself' and the resulting divide between phenomena and the noumena.

The tension around this divide is loosened by the German scholar Gerold Prauss, who notes in a careful study of Kant's texts, that the idea of a thing-in-itself is really short hand for *Ding an sich selbst*, the 'thing considered as it is in itself' (quoted by Madrid, 2014).[3] This scholarly formulation, which has numerous textual references in Kant, shifts the emphasis from an ontological formulation to an anti-metaphysical one 'whereby, in order for things to appear in intuition, they have to be thought of in and of themselves beforehand' (Madrid, 2014). However, such formulations do not solve the problem of the unassimilable, but move it away from a fixed ontology of impasse to a consideration of it as an epistemic concern—how a thing is being considered rather than the kind of thing it is or the way in which it exists. Oddly, this moves Kant somewhat closer to Hegel or, at least, to a certain reading of Hegel.

For Kant, it is not possible to intuit or know by pure reason anything about the noumena or thing-in-itself. It is this issue of the unknowable, undecidable noumena that Giegerich rejects and sees as standing behind the positions of Jung and me. As I have noted, for Giegerich as for Jung, Kant 'erected a barrier across the mental world which made it impossible for even the boldest flight of speculation to penetrate into the object' (Jung, 1977, p. 772, para. 1734). However, Giegerich re-translates this comment of Jung as 'a wall at which human inquisitiveness *turns back*', thus giving it a meaning that fits with his own criticism of limits (of the unknown) which Kant and Jung find essential (Giegerich, 2014b, p. 298). I will argue that Jung and I, and Kant himself for that matter, do not turn our backs on the unknowable, but rather engage it otherwise than Hegel or Giegerich.

Giegerich notes that in the face of impasse, the proper act for the psychologist is to leap into it. This speculative leap finds its springboard in Hegelian philosophy, in a dialectical move that radically alters the object in question. I would argue that rather than seeing Jung and me as turning our backs on the unknowable object, Giegerich via Hegel sidesteps it in a switch-and-bait strategy. What gets switched is Kant's idea of the thing-in-itself as a mind independent object, which Hegel and Giegerich transform into the thing-in-itself for consciousness. By this banishing and conjuring ritual, the dark and truly undecidable other is placed within the light of consciousness as if belonging to it as its 'truth'. The original object through the magic of sublation is relegated to an earlier and inadequate state of awareness and hierarchically surpassed, a true *caput mortuum* of Hegel's and Giegerich's distillation process. The spiritualized vapors of the thing-in-itself are a result of sublation, of being preserved, uplifted, and carried forward as a new phase of the soul's logical life. This heroic act reduces Kant's epistemic concerns about the unknown and the limits of reason to his 'fear of error' which Hegel says is the error itself and thus a fear of truth. Kant's painstaking philosophical critique is reduced to a psychology of fear and an ad hominem, psychological argument. Hegel's dialectic does not solve the problem of Kant's thing-in-itself. It dissolves it, loses interest in it, sidesteps it—but the issue is not closed. Consciousness, for Hegel and Giegerich, is now said to have progressed and to contain two objects: the original thing-in-itself and what experience and the dialectical procedure have made of it. Finally, for Hegel and Giegerich, consciousness arrives 'at a point at which it gets rid of its semblance of being burdened [as Kant was] with something alien and unknown'. Appearance now becomes identical with essence as consciousness grasps its own other and eventually leads through a long path of approximation to absolute knowing.

In the *Phenomenology*, Hegel speaks of the goal of absolute knowing as a 'Spirit that knows itself as Spirit … absolute Spirit, the actuality, truth, and certainty …' (1977, p. 493, para. 808). He uses the word 'absolute' in many different contexts with different meanings; often adjectivally, for example, in absolute idea, absolute knowing, absolute religion, absolute spirit. He uses the ontological substantive, the absolute, less frequently. In spite of the many ways Hegel uses the term 'absolute', his position conveys 'a single, central insight: [that] philosophy culminates in the comprehension of experience as a structured whole, or totality, whose interrelations are known with necessity' (Rockmore, 1996, p. 62). Throughout his thought, Hegel and Giegerich after him defend a view intended to overcome difference through a speculative (if differentiated) unity.

It is this notion of absolute knowing that has led to the judgment that Hegel is 'not a philosopher' at all (Magee, 2001, p. 3). 'He is no lover or seeker of wisdom—[rather] he believes he has found it' (Magee, 2001, p. 3). In his own words, Hegel states his intention '[t]o help bring philosophy closer to the form of Science, to the goal where it can lay aside the title "love of knowing" and be *actual* knowing—that is what I have set myself to do' (1977, p. 3, para. 5, emphasis in original). Leaving love behind, Giegerich takes off from Hegel's notion of the absolute and develops an interrelated number of basic concepts that form and frame his approach to psychology proper. Based in the idea of total interiorization of otherness and following Giegerich, the work of PDI has built a wall, a concept wall, and imagines that we Jungians will pay for it! The key ideas include the tautological presupposition, notional practice, the psychological difference, and, ultimately, absolute negative interiority. These ideas work together to absolutely overcome any 'trace' of a remainder. Absolute negative interiority leaves the psyche with no point outside itself, nothing literal, substantial, positively existing or 'actual'—no skin in the game, no dog in the fight.

Mogenson (2015) in his rich and provocative papers on Rilke and 'divine inseeing' shows the implications of Giegerich's idea of absolute interiority in which an 'actual' dog is negated, sublated from the outset. The dog that is not a dog, but something conceptual, noetic, linguistic—it is not an animal in nature—not a dog that is of interest to the psychologist or poet. The 'actual' dog, my friend, my companion, is bypassed and given over to scientific perspectives, but for me this move loses something important: my relationship to my 'actual' dog. I recently had to euthanize Curtis, a deeply loved companion over many years. I held out doing so until his suffering was undeniable and I felt it cruel to hold onto him for my sake. In my last hours with Curt, I lay with him in his bed, held him as my grief deepened. His breathing was hard and obstructed, and he had lost the use of his legs. I looked into his eyes as if hoping for an acknowledgment of what was to come. I inhaled his outward breath and he inhaled mine. This went on for some time and at one moment he licked my face and this gave me the capacity to move forward. The next morning, Curt was euthanized. I held him as the needle pinched him in the back of the neck and he slowly drifted away from his pain in a deep relaxation, release, and the oblivion of sleep. Then, the injection of chemicals followed that would transform him from living animation to a lifeless form. I continue to grieve Curtis, who was cremated, and whose remains sit at home and continue to fill me with a mixture of grief, love, and wonder. Curt remains for me something more than a conceptual, noetic, linguistic dog. He was my friend, actual, independent, objective, and deeply natural. I know that the noetic has its objectivity too and I do believe there is an intrinsic soul-bond with Curtis. Something noetic, sublated from the beginning, but my relationship to him also leads me back to Jacobi's early criticism of Fichte's and Hegel's idealism. For Hegel and Giegerich, the subject's realization of its final identity is with what seemed other to it. The object world turns out to be thinking itself, where substance is subject and one meets oneself beyond the vale. Yet, for me, this formula does not fully satisfy my relationship with Curtis and I hold with Jacobi that what really matters lies both before and outside an idealistic reduction to knowledge.

From the place of Giegerich's uroboric understanding of psyche, otherness remains internal to itself, logically not inner or outer, everything becomes mental and noetic. There is no subject-object. The traditional divide is overcome. No more tension between inner and outer. Spatial relations are dissolved. Psyche becomes totally autonomous, thinking itself essential truth in an act of self-knowing—psychic reality gone wild—on steroids! The 'actual' other is dismissed and my dog becomes my mind and my mind my dog. This view does not satisfy me, nor account for the reality of my relation to Curtis.

Ultimately, Hegel makes the claim 'that thought and being are one: the categories of thought are the categories of being' making an autonomous absolute whole, though internally differentiated (Magee, 2010, p. 28). It is a claim that is philosophically suspect. While Giegerich appears to reject the idea that he is making ontological claims, it is the case that the soul's logical life becomes its own substrate, its own ground, its own reality, and its own absolute, fully autonomous truth, i.e. absolute negative interiority. However, if it looks like ontology, smells like ontology, well—it still may be undecidable! What is *not* undecidable is that Giegerich's criticisms of Jung, Hillman, and me rely on the idea of this total negation that attempts to move beyond every trace of naturalism, empiricism, and the dark remnant of the unknowable other.

In his remarkable essay '"The Unassimilable Remnant"—What Is at Stake? A Dispute with Stanton Marlan', Giegerich forges his criticism of my approach to *sol niger*, the alchemical *mortificatio*, and the idea of an unassimilable remnant. My work began with the recognition that the image of the black sun resisted conscious assimilation—that it would not yield or be incorporated, did not dissolve, go away, go under, get lifted up, but rather remained to challenge one's psychological narcissism to the core, experiences of brokenness, incision, wound, castration, cut, negation, and with an ultimate 'no' to consciousness. *Sol niger* appeared to be intrinsic to the alchemical operation of the *nigredo* and *mortificatio*, an archetypal principle refusing integration into consciousness. Yet, my engagement with this dark enigma emitted an odd light, what the alchemists called the 'light of darkness itself' (Jung, 1953/1968, p. 160, para. 197; see also Marlan, 2005, p. 97). It was this light, intrinsic in the darkness itself, that opened the way to consider the ancient idea of the Philosophers' Stone. To bring the stone into focus was *not* to leave the black sun behind, nor to simply move beyond it to an animus *albedo*, or logical psychology. Rather, it led me to pursue my suspicion that the Philosophers' Stone has been there all along in the phenomenal *shine of darkness itself.*

One of the fundamental ideas that is in question in the differing perspectives between my thought and Giegerich's revolves around the question of this absolute negative interiority and his notion of the totally autonomous nature of psyche. I began to consider the darkness as an indispensable *caput mortuum*, the dross or residue that remains even as the light of consciousness struggles to show itself in its limits. Just as darkness exceeds itself in the *lumen naturae*, the stone that is not a stone exceeds its own light in darkness. *Sol niger* and the Philosophers' Stone, each in their own way, resist pure transparency. Whether in the language of revivification and Aphroditic pleasure or in the sublation to pure mercurial liquidity—there always remains a dark remnant in the retort after distillation. It remains other and opaque to consciousness and maintains its resistance to being accounted for by a movement in a dialectic intending to make it serve as a mark of differentiation of a higher sublation. But, for Giegerich, my negation, my description of the *nigredo* and *mortificatio* remain 'decidedly naturalistic' (2008, p. 202). They rely on 'experiential, sensible image, ritual behavior, *mystical* death of the ego' (2008, p. 202). He cites my strategy in *The Black Sun* (2005) as an example, saying that my intent 'was to hesitate before this darkness, to pause and then to enter its realm of corpses or coffins, of monsters and monstrous complexity' (Giegerich quoting Marlan, 2008, p. 202). He notes that my images of negation do not go far enough, do 'not come home to' themselves, and do not cut themselves loose from their 'tie to an immersion in immediate experience and natural(istic) image' (2008, p. 202.), that 'the cut did not really cut' itself (2008, p. 203)—it is not a full-fledged cut. While I have shown how experiences of *sol niger* desubstantiate the ego and drive the psyche to an archetypal pivot point, it does not drive it to the other side, to absolute negative interiority without remainder, to an ultimate and total liquification. Giegerich interprets my hesitating to go to this level as a resistance to go all the way, 'to "let ... go" without reserve' (2008, p. 204) and as a resistance to going under into thought proper. Thus, for Giegerich, my perspective remains under the *spell* of images and is *lured* back into the experiential field, into the past *held captive* in *myth, metaphor, metaphysics*—I confess. But it is worth noting that Giegerich himself sees such a position as intrinsic to the soul, an irrefutable madness.

Like Hillman, I put on the brakes, find a limit, tarry at the threshold of an ontological pivot, avoiding at all costs the poisonous state of splendid solar isolation, refusing both the peaks of spirit at one end and total literalism at the other. But what I do not confess to is Giegerich's accusation that I, like Hillman, maintain an anima-like innocence, reverently gazing in silent wonder at hypostasized mysteries as an immunization against wounding. At another moment, Giegerich recognizes that my position factually does achieve the negation that he speaks about, a cut that reaches the most terrible perturbations of the ego, of ego death—and thus arrives at the recognition of the *lumen naturae* and the light of darkness itself. But, for Giegerich, I do not theoretically catch up with the position I have already factually achieved. I resist the cut that moves my position into logical agreement—in agreement with his psychology? What Giegerich does not entertain is that I might understand his position, even appreciate it, but view psychology otherwise than he insists 'I/we' must. If one does not hold the position of absolute negative interiority, of total Dionysian liquification as an end result, and the view of an absolute rather than a relatively autonomous psyche, how else, he asks, could there be a psychology adequate to the soul? For him, a psychology that questions his self-proclaimed modernist assumptions, his essentialism, his logocentrism, and his logical symphony of ideas can only 'faddishly' insist on 'fundamental difference and otherness' (2008, p. 221).

Giegerich then asks if I disagree with Heraclitus' notion that 'you can never come to a boundary of the soul no matter what road you take and how far you travel' (2008, p. 215). If I don't disagree (again the refrain), 'how then did Jung get to his barrier and Marlan, with all the philosophers he cites behind him, to the insurmountable "not"?' (2008, p. 215). Did they disprove Heraclitus and show that there 'is' a limit after all?

It is to the question of limit that I now turn and, yes, there are many philosophers who claim such a limit. I have already noted my own hesitation/resistance simply to bypass limits by leaping headlong into stone walls, to privilege thinking and tilting the balance away from the metaphoric toward a hierarchical 'superiority' of the rational and absolute negative interiority in which image and metaphor can be reduced to instrumentality. I have noted in another place a group of thinkers supporting such a hesitation: Dominick LaCapra, Edgar Morin, Martin Heidegger, and Jacques Derrida, to name only a few (Marlan, 2006, pp. 9–10).[4] Heidegger, for instance, critiques Hegel's interpretation of negativity as an inauthentic modification of an insurmountable 'not'. He comments that the 'not' or 'negative' moment in the Hegelian dialectic cannot be simply overcome or assimilated by *reason*. The 'not' is more than a dialectical alienation on the way to sublation. In fact, the 'not' resists incorporation into the movements of thought; and for Heidegger, as for Jung, the negation of negation does not culminate in an unconditional 'yes' (a full assimilation of the 'not'). The 'not' remains a 'not yet' and a not at all. It is a 'not' that cannot be surpassed logically, but can serve as an access point that transitions from a logical understanding of the soul to a poetic one.

Giegerich, however, argues that the 'not' that Heidegger speaks of is not a dialectical one in the first place. It is a hypostatized or posivitized 'not', one extracted from the 'real process' [but whose process? his? Hegel's?]. Giegerich argues against Heidegger's idea that the 'not' is something in its own right and his claim that Hegel's attempt to assimilate the 'not' is illegitimate. But just what is this hypostatized 'not' if not the first 'not' of Kant's thing-in-itself, which from Hegel's and Giegerich's dialectical perspective must get transformed into a thing-in-itself, a 'not'—for consciousness. It is this dialectical position, as we have seen, that inauthentically bypasses (according to Heidegger) the poetic sign and the unknown, as a true recognition of limit.

Heidegger among contemporary philosophers is not alone in his criticism of Hegel's attempt to move beyond limit. For Hegel, a limit that is truly limited becomes a *caput mortuum* relegated to the margins of thought, left behind, declined, side-stepped, and sidelined, hierarchically risen above, making such a limit unimportant, a historical trace replaced by a new object that allows itself to be held in consciousness, complying with it, overcoming its aporetic status. For Derrida, on the other hand, an aporia is an absolutely impossible situation, one which cannot be resolved through rational analysis or dialectical thought. For him, the problematic that emerges with an aporetic situation cannot be answered by a discourse that would be capable of taking the aporia as an object of knowledge (Wortham, 2010, p. 15). Like Heidegger and Jung, the poetic, metaphoric, and symbol/sign is resistant to the clear light of consciousness. Derrida recognizes, as Hillman does (in the words of Heraclitus), that 'nature loves to hide' and 'omens and oracular mysteries do not speak clearly; they give only signs' (Hillman, 1995, p. 42). In his book *Margins of Philosophy*, Derrida takes up Hegel's view of signs and, like Heidegger, challenges the idea that attempts to include its own limit within itself, mastering it, dispensing with or transgressing it, making limit its own limit, a state of consciousness in which the limited is no longer foreign to it. The Hegelian approach believes that it can control the margins of its volume by thinking its other and in this way the so-called reified 'not' ends up in the margins of psyche. For Derrida, by thinking limits as its own 'proper other' and by 'recognizing it ... one misses it or, rather one misses (the) missing (of) it' (1982, p. xi). So what is missed is the real limit, that which resists being known and incorporated. While not known, and as a limit, it works to stimulate desire, passion, wonder, imagination, even love—the a-rational dark other of logical light—that is not even properly other, nor is it improper. Derrida's strategy is not to play into the hands of the dialectic by simply opposing it, but rather to approach it otherwise, obliquely, by luxating it, unhinging it, placing '*loxos* in the *logos*' (1982, p. xv) which creates some 'carnage of language', 'breaks open the roof' of 'the closed spiral unity of the palate ... to the point of no longer being *understood*. It is no longer *a* tongue' (1982, p. xv, fn8). It is an insurgence made to 'decry its law' and to engage philosophy by not 'permitting oneself to be encoded by philosophical logos, or to stand under its banner' (1982, p. iv). There are no surprises and all is reason from within 'the vault of [a hermetically-sealed] autism', seeded in hierarchy and exclusivity (p. xvi).

The unhinging of the dialectic resounds in the fact that the subterranean Persephone is everywhere associated with what resists consciousness, with what is unthought, the suppressed and repressed of philosophy. For Derrida, becoming unhinged evokes Persephone, her name corresponding to the French earwig: *perce-oreielle* and in her resistance to logos, she disrupts the philosopher's ear 'with twists, spirals, helixes, curves, floral curls, springs, corkscrews: figures which open, puncture, wind about and course through the linear image of the limit' (Wortham, 2010, p. 91) to the point of a poetic undecidable. Such a luxation casts an odd light obliquely and by surprise challenges philosophical and psychological idealism. The poetic, imagistic, symbolic sign illuminates differently, otherwise than spirit's claim of interiority. Its a-rational character proves refractory to any kind of dialectical incorporation. Perhaps oddly, Jung describes his own empiricism as a reaction to philosophical systems such as Fichte's and Hegel's. In his empiricism, he encounters chaos and chance, a not knowing which keeps wonder alive, an open and wandering spirit that stirs in the margins of the soul beyond what is known. One might say that it goes on behind the back of consciousness in the margin of the pit, the abyss, of what Jung called the unconscious—unconscious to the ego—but perhaps as well a formal unknowing that belongs to the form of the human condition. For Derrida, there is a real limit. The issue would be less to displace a 'given' determined limit than to work toward the concept of limit and the limit of the concept. Jon Mills, a Freudian psychoanalyst and Hegelian scholar, recognizes such a limit, knowing that even though the unconscious undergoes dialectical evolution, it is never fully sublated and it remains a repository, a pit of images beyond the call of spirit. He poses this idea as a question and further asks, 'Is not the pit bound to leave its residue? And what would this residue be? Could it perhaps be fragments of inclinations and passions that co-exist with spirit in its transcendence toward reason?' (Mills, 2002, p. 10).

Mills suggests that the unconscious abyss exceeds the elevating process of the dialectic and notes that even if the abyss were to become subordinated to spirit, 'would not the pit bring with it its own material, its nightness that would be absorbed in spirits universalization?' (Mills, 2002, p. 10). Mills asks if 'the host of images drawn from the pit [is] susceptible to the *sway of desire* that seeks life and fulfillment of its own' (Mills, 2002, p. 10; my emphasis). In her book interestingly titled *The Sway of the Negative*, Karin De Boer challenges the optimism of Hegel's dialectic, which for her like Mills is in tension with another aspect of Hegel's awareness, which she believes is not given enough recognition as playing an equal role in the dialectic itself. The aspect she highlights is the recognition of the 'tragic', which for De Boer cannot be fully sublated, but remains 'entangled' with the advance of spirit and continues as an equal principle, a logic of entanglement on par with Hegel's notion of absolute negativity (2010, pp. 2–4). For Mills and Giegerich, the resistance to dialectical advancement is basically attributed to illness, neurosis, and madness, but for De Boer, it becomes a principle on par with the forward movement of the dialectic itself. In his work *What is soul?* Giegerich too recognizes the dual intentionalities of the soul, what he calls the need for initiation alongside the need for emancipation. The need for initiation implies grounding, embeddedness in imagination, myth, and metaphysics, but ultimately Giegerich believes that the soul must cast off its mythological garments and it is in this gesture that modern man exceeds the *imaginal life* to find human dignity in the soul's *logical life*. What temporarily holds the soul back from this achievement is neurosis, a condition he believes ultimately can be surpassed, when the full price is paid for a departure from a previous stage of consciousness. It is precisely this optimism that is questioned by Mills and De Boer.

While Mills and Giegerich find resistance to the absolute movement out and beyond the unconscious primarily in illness and neurosis, De Boer raises the resistance to a more formal principle, a logic of entanglement. Such a principle of entanglement questions the supremacy of the logical and the rational making equal room for imagination and phantasy. John Sallis, a well-regarded philosopher, even places imagination beyond reason. He asks whether phantasy exceeds reason—or, more generally, is imagination in excess of spirit? For him, the question leads one to envision imagination as being out of the realm of the dialectic, on the periphery of spirit, not susceptible to its movement, transcending spirit's power to determine the activity and content of the abyss. Such a possibility has greater implications for understanding the potential faculties of the abyss independent of spirit. For Sallis, this implies that the abyss would seemingly appear to have a will and purpose of its own. He asks if the spirit is drawn back to the pit of its feeling life and if such a tendency 'could perhaps broach a wonder that one could never aspire to surpass' (1987, p. 157).

For Aristotle, all knowledge has its beginning in 'wonder'. For Hegel, the reason for this is that at the beginning, there is a tension between the irrationality with which the object is burdened and the merely intermediate certainty that spirit has of binding itself in that object, and it is precisely because of this tension that one is at the beginning inspired with wonder. But then the self-presentation of spirit is to *resolve* that particular tension and, thus, philosophical thought has to raise itself above the standpoint of wonder. This is a position taken by Giegerich as well. Sallis, on the other hand, asks whether there is, in the play of images, a dark residue, something not recoverable in universality, something resistant to the subjugating of images that would make them in the end only the mirror of spirit. Is there a residue that is absolutely lost beyond all hope of recovery? And would such a residue, with still more finality, be left behind, drawn back, toward the pit from which it came, for example, when the sign itself comes in Hegel's own sober text to be called a pyramid? For Derrida, the pyramid's 'materiality, ... and externality of signs obstruct the idea's return to complete self-ownership' (Sloterdjick, 2009, p. 54). In this manner, the soul exists in this externality—ecstatic in that which resists return to self, a dark energy in a pharaonic grave. From this perspective, it is not difficult to see why Hegel's interest in signs moves in a direction leading as far away as possible from Egypticism. If he is to bring his theory of the spirit to its goal, he cannot waste too much time with the weight of the pyramids or the enigmatic nature of hieroglyphics. While Hegel proposes the labor of the concept, negation cuts absolutely right through until spirit can clothe itself in a shell of language whose lightness and translucence allow it to forget that it requires any external supplement. This is not to say that Hegel is a lightweight. His own tombs are pyramid-like, not unlike magical grimoires and alchemical texts, difficult to interpret and perhaps ultimately indecipherable. Yet, for Hegel, the Egyptians remain external like the Chinese whose language and writing form one of the great barriers and disturbances that render impossible the fulfilled moment of absolute negative interiority in which the spirit remains intent on hearing itself speak. For Derrida, the pyramid then 'constitutes the archetype of cumbersome objects that cannot be taken along by the spirit on its return to itself' (Sloterdjick, 2009, p. 57). And yet, for Derrida, there is an oblique path different from Hegel's by which this cumbersome object can be brought back from Egypt as a transportable form, lighting and 'lightening through textualization' (Sloterdjick, 2009, p. 62). For a moment, 'the ghost of the Pharaoh' (Sloterdjick, 2009, p. 63) marks its return to us as an absent presence, as a darkness that shines. But, just as *sol niger* and the Philosophers' Stone exceed their darkness in light, so their light remains a darkness, a remainder which goes on behind the back of consciousness. The path remains circular and while the pyramid enters consciousness, it also returns to the pit that will always already have been the *lumen naturae* of the tomb, vault, crypt, and grave. It speaks with the voice of its own been-ness—the voices of our own dead, at the pivot point, both between pit and pyramid and pit and pyramid sublated and logically simultaneous, a unity of unity and difference.

For Giegerich however, being at the pivot point is not enough. The soul wants to push further to absolute negative interiority, but, as he has noted, the soul *also* needs initiation and thus remains attached to its dark light in myth, metaphysics, image, and symbol. In the soul's resistance to itself, it is more than a logical epiphany in an eternal space-less moment. It is also entangled in time and narrative, which Paul Ricoeur calls 'emplotment' (as quoted in Dowling, 2011, p. 10). It is also immersed in what Hillman has called the vale of soul making, the mess of anima, and not in simply pushing off from it. It is in a dark light, other and always with, but not reduced to the unity of logical light. The soul is not entirely contained in absolute negative interiority which privileges unity over diversity even as it tries to include it as its own difference. Giegerich's dialectical formula, the unity of unity and difference, is left wanting since it continues to tincture a syzygy that privileges unity as its major trope. As Giegerich has noted, his '[p]sychology boldly *privileges* unity by preferring the *coniunctio* over dissociation' (2008, p. 220).

But, preferences aside (which are not logically determined), the *coniunctio* always falls apart and, to do justice to the soul, I have suggested that the formula, the unity of unity and difference, needs to be supplemented with the idea of the difference of unity and difference, a difference which resists being totally lit up by consciousness. The remainder becomes the *caput mortuum*, a residuum that is left over after alchemical distillation and Hegelian sublation. Ultimately, it is the residue at the bottom of a heated flask, after the solution's 'noble' elements have been sublimated. It is the disregarded dross, the epitome of decline and decay, a disregarded thing-in-itself, a trace and a pigment, a *caput mortuum*, called 'death's head' (Caput mortuum, 2016). As *caput mortuum*, it is a color and a pigment sometimes called Egyptian or mummy's brown, and it is made ghoulishly out of the ground-up remains of mummies. The use of this pigment was discontinued in the nineteenth century when artists became aware of its ingredients. The color was often used to paint the robes of religious figures and important personages, as well as for shadowing human flesh and landscapes cast in darkness. Emitting a somber quality of dark light, it shadowed the royalty and landscapes of logical consciousness with a much-needed dark magic of Pharaonic corpses putrefied and signifying both eternal life and death, consciousness and the unconscious, at the core of its odd illumination. The art of illumination has a materiality that remains partially hidden in the odd glow of dark light.

Pierre Hadot has elaborated another idea of Heraclitus, the idea that 'Nature loves to hide' (2006, p. x) and noted that '[t]he occultation of nature will be perceived not as a resistance that must be conquered', stripped to its bare truth, 'but as a mystery into which human beings can gradually be initiated' (2006, p. 92). For Hadot, stripping the veil from Isis reflects a dominating Promethean orientation to truth, while initiation he considers aesthetic and Orphic.

The Promethean and Orphic attitudes represent two differing, perhaps opposed, yet simultaneous historical developments bound together like a double helix around a single historical axis: the master metaphor of nature's secrets. For Alan Kim (2007), 'Grand and tendentious philosophical narratives, be they of the Hegelian, neo-Kantian, or Heideggerian variety, necessarily ignore inconvenient facts, sometimes by calling into question their importance vis-à-vis history's "deeper" motion'. By contrast, Hadot's attention to the finer grain of facts reveals an integrating and wholly unexpected 'dialectic' between the Promethean and Orphic orientations to nature: dialectic not as successive sublimations, successionist degradations, and hierarchies, but as an unending conversation between two equal partners. I have imagined Jung, Hillman, and Giegerich as such partners, a community of thinkers I am comfortable partnering with. However, I would claim that it is not by methodological decisions, presuppositions, and acts of thinking alone, not in the practical, down-to-earth, and very sober, that we do justice to the dark shine of otherness. For Giegerich, truth is nothing unspeakable, but this truth alone does not deepen the erotics of the soul, setting it on fire or activating the fullness of human experience symbolized by the Philosophers' Stone. For him, what is important is not the human subject at all, but the logical subject who wants to do psychology. How then to speak of this shining that is a mortification of light and thought that remains outside and other, opaque and resistant to the dialectic and being accounted for by a movement of spirit intending to make it serve as a work of differentiation of a higher sublation, of a pure psychology too pure to treat ordinary human beings in the consulting room. Rather, psychology for me is a darker art, mongrel, a mix dismissed by Giegerich. If the stone can be thought of in terms of absolute negative interiority, it can also be seen as absolute negative exteriority, the mattering of idealist thought, a white earth exterior and ecstatic, and a dark sky marked by tracing a dark light, stars in a night sky, an Egyptian goddess Nuit, scintilla-like leaning over us—an erotic presence calling us toward her to an absolute that is not an absolute, seducing us to a wonder beyond the language of truth—on this white earth, *black light matters*.

Notes

1 Published in this volume as Chapter 10, Part A.
2 Published in this volume as Chapter 9.
3 This is Henry E. Allison's English translation of Kant, as quoted by Prauss in his German work and quoted by Madrid, 2014.
4 Published in this volume as Chapter 9.

References

Caput mortuum. (2016). In *Wikipedia*. August 14, 2016. Retrieved from https://en.wikipedia.org/wiki/Caput_mortuum, last modified on July 8, 2016.

De Boer, K. (2010). *On Hegel: The sway of the negative.* New York: Palgrave MacMillan.

Derrida, J. (1982). *Margins of philosophy.* (A. Bass, Trans.). Chicago, IL: University of Chicago Press (original work published 1972).

Dowling, W. C. (2011). *Ricoeur on time and narrative: An introduction to Temps et récit.* Notre Dame, IN: University of Notre Dame Press.

Giegerich, W. (2005). Afterword. In W. Giegerich, D. Miller, & G. Mogenson (Eds.), *Dialectics and analytical psychology: The El Capitan Canyon seminar* (pp. 107–112). New Orleans, LA: Spring Journal Books.

Giegerich, W. (2008). The unassimilable remnant: What is at stake?: A dispute with Stanton Marlan. In S. Marlan (Ed.), *Archetypal psychologies: Reflections in honor of James Hillman* (pp. 193–223). New Orleans, LA: Spring Journal Books.

Giegerich, W. (2014a). Jungian psychology as metaphysics? A response to Sean McGrath. International Journal of Jungian Studies, 7(3), 242–250.

Giegerich, W. (2014b). *Dreaming the myth onwards: C.G. Jung on Christianity and on Hegel – Part 2 of The flight into the unconscious, collected English papers, volume VI.* New Orleans, LA: Spring Journal Books.

Hadot, P. (2006). *The veil of ISIS: An essay on the history of the idea of nature.* Cambridge, MA: The Belknap Press of Harvard University Press.

Hegel, G. W. F. (1977). *Phenomenology of spirit* (A. V. Miller, Trans.). Oxford: Oxford University Press (original work published 1807).

Hillman, J. (1995). Pink madness. *Spring: A Journal of Archetype and Culture*, 57, 39–71.

Hoedl, J. (2015). Reflections on the Jungian nature of psychology as a discipline of interiority: A response to Saban's 'misunderstandings'. *Journal of Analytical Psychology*, 60(5), 698–716.

Jung, C. G. (1953/1968). *Alchemical studies. The collected works of C.G. Jung, vol. 13* (G. Adler, Ed.; R. F. C. Hull, Trans.). Princeton, NJ: Princeton University Press.

Jung, C. G. (1977). *The symbolic life. The collected works of C.G. Jung, vol. 18* (G. Adler, Ed.; R. F. C. Hull, Trans.). Princeton, NJ: Princeton University Press.

Kim, A. (2007). Review of Pierre Hadot's *The Veil of Isis: An Essay on the History of the Idea of Nature* (Michael Chase, Trans.). Cambridge, MA: Harvard University Press, 2006. *Notre Dame Philosophical Reviews*, May 6, 2007. Retrieved from https://ndpr.nd.edu/news/the-veil-of-isis-an-essay-on-the-history-of-the-idea-of-nature/.

Madrid, A. (2014). *The thing in itself*. Retrieved from https://aureliomadrid.wordpress.com/2014/01/19/the-thing-in-itself/.

Magee, G. A. (2001). *Hegel and the hermetic tradition*. Ithaca, NY: Cornell University Press.

Magee, G. A. (2010). *The Hegel dictionary*. London: Continuum.

Manning, R. J. S. (1993). *Interpreting otherwise than Heidegger: Emmanuel Levinas' ethics as first philosophy*. Pittsburgh, PA: Duquesne University Press.

Marlan, S. (2005). *The black sun: Alchemy and the art of darkness*. College Station, TX: Texas A&M University.

Marlan, S. (2006). From the black sun to the philosophers' stone. *Spring: A Journal of Archetype and Culture*, 74, 1–30.

Marlan, S. (2016). The psychologist who is not a psychologist: A deconstructive reading of Wolfgang Giegerich's idea of psychology proper. *Journal of Analytical Psychology*, 61(2), 223–238.

McGrath, S. (2014). The question concerning metaphysics: A Schellingian intervention in analytical psychology. *International Journal of Jungian Studies*, 6(1), 23–51.

Mills, J. (2002). *The unconscious abyss: Hegel's anticipation of psychoanalysis*. Albany, NY: State University of New York Press.

Mogenson, G. (2015). Inwardizing Rilke's dog of 'divine inseeing' into itself. *Journal of Analytical Psychology*, 60, 245–266.

Rockmore, T. (1996). *On Hegel's epistemology and contemporary philosophy*. Atlantic Highlands, NJ: Humanities Press International.

Saban, M. (2015). Two in one or one in two: Pushing off from Jung with Wolfgang Giegerich. *Journal of Analytical Psychology*, 60(5), 679–697.

Sallis, J. (1987). *Spacings—of reason and imagination in texts of Kant, Fichte, and Hegel*. Chicago, IL: University of Chicago Press.

Sloterdjick, P. (2009). *Derrida, an Egyptian: On the problem of the Jewish pyramid* (W. Hoban, Trans.). Cambridge: Polity Press.

Wortham, S. M. (2010). *The Derrida dictionary*. New York: Continuum.

Chapter 11

What's the matter—with alchemical recipes? Philosophy and filth in the forging of Jung's alchemical psychology

Prelude

There's an old alchemical dictum: "it is found in filth" (Jung, 1963b, ¶791) and another that says: "Despise not the ashes ... for in them is the diadem, the ash of the things that endure" ("Tractatus Micreris" (Jung, 1963b, ¶691, fn. 102). In fact, what matters in filth and endures in ashes is at the heart of alchemical recipes, but is often rejected and even despised. As some spiritually oriented alchemists began their work of sublimation and purification, the cry was: out with the foul, the obscene, and unclean, the garbage, grit, dirt, and grime. In the mind and under fire, feces and falsehoods are all refined, demons burn as flesh is roasted. Basilisks and blood also calcined and in a flash all foolishness undermined. As the volcano cools and leaves behind a blackened earth for us to find, all ash is left within the mind, blackness cools but will they find the lava goddess left behind?

Jung as philosopher

As Jung moved toward his idea of a psychology of alchemy and away from its simply literal, material practices, he recognized the importance of philosophy for understanding it and its goal: the Philosophers' Stone. In *Psychology and Alchemy* (1968), he cites Richardus Anglicus, who states:

> Therefore all those who desire to attain the blessing of this art should apply themselves to study, should gather the truth from the books and not from invented fables and untruthful works. There is no way by which this art can truly be found ... except by completing their studies and understanding the words of the philosophers
>
> (Jung, 1968, ¶362)

Likewise, he notes Raymond Lully who

> says that owing to their ignorance men are not able to accomplish the work until they have studied universal philosophy, which will show

them things that are unknown and hidden from others. 'Therefore, our stone belongs not to the vulgar but to the very heart of our philosophy'

(Jung, 1968, ¶365)

to what Jung called the *aurum non vulgi* or *aurum philosophicum*, a philosophical gold (1963a, p. 210, fn. 11). The emphasis on alchemy's true goal in the minds of Anglicus and Lully reflected a religious Christian view that was quite critical of the materialist, mundane, and so-called demonic practices of those alchemists whom they considered foolish and vulgar. For Jung, the emphasis on the philosophical dimension of alchemy helped to dispel the literalism of many alchemical operations and recipes, which were seemingly nothing more than a "witch's brew" of vile ingredients that sometimes led to chemical discoveries, but more often than not ended in no value—or worse, in poverty, sickness, and/or the death of the alchemist.

As Jung notes, Anglicus rejected all the assorted "filth" with which the alchemists worked in typical alchemical recipes: "eggshells, hair, the blood of a red-haired man, basilisks, worms, herbs, and human feces." Anglicus stated that "Whatsoever a man soweth that also shall he reap. Therefore if he soweth filth, he shall find filth."

> Turn back, brethren, to the way of truth of which you are ignorant; I counsel you for your own sake to study and to labour with steadfast meditation on the words of the philosophers, whence the truth can be summoned forth
>
> (Jung, 1968, ¶365)

In contrast to the misguided and materially oriented alchemists, Dionysius Zacharias relates his experience of turning away from such degrading practices. He

> relates that a certain 'religiosus Doctor excellentissimus' advised him to refrain from useless expense in 'sophisticationibus diabolicis' and to devote himself rather to the study of the books of the old philosophers, so as to acquaint himself with the *vera materia*

the true material. Jung relates Zacharias' process as reviving from a "fit of despair" with the help of the Holy Spirit and applying himself "to a serious study of the literature," which he

> read diligently and meditated day and night until his finances were exhausted. Then he worked in his laboratory, saw the three colors appear, and on Easter Day of the following year the wonder happened: 'Vidi perfectionem'—'I saw the perfect fulfillment': the quicksilver was
>
> (Jung, 1968, ¶365)

converted into pure gold before his eyes. Jung states that "[t]here is an unmistakable hint here that the work and its goal depended very largely on a mental condition" (Jung, 1968, ¶365). Here, Jung is building his case for a psychological understanding of alchemy, but the "mental condition" in these passages is an expression of the religious philosophy of Zacharias and Anglicus whose work served to help Jung recognize the importance of mind and spirit for understanding his psychological approach to alchemy, but it also degraded the importance of "matter" and "nature."

Jung's close follower Marie-Louise von Franz (2006) has noted that in both Arabic religiosity and Western Christianity, the idea of matter became more and more "spiritualized." She points out that the "masculine element of logos slowly prevailed over matter," to the extent that there was a "loss of the dimension" of materiality, to which she ultimately ascribed the highest value, even calling it "Divine Matter" (p. 29).

Jung's reclaiming of the filth

While spiritual philosophy was a stepping stone to Jung's recognition of the mental aspect of the alchemical opus, it was also a rejection of the shadow of what it called "filth." Spirituality split off, turned away from worms, feces, blood, and basilisks,[1] from what the religious doctrines called diabolical—but Jung was not one to turn away from the daemonic, the darkest and most repulsive aspects and deepest roots of the repressed and unknown dimensions of nature. In fact, alchemy's attention to the *nigredo* and nature in all of her aspects was one of its important responses to Christian religious philosophy.

While for Jung Christian philosophy was central to the development of the Western psyche, it fell short of adequately resolving the split between spirit and matter. Thus, alchemy with its emphasis on nature and the material world was an important compensation to the over-spiritualization of religious philosophy.[2] In contrast to a metaphysical ontology of spirit, Jung spoke of the significance of the shadow of materiality and of the daemonic. At a 1952 Eranos Conference, religious scholar Mircea Eliade interviewed Jung, who spoke of the serious problem of integrating the opposites. Jung noted that in *C.G. Jung Speaking* (1977), he "had the occasion to interest [himself] in the integration of Satan," remarking that to the extent Satan was "not integrated, the world is not healed and man is not saved." The alchemists' ideal of the Philosophers' Stone "was to save the world in its totality" (p. 227). The very things rejected from alchemical recipes by religious philosophers were ultimately included by Jung in his formulation of the alchemical work. He stated: "The work is difficult and strewn with obstacles; the alchemical opus is dangerous. Right at the beginning you meet 'the dragon,' the chthonic spirit, the 'devil' or, as the alchemists called it, the 'blackness, the *nigredo* ..." (p. 228).

By confronting the chthonic and the demonic, Jung plunges into a witch's brew of his own and struggles to come to terms with the unconscious and with what he called the shadow that is just below the surface of our civilized and often pious identities. Jung goes on to describe this alchemical and psychological work with the often so-called repulsive "*prima materia.*" "The prima materia is 'Saturnine,' and the malefic Saturn is the abode of the devil, or again it is the most despised and rejected thing. 'Thrown out into the street,' 'cast on the dunghill,' 'found in filth'" (Jung, 1967, ¶209). For Jung, the central mystery of alchemy comes in the linking of conscious and unconscious in a *coniunctio* that aims at "synthesis" and "assimilation," but he also notes that this process of linking above and below produces suffering and intense struggle. The soul finds itself in the throes of melancholy in which "matter" itself is said to "suffer" (1977, p. 228). For Jung, the coming together of conscious and unconscious, Sol and Luna, masculine and feminine, spirit and matter, the pure and the impure, often has "undesirable results to begin with: it produces poisonous animals such as the dragon, serpent, scorpion, basilisk, and toad" (1963b, ¶172).

Struggling with such creatures is working with the unconscious and with those elements of it that were rejected by spiritual philosophy, but nevertheless are essential to the development of Jung's psychology. As Jung discovered and engaged the symbolic life of the unconscious, he found ouroboric dragons, suffering matter, the peacock's tail, red and green lions, kings and queens, fishes eyes and inverted philosophical trees, salamanders, hermaphrodites, black and white earth, *sol niger*, the black sun, and all of the "chthonic filth" of materiality that had been rejected and fallen into the shadow or that had not yet become conscious. It would be too easy to simply consider these images as psychological and symbolic fantasies that were projected onto the reality of the material world; yet, Jung has demonstrated that the withdrawal of such projections can yield profound insights into our subjectivity. But is there something more to an ouroboric dragon or a philosophical tree that remains unknown and unappreciated?

Typical of Jung's style, he defines a symbol as the best possible expression of an as yet unknown fact, which is "none the less known to exist or is postulated as existing" and "cannot be differently or better expressed" (1971, ¶814). In this definition, the symbol points both to and beyond itself to a mysterious presence/absence, both to the flesh of a visible mystery and to the mystery of an invisible arcane substance. The archetype-in-itself is an unconscious absence not unlike the notion of God or the Philosophers' Stone. Both have multiple divine and symbolic names, but, as Jung points out, just what the philosophers meant by the arcane substance has never been quite clear. In a 1946 letter to Pastor Max Frischknecht, Jung wrote "the concept of the unconscious *posits nothing*, it designates only my *unknowing*" (1973, p. 411). Still, for Jung, we can proceed "as if" we know something by virtue of the filth and flesh of archetypal images, as our best expressions and manifestations of psychic reality, without taking this reality literally in traditional metaphysical terms—either as simply psychological or simply material.

James Hillman, a Jungian analyst, writes:

> The work of soul-making requires corrosive acids and heavy earth, ascending birds; there are sweating kings, dogs, and bitches, stenches, urine, blood .... I know that I am not composed of sulfur and salt, buried in horse dung, putrefying or congealing, turning white or green or yellow, encircled by a tail-biting serpent, rising on wings. And yet I am! I cannot take any of this literally, even if it is all accurate, descriptively true.
>
> (1978: 37 and 39)

Hillman describes the soul, which includes filth, sweat, stench, urine, blood, horse dung, etc., and resists translating these images into psychological (or philosophical) abstractions that leave these images behind. For Hillman, it is not adequate to translate the "White Queen and Red King" into "feminine and masculine principles," "their incestuous sexual intercourse" into "the union of opposites," or "the freakish hermaphrodite and uniped, the golden head," into "paradoxical representations of the goal, examples of androgyny symbols of the Self" (2010, p. 15). For Hillman, keeping the image alive requires the offense and stench, the preservation of the flesh, the vital quality bypassed by spiritual purification where what's the matter with alchemical recipes is that the matter was rejected and thrown out. By refusing to translate images into concepts, Hillman preserves the mysterious, often bizarre and repulsive, but vital quality of psychic reality, resonant with Gerhard Dorn's challenge to "Transform yourself from dead stones into living philosophic stones" (Eliade, 1971, p. 158). Finally, for Hillman it is not a matter simply of image versus concept, a literal move, but of keeping the metaphoric vision of the alchemical imagination alive as it returns the soul to the world.

The self for Jung and soul for Hillman were radical ideas that recognized "the identity of *something* in man [self/soul] with *something* concealed in matter [body/world]" (Jung, 1968, ¶378; emphasis added). In the last chapter of the *Mysterium*, Jung analyzes Dorn's alchemical recipe to achieve the magnum opus, a conjunction which is the goal of the alchemical work. It is an operation that involves the relationship between the mind/spirit unity and soul, body, and world that takes place in stages and begins with the creation of the *unio mentalis*, the union of the soul with the mind, separated from the body and the natural world. The importance of this separation was to "establish a spiritual position supraordinate to the turbulent sphere of the body" (1963b, ¶671) and to create "a state of equanimity transcending the body's affectivity and instinctuality" (1963b, ¶470).

Psychological development requires not being controlled by instincts and/or bodily emotions—but leaving our natural vitality behind cripples life, creates dissociation, can be too pure, too literal, and ultimately a condition that limits the fullness of life. Something more is required, another step, namely, the reintegration of the *unio mentalis* (soul and mind) with the body. This second conjunction is particularly important, since it moves from an intellectual/philosophical and abstract spirituality to a more fully developed existential life.

The question for Jung was: how does this further integration happen? Following Dorn, Jung sees that only part of the process takes place in the "psychological" sphere. The rest of the procedure requires the use of magical substances said to be hidden in the body. Dorn called it the "*caelum*" or "sky stuff," that was to be prepared to serve as a medium for the unification of the *unio mentalis* with the body. It would be a quintessence that would hold together opposites and binaries.

> Beginning with the *caelum*, other ingredients are added to make a robust 'arcane substance' that will hold the body and spirit together in a *coniunctio*..... Jung finds an analogy between this stage of Dorn's *coniunctio* and the creation of the Jungian *self*. The *self* repairs the dissociation that is both individual and collective
>
> (Power, 2017, 46–47)

Dorn describes the ingredients of his alchemical recipe as requiring a mixture of the *caelum* with honey, chelidonia, Mercurialis, rosemary, red lily, and blood. According to Von Franz, the result of Dorn's recipe leads to the secret of the Philosophers' Stone. The stone:

> is identical with the God-image [the self] in the human soul. The whole procedure is like an active imagination performed with symbolically meaningful substances .... The end result is also described as a four-petaled yellow flower, exactly as in the Chinese text of *The Secret of the Golden Flower*. The whole recipe runs: Take the inner truth, add your *elan vital* to it, the inspiration of the Holy Ghost, and the capacity to link opposites. Put into this mixture heavenly and earthly love (sex) and then you have an essence with which you can unite heaven and earth. All ingredients assemble round the four-petaled yellow flower, i.e., the Self.
>
> (1979, pp. 113–114)

These complex ingredients are rich with symbolic resonances which render understandable at the psychological level why they would be valuable in promoting a reunification of body and soul.

In these ingredients, one finds material support for the second conjunction linking the *unio mentalis* to the body. In addition, Jung's amplifications also address the shadow and the archetypal bipolarity of these ingredients that can interfere with, poison, negate, and blacken the *coniunctio*. The process and production of the second *coniunctio* requires careful consideration of the *pharmakon*—both the healing and poisonous dimension of the recipe, whether literal or symbolic.

It is not easy to define the meaning of the *caelum* which, like the Philosophers' Stone, has many names—"the quintessence, the 'philosophical wine,' a 'virtue and heavenly vigor,' ... the 'truth' .... the panacea .... the *imago Dei*," etc. (Jung CW14: ¶681). Jung was able to understand these descriptions in a psychological and symbolic way as images of the self and the individuation process, but he was also aware that "[t]he production of the *caelum*" took place for Dorn as "a symbolic rite performed in the laboratory"—perhaps as an alchemical form of active imagination (Jung CW14: ¶705). How can a philosophical position account for these phenomena?

For Jung, the engagement with this elusive and mercurial *materia* requires unusual concentration, religious fervor, meditation, and imagination. . Using Ruland's definition, Jung describes meditation as "an inner dialogue with someone unseen." (CW12: ¶390) This engagement is not "mere cogitation, but explicitly an inner dialogue and hence a living relationship to the answering voice of the 'other' in ourselves, i.e., of the unconscious." (CW12: ¶390). But, as Jung has described it, the unconscious is not simply "in us." It is as much, and perhaps more, outside us (see CW12: ¶.396). Such ambiguity is captured by Martin Heidegger who noted that the call of conscience summons us. It is a call that "comes from me and yet from beyond me" (1962, 271/316). What is this "outside"? What is this "beyond me"? What are we summoned to? Is there any there there, as they say?

For Paracelsus and Ruland, it is the imagination that sees into the beyond and is an "astrum" or "star in man, the celestial or supercelestial body" (Ruland, quoted in Jung CW12: ¶394), a quintessence which should not be conceived as "immaterial phantoms" which "we readily take fantasy-pictures to be, but as something corporeal, a 'subtle body,' semi-spiritual in nature" (Jung CW12: ¶394). Jung explains the subtle body as

> a hybrid phenomenon ... half spiritual, half physical; .... The *imaginatio* or the act of imagining is thus a physical activity that can be fitted into the cycle of material changes that brings these about and is brought about by them in its turn. In this way the alchemist related himself not only to the unconscious but directly to the very substance which he hoped to transform through the power of imagination. .... Imagination is therefore a concentrated extract of the life forces, both physical and psychic... But, just because of this intermingling of the physical and the psychic, it always remains an obscure point whether the ultimate

transformations in the alchemical process are to be sought more in the material or more in the spiritual realm.

(CW12: ¶394)

The strange middle ground and ambiguity of Jung's psychological/philosophical position received criticism from both sides of the divide between material and spiritual orientations. Actually, for Jung, it was not a question of either-or, but of "an intermediate realm between mind and matter, i.e., a psychic realm of subtle bodies whose characteristic it is to manifest themselves in a mental as well as a material form" (CW12, ¶394).

The symbolic, magical, mythological, and alchemical meanings of the substances are amplified by Jung. Still, Jung is not completely convinced that it is adequate to interpret these ingredients only symbolically or whether and to what extent it is important to acknowledge their literal or magical importance.

Critiques of Jung: idealist and naturalist

The tension between the symbolic and the literal places Jung between two alternative philosophical orientations: idealism and naturalism—and he is criticized from both perspectives. Jungian analyst Pamela Power (2017) is critical of Jung's reading of Dorn's alchemical recipe, arguing that Jung remains too attached to a symbolic understanding and does not go beyond it into thinking proper. She holds that, given Giegerich's notion of absolute negative interiority, all such symbols and substances, images and imagination, must be surpassed, negated, cut through, over and over again. The aim of this would be to achieve a purification approaching a more sophisticated version of the Christian philosophers' view of purity and a homeopathic distillation that leads to a logical level such that "it no longer contains any molecules of … specific ingredients at all" (p. 47). For Giegerich and Power, any trace of a remainder of natural substances in Jung's formulation disqualifies his psychology from becoming the highest expression of the soul's logical life.

Power's description of Giegerich's system of "applying negation after negation, negating highly sensuous ingredients" as parallel to homeopathic remedies is apt (p. 47), but I do not see this level of purification as achieving the potency of Jung's grittier spagyric formulations. "Homeopathic remedies are created by extracting a substance" to such an extent that it leaves only a "vibrational signature of the original material … with none of its physical characteristics. … [This] total annihilation of the substance's physical being is … [the homeopathic character of] Hahnemann's work" (Nilsson, 2006).

Jung's approach is more like Paracelsus' spagyric formulas:

> Paracelsus repeatedly stressed the importance of [not eliminating or surpassing the sensuous reality of materials that still contain] deep color,

intense flavor, and low dosage.... The difference between ... spagyrics and any homeopathics, then, is ... apparent to the ordinary senses.
(Nilsson, 2006)

In a similar manner, it is the presence and importance of the imagistic subtle body and sensate dimension of Jung's work that gives it its healing power.

From a nearly opposite perspective, chemists and natural science historians Lawrence Principe and William Newman (2001) reject Jung's psychological and symbolic understanding of alchemical recipes as not literal enough, noting that all the ingredients, the "alien," "strange," "bizarre" (p. 418), and "outlandish" (p. 417), are not symbolic in Jung's sense, but are rather signs and code names (Decknamen) for ***natural substances*** used by alchemists in the laboratory. For them, there is no need to explain alchemy in any way that exceeds the metaphysical world view of "natural philosophy."

Following the actual notebooks of the alchemist George Starkey (a.k.a. Philalethes), Principe unmasks the seemingly symbolic processes by creating a chemical version in his own laboratory of "'animated' Philosophical Mercury" and its production of a "philosophical egg" out of which, over time and with proper heating, there emerged a glittering and fully formed tree in a laboratory flask (2013, p. 165). For Principe, this was "the 'Tree of Hermes,'" the philosophical tree which for the alchemist would have been "vivid and unquestionable proof that he had found the 'entrance to the palace of the king,' that is, the crucial threshold leading to the Philosophers' Stone" (p. 165). Principe reflects that "[f]or the historian, the reality of this Philosophical Tree indicates unambiguously that at least some of the imagery of chrysopoeia [gold-making, seeking the Philosophers' Stone], bizarre as it might seem, stems from the literal appearance of reacting chemicals" and must be taken literally (p. 165). For Principe, the results of such experiments must have served to encourage the alchemists in pursuit of their goals. Yet, while this discovery is indeed very provocative, it is also interesting that

> Starkey's continued experimentations apparently did not lead to the Philosophers' Stone; otherwise, it is doubtful he would have ended up in debtor's prison. The failure finally to obtain the stone, despite encouraging results such as gold's volatilization or its germination into a glittering tree
>
> (p. 166)

raises for me the question: Why were there so many alchemical failures to produce the Philosophers' Stone? From my perspective, the reason for this is that limiting the philosophical tree to a naturalistic perspective reduces it to a literal, chemical phenomenon. It is interesting to compare Principe's version of the philosophical tree with the way Jung imagined it.

Jung acknowledges "that the adept [can literally see] branches and twigs in the retort" (1967, ¶374). However, for Jung, the tree is an archetypal image with broader-ranging meaning. What Principe did not do in his experiment was what the alchemists advised: to "contemplate [the tree's] growth, that is, to reinforce it with active imagination." According to Jung, for the alchemist Senior, "[t]he vision was the thing to be sought" (1967, ¶374). Recognizing this,

> [h]ermetic philosophy had for its goal an explanation that included the psyche in a total description of nature. The empiricist [e.g., Principe] tries, more or less successfully, to forget his archetypal explanatory principles, that is, the psychic premises that are a *sine qua non* of the cognitive process, or to repress them in the interests of 'scientific objectivity'.
>
> (Jung, 1967, ¶378)

But, for Dorn and Jung, the philosophical tree is far more than the literal chemistry of the flask. It is

> a metaphorical form of the arcane substance, a living thing that comes into existence according to its own laws, and grows, blossoms, and bears fruit like a plant. ... Dorn ... makes a distinction between the 'living things of nature' and those of matter. ... But,

Jung points out, "it is not so clear what the former are meant to be." They don't seem to be

> 'vegetabilia materiae' nor are they found in nature, at least not in nature as we know it, though they may occur in that more comprehensive, Platonic nature as Dorn understood it, that is, in a nature that includes psychic 'animalia,' i.e., mythologems and archetypes
>
> (Jung, 1967, ¶382)

Active imagination and the forging of Jung's psychology of the unconscious

From the beginning, Jung felt that the goal of his psychology was to make a contribution to the science of modern psychology, but a powerful experience of the archetypal psyche led him to enlarge and deepen the course of his work. Jung writes:

> But then, I hit upon this stream of lava, and the heat of its fires reshaped my life. That was the primal stuff which compelled me to work upon it, and my works are a more or less successful endeavor to incorporate this incandescent matter into the contemporary picture of the world.
>
> (1963a, ¶199)

It is this experience of psyche that opened Jung to a vision of reality beyond the natural science of his day. Jung's dreams and active imagination helped him move beyond fantasy to psychic reality and to the signature of things, to an embodiment not simply logical (Giegerich) or literal (Principe), but mysterious and hard to define. For Jung, the imaginal is not simply a mental process, but also a subtle body, corporeal yet semi-spiritual, not unlike the alchemist's idea of Mercurius: it is said "sometimes Mercurius is a substance like quicksilver, sometimes it is a philosophy" (1959, ¶240). Mercurius is both "material and spiritual" and "the process by which the lower material is transformed into the higher and spiritual, and vice versa" (1967, ¶284). Likewise, active imagination is a mercurial process, an embodiment of imaginal life incarnating the spiritual and psychizing nature.

Active imagination

Typically in active imagination, it is of value to begin with a dream, an event, a memory, or a fantasy, and to fix it in writing, painting, sculpture; then to engage with its embodiment, honoring it, dreaming it onward, imagining it forward, dialoguing with it, etc. Over the years of working with this process, I have found it of value to help patients expand the process in such a way as to suggest the value of pursuing memories, dreams, and images by enactments, an acting in and out that sometimes leads beyond typical ways of getting at what the psyche presents—not unlike enacting magical rituals or practicing alchemical recipes in a laboratory. Such enactments often lead to a deepened and expanded sense of a psychic experience and to moments of mythical and magical realism that set the stage for synchronistic occurrences which can open to a world beyond our everyday experience.

The following active imagination is of a patient who had many losses and an extremely difficult family life. He was in a marriage that was not working. His inner life was an intense struggle and one might alchemically characterize his life as being in a state of *nigredo*, of blackness and burnout. He is highly intelligent and a person who has worked with his dreams, active imagination, and magical enactments that have helped to activate a deep psychic process. He later reported a vision of entering into a space where the earth is pitch black, burnt, and crusted, like volcanic rock and ash. He is looking at the landscape when he observes a movement of the earth taking shape in the contour of the voluptuous body of a woman who emerges from the blackened ground. Her skin is extremely dark and smooth. He wants to get to know this woman better. Engaging her is hot—pools of lava, melting everything, flowing in circular patterns. He sees her torso and breasts (Figure 11.1).

She's heating up from inside out. Her black skin glows red beneath the surface. She has an animal ally standing with her, a large, hooded falcon. When the hood is removed, the falcon looks directly at him. He holds out his hand with a gift offering—a mirrored stone, silver and shiny, like a drop

Figure 11.1 Pele, Goddess of Fire. (Courtesy of the Illustrator: Kim Herbst.)

of mercury reflecting light. The falcon extends its wings and claws, grabbing the mirrored stone, and in a flash of light the stone becomes an egg brightly glowing. Intricate, iridescent triangles appear in the egg, overlapping in a complex design, some kind of code—like DNA. The triangular lines are made of beads of light strung together— cellular. My patient reaches inside the egg with two fingers and a thumb—something grips him (Figure 11.2).

Pulling out a long snake or eel, he shakes it off, violently waving his arms—terrified! The creature lets loose but moves toward him, mouth open. Frightened, he evades contact and it moves away over his shoulder. He reaches into the egg once again—a glowing human skull emerges terrifying him. He now recognizes that what he is doing is dangerous and he needs to protect himself. Carefully, reaching down again, he pulls out a handful of

Figure 11.2 The philosophical egg. From Codex Palatinus Latinus (15th c.) Shelf-mark: Pal.lat.412.- p.85v Author/s: Graf, Agnes, Title: Hildegard von Bingen bei Winand von Steeg, Adams colluctantium aquilar Volume/Year: 61–83*, tavv. XI–XII, XIV–XV, XVII–XVIII. ©2020 Biblioteca Apostolica Vaticana. Reproduced by permission of Biblioteca Apostolica Vaticana, with all rights reserved.

orange powder. He rubs his hands together. The substance coats his palms like chalk. He holds his hands up to the sky and the cosmos attaches to them like gloves made of purple, black, and glittering light. No longer apprehensive, he experiments, pressing his hands together and pulling them apart, creating an energy field between them. He is able to manifest forms, but cannot control what he manifests. He can only choose how to interact with what emerges. He takes a breath and reaches down inside the egg once more—a large beam of light begins to grow into the form of a pillar, arrow-like, erect, pointing toward the sky. He feels an affinity with this energy and good about interacting with it. As this happens, he looks down in the midst of the blackened earth, volcanic rocks, and ash. He is surprised to see very green plants and grasses growing. The air becomes humid, but only around the pillar. It's like a rainforest drizzle. Branches begin to grow out of the pillar of light that is now also a tree—a single, verdant light-filled growth on the blackened earth.

The emergence of moisture, rainforest air, humidity,[3] the growth of a tree of light in the midst of rocks and ashes, is a painful and transformative image that spurred a further active imagination with the intent to nourish and care for the tree, which is now glowing brightly with yellow-white light. As he walks toward it, he feels the warmth of the volcanic landscape underneath his bare feet. As he approaches the tree, he sees that the branches have grown and are now full and golden. They look almost like neurons. From a distance, the full branches on the tree look like a large, radiant brain, glowing filaments of life. In a final moment, my patient realizes that the tree is sentient, fleshy. He looks at it and it looks back at him. Its eyes are deep and very ancient. The tree is a living presence and he wants to talk to it and share his pain, and he begins to cry. The sparks of light gather together in a swarm and congeal into an image of his son illuminated in the trunk of the tree. He feels overjoyed and embraces his child. He feels complete.

While I will not elaborate all the personal meanings and development of my patient's process, it is interesting to revisit some of the archetypal images and moments that emerged in the process: the blackened earth of hardened lava, the ash; the energizing volcano goddess, the shine of darkness itself, the incandescent lava fires and crystal stone, the mirror and mercury flashes and sparks of light, the gift, the transformation from bird to egg, the emergence of a poisonous snake or an eel as electrifying irruptions he tries to shake off. He came to see the glowing skull as the light and illumination that comes from death, and beyond it there is a starry cosmos, the sky stuff like the *caelum*, the towering phallus and the philosophical tree, the blessed greenness, moisture, humidity, and growth in the most burnt and dried out ground of the soul. It is a tree that continues to glow and grow full and golden. It is sentient or super-sentient. It looks back and is a living presence that hears and reaches out to the patient. The fertile waters are also tears that soften and smooth. It mirrors his inner and outer child in sparks of light and heals his wounds, opens his heart and senses, leaving him feeling complete.

In this active imagination, there is a profound transformation from the deep *nigredo*, the filth and the dirt of the blackened earth, to a vital renewal symbolized by the growth of an archetypal and philosophical tree of life and light. It is interesting to compare the notions of the philosophical tree created by the chemist Principe in the context of natural scientific philosophy and the ones elaborated by the dreams and active imaginations of my patient, the alchemists, and Jung. For all of them except Principe, the tree requires the "true imagination"[4] of the alchemists if the tree is to flower as a philosophical tree—an illuminated tree of light (Figure 11.3).

Figure 11.3 Illuminated tree. (Courtesy of the artist: Demetrio Garcia Aguilar.)

In an archetypal image of the philosophical tree as reported by Jung in *Memories, Dreams, Reflections*, in his now famous Liverpool dream, Jung reports finding himself in Liverpool, "in a dirty, sooty city" (1963a, p. 197). He was walking

> through the dark streets. ... The various quarters of the city were arranged radially around the square. In the center was a round pool, and in the middle of it a small island. While everything round about was obscured by rain, fog, smoke and dimly lit darkness, the little island blazed with sunlight. On it stood a single tree, a magnolia, in a shower of reddish blossoms. It was as though the tree stood in the sunlight and were at the same time the source of light. My companions commented on the abominable weather, and obviously did not see the tree. They spoke of another Swiss who was living in Liverpool, and expressed surprise that he should have settled here. I was carried away by the beauty of the flowering tree and the sunlit island, and thought, "I know very well why he settled here." Then I awoke.
>
> (p. 198)

Jung comments:

> The dream represented my situation at the time. I can still see the grayish-yellow raincoats, glistening with the wetness of the rain. Everything was extremely unpleasant, black and opaque—just as I felt then. But I had had a vision of unearthly beauty, and that was why I was able to live at all. Liverpool is the "pool of life." The "liver," according to an old view, is the seat of life—that which "makes to live."
>
> This dream brought with it a sense of finality. I saw that here the goal had been revealed. One could not go beyond the center. The center is the goal, and everything is directed toward that center. Through this dream I understood that the self is the principle and archetype of orientation and meaning. Therein lies its healing function.
>
> (1963a, 198–199)

A final question remains about the nature of the subtle body and the images of active imagination. In the alchemical sense, this was a mixture of psyche, soul, body, and what the alchemists considered to be matter and the nature of the world. However, at one point, Jung suggested that what the alchemists projected onto matter had nothing to do with matter as we know it today. What can the crazy images of the psyche have to do with our knowledge of scientific reality?

Unus mundus as a philosophy of the integration of self and world in Jung's psychology

Jungian analyst Gary Sparks (2007) gives an example of the importance of heeding dreams, images, and emotions for scientific discovery. He elaborates the discovery of the benzene ring by Kekulé who demonstrated how dreams helped him to develop insights into the structure of matter. Kekulé shows how in his dream vision, a snake seized hold of its own tail, leading him to have an intuition about the scientific structure of the benzene ring. The snake biting its own tail is an archetypal symbol of the ouroboros of the Greek alchemists, "one of the central, recurring symbols representing the structure of the psyche" (p. 81).[5]

> In the case of Kekulé we can clearly see the relation between an archetypal image and the form in which matter is constructed, an example of the psychoid dimension of the archetype that [Wolfgang] Pauli [the world-renowned physicist] felt could be constructively applied to our understanding of how scientific creativity works—in the way both outer matter and inner psychology overlap. The archetype pertains to both psyche and matter and is what allows the former to see into the structure of the latter. Thus, Pauli was keenly interested in the influence of archetypal images on the development of science.
>
> In conclusion, the hypothesis of the psychoid archetype spoke to both Jung and Pauli with respect to the parallel structures of matter and psyche. Both saw that continued research in their respective fields might shed light on the psychoid archetype.
>
> (Sparks, 2007, p. 81)

It is provocative to imagine what other archetypal images, "dragons of the mind," may lead to discoveries of material reality as yet unknown. The movement from the ouroboros to the benzene ring is a one-way direction, but all forms of matter also contain denizens of the deep that are unknown aspects of the psyche waiting to be discovered, a chemistry of the depths, an alchemy of the soul beyond our laboratory products. The play between psyche and matter is itself ouroboric, and awaits a new alchemical recipe, a psychoanalysis, and a philosophy that can do justice to the circular movement of the soul. Such a connection between the soul and material reality was also part of the vision of Dorn's third *coniunctio* "in [which the] conjunction [of] the combined spirit-soul-body now merges with the universal ground of being" (Mather, 2014, p. 163). Matthew Mather (2014) points out that this union with the *unus mundus* is described by Jung as the *mysterium coniunctionis*.

The perplexity of this psychoid union was important to both Jung and Pauli, each of whom took up the question from his own perspective. Pauli continued to seek for a rational, scientific explanation, as Jung did, but Jung's perspective was always enlarged by his discovery of the archetypal layers of the psyche, which played an essential role in his conception of reality. The philosophical issue of psychoid reality has also been considered by Mills (2014) in his development of a psychoanalytic metaphysics. I believe Mills is on the right track by insisting on the importance of philosophy as essential in improving our understanding of Jungian psychology. For me, philosophy is an important part of the mix, which can add more clarity to our understanding of Jung's ideas and the forging of his psychology.

If we are to consider Jung a philosopher, it is as an alchemical and philosophical doctor of the soul—Paracelcian and spagyric, intent on coming to terms with the unconscious and with saving the phenomena. As a thinker, Jung allowed himself to be shaped by volcanic, incandescent fires and their lava, and by illuminated, philosophical trees of light found in the midst of darkness and soot. For Jung, psyche's serpentine and ouroboric revelations spoke to the depths of reality, both visible and invisible, intertwined in a chiasm,[6] and manifested in the flesh of images and symbols. As a philosopher of psychic depths, Jung was led by these images to resist static formulations and to develop a philosophical and creative way of thinking that requires doing justice to what he called "the protean mythologem and the shimmering symbol" (Jung, 1967, ¶199)—with the recognition that filth and images are not left behind.

Notes

1 Basilisks are mythical creatures often related to lizards and are considered kings of the serpents. They are feared because of their power to cause death with a single glance.
2 For a fuller discussion of these points, see Marlan, 2006, p. 270. Also published in this volume as Chapter 1.
3 "For the alchemists the prima materia was the *humidum* radicule (radical moisture), the water, the *spiritus aquae*, and *vapor terrae*; it was also called the 'soul' of the substances, the *sperma mundi*, Adam's tree of paradise with its many flowers, which grows on the sea" (Jung, 1967, ¶173).
4 "True imagination" is a term the alchemists used as having to do with the intimate connection between psyche and matter. "Jung understood 'true imagination' as the creation and evocation of images which have a life of their own and which develop according to their own logic ... [and] which grasps inner facts and portrays them in images true to their nature" (Salman, 2006, p. 176).
5 The question whether the relationship of archetypal images and the structure of matter is genuine in Kekulé's case has been raised by the chemist John Wotiz, who accused Kekulé of fabricating his dream interpretation in order to obscure the fact that others had discovered the structure of the benzene ring before he did. What Wotiz doesn't consider is the possibility that Kekulé's account is true and that it is also the case that there were earlier renditions of the structure of the benzene ring. His view that Kekulé simply lied is an assumption for which I have not seen any conclusive evidence (Browne, 1988).
6 Chiasm and flesh refer to Maurice Merleau-Ponty's *The Visible and the Invisible*.

References

Browne, M.W. (1988). The benzene ring: Dream analysis. *The New York Times*. Retrieved from http://www.nytimes.com/1988/08/16/science/the-benzene-ring-dream-analysis.html.

Eliade, M. (1971). *Forge and crucible: Origins and structures of alchemy.* New York: Harper & Row.
Heidegger, M. (1962). *Being and time.* (J. Macquarrie & E. Robinson, Trans.) New York: Harper & Row.
Hillman, J. (1978). The therapeutic value of alchemical language. In R. Sardello (Ed.), *Dragonflies: Studies of Imaginal Psychology*, Vol. 1(1). Irving, TX: University of Dallas.
Hillman, J. (2010). *Alchemical psychology*, Uniform edition of the writings of James Hillman (Vol. 5). Putnam, CT: Spring Publications.
Jung, C.G. (1959). *Aion,* The collected works of C.G. Jung (Vol. 9ii). G. Adler (Ed.). R.F.C. Hull (Trans.). Princeton, NJ: Princeton University Press.
Jung, C.G. (1963a). *Memories, Dreams, Reflections.* A. Jaffé (Recorder & Ed.). R.C. Winston (Trans.). New York: Pantheon.
Jung, C.G. (1963b). *Mysterium Coniunctionis,* The collected works of C.G. Jung (Vol. 14). G. Adler (Ed.). R.F.C. Hull (Trans.). Princeton, NJ: Princeton University Press.
Jung, C.G. (1967). *Alchemical studies,* The collected works of C.G. Jung (Vol. 13). G. Adler (Ed.). R.F.C. Hull (Trans.). Princeton, NJ: Princeton University Press.
Jung, C.G. (1968). *Psychology and alchemy,* The collected works of C.G. Jung (Vol. 12). G. Adler (Ed.). R.F.C. Hull (Trans.). Princeton, NJ: Princeton University Press.
Jung, C.G. (1971). *Psychological types,* The collected works of C.G. Jung (Vol. 6). G. Adler (Ed.). R.F.C. Hull (Trans.). Princeton, NJ: Princeton University Press.
Jung, C.G. (1973). Letter to Pastor Max Frischknecht. In G. Adler (Ed.) in collaboration with A. Jaffe. R.F.C. Hull (Trans.), *C.G. Jung: Letters, Vol. I: 1906–1950.* Princeton, NJ: Princeton University Press, pp. 408–412.
Jung, C.G. (1977). *C.G. Jung speaking: Interviews and encounters.* W. McGuire & R.F.C. Hull (Eds.). Princeton, NJ: Princeton University Press.
Marlan, S. (2006). Alchemy. In R. Papadopolous (Ed.), *The handbook of Jungian psychology: Theory, practice and applications.* London: Routledge, pp. 263–295.
Mather, M. (2014). *The alchemical Mercurius: Esoteric symbol of Jung's life and works.* New York: Routledge.
Merleau-Ponty, M. (1969). *The visible and the invisible.* Evanston, IL: Northwestern University Press, 1969.
Mills, J. (2014). "Jung as philosopher: Archetypes, the psychoid factor, and the question of the supernatural." *International Journal of Jungian Studies,* 6(3): 227–242. DOI: 10.1080/19409052.2014.921226.
Nilsson, M. (2006). "Spagyrical homeopathy." *Alchemy Journal,* 7(1). Retrieved from https://www.alchemylab.com/AJ7-l.htm#Spagyrical_Homeopathy.
Power, P. (2017). 'The psychological difference' in Jung's Mysterium Coniunctionis. In J.M. Sandoval & J.C. Knapp (Eds.), *Psychology of as the discipline of interiority: "The psychological difference" in the work of Wolfgang Giegerich.* London: Routledge, pp. 43–54.
Principe, L. (2013). *The secrets of alchemy.* Chicago, IL: University of Chicago Press.
Principe, L. & Newman, W. (2001). Some problems with the historiography of alchemy. In W.R. Newman & A. Grafton (Eds.), *Secrets of nature: Astrology and alchemy in early modern Europe.* Cambridge, MA: MIT Press, pp. 385–431.

Sparks, G.J. (2007). *At the heart of matter: Synchronicity and Jung's spiritual testament.* Toronto: Inner City Books.

Von Franz, M.-L. (1979). *Alchemical active imagination.* Dallas, TX: Spring.

Von Franz, M.-L. (2006). Psychological commentary. In Muhammad Ibn Umail & T. Abt (Eds.) *Corpus alchemicum arabicum: Book of the explanation of the symbols, kitāb hall ar-rumūz.* Zurich: Living Human Heritage Publications.

Chapter 12

The Philosophers' Stone as chaosmos

The Self and the dilemma of diversity

The Philosophers' Stone was considered to be the ultimate achievement of the "Great Work" of alchemy and the elusive goal of alchemical transformation. The Philosophers' Stone has been described in numerous ancient manuscripts, and in many recipes, with considerable disagreement about its nature and its appearance, as well as how it was to be discovered or made. These disagreements have followed the Stone throughout its history and into its transformation to its psychic equivalent: the Self of contemporary Jungian analysis.

Both the Stone and the Self continue to be difficult notions to understand. Warren Colman notes that Jung's thinking about the Self is "full of complexities, paradoxes and uncertainties" (2000, 4). Roger Brooke has described Jung's concept of the Self as an "enigmatic complexity" (2009, 601). Lyndy Abraham calls the Stone the "arcanum of all arcana" (1998, 145), and, in *Psychology and Alchemy*, Jung writes: "What the old philosophers meant by the *lapis* has never become quite clear" (1953/1968, CW12, ¶555). Although the Stone was often identified with the *unus mundus*—the principle of the one world—it has also been known by a variety of names, many of which were collected by William Gratacolle in his "Names of the Philosophers' Stone," from the 1651–1652 publication, *Five Treatises of the Philosophers' Stone*. Among the names of the Stone, we find it referred to as "Chaos, a Dragon, a Serpent, a Toad, the green Lion, the quintessence, our Stone Lunare, Camelion, … blacker than black, … radicall humidity, unctuous moysture, … urine, poyson, water of wise men …." and the list goes on, disseminating into a continuing complexity of images. (67)

Complexio oppositorum

Seeing the Stone as both *unus mundus* and a multiplicity is an aspect of the paradox Jung calls a *complexio oppositorum* (1950/1968, CW9i, ¶555), which is an attempt to render a description of what appears as incompatible dimensions of the Stone and one of alchemy's great mysteries. Jung writes: "In order to attain this union, [the alchemists] tried not only to visualize the opposites together but to express them in the same breath" (1955–56/1970, CW14, ¶36). *Hierosgamos*, sacred marriage, chemical wedding, *filius philosophorum*, *Mercurius duplex*, *mysterium coniunctionis*, Anthropos, Abraxis, Adam Kadmon, *coniunctio, lapis philosophorum*, and so on were Jung's attempts to render complexity and multiplicity in a single gesture. To this list, I would like to add the term *chaosmos*, which was used by James Joyce to describe the structure of his book *Finnegan's Wake* and is a term that brings together chaos and cosmos, unity and multiplicity. *Finnegan's Wake* has been called Joyce's "Philosophers' Stone" (DiBernard 1980, 8), and I contend that the notion of chaosmos applies equally well to his other major work, *Ulysses*. In both works, separation and synthesis are oddly expressed together, in one breath, as it were.

Mysterium Coniunctionis

In *Mysterium Coniunctionis*, Jung gives his late life account of grappling with these complexities. The subtitle of his book, "An Inquiry into the Separation and Synthesis of Psychic Opposites in Alchemy," prefigures the focus of this work. Jung opens the book with "[t]he factors which come together in the coniunctio are conceived as opposites, either confronting one another in enmity or attracting one another in love" (1955–56/1970, CW14, ¶1). It has been traditional to treat Jung as privileging love over enmity, synthesis over separation, convergence over divergence, and to see him as unifying diversity into oneness, chaos into cosmos, and suffering into healing and wholeness. As Jung states, "the desperately evasive and universal Mercurius—that Proteus twinkling in a myriad shapes and colours—is none other than the 'unus mundus,' the original, non-differentiated unity of the world or of Being" (¶660) or its "equivalent," the Philosophers' Stone (¶661). Jung spent a good part of his later life attempting to describe this goal of psychic life, but, despite all his efforts, the *coniunctio* remains anything but a simple unity. The entire *Mysterium Coniunctionis* testifies to the complexity of Jung's vision. What remains clear is that the unification of opposites requires continuing investigation. Despite all of Jung's attempts to see beyond the opposites and the plurality of psychic life, he recognized that the idea of unity and the *unus mundus* remain a "metaphysical speculation" (¶660). Elsewhere, he observed that, while the tensions between psychic pairs of opposites "ease off" over time, "the united personality will never quite lose the painful sense of innate discord. Complete redemption from the sufferings of this world is and must remain an illusion" (1946/1966, CW16, ¶400).

The forces at work, according to the *Mysterium*, are enmity and love, and it is important to realize that these "energies" are more than personal. They are archetypal phenomena that do not simply give up their force. Love and hate continue to be generators of psychic processes, and they spur ongoing tensions and remain active in some form, even when relaxed and refined in the production of the lapis. The lapis can then be seen to be as much a multiplicity as a unity. The symbols that attempt to capture what Edinger called "a transcendent, miraculous substance" are multiple, wide-ranging, and diverse, and as much harmonious as dissonant (1985, 9).

Jung's struggle with unity and multiplicity had a historical and archetypal background. From the Presocratics to the postmoderns, in the philosophies of the East and West, the perennial problems of unity and diversity, the one and the many of monism and pluralism, continue to challenge us to this day.

Mercurius

Jung proposed a solution to the perennial problem of unity and multiplicity in the figure of Mercurius, who lies between opposites and is the means of bringing them together. As the mercurial body that bridges the divide, he was called a "mediator" (1943/1948/1968, CW13, ¶283). Mercurius links heaven and earth and, as such, is both "prima materia" and "ultima materia" (¶282)—and, therefore, called "lapis" (¶283) and "the stone" (¶282), as the great principle of unification. But Jung was also aware that this unity was subject to a deconstruction and a division. He notes that Mercurius "is named a unity in spite of the fact that his innumerable inner contradictions can dramatically fly apart into equal numbers of disparate and apparently independent figures" (¶284).

Ulysses

Jung's most formal and comprehensive attempt to deal with this dilemma of diversity was in *Mysterium Coniunctionis*; however, in his reflections on James Joyce's *Ulysses* (1932/1966, CW15, ¶163–203), we get an intimate view of Jung's personal struggle to confront the problem of chaos and multiplicity. His reading and critique of Joyce are open, vulnerable, passionate, and self-revealing, and for this reason, it is particularly instructive in a way not unlike reading his *Red Book*. In "'Ulysses': A Monologue," Jung's premodern assumptions find themselves in crisis. His passionate attempt to wrest a unified meaning from the book—a text that appears to resist all such attempts—is frustrated as he walks a tightrope between his premodern sensibilities and his developing modernism. Jung writes that *Ulysses* "reflects life's ten thousand facets and their hundred thousand gradations of colour." He complains that, in his reading of Joyce's "seven-hundred and thirty-five pages," there is "not a single blessed island where the long-suffering reader may come to rest; no place where he can seat himself." Jung, as the long-suffering reader, finds the process so "unbearably tense" that he reaches the "bursting point" (¶164). As he describes in another context:

"The individual's specious unity ... breaks down under the impact of the unconscious" (1946/1966, CW16, ¶399). For Jung, this implies going under, a descent into the unconscious and a deconstruction, a *solutio* of a unity that could not hold. In such a process, the center is displaced, deferred, and, for Jung, the experience was hellish.

Jung's reading of *Ulysses* reminded him of his uncle, whom he described in contrast to Joyce as "always to the point" (1932/1966, CW15, ¶165). He recalls his uncle asking: "Do you know how the devil tortures the souls in hell?" And answering, his uncle says: "He keeps them waiting." For Jung, this is the hell of *Ulysses:* the interminable, endless, and ongoing deferral of graspable meaning, which he took as a maddening defeat of his intelligence. Jung confesses his prejudice: "I am naïve enough to suppose that a book wants to tell me something, to be understood—a sad case," he says, mocking himself, "of mythological anthropomorphism projected on to the book!" (¶167). Jung believes that a book must represent something, but he suspects "that Joyce did not wish to 'represent' anything." Here, Jung's premodern temperament meets a postmodernist insult. What felt to him like his uncle's idea of the devil left him not only impatient, but also without hope of understanding. This was a defeat for Jung's ego, and, initially, without any trace or appearance of a compensatory self or vision of mandala-like salvation, it left him with only deferral and the void. Jung's honesty and self-exposure give us a look at the condition of the soul of a "modern man" at the edge of postmodern plurality, multiplicity, and chaos—an alchemical *solutio* of the kingship of the conscious ego.

In contrast to Jung's experience, it is instructive to consider the sensibilities of Jacques Derrida, whose philosophy is one of continuing deferral and whose view of "the book" articulates a post-structural sensibility. For Derrida, a book with its beginning, middle, and end, front and back covers, its first and last pages, its vision of completion, wholeness, and closure, reflects the logocentrism of our Western philosophical tradition. Derrida, like Joyce, turns the tables on this search for unity and a singular vision of the world. He seems to have overcome what, for Jung, was a self-confessed "naïveté" and mythological anthropomorphism by withdrawing any projection that a book wants to tell us something. For Derrida, the era of the book is "approaching ... its own *exhaustion*" and its end is a serious assault on logocentric thinking (Derrida 1976/1997, 8).

Tired and treading the waters of *solutio*, Jung writes sardonically: "In its destruction of the criteria of beauty and meaning that have held until today, *Ulysses* accomplishes wonders. It insults all our conventional feelings, it brutally disappoints our expectations of sense and content, it thumbs its nose at all synthesis" (1932/1966, CW15, ¶177). And he later notes, "... the shattering thing about *Ulysses* is that behind the thousand veils nothing lies hidden; it turns neither to the world nor to the spirit but, cold as the moon looking on from cosmic space, leaves the comedy of genesis and decay to pursue its course" (¶186). One might imagine implicitly that Jung, in his concept of the Self, anticipated a postmodern sensibility and that the dynamism of the Self is akin to the dynamism of deconstruction.

The turning

One could as well summon *Sol niger* as the moon in recognition of what, for Jung, amounts to a toppling of "the old ideals" (1932/1966, CW15, ¶178) and the "shaking off a world that has become obsolete" (¶179). This is a moment of turning, a moment that echoes in the work of Nietzsche, Freud, Derrida, and others who turn our attention away from our premodernist convictions and hopes and into the stark realities of what Jung calls "a *Mahabharata* of the world's futility and squalor" (¶194). He quotes Joyce: "From drains, clefts, cesspools, middens arise on all sides stagnant fumes." And yet, astonishingly, Jung turns to see something of value in what he now calls Joyce's "creative destruction" (¶180). "It seems to me now that all that is negative in Joyce's work, all that is cold-blooded, bizarre and banal, grotesque and devilish, is a positive virtue for which it deserves praise" (¶194).

Perhaps this recognition, the importance of exposing shadows, is the dark sparkle in Jung's eye that allows him to link Joyce's just-so story to the Hindu notion of *Tat tvam asi*—"That art Thou"—the Self that is just what it is and is also the thousand things of life. Jung notes that whenever he reads *Ulysses*, what comes to mind is the image of a yogi (or alchemist) from the Chinese picture published by Richard Wilhelm. This picture images the movement from ego to Self and represents a vision of the ultimate goal of Eastern alchemy.

If it were not for my respect for Jung's psychic integrity, I might wonder, from an analytic perspective, if Jung was not simply caught up in a massive compensatory reaction and virtual *enantiodromia* as he waxes enthusiastic about *Ulysses* and states that what Joyce has achieved is "what a Jesus or a Buddha achieved, and what Faust also strove for—the overcoming of a fool's world, liberation from the opposites" (1932/1966, CW15, ¶191) and the appearance of the Self. But just what does Jung mean by Self in this context? The Self is, oddly, not only Christ, but also an Antichrist. This heretical vision is, for Jung, not only a Christian one, but also "a Buddhist, Shivaist and a Gnostic" one (¶195).

Quoting from Joyce's mantra-like, playful, and devilish chant of voice and image, Jung links the highest with the lowest, in deadly serious humor: "… White yoghin of the Gods. Occult pimander of Hermes Trismegistos. …. Shakti, Shiva! … Aum! Baum Pyjaum! I am the light of the homestead, I am the dreamery creamery butter" (1932/1966, CW15, ¶195).

As above, so below

In this melding of sacred and profane, of divine humor and joke, Jung sees with Joyce that spirit is intimately linked to the playful and vulgar dimensions of life. In this alchemy, he notes that, "Old Hermes, father of all heretical bypaths, is right: 'As above so below.'" If the linking of heaven and earth can be said to transcend the opposites, it is not in any kind of transcendental purity beyond the world, but rather in the midst of things—in a oneness that is not a oneness, in a multiplicity that is not simply multiple. For Jung, Joyce's perspective provokes a vision of "a hundred-eyed Argus," a demiurge that "has thought up ... a world and an anti-world, filling them with objects without which [one] could not be conscious ...." (1932/1966, CW15, ¶197).

Jung imagines a view of the Self as "a being who is not a mere colourless conglomerate soul composed of an indefinite number of ill-assorted and antagonistic individual souls, but consists also of houses, street-processions, churches, ... several brothels, and a crumpled note on the way to the sea— and yet possesses a perceiving and registering consciousness!" (1932/1966, CW15, ¶198). In short, what seems to express the transcendence of opposites is a world just as it is, conscious of itself in nuance and complexity as a living being in a way that reminds one of Hillman's calls to return soul to the world. Like Jung, Hillman finds it particularly strange how personal life reflects the objective psyche. It is a "me-ness that is simply thatness" (Hillman 1993, 252)—a deeply subjective expression that is also an objectivity.

Hillman likewise describes the Stone in a spirit not unlike Joyce's and Jung's: "All that other people are and the world is, from rivers and elephants to ashtrays and toasters is essentially what I call 'me' as part of an ensouled *anima mundi* and yet utterly depersonalized ...." (1993, 252). And yet what a strange vision of Self! In these, at times, infernal and sacrilegious chants of psychology, literature, and life, we find a variegated multiple world, rich beyond any organizing principle of the ego, a Self who is a dark father and demiurge, a hundred-eyed Argus, and so, for Jung, "a monstrosity [that] drives one to speculation" (1932/1966, CW15, ¶198).

One might ask: what kind of alembic is necessary to distill this new vision of consciousness? Toward the end of Jung's essay on *Ulysses*, he imagines a distilling vessel, "eighteen alchemical alembics piled on top of one another, where amid acids, poisonous fumes, and fire and ice, the homunculus of a new, universal consciousness is distilled!" (1932/1966, CW15, ¶201).

Alchemy is an art of multiple, careful distillations and tinctures, and the continuing refinement of the play between unifications and differentiations, all of which yield subtle nonessentialist essences and soft rather than hard lines of demarcation, like the Philosophers' Stone itself. As an alchemical book, *Ulysses* is different from the hard-edged book that Derrida claims is at an end. By being flexible, like wax or soft gold, *Ulysses* as an image of the Philosophers' Stone defeats logocentrism. If the distillation of this new consciousness can be said to reflect the Self and the Stone, or if the Stone and the Self reflect this new consciousness, perhaps we can also imagine that, when it does so mythically and religiously, it parallels images such as Christ, Buddha, Atman-Brahman, and the multi-eyed Argus. But when this new consciousness is seen through the scintillae of these multiple eyes, the demiurgic creativity is expressed in the multiplicity and free play of life as it is in its everydayness. However, when this play is frozen into one or the other of the opposites, it produces a one-sided vision requiring yet another tincture. Unity becomes a Cyclops, and multiplicity, a hundred-eyed Argus. Both are monsters. My intention here is to emphasize that unity and multiplicity are both legitimate aspects of the Self, but when they are imagined as simple opposites, the complexity of the Self is lost.

The Cyclops sacrifices heterogeneity, and the hundred-eyed Argus lacks integral unity.[1] Rather, one might imagine this everydayness, this flow of life, like a Heraclitian river, or moving like the Tao of Lao Tse and playful like the Lila of the Hindu sages. It also might be seen as a "paradoxical co-incidence of order and disorder, cosmos and chaos" (Kuberski 1994, 3), a "quantum weirdness" (2), or chaosmos of the natural world—anything but the static frozenness of categories and fixed meaning.

Perhaps then we can add the notion of chaosmos to the effort to express what Jung was after when speaking of the *complexio oppositorum*. Its further exploration can add contemporary nuance to our mercurial understanding of just what we mean by the unity of opposites, which is never a simple unity or stable presence but rather a "dynamic hybridity" (Evans 2009, 28), a unity that does not require that differences subordinate themselves to a unifying principle. Such a unity "affirms the very heterogeneity that would appear to dissolve it" (4). As such, it is a unity in continuing self-deconstruction and so, an errant fugitive that maddeningly continues to escape our grasp while teasing us into conjunctions.

After grappling with Joyce's *Ulysses*, Jung became aware that at the core of the Self, beyond a defeat for the ego, there was a process of ongoing deconstruction so destabilizing that even the constellation of the Self was no stable island where the soul could shield itself from falling apart, from multiplicity, from its own shadow. I believe that at the end of his essay on *Ulysses*, Jung retreats from this recognition to a surprising but secure vision of Homer's Penelope rather than staying with Joyce's Molly Bloom, Penelope's contemporary counterpart and shadow. Jung briefly quotes from Molly's famous soliloquy, but in ending quickly turns to a vision of Ulysses returned home with Penelope—and in this *coniunctio*, Jung finds, at the end, what he could not find at the beginning. Penelope no longer has to weave her never-ending garment but can "take her ease in the gardens of the earth" and with her Jung can rest his soul and reflect on "[a] world [that] has passed away and is made new" (1932/1966, CW15, ¶202).

At this point, we have an image of Ulysses, home at last, a reunion of king and queen, male and female, an alchemical *coniunctio*, leading to peace, rest, and reflection. Here, Jung envisions a world observed from a distance, as if from some "window of eternity" or behind the walls of a "golden fortified castle." One gets a sense of an observer, removed and protected from the ravages of time, space, and change. In this vision, Jung finds comfort, situated "somewhere beyond the cosmic illusion woven by Maya ...." (Eliade 1970, 3). Now Penelope has no need to continue weaving the illusion of doing and undoing, of never-ending deferral to put off those suitors who desire to possess the queen, in absence or death of the old king. Weaving the shroud of Laertes has served its purpose of delay and treachery.

With the return of Ulysses, the kingdom is preserved, set right, stabilized, and renewed. The death and change of the old structure are halted. One might wonder about the meaning of this image that stabilized Jung at the end of his Ulysses-like journey of reading Joyce's epic novel. This vision of the *coniunctio* indicates the constellation of the Self, part of whose function is to compensate for feelings of fragmentation and destabilization and to bring order to chaos.

I characterized this vision as a defense against chaos, but it is also a genuine, if temporary, achievement. In this transcendental vision, Jung achieves a sage-like perspective—an untouched witness to the ordinary flow of life—but it is also a perspective that transfers something of itself to the empirical ego. Although the Self is understood as a transcendental archetype, when it constellates and is related to by the empirical person, the ego takes on some of the characteristics of the Self. Jung does not equate himself with the archetype, but its effects open a vista for the soul and connect it with a larger and transformed vision of the world. In *Memories, Dreams, Reflections*, Jung speaks of his personal experience of an expanded vista:

> At times I feel as if I am spread out over the landscape and inside things, and am myself living in every tree, in the splashing of the waves, in the clouds and the animals that come and go, in the procession of the seasons ... I chop the wood and cook the food. These simple acts make man simple; and how... difficult it is to be simple! .... In Bollingen, silence surrounds me almost audibly, and I live "in modest harmony with nature." Thoughts rise to the surface which reach back into the centuries, and accordingly anticipate a remote future. Here the torment of creation is lessened; creativity and play are close together.
>
> (1963, 225–226)

Later on in *Memories, Dreams, Reflections*, Jung notes just how important such a perspective is:

> The decisive question for man is: Is he related to something infinite or not? That is the telling question of his life. Only if we know that the

thing which truly matters is the infinite can we avoid fixing our interest upon futilities, and upon all kinds of goals which are not of real importance ... If we understand and feel that here in this life we already have a link with the infinite, desires and attitudes change. In the final analysis, we count for something only because of the essential we embody, and if we do not embody that, life is wasted.

(1963, 325)

For Jung, the Philosophers' Stone and the Self are such fundamental images of this link to eternity.

Penelope and Molly Bloom

Jung's vision amplifies his fantasy at the end of *Ulysses* and underscores a reading of the Self as a transcendental perspective that privileges the changeless over the changing, unity over multiplicity, and the fidelity of the sun over the infidelity of the moon. Perhaps this is the reason why at the end of reading *Ulysses*, Jung turns to Homer and Penelope rather than to Joyce and Molly Bloom. It would appear that the anxiety produced by the flux and fragmentation associated with a postmodern sensibility played a role in Jung's retreat to a more stable, fixed vision of what "conjunction" was all about.

Penelope whose fidelity can be trusted is a figure of virtue and consistency whose eye is always fixed on the return of the old king, a perfect anima for linking to a sense of the stabilized Self. As an anima figure, she is more like Hera, goddess of home and hearth, but she is not an anima that supports the deconstruction at the core of the Self, of passion and change. It is interesting to imagine what the vision of the Self might look like if Jung's coming to terms with *Ulysses* continued farther on the path on which it was headed and he had embraced the more contemporary Aphroditic figure of Molly.

Just prior to the Penelope fantasy, Jung quotes a small part of what he refers to as the voice of "easygoing" Mrs. Bloom (1932/1966, CW15, ¶200), which is a fragment of what has become Molly's famous soliloquy. It is a long speech of which I will quote a longer passage than the one quoted by Jung:

> ... I got him to propose to me yes first I gave him the bit of seedcake out of my mouth and it was leap year like now yes 16 years ago my God after that long kiss I near lost my breath yes he said I was a flower of the mountain yes so we are flowers all a woman's body yes that was one true thing he said in his life and the sun shines for you today yes that was why I liked him because I saw he understood or felt what a woman is and I knew I could always get round him and I gave him all the pleasure

> I could leading him on till he asked me to say yes and I wouldn't answer first only looked out over the sea and the sky I was thinking of so many things he didn't know .... O and the sea the sea crimson sometimes like fire and the glorious sunsets and the figtrees in the Alameda gardens yes and all the queer little streets and pink and blue and yellow houses and the rosegardens and the jessamine and geraniums and cactuses and Gibraltar as a girl where I was a Flower of the mountain yes when I put the rose in my hair like the Andalusian girls used or shall I wear a red yes and how he kissed me under the Moorish wall and I thought well as well him as another and then I asked him with my eyes to ask again yes and then he asked me would I yes to say yes my mountain flower and first I put my arms around him yes and drew him down to me so he could feel my breasts all perfume yes and his heart was going like mad and yes I said yes I will Yes.
>
> (Joyce 2008)[2]

Critics have described Molly's voice as the "essence of female creative energy, with its constant recurrent 'Yeses' and its streamlike structure as her inner discourse flows from one subject to another. The soliloquy is full of images of nature, of mountains and flowers and rivers and seas" (Kennesaw State University 1998). Molly's character with all its stereotypes pointed out by feminist critics was Joyce's attempt to render a fuller vision of women. Molly, in contrast to Penelope, is frustrated in her marriage that

> lacks the sexual freedom she needs. [She] fantasizes about her sexual desires and dreams because it is a human quality that she is not willing to suppress. And she makes no apologies for it. Some critics appreciate Joyce's characterization of Molly as a step forward to paint a free woman in Western literature.
>
> (Sahoo 2009)

Molly does more than fantasize; she has affairs. But her character is far more complex than simply living out her sexual needs.

> While [Molly's] sexuality is undeniable and lush, she is not strictly representative of a Magdalene archetype. She speaks in the tones of a Gaia figure, her voice encompassing rich natural metaphor, and her own wit and quick mind flesh her out as a woman who sees beyond the scope of what men see. Her train of thought is honest, rich, and associative, informing us with unsparing honesty in each of her smallest personal rituals and bodily functions. Her menstruation and urination reinforce the metaphor of her voice as streamlike, of the cyclical river of consciousness which celebrates the physical, the earthly, and the real.
>
> (Kennesaw University 1998)

The voice of Molly, in this chapter, is not rambling, or incoherent. But it has something in it of a doubling-back, a word-association—puns leading to other thoughts, jokes made to herself ... sudden

> swoops of romanticism, punctuated by menstrual cramps. So: she is *everything*. She becomes—oddly enough—the *entire human race*, in all its messiness, beauty, pettiness, and physical limitations. But her voice itself is hypnotic, almost scary at first... we are so deeply inside her, and up until this point in the book we have only heard things about her, and judged her behavior ... and Joyce does not prepare us for what happens in the last episode. He does not set us up carefully so we will be "ready." He throws us in. here: swim.
>
> (sheila 2008)

And swim we must! Critics male and female, feminist and patriarchal, generally focus on the metaphor of "flow" (Attridge 1989), like a "plunge into a flowing river" (Blamires, quoted in Attridge). Roy K. Gottfried has noted that Molly represents "the extreme of language at its loosest and most flowing" (quoted in Attridge; Gottfried 1980, 35). "The flow is the flow of Nature" (Blamires quoted in Attridge; Blamires 1996, 608), and it is in Molly's character and language that Harry Blamires finds "refreshing life-giving waters" (quoted in Attridge). It is interesting to speculate about the play of anima images in Jung as they affected both his personal life and theoretical reflections. Though too simple, might we imagine both Emma and Penelope as supporting the importance of stability, and Sabina, Toni, and Molly as marking a place for dynamic and deconstructive passions that keep the spirit sexy and embodied, creating a tension that always challenges the spiritualization of language? With these dynamic anima figures, the language of Stone and Self is eroticized and made complex. When this complexity falls apart, the anima and the Self become fixed and rigid, controlled by the senex or abandoned to Dionysus, a split between the stable and dynamic aspects of the soul that affect both theoretical understanding and personal life. I believe it is in the mutual engagement of these archetypal energies that one can find the dynamic hybridity that links chaos and cosmos, an integration that Jung intended but didn't always achieve. This linkage between chaos and cosmos is what I have here called *chaosmos*—another name for the Philosophers' Stone and another perspective through which we can reconsider and reread Jung's idea of the Self.

Notes

1 Personal communication from Fred Evans, 2010.
2 Jung's quote begins with "O and the sea ...." and ends "yes I said yes I will Yes."

References

Abraham, Lyndy. 1998. *A dictionary of alchemical imagery.* Cambridge: Cambridge University Press.

Attridge, Derek. 1989. Excerpt from Molly's flow: The writing of "Penelope" and the question of women's language. *MFS Modern Fiction Studies* 35(3): *Project MUSE*, http://muse.jhu.edu/login?auth=0&type=summary&url=/journals/modem_fiction_studies/v035/35.3.attridge.html (accessed October 29, 2012).

Blamires, Harry. 1996. *The new Bloomsday book: A guide through Ulysses.* London: Routledge.

Brooke, Roger. 2009. The self, the psyche, and the world: A phenomenological interpretation. *Journal of Analytical Psychology* 54: 601–618.

Colman, Warren. 2000. Models of the self. In *Jungian thought in the modern world.* Edited by E. Christopher and H. Solomon (pp. 3–19). London: Free Association Press.

DiBernard, Barbara. 1980. *Alchemy and Finnegan's wake.* Albany, NY: State University of New York.

Derrida, Jacques. 1976/1997. *Of grammatology.* Baltimore, MD: The Johns Hopkins University Press.

Edinger, Edward F. 1985. *Anatomy of the psyche.* La Salle, IL: Open Court.

Eliade, Mircea. 1970. *Yoga: Immortality and freedom.* Princeton, NJ: Princeton University Press.

Evans, Fred J. 2009. *The multivoiced body: Society and communication in the age of diversity.* New York: Columbia University Press.

Gottfried, Roy K. 1980. *The art of syntax in Ulysses.* Athens: University of Georgia Press.

Gratacolle, William. 1652. "The names of the philosophers stone." In *Five treatises of the philosophers stone.* Edited by Henry Pinnell (pp. 65–72). London: Thomas Harper.Hillman, James. 1993. Concerning the stone: Alchemical ideas of the goal. *Sphinx: Journal of Archetypal Psychology and the Arts* 5: 234–265.

Joyce, James. 2008. Molly Bloom's soliloquy. Poetry Dispatch No. 242 I. June 16, 2008, Molly Bloom's Soliloquy – The Art of Writing: Lesson # 336, poetry dispatch and other notes from the underground. http://poetrydispatch.wordpress.com/2008/06/16/james-joyce-molly-blooms-soliloquy/ (accessed October 29, 2012).

Jung, Carl Gustav. 1932/1966. "Ulysses": A monologue. *The spirit in man, art, and literature.* CW15.

———. 1943/1948/1968. The spirit of Mercurius. *Alchemical studies.* CW13.

———. 1946/1966. The psychology of the transference. *The practice of psychotherapy.* CW16.

———. 1950/1968. A study in the process of individuation. *The archetypes and the collective unconscious.* CW9i.

———. 1952/1969. Answer to job. *Psychology and religion: West and East.* CW13.

———. 1953/1968. Epilogue. *Psychology and alchemy.* CW12.

———. 1955–1956/1970. *Mysterium coniunctionis.* CW14.

———. 1963. *Memories, dreams, reflections.* Edited by Aniela Jaffé. Translated by Richard and Clara Winston. New York: Pantheon.

———. 2009. *The red book: Liber novus.* Edited by Sonu Shamdasani. Translated by M. Kyburz, J. Peck, and S. Shamdasani. New York: W.W. Norton & Company.

Kennesaw State University. 1998. Fall Semester 1998 KSU English Senior Seminar, episode by episode guide to James Joyce's *Ulysses*. "Report on James Joyce's Ulysses, Episode 18—PENELOPE (738–783)." http://ksumail.kennesaw.edu/~mglosup/ulysses/penelope.htm (accessed October 29, 2012).

Kuberski, Philip. 1994. *Chaosmos: Literature, science and theory.* Albany: State University of New York Press.

Sahoo, Sarojini. 2009. The myriad of Molly Blooms. *Sense & sensuality: Redefining feminism.* (March 2). http://sarojinisahoo.blogspot.com/2009/03/scene-from-wilde-irish-productions_02.html (accessed October 29, 2012).

sheila. 2008. The books: "Ulysses"–the Penelope episode (James Joyce). *The Sheila Variations.* (January 24). http://www.sheilaomalley.com/?p=7642 (accessed October 29, 2012).

Chapter 13

The Azure Vault

Alchemy and the cosmological imagination

In the last chapter of his book *Alchemical Psychology* (2010) entitled "The Azure Vault: Caelum as Experience," James Hillman opens a door to a new dimension of his archetypal and alchemical psychologies. It is a chapter that builds on an earlier paper "Back to Beyond: On Cosmology" (1989a), where he notes: "Something further is needed" (p. 214). In that earlier work, Hillman challenges himself to go beyond his self-imposed limits. He believes that sticking to the image and sticking to the soul have become "literalized" and stuck in soul, in a via negativa that rejects the soul's need to go beyond itself—skyward to fill its own absence and longing for something positive, something more, a homecoming.

Responding to this need, Hillman moves to open a new frontier of cosmological praxis, a vast aesthetic bluing of psychology that can entertain a living metaphysics. Here with Hillman, we are heading to the edge of psychology and philosophy, of metaphor and metaphysics, of alchemy and astrology, and to a cosmological pivot point, both personal and transpersonal. At the end of his work on alchemy, Hillman (2010) leaves us with a new vision of the beyond, the blue sky as a "breath of life," heaven, "the abode of the gods," "the upper firmament or covering dome," a caelum of experience with "a thousand names" and, like the Philosophers' Stone, a "final realization of the alchemical opus" (p. 318).

It is to this expanded cosmological beyond that Hillman points, to a new home for the soul, and to a new dimension of his psychology. How then to proceed in response to Hillman's provocation? In what direction can we go to advance Hillman's archetypal and alchemical psychologies as a cosmological praxis and a living metaphysics? In going back to beyond, I am first thrown back to the beginning of *Alchemical Psychology*, to its Preface and to the book as a whole, but specifically to a number of important papers that set the stage and give context to Hillman's revisioning of the soul's goal.

I would like to suggest seeing the Azure Vault in relationship to Hillman's larger corpus, particularly to a number of his insights in "The Therapeutic Value of Alchemical Language: A Heated Introduction" (2010), in "Peaks and Vales" (1979), in "Concerning the Stone: Alchemical Images of the

Goal" (2010), and in "Alchemical Blue and the *Unio Mentalis*" (2010). I have already mentioned the importance of "Back to Beyond: On Cosmology" (1989a). I would add here that we also consider Ed Casey's response to Hillman's "Back to Beyond" entitled "Back of 'Back to Beyond' and Creeping Dichotomism," along with Hillman's response to Casey's criticism at the end of Griffin's book *Archetypal Process* (1989). And finally, as a spring board to forwarding Hillman's archetypal and alchemical legacies, that we consider, carry on, enter into, and forward the three conversations between Hillman and Casey published in the last chapter of *Philosophical Intimations (*2016). These contexts enrich and deepen our reflections on the extension of Hillman's work. I do not believe, in spite of Hillman's self-criticism, that he is either simply stuck in soul, literalizes it, or that in his idea of seeing through he is *locked* into a via negativa. My contention is that, though Hillman is critical of his past limitations, in reviewing and re-membering his ideas, we find a fertile, imaginative, and ongoing process that is resonate with and gives support to his emerging vision.

In "The Azure Vault," Hillman (2010) links soul and spirit—in the concreteness of the alchemical imagination, in the puer-psyche marriage, in the Stone as *unus mundus*, in the objectification of the subject, and in a circular iteration, where telos returns to itself, and where libido is seen as a cosmic erotic dynamic that permeates all life, crowning matter as "[t]he soul descends ... from heaven, beautiful and glad" ... "into the world's material body" (p. 261; first part is from *Le Rosaire des philosophes*).

In the movement skyward, the blue of self-reflective feeling becomes paramount. Imagination is seen as fundamental. Its aesthetic is expanded and more brightly illuminated in the Azure Vault. Here, blue moves from the *unio mentalis* to the *unus mundus*, from integrated mind to the integrated world—Cézanne-like. For Hillman, the Azure Vault answers to the soul's desire to go beyond itself to a positive but not positivistic metaphysics. Hillman's vision of metaphysics is anything but traditional metaphysics as we know it from Aristotle to Hegel and beyond. Its emphasis is not hierarchical and spiritually progressive. Hillman (2010) follows Jung, the psychologist of the soul, and not simply Jung, the metaphysician of the spirit, in order to recover the ancient idea of "sav[ing] the phenomena" (p. 7) by continuing his focus on images of the sensate imagination as they present and display themselves. The soul's desire to go beyond itself, to come home to itself, requires a different vision of metaphysics. It's not our father's Oldsmobile or our grandfather's Buick that will get us there; that is, it is not our ancestors' metaphysics, not a grand, noble system that encompasses images and ideas in an overarching "explanatory theory" of "universal symbols" and/or ideas (p. 7). It is not a metaphysics of spirit that translates images into concepts and then proceeds to lose the images. It is neither a transcendence into colorless abstractions or mathematical purity, nor a spiritual via negativa or metaphysics of the void. It is not an application of directed thinking to fantasy thinking. It does not create fixed, abstract, repetitive categories, boxes drained of color and blood. It is not in nominalism, Apollonic consciousness, and day world concepts. In short, it is not in little boxes of conceptual rationalism that the soul finds itself at home.

What then does Hillman mean by metaphysics? What is that positive cosmic home that the soul longs for and aims at as its goal? We know from "Concerning the Stone" that this goal is a goal of a lifetime. The "extraordinary" goals "like gold and pearls, elixirs and healing stones of wisdom" are deliteralized right at the beginning (2010, p. 232). They are fictions that "impel the psyche into the opus"—that motivate us to stay the course of our lives. These images are the impetus that urges us, pulls us, toward a beyond—an opus aimed at sustaining value—not this or that value or purpose, but "purposiveness itself.... [n]ot the attainable but the idea of the unattainable" (p. 233). It is the receding blue that is at the core of desire and the divine energy of the soul.

As noted, to further extend his understanding of the soul's need to go beyond itself, Hillman felt that his work needed to go back to "beyond," to an extension and furthering of the imagination in the Azure Vault. This move began for him in jottings and in a collection of likely stories—Timaeus-like[1]— stories of magical moments of bluing, the intrusion of the imaginal psyche into the lives of well-known figures, including patients, psychologists, poets, painters, musicians, writers, philosophers, and even Jung himself. Among these figures, we find Anna O., Gustav Fechner, Æ George William Russel, Miles Davis, Novalis, Wilhelm Reich, Paul Cézanne, Friedrich Hölderlin, Martin Heidegger, Marcel Proust, Wolfgang Pauli, Wallace Stevens, and, as just noted, Jung.

These stories coalesce around transformational moments of vision, out of a black hole, a "night world," "out of a dull chrysalis"[2] into experiences of intensification, revivification, and wonder. Psychic joy rises Faust-like from gloomy thoughts about the life of the mind to the emergence of an aesthetic attitude. Images of gas lamp angels, "blue vapor without end,"[3] blue flowers and blooming gardens, "the shining of [a] plant's soul,"[4] "a magic sword with a hilt of silver and a blade of blue steel,"[5] "a glittering dragon-fly"[6]; "[c]limbing through a strange geography"[7]; azure intoxication, "impressions of coolness, of dazzling light"[8]; a "world clock,"[9] and the "visible spirit of Song"[10]—all "played upon Wallace Steven's blue guitar" (p. 337), a cosmic vision, where a gathering of depth shines forth only as it veils itself—light without visible source. With all this comes a sense of the holy and "'inexpressible sanctity' that had a 'magical atmosphere'"[11] and a feeling of harmony and eternity.

Hillman notes his temptation to account for these experiences and images in metaphysical terms, to leave the earth for "the [wild] blue yonder" of earthly transcendence (2010, p. 327). He asks: "Have we not been encountering the Celestial Kingdom, the 'effulgent blue light'" of the body of Buddha "the visitations of ethereal Sophia, of Mary in her blue dress, the ultimate transcendent anima?" (pp. 327–328) And, I would add, Nuit, the Egyptian sky goddess?

Hillman answers his own question as to whether these experiences are truly transcendental, saying: "Not quite; not yet; not today" (p. 328). All the above cannot be accounted for by traditional metaphysics, by spirit in splendid isolation, and/or spiritual ascension. It does, however, require a going back to the "beyond," now seen from the point of view of a living metaphysics, one in which the sensate imagination keeps the high-flying spirit connected to the lived body and into a longing made poignant and visceral by the withdrawing nature of blue, by its absenting and voiding itself. It is in nostalgia, lack, mourning for what's "not here," "not yet" or long ago, in the hollow ache that the soul is moved homeward. Following Derrida, Hillman recognizes that the essence of the eye is not sight, but seeing "by means of tears" (pp. 337–338), the feeling of pathos that deepens and enriches the *caelum* as it expands skyward. As it expands skyward, the deep ache of absence is also fullness.

> A blue mind may be a deep mind and a wide mind, but also it is a place of pleasure, the pleasure of thinking, the libidinal pleasures of secret study, of teasing meanings in the dark; revelations, uncoverings, fresh insights laid bare.
>
> (pp. 336–337)

Heaven pulls each of us into its arms.

In this, there is a fullness of imaginal life of the blue world as it appears in analogies—things refer, imply, connote. There is likeness everywhere. Things cure one another by means of similarity, objects exist together, edges soften, at times disappear. The human soul recognizes itself in the world and as the world. There is a healing magic in art, and the poet becomes the transcendental doctor leading us back to beyond. Here, one finds the power of the objective psyche to display and objectify itself in all its shining beauty. An expression of this bluing power is found in the next image where it appears that the blue-green instinctual energy expressed by the serpent is the key that opens the gate to a magical illumination (Figure 13.1).

The Azure Vault, like the Egyptian goddess Nuit, leans over us scintilla-like, an erotic presence calling us toward her, seducing us to a wonder beyond the language of truth. The heart expands to claim the world, blue vapor without end. Things cast a light of their own. The sweet shock of beauty instructs and educates the soul, leaving us to ponder, wonder, and enjoy. *Unio mentalis* (the unity of the mind) becomes the *unus mundus*, the one world *caelum* embraced in blue. "I am the sky itself," writes Hillman quoting C. Smith (2010, p. 329), mind/imagination/world conjoined—what Hillman called the poetic basis of mind beyond even metaphor.

In assessing Hillman's legacy, it is important to consider Ed Casey's (1989) idea of creeping dichotomism. Casey has raised the concern that affirming and re-affirming the fundamental "ultimacy of the image" and thus "the

Figure 13.1 "Gates to the Garden." Acrylic on canvas by Courtney Padrutt, Artist and Magickal initiate. In the original colored image, a blue-green snake expressing instinctual energy is the key that opens the gate to a magickal illumination. (Courtesy of the artist.)

secondariness of all that is non-image" can lead to all the problems of philosophical dualism and away from "the polyadic cosmos—or the plural *cosmoi*" (p. 235). For Casey, this tension is in danger of creeping toward ontological divisions when the bipolar tensions between image and concept, image and word, and animated and de-animated split into conceptual rationalisms. Another term is needed to contain both sides of this separation, and Casey suggests the word "phenomenal." Phenomenal, he notes, is not a third term between dichotomies, but a term that encompasses both. Casey links this idea to both Kant's definition of "determinate appearance," in which intelligibility is inherent in appearances, and Heidegger's idea of "that which shows itself from itself" (p. 237). Metaphysical vision that goes back to beyond does not go into the beyond of metaphysics, but stops short of the "beyond of 'meta'" (p. 233). It is a matter of the back of beyond or, rather, as he says, "of its *front*, its face," an "immediately given aspect of the universe" (p. 233). I believe that for Casey, as also for Hillman, the cosmic comes configured as a phenomenological display.

Hillman's (1989b) response to Casey is not to deny these dichotomies. In fact, he references more of them, including peaks and vales, underworld and day world. He, however, looks at this divide in another way and asks what else is going on in this tension? What is the value of the separation, following Pat Berry's recognition that there can be artfulness in tensions? Hillman moves the idea of tensions from a philosophical perspective to a psychological and aesthetic one, not logical or ontological, but practical, "fecund," and specifically "poetic" (p. 252). Hillman uses this strategy with regard to soul and spirit in "Peaks and Vales," where he notes, "I have been aiming to draw apart these images in order to contrast them as vividly as I can" (1979, p. 57). Underlying this strategy is the emotion of *"eris* or *polemos*, which Heraclitus … [has said] is the Father of all" (p. 58). For Hillman, contrasts are an important aesthetic principle. But he also makes an accommodation by linking differences together (puer-psyche marriage)—possibly in the spirit of Casey's idea of phenomenality? A question that might be asked is whether this marriage of soul and spirit in the name of a living metaphysics and cosmological praxis attains to the polyadic cosmos that has been the mark of archetypal psychology. I would argue that Hillman's work lends itself to a phenomenality in Casey's sense, but that the question remains an ongoing and important one for Hillman's legacy.

Some of the important issues at stake with regard to the nature and place of images and a phenomenological metaphysics are taken up in the last chapter of *Philosophical Intimations*, where Hillman and Casey engage in three provocative conversations. These dialogues give context, set the stage, and are a valuable starting point for continuing reflection on Hillman's legacy and the development of an archetypal/alchemical psychology that opens the soul to the deepest wonders of the cosmos. For Hillman and Casey, conversation becomes one of the important places and carriers of image and imagination, and it is in this spirit that I imagine Hillman's legacy being carried on by the Dallas Institute's publications of *Conversing with James Hillman*.

John Sallis (2012), a philosopher writing about elemental cosmology and the expanse beyond, writes:

> Nothing more readily evokes wonder or awakens aspiration than the sky. Set beyond all things, it is the elemental that most insistently resists being conceived as a thing. It is the elemental that most expansively bounds the domain in which things show themselves and humans pursue their sundry concerns. As elemental, it towers above the earth in such a way as to encompass the entire enchorial space in which virtually everything comes to pass.
>
> The nocturnal sky is most wondrous. The spectacle of the starry heaven above, of the vast array of stars revolving in their orderly courses, has never ceased to evoke the most wonderful fancies and the most profound questions.….

Soaring above even the loftiest mountains, the sky conveys to humans a sense of height, of an absolute elevation that in its very unattainability is utterly enthralling. It is primarily from the diurnal sky that the warmth necessary for life is received and that the light that spreads over and illuminates all things is bestowed. As the supreme source, the solar sky awakens aspiration. Humans look up to the supernal and long to draw nearer to it, to gain, in some sense (if not the most literal), proximity to it.

(p. 244)

We might then ask: Does Hillman's vision of a living metaphysics and cosmological praxis bring us closer to being at home in this mystery?

Notes

1 For Plato, the Timaeus' view of the cosmos is an eikôs logos, a likely story.
2 Hillman 2010, p. 321; quoting from *Song and its Fountains*.
3 Ibid., p. 319; quoting Lisel Mueller.
4 Hillman quoting W. Lowrie, p. 321.
5 Ibid., p. 321; quoting from *Song and its Fountains*.
6 Ibid.
7 Ibid., p. 322.
8 Ibid., p. 326; quoting Proust.
9 Ibid., p. 326; referring to Pauli.
10 Ibid., p. 338; quoting Novalis.
11 Ibid., pp. 324–325; quoting Jung.

References

Casey, E. (1989). "Back of 'back to beyond' and creeping dichotomism." In D.R. Griffin (Ed.) *Archetypal process: Self and divine in Whitehead, Jung, and Hillman* (pp. 233–237). Evanston, IL: Northwestern University Press.

Griffin, D.R. (Ed.) (1989). *Archetypal process: Self and divine in Whitehead, Jung, and Hillman*. Evanston, IL: Northwestern University Press.

Hillman, J., et al. (1979). "Peaks and vales." In J. Hillman (Ed.), *Puer papers* (pp. 3–53). Dallas, TX: Spring Publications.

Hillman, J. (1989a). "Back to beyond: On cosmology." In D.R. Griffin (Ed.) *Archetypal process: Self and divine in Whitehead, Jung, and Hillman* (pp. 213–231). Evanston, IL: Northwestern University Press.

Hillman, J. (1989b). "Responses: Response to Edward Casey." In D.R. Griffin (Ed.) *Archetypal process: Self and divine in Whitehead, Jung, and Hillman* (pp. 251–258). Evanston, IL: Northwestern University Press.

Hillman, J. (2010). *Alchemical psychology* (Uniform ed., vol. 5). Putnam, CT: Spring Publications.

Hillman, J. (2016). *Philosophical intimations* (Uniform ed., vol. 8). E. Casey (Ed.). Thompson, CT: Spring Publications.

Sallis, J. (2012). *Logic of imagination: The expanse of the elemental*. Bloomington: Indiana University Press.

Chapter 14

Divine Darkness and Divine Light

Alchemical illumination and the mystical play between knowing and unknowing

The art and alchemy of transformation is a large and complex subject. There are many approaches to understanding the *opus alchemicum* and its goals of solification and the Philosophers' Stone. My approach to this work is from the perspective of a Jungian analyst, which means privileging a certain orientation and point of view. It is a point of view that continues to develop within, around, and on the edges of the Jungian tradition and, for me, it remains an open inquiry that continues to intrigue and surprise me.

Like Jung, the alchemists were interested in fundamental and elemental change, classically imagined as the transformation of lead into gold, a base substance into a noble one. Jung's (1968) revolutionary insight was that the alchemists were not simply concerned with the "material world," but were speaking in symbols about the soul and were working simultaneously as much with the "imagination" as with the literal substances of their art.

This shift of focus from the literal to the imaginal, from substance to image and imagination, had its roots in the idea that the alchemists were projecting into a mysterious unknown called "matter" another unknown—the unconscious psyche. Thus, Jung (1968) proclaimed "*ignotum per ignotius*" (¶345), his attempt to understand the unknown by the greater unknown.[1] While knowledge about both matter and psyche was obscure in the deepest sense, using the developing idea of the unconscious psyche to understand alchemy opened a new and creative vista. This opening of a psychological approach allowed Jung to understand the alchemical *opus* in a new way that both revealed and yet preserved the mysteries of transformation. Jung concluded that the "gold" the alchemists were trying to produce was not simply the common vulgar gold but the aurum non-vulgi or the *aurum philosophicum*, a philosophical gold.

This imaginal, philosophical, and psychic reality was a new category used to understand the mysteries of alchemy. It became clear to Jung that alchemy was interested not just in the perfection of nature, but also in the creation of a higher-level human being, divine salvation, and the transformation of the cosmos, with what Aaron Cheak (2013) calls both "gold-making and god-making" (18). Alchemy then was an *opus divinum*, a sacred work and far more than simply the protoscience of chemistry. It was *also* a religious philosophy and a psychological and transformational art. Jung came to see alchemy as a precursor and confirmation of his psychology of the unconscious. The wealth of alchemical symbolism and the complexity of its system of transformation added to the richness and depth of Jung's psychology.

Over the years, many analysts and scholars influenced by Jung's work have continued to make important contributions to alchemical studies. My own work has been primarily influenced by Marie-Louise von Franz, Edward Edinger, James Hillman, and Wolfgang Giegerich. Each of these thinkers has approached alchemy in different ways. Von Franz and Edinger both amplified and helped others gain access to what they saw as Jung's fundamental and profound insights. Hillman and Giegerich challenge Jung, are iconoclastic, and offer alternative, if related, ways of imagining and thinking about alchemy.

My own perspective is rooted in and responds to the tension of ideas catalyzed by the differing ways of coming to terms with the alchemical imagination still unfolding in the Jungian tradition and elsewhere. I once wrote about my perspective using the metaphor of the alchemical stove with its many burners and degrees of heat (Marlan 2006, 3).[2]

At the time, I imagined Jung in one alembic on a back burner, cooking over a low and steady heat, with Hillman and Giegerich in differently shaped vessels boiling up-front, as I was trying to prepare my own concoction utilizing the vapors produced by them and others to further distill and coagulate the essences necessary for the difficult work of understanding and forwarding an alchemical psychology and its elusive and mysterious goal. Since that time, my experiment in understanding alchemy has shifted a bit. Jung's ideas are back up-front and I find myself returning to consider his work again and again (Figure 14.1).

Currently, I have been focusing on Jung's *Mysterium Coniunctionis* (1970), his last great work on alchemy. As a book, and as an archetypal idea and image, it is at the core of the alchemical *opus* and central to Jung's psychology. The *Mysterium Coniunctionis* as a book has been described as the "*summa* of Jungian psychology" (Edinger 1995, 17). Its first chapter, entitled "The Components of the Coniunctio," describes the overarching theme of the alchemical work. Jung (1970) states: "The factors which come together in the coniunctio are conceived as opposites, either confronting one another in enmity or attracting one another in love" (¶1). One way of reading this description is to observe that the archetypal energies of enmity and love are fundamental forces in the eternal play of opposites. These forces are both cosmic and universal, as well as aspects of the human soul. The opus of the alchemists then can be understood as entering into relationship with these energies in an attempt to produce a mysterious conjunction essential to the goal of the work.

Figure 14.1 Alchemical homunculus by Franz Xaver Simm, 1899. (Public domain.)

It is not surprising then that Jung (1970) refers to Karl Kerenyi on the Aegean Festival in Goethe's *Faust* and its literary prototype of the *Chymical Wedding* of Christian Rosenkreutz as motivating his writing in the *Mysterium*. Jung likewise notes that the idea of the "chymical wedding" is "a product of the traditional hierosgamos symbolism of alchemy" (xiii). Hierosgamos is a Greek word for a sacred marriage, often signifying a ritualized sexual union symbolically inclusive of many levels of the *coniunctio*. It is a union of opposites and a way of opening and linking the deepest recesses of the soul and the cosmos, both human and divine. The *Mysterium* as a book is the final major statement of Jung's understanding of the alchemical *opus*. It is also difficult to read, understand, and assimilate—some say as difficult as understanding the alchemical texts themselves. Interpretations of the *Mysterium* are divided, some giving it high praise and profound respect (Edinger 1995), others relativizing its value (Hillman 2010), and still others minimizing it as generally outdated (Giegerich [1998] 2001; Power 2017).

Hillman (2010) tries to avoid "any grand narrative that encompasses alchemy within an explanatory theory, such as Jung's conjunction of opposites and the realization of the self, eschewing the temptation to give meaning by translation into universal symbols and noble metaphysics" (7). Both Giegerich ([1998] 2001) and Power (2017) claim that the *Mysterium* is largely of historical interest only and needs to be developed further, i.e. sublated. For Edinger (1995), on the other hand, it is so important that he believes that it "will be a major object of study for centuries" (17). I agree with Edinger that the *Mysterium* is an important text, though I have no prediction of how it will be regarded in the future. It is Jung's crowning achievement. It describes the opus of alchemy from beginning to end in breathtaking scholarly and psychological depth and is organized around images that illuminate the archetypal psyche. Edinger (1995) demonstrates how Jung guides his readers through over one hundred images that mark the path of alchemical transformation, from the war of opposites through the mercurial and central mystery of the *coniunctio*, to the emergence of the arcane substance, the Philosophers' Stone, and the self. While my own style of thinking about alchemy is in many ways closer to Hillman's Archetypal Psychology, I nevertheless find the *Mysterium Coniunctionis*, both as a book and as the central image of the *coniunctio*, to be an essential key to understanding the dynamics of psychological transformation (Figure 14.2).

Jung was not always systematic in the way he spoke about the idea of the *coniunctio*. In a masterful chapter on the opposites, David Henderson (2014) provides a historical and scholarly account of the *coniunctio* as Jung presents it over the corpus of his Collected Works. Henderson differentiates the *coincidentia oppositorum*, the *complexio oppositorum*, the *coniunctio oppositorum*, and the unity of opposites. For Henderson, these differing descriptions reflect not only subtle differences in the meaning of the *coniunctio*,

Figure 14.2 Rati-asana (detail). Stone, Khajuraho, Vishvanatha temple, 1059–1087. (Credit Oversnap 471246509/iStock.com).

but also a progressive development of the idea over time (56–70). I will not reiterate the subtleties that Henderson describes, but in general the *coniunctio* and the transcendent function are attempts to describe what for Jung is an irrational, instinctual, half-bodily/half-spiritual, symbolic process of the transformation of opposites/contraries/differences, into some kind of unified transcendence. For Jung, the *coniunctio* opens toward images of wholeness: the birth of the *filius philosophorum* (the philosophical child), the Self, and the most famous of all alchemical images, the Philosophers' Stone, an emergent image of transcendental wholeness. The stone then is the alpha and omega of the process, and, like Mercurius, it is the mediator and the intermediary of the goal of the work and has the power to transform earthly man into an illuminated philosopher (Abraham 1998, 145).

The Philosophers' Stone is said to have a thousand names, and yet it is also nameless and ineffable. Gratacolle (1652) mentions "a Dragon, a Serpent, a Toad, the green Lion, the quintessence, ... Camelion, ... Virgins milke, radicall humidity, unctuous moysture, ... urine, ... water of wise men," and other images (67). A number of the images are related to light and illumination: "Gold, Sol, Sun, ... lightning, ... afternoone light, ... a crowne overcoming a cloud. ... fire, ... the fulle moone, ...the light of lights, ... our stone Lunare," but he likewise tells us that the stone is also known as "blacker than black," and the list goes on and on disseminating itself into a continuing complexity of images (67).

Since the black sun/*sol niger* is both *prima materia* and *ultima materia*, they are equally names of the Philosophers' Stone, linking light and darkness and other opposites. I have recently added the notion of chaosmos, the unity of chaos and cosmos (Marlan 2013[3]). Each of these images of the Philosophers' Stone contains a subtle phenomenology that, if followed, opens a unique epiphany, a way into understanding the Stone's multiplicity. Despite the many names of the Stone, the alchemists stressed that it personified unity and consisted in one thing and one thing only. Morienus wrote: "For it is one Stone, one med'cin in which consists the whole magistery," and the *Scala philosophorum* stated: "The Stone is one: Yet this one is not one in Number, but in kind" (in Abraham 1998, 148). Perhaps what the alchemists had in mind was embodied in the Stone's most paradoxical and mystical description *lithos ou lithos*, the "stone that is no Stone." In this description, the enigmatic quality of the Stone shines forth—ultimately what Abraham called the "arcanum of all arcana" (145).

Is this then the mystery of the great work, the goal of the opus, the mysterious Philosophers' Stone? Is this then the "med'cin" Morienus wrote about that contains the whole magistery? Does it then carry its self-negation within itself, a *via negativa* that separates it from literal nature and from any simple positive being or presence? Or rather, is it an unknown, an absence, an obscurity, a darkness, or perhaps, more accurately, a fundamental paradox that links all binaries into an expression of the *mysterium coniunctionis*?

If this is so, the "med'cin" is also a *pharmacon*—a poyson as well as a healing draught.

One such *pharmacon* is *sol niger*, the black sun, one of the many symbolic expressions of the Stone. As an emergence from the *mysterium coniunctionis*, it is a conjunction and primal expression of Divine Darkness and Divine Light, unconscious and conscious, knowing and unknowing, ego and self, and the mystical play between these opposing tensions—in general, it reflects a dynamic condensation of the polar character of the archetypal psyche.

In the phenomenon of *sol niger*, one discovers the blacker-than-black aspect of the psyche—the presence of a dark light, a light that Jung and the alchemists called the light of darkness itself, the *lumen naturae*, the unnatural light of nature. My major focus when writing about the black sun was to explore its darkest aspects, to lean toward the exploration of darkness in its darkest depths (Marlan 2005). But I am also indebted to the study of *sol niger* for its revelation of an intimate linking between it and the mysterious other that shines in the darkness. At the end of *The Black Sun*, my interest turned more directly to this other light and my work began to lean in the direction of exploring it as a manifestation of the goal of the alchemical work, the illuminated Philosophers' Stone. Turning toward illumination is not simply moving beyond darkness, but seeing further into its paradoxical and mercurial complexity, hesitating at the ontological pivot point between presence and absence, inside and outside, consciousness and unconsciousness, knowing and unknowing, relativizing them but leaning toward the illumination that emerged in the deconstruction of these binaries (Figure 14.3).

What is the point, the ontological pivot point? In the "Paradoxa" chapter of the *Mysterium*, Jung takes up the symbolism of the point, which for him is a creative center where things and beings have their first origin. As such, the point is an expression of the divine, which, like Mercurius, appears to be before, beyond, and between binaries. In *Mysterium*, this point also symbolizes the Godhead, and the light and fire that connect the divine to the *scintillae*, to sparks that shine in the darkness and then are related to the *solificatio*, illumination, enlightenment, *gnosis*, and the illuminated body that dwells in the heart of man. As the light of nature, it is also the radical moisture and healing balm that is the gold of wholeness, which Jung called the Self (Edinger 1995, 58).

While working on the black sun and the multiple names for the Philosophers' Stone, I noticed a parallel attempt to describe a supreme principle or archetype of divinity in the work of the mystical theologian Pseudo-Dionysius (1987), also known as Dionysius the Areopagite, hereafter referred to as Dionysius. In his *The Divine Names*, he attempts to express and understand God by examining a long list of attributes taken from the Old and New Testament scriptures. Like Gratacolle, with regard to the multiple

Figure 14.3 Illuminatio. From *Artis Auriferae,* 1572. (Photograph by author).

images of the Philosophers' Stone, Dionysius (1987) elaborates names associated with God, including:

> 'being,' 'life,' 'light,' ... the 'truth.' ... good, beautiful, wise, beloved, God of gods, Lord of Lords, Holy of Holies, eternal, existent, Cause of the ages. ... source of life, wisdom, mind, word, knower, ... powerful, and King of Kings, ancient of days, ancient of days, the unaging and unchanging, salvation, righteousness and sanctification, redemption, greatest of all and yet the one in the still breeze. (55)

The list of positive, affirmative names, referred to as *kataphasis*, is followed by his work *The Mystical Theology*, often referred to as an apophatic approach, which suggests the limitation of any and all positive attempts to describe God. In *The Mystical Theology*, the positive attributes are surpassed by introducing the *via negativa*, which leads to a new level of mystical understanding of darkness and the hyper-essential designations of the reality of the divine. Just as in alchemy, the stone is not a stone, so in mystical theology, God is not God. This image of God as a Divine Darkness is illustrated by Meister Eckhart's enigmatic prayer to God "that we may be free of God" (in Kroll-Fratoni 2013, 146). The *via negativa* is elaborated in *The Mystical Theology*, which begins with the question, "What is Divine Darkness?" In this treatise, Dionysius (1949) gives instructions to an initiate intended to guide him to the:

> ultimate summit of Thy mystical Lore, most incomprehensible, most luminous and most exalted, where the pure, absolute and immutable mysteries of theology are veiled in the dazzling obscurity of the secret Silence, outshining all brilliance with the intensity of their Darkness, and surcharging our blinded intellects with the utterly impalpable and invisible fairness of glories surpassing all beauty. (9)

The themes of illumination, Divine Darkness and Divine Light, are richly differentiated and amplified in the work of Henri Corbin and in the scholarly, experiential, and vital presentation of his work by Tom Cheetham (2002). Cheetham writes about the *via negativa*, the emptying God in Christian theology, kenosis, and the Destiny of the West, the hermeneutics of absence, and the faces of darkness, and the Faces of Light. Cheetham differentiated "two kinds of darkness, two sources of bewilderment" (67). He describes a "Darkness that is only Darkness, a darkness that refuses Light and is demonic," unconscious and evil. He distinguishes this from another kind of darkness "that is not merely black, but is a luminous Night, a dazzling Blackness, a Darkness at the approach to the Pole" (the point?).

This is the black light of what Corbin calls supraconsciousness. Cheetham notes that "[t]he appearance of Black Light marks a moment of supreme danger" (67). The black light signals "the annihilation of the *ego* in the Divine Presence" and its "unknowable origin." "It announces the Nothing that exists beyond all being, beyond all the subtle matter that mirrors it[s] uncanny light. The Black Light marks the region of the Absolute, *the Deus absconditus*, the unknown and unknowable God" (67).

How this God's absence is encountered and experienced makes all the difference and is considered a "moment of the greatest danger": one can become hopelessly swallowed up in the majesty of demonic darkness or emerge initiated and resurrected in the beauty of theophanic revelation—a man of light perhaps not unlike the solification of the alchemist. Ultimately for Corbin as for Dionysius, Divine Darkness and Divine Light are logically and mystically inseparable and simultaneous, and there is "a constant interplay between the inaccessible Majesty of Beauty and the fascinating beauty of inaccessible Majesty" (Cheetham 2002, 68, quoting Corbin 1994, 103)— what I have called alchemical illumination and the mystical play between Divine Darkness and Divine Light. Cheetham (2002) writes that for Corbin, "this duality is the central feature of all Creation: without the blossoming of Beauty as theophany man could not approach the sublimity of the *Deus absconditus*" (68, quoting Corbin 1994, 150, n. 64) as "the Light of Glory" (73). Illumination and the resurrection into life require a step more deeply into the interior of the *via negativa*, a radical *via negativa*, described as "the annihilation of annihilation" (68, quoting Corbin 1994, 117).[4] This level of negation "signifies the recognition of the Unknowable in 'a supreme act of metaphysical renunciation,' .... the real meaning of [mystical] poverty... *darwish*" (68).

It is of interest to consider a psychoanalytic parallel other than Jung's to this mystical notion of poverty. In a study of psychoanalysis and mysticism, Mark Kroll-Fratoni (2013) compares the work of Jacques Lacan and Meister Eckhart and concludes that Lacan's "psychoanalysis and [Eckhart's] mysticism are guided by a similar logic and structure as they are both oriented around [an emptying of the self and] processes of change" (v). Just as Jung's idea of the Self required a defeat for the ego, so Lacan, following Freud, recognized that the ego is not "master in its own house" (Kroll-Fratoni 2013, 1, quoting Freud). Along with the idea of the unconscious comes the introduction of the Other into the heart of the Self, which displaces the centrality of the ego. With Lacan, this notion of the Other is radicalized and is a view of the unconscious and unknown which cannot be "colonized or tamed" (Kroll-Fratoni 2013, 2). For Lacan, the self remains precisely "not-whole, and irreducibly heterogeneous" (Kroll-Fratoni 2013, 2) and decentered. Its "lack" is at the heart of continuous transformation and represents more than "a negative *moment*" in the dialectic of consciousness. It precludes "any attempt by the ego to constitute itself as a unity" (2). Lacan instead aims at acceptance of the unconscious as an alien, a radical "otherness" within the self, intrinsically lacking and self-emptying.

Kroll-Fratoni goes on say that, in a parallel way, Eckhart rejects the idea of a unity with a static notion of God as a being and instead seeks a unity with God as an ongoing activity of creation—with the self-emptying kenotic process that awaits the "*event*" of God's birth in the soul of man (Kroll-Fratoni 2013, 94). Such a birthing process does not create wholeness or fullness, but rather opens an abyss which for Eckhart is the *grunt* or ground—a non-ontotheological understanding of God, a mystical view resonant with Lacan's. Lacan and Eckhart stay close to the *via negativa* and cast doubt on the *via positiva*. Any movement toward transcendence that tries to compensate for feelings of anxiety or incompleteness in the face of lack or annihilation is seen as defensively fleeing from the divine and/or finitude. It is a flight from the trauma of the abyss and from our creatureliness.

For Eckhart, releasement (*Gelassenheit*), not defending against the abyss, "means letting go of the need for grounds and living without" a need to even ask the question "why?" (Kroll-Fratoni 2013, 225)—why things occur in the way they do. To let go this question approaches the nothingness of the *via negativa*—being close to dying. In this regard, it is interesting to recall the last reported words of Timothy Leary before he passed away.[5] It was recorded that at one moment Leary sat straight up in his bed and asked: "Why?" (as if to recognize Eckhart's point). Then, there was a long, silent pause, and he responded much more softly, a number of times, "Why not? Why not?" At another moment, as though he was describing something he was seeing, he said "Beautiful"—as if intimating something more in the midst of approaching the nothingness of dying. A few days before he passed on, one of his disciples asked him, "Who are we?" He responded, "We are bearers of the light—light bearers." Another question followed and he was asked, "What is our purpose?" and he responded, "We can shine it to illuminate others." Such a shine of light is what Corbin captures in his mystical and gnostic vision of illumination. Is this simply a defense against the abyss of the *via negativa* illusions that Lacan describes as imaginary? I would claim "no" (Figure 14.4).

In an essay, Warren Coleman (2006) makes a distinction between Lacan's view of the "imaginary" and Corbin's view of the Imaginal or real imagination. The "imaginary" in Lacan's sense emerges as a defense against negation and loss and flees from it, creating the kind of fantasy that Kant (1915) called "schwärmen," a kind of madness and undisciplined metaphysical speculation, a "land of shadows ... nursery tales, and monastic miracles" (37). Such fantasies lack depth, substance, and psychic reality. The real symbolic and imaginal are products of the transcendent function rather than of transcendence in Kant's sense. Jung (1971) notes that the transcendent in "transcendent function" "does not refer to a metaphysical quality but merely to the fact that this function facilitates a transition from one attitude to another" (480). It is a function in which the opposites, like absence and presence, light and dark, conscious and unconscious, are at play shuttling to and fro in a tension out of which a new attitude emerges and in which these binaries can be seen to be interpenetrative, a primordial expression of the mysterium coniunctionis. From this perspective, the *via negativa* is also a *via positiva* and more. Similarly, in alchemy, the prima materia is also the ultima materia both logically and mystically. Such combinations might as well be spoken of, in the way they are in mystical theology, as hyper-essential or divine. Divine Darkness and Divine Light imply one another; both are supra-abundant illuminations. I believe that this is the kind of illumination of which Corbin speaks.

While Lacan and Eckhart resist moving away from the *via negativa*, they both also recognize that the abyss carries another potentiality within itself. The revelations that occur within the midst of emptiness and the darkness of the *via negativa* are expressions of a bipolar archetypal reality, a *via negativa* intrinsically linked to a *via positiva*. This bipolarity is at the heart of our finitude and lack. There is considerable similarity between Eckhart's notion

Divine Darkness and Divine Light   263

Figure 14.4 Nicolas de Locques: Les Rudiments de la Philosophie Naturelle. Paris, 1665, frontispiece (N. Bonnart). (Credit: Beinecke Rare Book and Manuscript Library, Yale University).

of "wandering joy" (Kroll-Fratoni 2013, 185, quoting R. Schärmann) and Lacan's idea of jouissance.[6] *Jouissance* is a difficult notion to understand, and Lacan develops its meaning through several of his successive seminars. In simple terms, *jouissance* describes a kind of ecstatic sexual joy that is released in an acceptance of castration, lack, finitude, and death as fundamental truths of our human limits.

This acceptance is at the same time a release, an "excess of life" and a "superabundant vitality," that Lacan graphically states "[b]egins with a tickle and ends with blaze of petrol" (in Hewitson 2015). This mystical sexual energy linking pain and pleasure has what Hewitson, referring to Freud, calls a sexual coloring, and which Lacan describes as "the colour of emptiness, suspended in the light of a gap" (in Hewitson 2015). This gap, it would seem, is the space between human limits and divine plentitude. The experiences of both Eckhart and Lacan identify something that exceeds and yet is one with negation, a pleasure in nothingness. The nothing of the ecstatic is also elaborated by Henderson (2014) who shows that in addition to *kataphasis* (affirmation) and *apophasis* (negation), Dionysius includes *ekstasis* (ecstasy) as a third dimension of his mystical theology (13).

It is important to note that the mystical experiences of affirmation and negation are not distinct moments in time, or aspects of a linear process—but are logically and mystically simultaneous. Negation is not the simple opposite of affirmation, but is "at work at the heart of Dionysius' kataphatic celebrations of the divine" (Henderson 2014, 17). If these mystical and ecstatic experiences occur simultaneously in a moment, it is also the case that we are separated from this moment in the ordinary temporal reality of our lives. We do not live continuously in "wandering joy" (Kroll-Fratoni 2013, 185, quoting R. Schürmann) or in an eternal *coniunctio* or *jouissance*. The *coniunctio* falls apart, and we find ourselves outside of eternity and are mostly unconscious, everyday, all-too-human human beings. How then can we imagine the goals of alchemy, analysis, and mystical theology from our egoist position in time, as temporal beings in a process of development, growth, and individuation?

Alchemy, psychoanalysis, mystical theology, and gnosis all describe initiatory processes and a phenomenology of a path leading to the goal of their respective disciplines. Comprehensive descriptions of these paths and processes are available in the respective literature and traditions of these disciplines. In all of them, there are unique and individual variations on an archetypal process. There are no simply accurate cookbooks, and we are all thrown back on our unknowing. We enter analysis or spiritual disciplines for guidance. Dreams, fantasies, and visions give us access to the imaginal life, its images and symbols, that appear to have a telos and which Jung (1971) describes as the best possible expression of an as yet unknown reality. One might say that images and symbols stand in the "gap" between the known and the unknown, illuminate us, and point the way to our unique possibilities.

Illumination is an archetypal expression of the teleological function of symbolic images, as well as a manifestation of the numinosity of consciousness as it discovers its own radiant relationship to its unknown aspects. It is also an expression of conscious life within darkness itself. Dark light and the light of darkness, the *lumen naturae*, opens us to an uncanny recognition of an autonomous, or at least semi-autonomous, intelligence to whom we are drawn and who is also drawn to us. Recognition of this otherness can play a role in the unfolding of our lives, call us to a beyond, to a purpose that exceeds our own narcissism and opens us to the larger mystery of the *anima mundi*, or world soul. It is a critical moment in psychic development when we realize that the unconscious (and what we thought was our inorganic material world) shows itself to have a consciousness of its own, a subject that looks back at and responds to us as we look at it. Edinger (1995) writes: "It is a major transition from the discovery of lights shining in the darkness of the unconscious to the discovery of eyes looking at us from within that darkness" (64).

Edinger (1995) continues, "The presence of eyes indicates that the light residing in the unconscious has a subject," and notes that Jung has said, "The eyes indicate the lapis is in the process of evolution and grows from these ubiquitous eyes" (64; quoting Jung 1970, ¶45). This is indeed an uncanny moment, connected to the archetype of "the eye of God" (65). How we relate to this moment can create considerable anxiety. The archetype of the Eye of God is bipolar: on the one hand, imagined as God looking after us, seeing us, knowing us; on the other hand, of being watched and scrutinized, an experience at the core of paranoia. Edinger suggests that the danger comes when we turn away from this recognition, not looking at or refusing to acknowledge it. When this occurs, "the experience of being looked at is replaced by being nagged by an obsessive complex" (65). Understood properly, this moment speaks to the fact that the unconscious requires attention and indicates that the individual is ready for an important step in individuation, "ready to relate to the unconscious as a light-bringer" and that "the ego is not the sole source of light" (61).

I remember Edinger's once telling me about dreams. After years of looking at them, observing their capacity to point out meaningful insights about the Self, he realized that dreams also look back at us, that the unconscious "other" has a subjectivity of its own. Seeing the other as alive can be a truly numinous experience. While working on this paper, I had the following dream:

> I discover that an animal is living with me. I am in my den sitting on the couch, and a large, sleek panther or jaguar comes over to me. He has a shining black coat and golden-yellow, intense eyes. I look into his eyes and realize that they don't seem to have a pupil, but there are fields of yellow gold lying over one another, the way a camera's aperture opens and shuts when a picture is snapped. His head is large, muscular, and

Figure 14.5 Black jaguar. (Credit: Ryan Ladbrook/istockphoto.com).

oddly shaped. I am frightened, but reach out tentatively petting him, not knowing if he will turn on me instinctually like a wild animal—or if he will befriend me. He seems to like the attention I am giving him. He stays a moment, then walks away and returns as if he wants me to stroke him again. I wonder if he has been in the house all along or if he was ever outside. I wonder about letting him out, but fear he will run away and/or be a danger to others. At one point, I am stroking him with a pen, pushing it into his fur, and he seems to like it and comes back as if asking me to do it again.

I suspect that the jaguar, as autonomous psyche, enjoys being written about and so, as I put my pen to this paper, I feel this jaguar—perhaps a totem animal accompanies and supports my effort to express something of the illumination present in the *anima mundi* (Figure 14.5).

In this chapter, I have explored some of the mutual overlap and goals between certain psychoanalysts, and mystical philosophers and theologians. Relying primarily on Jung, Hillman, Lacan, Pseudo-Dionysius, and Henri Corbin, I have followed the thread of the *via negativa* in analysis, alchemy, mystical theology, and the gnostic imagination. In and through these traditions, the *via negativa* plays a central role in the emergence and outcome of an experience of transformation. It is this experience of transformation that psychoanalysis and mysticism share. Many of the images of this outcome have been noted, from the solification of the alchemist to the man of light in gnostic theophanies, accompanied by an excess of life and abundant divinity, "wandering joy," and *jouissance*, an *ekstasis* that opens to a Divine Darkness and a Divine Light. These experiences of illumination, continuing self-negation, and intrinsic positivity do not lead to any static, ontological fixity, but to an ecstatic, ongoing, vital process in the midst of finitude and temporality. Between finitude and eternity, alchemical and mystical illumination, in light of analysis, does not erase mystery but activates and enlivens it, making it conscious and a significant part of psychological transformation. For me, mystery, imagination, and wonder can be like a wild animal, integral to psychological work—at a pivot point between being torn apart and/or experiencing a renewed vitality.

Notes

1 For Giegerich ([1998] 2001), this is merely a mystification (pp. 157–168).
2 Published in this volume as Chapter 9.
3 Published in this volume as Chapter 12.
4 This point is strikingly similar to the Madhyamika logic of the Buddhists—the voiding of the void.
5 This account is based on numerous reports of Leary's dying moments. For example, refer to Carol Sue Rosin's "Timothy Leary's Last Moments," http://www.earthportals.com/Portal_Ship/rosin.html.
6 For Kroll-Fratoni's discussion of this similarity, refer to Kroll-Fratoni (2013) pp. 230–231.

References

Abraham, Lyndy. 1998. *A Dictionary of Alchemical Imagery*. Cambridge: Cambridge University Press.

Cheak, Aaron. 2013. "Introduction: Circumambulating the Alchemical Mysterium." In *Alchemical Traditions from Antiquity to the Avant-Garde*, edited by Aaron Cheak, 18–43. Melbourne: Numen Books.

Cheetham, Tom. 2002. "Within This Darkness: Incarnation, Theophany and the Primordial Revelation." *Esoterica* IV: 61–95. http.//www.esoteric.msu.edu/VolumeIV/Darkness.htm (accessed October 4, 2017).

Coleman, Warren. 2006. "Imagination and the Imaginary." *Journal of Analytical Psychology* 51(1): 21–41.

Corbin, Harry. 1994. *The Man of Light in Iranian Sufism*. Translated by N. Pearson. New Lebanon, NY: Omega Publications.

Dionysius the Areopagite. 1949. *Mystical Theology and the Celestial Hierarchies*. Translated by the Editors of the Shrine of Wisdom. Godalming: The Shrine of Wisdom.

Edinger, Edward F. 1995. *The Mysterium Lectures: A Journey Through C. G. Jung's Mysterium Coniunctionis*. Edited by J. Dexter Blackmer. Toronto: Inner City Books.

Giegerich, Wolfgang. [1998] 2001. *The Soul's Logical Life: Towards a Rigorous Notion of Psychology*. Frankfurt am Main: Peter Lang.

Gratacolle, William. 1652. "The Names of the Philosophers Stone." In *Five Treatises of the Philosophers Stone*, edited by Henry Pinnell, 65–72. London: Thomas Harper.

Henderson, David. 2014. *Apophatic Elements in the Theory and Practice of Psychoanalysis: Pseudo-Dionysius and C. G. Jung*. London: Routledge.

Hewitson, Owen. 2015. "What Does Lacan Say about ... Jouissance." http://www.lacanonline.com/index/2015/07/what-does-lacan-say-about-jouissance/ (accessed October 4, 2017).

Hillman, James. 2010. *Alchemical Psychology, Uniform Edition of the Writings of James Hillman, vol. 5*. Putnam, CT: Spring.

Jung, C. G. 1968. *Psychology and Alchemy, The Collected Works of C. G. Jung*. Edited by Gerhard Adler and Translated by R. F. C. Hull, vol. 12. Princeton, NJ: Princeton University Press.

———. 1970. *Mysterium Coniunctionis. The Collected Works of C. G. Jung*. Edited by Gerhard Adler and Translated by R. F. C. Hull, vol. 14. Princeton, NJ: Princeton University Press.

———. 1971. *Psychological Types. The Collected Works of C. G. Jung*. Edited by Gerhard Adler and Translated by R. F. C. Hull, vol. 6. Princeton, NJ: Princeton University Press.

Kant, Immanuel. 1915. *Dreams of a Spirit-Seer*. London: New-Church Press Limited.

Kroll-Fratoni, Mark. 2013. "The Significance of Meister Eckhart's View of the Self for Psychoanalytic Theories of Subjectivity: A Radical Hermeneutic Study." PhD diss., Duquesne University. Retrieved from https://pqdtopen.proquest.com/doc/1426182497.html?FMT=AI.

Marlan, Stanton. 2005. *The Black Sun: The Alchemy and Art of Darkness.* College Station: Texas A&M University Press.
———. 2006. "From the Black Sun to the Philosopher's Stone." *Spring: A Journal of Archetype and Culture* 74: 1–30.
———. 2013. "The Philosophers' Stone as Chaosmos: The Self and Tire Dilemma of Diversity." *Jung Journal: Culture and Psyche* 7(2): 10–23.
Power, Pamela. 2017. "'The Psychological Difference' in Jung's *Mysterium Coniunctionis.*" In *Psychology of as the Discipline of Inferiority: "The Psychological Difference" in the Work of Wolfgang Giegerich*, edited by Jennifer M. Sandoval and John C. Knapp, 43–54. London: Routledge.
Pseudo-Dionysius. 1987. *Pseudo-Dionysius: The Complete Works.* Translated by Colm Luibheid and Paul Rorem. New York: Paulist Press.

Index

Note: *Italic* page numbers refer to figures and page numbers followed by "n" denote endnotes.

Abraham, Lyndy 233
absolute interiority idea 202
absolute negative interiority 165, 209
absolute religion 201
absolute spirit 201
The Abstracts of the Collected Works of C.G. Jung 10
active imagination 33, 222, 223
Adams, M.V. 124
Aion 9, 15
The Aion Lectures: Exploring the Self in C.G. Jung's Aion (Edinger) 10, 20
albedo psychology 168
Alchemical Active Imagination (Von Franz) 10, 17
'Alchemical blue and the *unio Mentalis*' (Hillman) 21, 152
alchemical marriage 185
alchemical operations 8
alchemical opus 215
alchemical philosophy 187
alchemical process 139
alchemical psychology 23, 81, 154, 160
Alchemical Psychology (Hillman) 21
alchemical soul 90–95
alchemical stove 165
Alchemical Studies 9, 46
alchemical symbolism 24, 254
alchemical themes 160
alchemical transformation 233
alchemical vision 121–135, *126–127*; shadow of vision 122
alchemy 160, 238, 253; and psychology 9
Alchemy: An Introduction to the Symbolism and the Psychology (Thomas) 10, 17

Alchemy in a Modern Woman (Grinnel) 11
'Alchemy: Jung and the historians of science' (Holt) 10
alchemy of desire 61–64, 78
The Alchemy of Discourse: An Archetypal Approach to Language (Kugler) 23
Ambix 11
amplification 87
analysand 139
analytical psychology 13
The Analytic Encounter: Transference and Human Relationship 12
Anatomy of the Psyche: Alchemical Symbolism in Psychotherapy (Edinger) 10, 14, 19, 20, 41, 148
Anglicus, Richardus 213, 214, 215
anima-like innocence 204
anima *vs.* animus psychologies 186
animus-laden shadow 144
"An Inquiry into the Separation and Synthesis of Psychic Opposites in Alchemy" 234
Anna O. 248
annihilation violence 155
anti-Heraclitian position 198
aphroditic language 6, 162
aphroditic quality 77
apocalypse 148
Appollonic archetype 107
Aquinas, Thomas 17
Arabic religiosity 215
Arcane Substance 87
"arcanum of all arcana" 233
archaic neologisms of alchemy 43
archetypal approach 143

Index

archetypal bipolarity 219
archetypal energy 71, 72
archetypal images 229
archetypal jouissance 66
Archetypal Process (Griffin) 146, 247
archetypal psychology 4, 61–64, 166, 256; shared medium of 64–65
archetypal shadow 139
archetype 33
Aristotle 50, 208
Artis Auriferae 52
The Artis Auriferae Volumina Duo 8, 13
art of fire 6
"art of psychological discourse" 171
art of transformation 1
"assimilation" 216
Atom and Archetype: The Pauli/Jung Letters, 1932–1958 (Zabriskie) 26
Aufhebung: Hegel's notion of 162; 'moment' of 167; operation of 167
aura seminalis 86–90
The Aurora Consurgens (Von Franz) 17, 41
aurum philosophicum 214
"The Azure Vault: Caelum as Experience" (Hillman) 21, 246–248, 249

"Back to Beyond: On Cosmology" 246, 247
Badiou, Alain 178
Bal, M. 134
banal cliché and catechism 151
Basilius Valentinus 87
Bass, Alan 101n16
Beckett, Samuel 172
Bennington, Geoffrey 172
Berry, Pat 11, 110; "Stopping As Mode of Animation" 110
Bion, W. 135
"birth of Man" 172
"blacker than black" dimension 147, 170
black light 154
blackness 15, 16, 147; individuation process 148; intention of 150; nigredo aspect of 147
The Black Sun: The Alchemy and Art of Darkness (Marlan) 2, 29, 138, *151*, 167, 170, 204
Blamires, Harry 243
bliss and blackness 153

Bloom, Harold 42, 44, 50
Bloom, Molly 241
Bly, Robert 72
bodily emotions 218
Bollingen Foundation 173
Bonus of Ferrara 40
The Book of Abraham the Jew 52
Bosnak, Robert 147
"breath of life" 246
Brooke, Roger 126, 127, 170, 233
Buddhism 191
Buddhism and the Art of Psychotherapy (Kawai) 29

Campbell, Joseph 110
caput mortuum 198, 209–210
Casey, Edward 163, 247, 249, 250
Cater, Nancy 160
Catholicism 67
Catholic tradition 113
Celestial Kingdom 248
centroversion 140
Cézanne, Paul 248
C.G. Jung Letters 10
C.G. Jung Speaking: Interviews and Encounters 9, 15, 215
Chang Chung Yuan 106
Chang Po-Tuan 115
Chassidim 140
Cheak, Aaron 253
Cheetham, Tom 260
Chi Po & the Sorcerer: A Chinese Tale for Children and Philosophers (Mandel) 116
Christianity 14, 15, 18, 35, 82, 113, 114, 131
Christian myth 18, 20
Christian philosophy 215
Churchill, Scott 11
Chymical Wedding 255
Cioran, Emil 148; *On the Heights of Despair* 148; Salvationist fantasies 149
classical development, ideas 17–20
Cleary, Thomas 29, 103, 106, 107
Cleo's Circle: Entering the Imaginal World of Historians (Meyer, Ruth) 48
clinical literalism 21
clinical vignettes 68–74
Collected Works 10
Complete Reality School (CRS) 116
complexio oppositorum 3, 233, 239

"The Components of the Coniunctio" 254
"Concerning the Stone: Alchemical Images of the Goal" (Hillman) 21, 58, 154, 160, 246–247, 248
coniunctio oppositorum 2
"conjunction" 241
conscious mind 68
consciousness 2, 42, 105
contemporary dream 130–133
Conversing with James Hillman (Hillman) 251
Corbett, Lionel 11
Corbin, Harry 25, 104, 129, 154, 162, 260
Corpus Alchemicum Arabicum: Book of the Explanation of the Symbols Kitab Hall ar-Rumuz (Von Franz) 18
Coward, Harold 29; *Jung and Eastern Thought* 29
"creative destruction" 237
Critchley, Simon 172
criticism 20–33
Cyclops 239

daimonic reading 40–57
darkness 137
Davis, Miles 248
dazzling darkness 153
"death" 139
'death's head' 210
De Boer, Karin 207; *The Sway of the Negative* 207
"*de-create* narratives of redemption" 172
Dee, John 52
deep emotion 138
demonic practices 214
depth psychology 81, 137
Derrida, Jacques 24, 34, 45, 62, 64, 65, 92, 126, 127, 128, 155, 167, 192, 205, 236; *Margins of Philosophy* 206
desendu ad inferno mystic 153
desire, alchemy of 61–64, 78
despair 148
destruction, dramatic process of 149
"determinate appearance," definition of 250
development, alchemy 20–33
dialectical and syntactic awareness 191
différance 62, 64, 79n3
"Different Moments in Dialectical Movement" 164

Dionysian energy 68
Dionysian freedom 186
Dionysian liquification 204
Dionysian psyche 71
discovery of alchemy 12–16, 51
dissemination 90–95
Divine Darkness 158, 258, 260, 267
Divine Light 258, 260, 267
"Divine Matter" 215
The Divine Names (Pseudo-Dionysius) 258
Divine Self 153
divinity 144
Dorn, Gerhard 17, 148, 217
Downcast Eyes (Jay) 127
The Dream and the Underworld (Hillman) 23
"dynamic hybridity" 239

Eastern alchemy 28
Eckhart, Meister 144, 261
ecstatic love, passion of 154
Edinger, Edward 2, 10, 14, 17, 18, 19, 20, 22, 40, 41, 42, 60, 124, 143, 148, 159n1, 160, 254, 265; *The Aion Lectures: Exploring the Self in C.G. Jung's Aion* 10, 20; *Anatomy of the Psyche: Alchemical Symbolism in Psychotherapy* 10, 14, 19, 20, 41, 148; *The Mystery of Coniunctio: Alchemical Image of Individuation* 10, 20; 'Psychotherapy and alchemy' 19
Edinger, P. 255, 256
ego 12, 64
ego assimilation 185
"egocide" 171
ego death, idea of 171
ego psychology 171, 185, 194
ego-Self identity 54
Eliade, Mircea 9, 215
Emerson, Ralph Waldo 172
empiricism 203
emplotment 209
enantiodromia 71
Encyclopedia Hebraica 9
"enigmatic complexity" 233
equal principle 207
1952 Eranos Conference 8, 215
esoteric occultism 8
essentialism 60–61, 78n2
eternal space-less moment 209
ethical dimension 140

ethical responsibility 140
evil 140
'Exiles and orphans: Jung, Paracelsus and the healing images of alchemy' (Zabriskie) 26
existential phenomenology: tension and development 127–128
explanatory theory 247, 255
extended metaphors 48
"eye of God" 265

"fabulous scene" 167
Faces of Light 260
false subject/object dichotomy 175
"fantastical gold" 164
fantasy images 143
fascinosum 89
Faulconer, James 65, 79n3
'Faust and Alchemy' 9
'fear of error' 201
Fechner, Gustav 248
feeling function 191
Felman, Shoshana 50
'Fermentation in Jung's alchemy' (Zabriskie) 26
fervor 90–95
fictional space 64–65
fictive element 48
filius macro cosmi 15
filius philosophorum 105, 129, 169, 257
"filth" 215
Finnegan's Wake (Joyce) 3, 234
fire in the stone 74–78
'Fire in the stone: an inquiry into the alchemy of soul-making' (Marlan) 24
Fire in the Stone: The Alchemy of Desire (Marlan) 11, 23, 24
Five Treatises of the Philosophers' Stone (Gratacolle) 233
Flamel, Nicolas 52
'flap of Persephone' 185
Fludd, Robert 68
Flynn, T. 134
Fordham, Michael 11
'Foreword to a catalogue on alchemy' 9
Foucault 132, 192
von Franz, Marie-Louise 160
freedom 189, 190; definition of 190
Freud and Philosophy (Ricoeur) 141
Freudian analysis 141
Freud, S. 86, 89, 94
Frischknecht, Max 216
'fruit cake' principle 42

Gad, Irene 12
Gathering the Light: A Psychology of Meditation (Odajnyk) 28
Gebser, Jean 25
General Bibliography 10
General Index 10
Giegerich, Wolfgang 2, 3, 4, 30, 31, 32, 34, 35, 41, 43, 144, 160, 198, 254; absolute interiority idea 202; alchemical themes 160–161; alchemy work 184; criticism of 191, 192; "gold," subtle view of 164; human person 184; Jung, criticism of 197; Jungian tradition 183; land of soul 154; mortificatio and putrefactio 149; negative interiorization work 164; Philosophers' Stone 167; "psychoalchemical" 173; 'psychology proper' view 183; soul, logical life of 154; *The Soul's Logical Life* 30, 31, 144, 160; sublation, notion of 163; *What Is Soul?* 183, 187
Gnostic imagination 28
Gnosticism 13
goal, revisioning 65–66
Goddess of Fire *224*
Goethe, Johann Wolfgang von 49, 50, 146
"gold" 164
Golden Flower 2, 105
"golden touch" 164
Gottfried, Roy K. 243
Gratacolle, William 233, 257; *Five Treatises of the Philosophers' Stone* 233
"Great Work" 160
Griffin, D.R. 247
Grinnel, Robert 11; *Alchemy in a Modern Woman* 11
Grof, Stanislov 153; *LSD Psychotherapy* 153

Hades: innocent soul, marriage of 153; sublime beauty of 153
Hadot, Pierre 210
Hanegraaff, Wouter 41, 43
Hannah, Barbara 10
Hartmann, Franz 85
Healing Fiction (Hillman) 50, 59
"heart of gold" 164
Hebrew 154
Hegel, G. W. F. 144; absolute spirit 201; *Aufhebung,* 'moment' of 167;

images, weight of 144; negativity, interpretation of 167, 205; post-Hegelian neo-rationalist thinking 166
Hegelian perspective 197
hegemony of vision 125–126
Heidegger, Martin 65, 166, 167, 192, 205, 206, 219, 248, 250
Henderson, David 256
Henderson, Joseph 11; 'Practical application of alchemical theory' 11
Heraclitus 104, 108
hermeneutic strategies 141
Hermes 87
hesitation/resistance 165
Hesse, Mary 94
Hierosgamos 234
Hillman, James 2, 4, 6, 11, 20, 21, 22, 23, 24, 31, 34, 35, 41, 43, 54, 58, 62, 63, 64, 65, 66, 68, 72, 73, 77, 78, 80n8, 81, 90, 91, 92, 93, 103, 107, 111, 114, 118, 124, 127, 128, 131, 132, 133, 139, 140, 147, 160, 209, 217, 246, 247, 251, 252, 254; 'Alchemical blue and the *unio Mentalis*' 21; *Alchemical Psychology* 21, 154; alchemical themes 160–161; archetypal psychology 166; 'The azure vault: the caelum as experience' 21; banal cliché and catechism 151; blackness, intention of 150; "Concerning the Stone: Alchemical Images of the Goal" 21, 58; *Conversing with James Hillman* 251; depression and melancholy 151; depth psychology 173; *The Dream and the Underworld* 23; goal, "idea" of 161; *Healing Fiction* 50, 59; image, understanding of 163; 'The imagination of air and the collapse of alchemy' 21; *mortificatio,* process of 149; mystical language 153; 'Notes on white supremacy: the alchemy of racism' 21; "Peaks and Vales" 107; *Philosophical Intimations* 247, 251; "psychotherapeutic cure of me" 171; religious darkness 153; 'Salt: a chapter in alchemical psychology' 21, 23, 81; 'The seduction of black' 21; "Silver and White Earth" 21, 118, 152; sublation, critique of 163; 'The therapeutic value of alchemical language' 21; 'The yellowing of the work' 21
historical realism 48

historical scholarship 47
Hoedl, John 192, 193, 197
Hokusai 152
Hölderlin, Friedrich 248
Holt, David 10, 11; 'Alchemy: Jung and the historians of science' 10; 'Jung and Marx' 11
Holy Spirit 214
Homer 82
human dignity 189
human feeling 191
human life and love 185
human person 184
human psyche 157
human relationship 25
Husserl, Edmund 25

idealism 220
"*ignotum per ignotius*" 253
illumination 265
"Illumination and Darkness in the Song of Songs" 153
images: Hillman, understanding of 163; and imagination 165–166; Jung, resuscitation of 166; paradoxical view of 144
"Image Sense" 163
imaginal life 142
imaginal psychology 185
imagination 165–166, 176, 253
'The imagination of air and the collapse of alchemy' (Hillman) 21
immateriality 149
"immaterial phantoms" 219
individuation 33, 60
'The influence of alchemy on the work of C.G. Jung' (Jaffé) 11
innovations 20–33
insofar 183
instinctual unconscious 110
intense confrontation 12
interiority, philosophical discipline of 186
International Congress in Rome 21
Introduction to Alchemy 115
Irigaray 132
irrevocable, feeling of 149

Jacoby, Mario 12, 202
Jaffé, Aniela 11, 49; 'The influence of alchemy on the work of C.G. Jung' 11
Jay, Martin 134
Jesus Christ 113, 114
Jewish mystical tradition 140

Johnson, Barbara 92
Johnson, H. Robert 68
Jones, Ernest 82, 86
jouissance 6, 153
Joyce, James 3, 234; *Finnegan's Wake* 3, 234; *Ulysses* 235, 236, 238
Jung and Eastern Thought (Coward) 29
'Jung and Marx' (Holt) 11
'Jung and Pauli: a subtle asymmetry' (Pauli) 26
Jung and the Alchemical Imagination (Raff) 27
Jung and the Making of Modern Psychology (Shamdasani) 48
Jung, C.G. 160; *Aion* 9, 15; *Alchemical Psychology* 246; *Alchemical Studies* 46; alchemical vision 161; alchemy, psychology of 213; *aurum philosophicum* 214; blackness 148; *The Book of Abraham the Jew* 52; *C. G. Jung Speaking* 215; filth, reclaiming of 215; *General Bibliography* 10; *General Index* 10; idealist and naturalist 220; images, resuscitation of 166; Kantian influence 144; *Memories, Dreams, Reflections* 8, 9, 10, 13, 47, 146, 227, 240; *Mysterium Coniunctionis* 3, 9, 15, 16, 17, 20, 28, 88, 95, 115, 144, 158, 234, 254, 256; objective psyche 183; "Paracelsus as a Spiritual Phenomenon" 45; *Psychology and Alchemy* 5, 9, 14, 15, 213, 233; *Psychology and Religion* 14; *Red Book* 235; self-expression through architecture 173; "the Telesphoros of Asklepios" 174; "*the experience of the self is always a defeat for the ego*" 171; thought *vs.* imagination 142
Jungian Analysis (Stein) 137, 141
Jungian-analytic parallels 109–115; dream 113–115; dream four years later 111–112; dream many years later 112–113; first dream 109–111
Jungian approach 143
Jungian psychoanalysis 137, 141
Jungian spirituality 27
Jung on Alchemy (Schwartz-Salant) 10
Jung's travel in Africa 122–125
Jung's Treatment of Christianity (Stein) 15

Kadmon, Adam 234
Kali's dance 170–171
Kali, Tantric goddess 139
Kalsched, Don 11
Kant 199–200
Kantian position 198
Kantian victory 199
Kant und die Epigonen (Liebman) 199
Kawai, Hayao 29, 30; *Buddhism and the Art of Psychotherapy* 29
Kekulé 229
Kerenyi, Karl 255
Kim, Alan 210
Kirsch, Jean 12, 40; 'Transference' 12
Kroll-Fratoni, Mark 261
Kugler, Paul 11, 23, 34; *The Alchemy of Discourse: An Archetypal Approach to Language* 23; *Raids on the Unthinkable* 178

"labor of concept" 164, 165
Lacan, Jacques 4, 6, 138, 153, 261
LaCapra, Dominick 166, 205
Lambert, Kenneth 141
language, importance of 142
"lapis" 235
Lawrence, D. H. 92
lead 91
Levin, D.M. 128, 192
liberation 191
library 51
Liebman, Otto 199
life 149
light and lumen 130–133
light of darkness 168
"Light of Glory" 261
light of nature 128–130
literal and destructive forms 150
logical life 185, 189, 207
logical psychology 185
logocentrism 62, 64, 238
logos: and patriarchy 82–86
LSD Psychotherapy (Grof) 153
Lully, Raymond 213, 214
lumen naturae 113, 128–130, 169
lunar symbolism: erotics of 86–90

McGoveran, Patrick 12
McGrath, Sean 192, 197
McLean, Adam 43, 44
Maier, Michael 137
Majesty of Beauty 260
Mandel, Oscar: *Chi Po & the Sorcerer: A Chinese Tale for Children and Philosophers* 116

Margins of Philosophy (Derrida) 206
Marlan, Stanton 34, 205; *The Black Sun* 138; 'The black sun: archetypal image of the non-self' 29; 'Fire in the stone: an inquiry into the alchemy of soul-making' 24; *Fire in the Stone: The Alchemy of Desire* 11, 23, 24; *Salt and the Alchemical Soul* 23, 81–102
marriage 185
Marx 192
masculine psyche 71
massa confusa 55
Mather, Matthew 229
'The matter of psyche' (Zabriskie) 26
"mediator" 235
"mediocrity of ataraxic rationality" 161
Memories, Dreams, Reflections 8, 9, 10, 13, 146, 227, 240
"mental condition" 215
Mercurius 87, 129, 235; dual aspect of 191; liquification of 191
Merleau-Ponty, Maurice 25, 155, 176; *The Visible and the Invisible* 155
metaphor of light 103–119, 121–135
metaphysical realm 27
"metaphysical speculation" 234
metaphysical systems 172
metaphysical vision 250
Meyer, Ruth 43, 48; *Cleo's Circle: Entering the Imaginal World of Historians* 48
Micklem, Neil 144
microcosmic ecology 92
Miller, David 61, 155, 163, 165, 171, 176; "Nothing Almost Sees Miracles" 155
Mills, Jon 207, 229
modernity 200
modern psychology 222
Mogenson, Greg 163–165, 202
Monick, Gene 69
monkey, archetypal figure 69
Morin, Edgar 167, 205
Morris, Marla 172
Morrison, Toni 152
mortificatio 148
Mundus Archetypus 146, 192
mundus imaginalis filius 105
Mutus Liber 1, 5, 41, 45
Mylius 146
Mysterium Coniunctionis 3, 9, 15, 16, 17, 28, 95, 115, 158, 170, 234, 254, 256
The Mysterium Lectures 10

The Mystery of Coniunctio: Alchemical Image of Individuation (Edinger) 10, 20
The Mystery of the Human Relationship (Schwartz-Salant) 24
mystical death 171–173
mystical language 153
The Mystical Theology 259

naturalism 203, 220
natural philosophy 221
"natural structure" 174
natural substances 221
Nazi images 140
Needham, Joseph 103
negative interiorization work 164
negativity, interpretation of 205
"negativity of image" 164
neo-Hegelian idealism 192
neo-Kantian/Heideggerian variety 210
Nerval, Gérard de 50, 51
Neumann, Erich 54, 132, 140; supra-ordinate unity 140
Newman, Kenneth 11, 143, 144; 'The riddle of the Vas Bene Clausum' 11
Newman, William 43, 44, 221
Nietzsche 192
nigredo aspect 150
non-self: archetypal image of 146; Buddhist idea of 155
'Notes on white supremacy: the alchemy of racism' (Hillman) 21
"Nothing Almost Sees Miracles" 155
Novalis 248
numinosum 67
Nye, A. 128

objective psyche 14, 183
Odajnyk, Walter V. 28, 29, 34, 35, 103, 106; *Gathering the Light: A Psychology of Meditation* 28
"One book opens another" (Rhazes) 41
Onians, Richard Broxton 66
On the Heights of Despair (Cioran) 148
opus alchemicum 253
opus divinum 1, 4
opus magnum 192, 193, 197
ordinary, perception of 172
Original Mind 105
Original Spirit 104

Panisnick, G.D. 185
Paracelsica 14

"Paracelsus as a Spiritual Phenomenon" 45, 85, 87, 130, 147, 170
paradoxical images 141
participation mystique 50, 54, 189
passionate reading 45
patriarchy: and logos 82–86
Pauli, Wolfgang 26, 248; 'Jung and Pauli: a subtle asymmetry' 26
"Peaks and Vales" (Hillman) 107, 163, 246, 251
personality, mysterious side of 139
personification 143
phantasmagoria 50
Pharaonic corpses 210
pharmacon 46
Philosophers' Stone 2, 3, 5, 44, 45, 46, 145, 203, 209, 213, 215, 253, 257; alchemical psychology 160; alchemical thinking 160; alchemy, "Great Work" of 233; mystical death 171–173; reiteration, sparks of 170–171; remainder, resistance of 165–170; stone, tinctures of 161–165; turning to stone 173–175
philosophical egg 221, *225*
philosophical gold 8
Philosophical Intimations (Hillman) 247, 251
Philosophical Tree 21, 221, 227
"picture thinking" 162, 163
Plato 50, 82
playfulness 94
plural psyche 34
The Plural Psyche (Samuels) 10
"poetic" 251
polysema 93
post-Hegelian Idealism 166
post-modernism: shared medium of 64–65
post-modern voice 61–64
Power, Pamela 220
'Practical application of alchemical theory' (Henderson) 11
The Practice of Psychotherapy 9
Prauss, Gerold 200
prima materia 109, 216, 235
Primordial Man 105, 129
primordial shadow 139
Principe, Lawrence 43, 44, 221
Proust, Marcel 248
Pseudo-Dionysius 258–260; *The Divine Names* 258

psyche 148; experience of 223; fundamental facts of 143; margins of 206; uroboric understanding of 202
Psyche and Matter (Von Franz) 18
psyche's purpose 59–60
psychic disposition 67
psychic facts 42
psychic life 139, 144; darkest aspects of 139; shadow and imaginal life 142
psychic reality 14, 33, 35, 55, 66
"psychoalchemical" 173
psychoanalysis 110, 137, 142
"psychoanalyst's stone" 172
psychoanalytic metaphysics 230
psychological development 218
'psychological difference' 192, 193
psychological drama 148
psychological life 148
psychological space 65
psychological theory 171, 194
Psychology and Alchemy 5, 9, 14, 15, 213, 233
Psychology and Religion 14
Psychology as a Discipline of Interiority (PDI) 198, 201
psychology of alchemy 34
psychology of consciousness 13
'Psychology of the transference' 9, 25, 27
psychology proper 4, 183, 198
psychotherapy 63
'Psychotherapy and alchemy' (Edinger) 19
Psychotherapy Grounded in the Feminine Principle (Sullivan) 12
"*Putrefactio*" 168

Quasha, George 50

radical interiorization 164
Raff, Jeffrey 27, 28, 35; *Jung and the Alchemical Imagination* 27
Raids on the Unthinkable (Kugler) 178
Rasaratnakara 77
Rati-asana (detail) *256*
ratnaraj 79n6
reality of psyche 19
'real psychology' 184
real transformation 67
rebis 89
"reborn in stone" 173
The Red Book 1, 235
Reich, Wilhelm 248

relativism 78n1
religion 144
resources, Jung's writings 10–12
resurrection 73
retrograde movement 138
return of the soul *73*
return to instinct 66–68
revivification process 66–68, *73*
revolutionary insight 253
Rhazes: "One book opens another" 41
Ricoeur, Paul 110, 141, 142, 166, 178, 209; *Freud and Philosophy* 141
'The riddle of the Vas Bene Clausum' (Newman) 11
Rilke, Rainer Maria 172
Romanyshyn, Robert 4, 105, 176
Roob, Alexander 104
Rorty, Richard 93, 94
Rosarium Philosophorum 13, 27, 30, 52, 111
Rosen, David 171
ruby dream 74–78
Ruland, Martin 77, 219
Russel, George William 248

Saban, Mark 192, 197
sacred marriage 2, 33
Sal Alkali 87
Sallis, John 174, 208, 251
salt 91; arcane substance 86–90; dissemination and fervor, alchemical soul 90–95; fixative quality of 91; Nietzschean example of truth 94
'Salt: a chapter in alchemical psychology' (Hillman) 21, 23, 81
Salt and the Alchemical Soul (Marlan) 23, 81–102
Salvationist perspective 147
Samuels, A. 26, 34; *The Plural Psyche* 10
Samuels, Andrew 141
Schelling 192
Schenk, Ron 11
Scheper, George 153
Schwartz-Salant, N. 9, 10, 24, 25, 34, 175, 177; *Jung on Alchemy* 10; *The Mystery of the Human Relationship* 24
science 144
scientific imagination 143
Secret of the Golden Flower 169
The Secret of the Golden Flower 13, 21, 28, 29, 103, 104, 105, 106, 107, 108, 114, 119

'The seduction of black' (Hillman) 21, 150
Self 12, 33, 46, 115, 126, 157–158, 233, 238, 258; Jung's concept of 233
self-accusation 91
self-deconstruction 158
self-expression through architecture 173
self-purification 91
self-realization 108
semantic modesty 199
semination 82–86
senex metaphors 161
"sensate intuition" 162
"sensory intuition" 163
separation process 66–68
shadow 141; and imaginal life 142; Jungian literature on 137–138; Jung's idea of 141
Shamdasani, Sonu 35n1, 43, 44, 46, 47, 48, 49; *Jung and the Making of Modern Psychology* 48
"sheer mereness of things" 172
Sherwood, Dyane 11; *Transformation of the Psyche: The Symbolic Alchemy of the Splendor Solis* 11
shine of darkness 168
"shining truth" 177
Shual, Katon 77, 80n7
Silberer, Herbert 4
"Silver and White Earth" (Hillman) 21, 118, 152
Smith, C. 249
Sol niger 29, 138–139, 146, 209; blackness of 168; darkest dimension of 148; phenomenon of 258; physiological destructive actions 148; vindictiveness of 150; *see also* The black sun
Solve et coagula 178, 186
The Song of Solomon (Morrison) 152
Song of Songs 153
Soror Mystica 5
soul 190; dream as access 68–74; logical life of 185; uroboric communication of 192
soul-making process 2; alchemy of 58–80; psyche's purpose 59–60
soul making vale 209
soul—Paracelcian 230
The Soul's Logical Life (Giegerich) 30, 31, 144, 160
Sparks, Gary 228

spirit: periphery of 208; self-presentation of 208
spirit/thought 165–166
spiritual embryo 2
spiritual intoxication 155
spiritualisation 35
spiritual literalism 35
spiritual philosophy 215, 216
Splendor Solis (Trismosin) 11, 169
Spring, readership of 160
Starkey, George 221
static ontological fixity 5
Stein, Murray 11, 40; *Jungian Analysis* 137; *Jung's Treatment of Christianity* 15; personality, mysterious side of 139
Stevens, Wallace 50, 172, 248
"Stopping As Mode of Animation" (Berry) 110
sublimation 67
substantial reality 124
Sufi concept 27
Sufi mysticism 154
Sullivan, Barbara Stevens 12; *Psychotherapy Grounded in the Feminine Principle* 12
"The Sun and its shadow complete the work" (*Atalanta Fugiens,* Emblem 45) 137
The Sun King 169
supra-ordinate unity 140
The Sway of the Negative (De Boer) 207
symbol, definition of 216
symbolic images 265
The Symbolic Life 9, 141, 142
symbolic structures 48
"synthesis" 216

Tanaka, Yasuhiro 32
Tanizaki, J. 133
Tantric tradition 153
Taoist alchemy 29, 104–109, 169; unification of "opposites" in 115–119
Tat tvam asi—"That art Thou" 237
Taylor, Charles 84
Taylor, Gladys 19
"the Telesphoros of Asklepios" 174
telos, revisioning 65–66
theoretical/metaphysical shadow 144
"The Therapeutic Value of Alchemical Language: A Heated Introduction" (Hillman) 21, 246
'"The Unassimilable Remnant"—What Is at Stake? A Dispute with Stanton Marlan' 203

thing-in-itself 200
Thomas, Una 17
Thoth-Hermes 68
thought/philosophy 166
thought *vs.* imagination 142
Tilton, Hereward 43
Tractatus Aureus 129
'Transference' (Kirsch) 12, 77
transformational art 254
Transformation of the Psyche: The Symbolic Alchemy of the Splendor Solis (Sherwood) 11
'Tree of Hermes' 221
Trismosin, Solomon 11; *Splendor Solis* 11, 169
'true gold' 190
"true imagination" 230n4
true psychology 165, 191, 199
The turning 237

"ultimacy of image" 249
"ultima materia" 235
Ulysses (Joyce) 235, 236, 238
Umail, Muhammad ibn ('Senior') 18
unconscious psyche 9, 68, 207, 253
Understanding the Meaning of Alchemy: Jung's Metaphor of the Transformative Process 11
unification 2
unio mentalis (soul and mind) 183, 218
Unus Mundus 18
Uraltes Chymisches Werck (Eleazar) 53

vale of soul making 209
'vegetabilia materiae' 222
violence of annihilation 155
The Visible and the Invisible (Merleau-Ponty) 155
vitalization 71
"voice of things" 4, 176
volcanic metaphor 153
Voluptas 77
voluptuousness 149
Von Franz, Marie-Louise 2, 10, 17, 18, 20, 22, 27, 40, 41, 42, 215, 218, 254; *Alchemical Active Imagination* 10, 17; *Alchemy: An Introduction to the Symbolism and the Psychology* 10, 17; *The Aurora Consurgens* 17, 41; *Corpus Alchemicum Arabicum: Book of the Explanation of the Symbols Kitab Hall ar-Rumuz* 18; *Psyche and Matter* 18
"vulgar gold" 164

Warnke, G. 134
Western Christianity 215
Westerners Taoism 106
What Is Soul? (Giegerich) 183, 187
White, Hayden 43, 47
whiteness 147
"White Queen and Red King" 217
wholeness, symbols of 157
Wilhelm, Richard 13, 103, 237
"window of eternity" 240
Wix, Linney 63
Woolf, Virginia 50
writings on alchemy 9–10

'The yellowing of the work' (Hillman) 21

Zabriskie, B.D. 11, 26; *Atom and Archetype: The Pauli/Jung Letters, 1932–1958* 26; 'Exiles and orphans: Jung, Paracelsus and the healing images of alchemy' 26; 'Fermentation in Jung's alchemy' 26; 'The matter of psyche' 26
Zacharias, Dionysius 214, 215
Zen Buddhism 42
Zen-like astonishment 178
Zosimos of Panopolis 14

Taylor & Francis eBooks

www.taylorfrancis.com

A single destination for eBooks from Taylor & Francis with increased functionality and an improved user experience to meet the needs of our customers.

90,000+ eBooks of award-winning academic content in Humanities, Social Science, Science, Technology, Engineering, and Medical written by a global network of editors and authors.

TAYLOR & FRANCIS EBOOKS OFFERS:

- A streamlined experience for our library customers
- A single point of discovery for all of our eBook content
- Improved search and discovery of content at both book and chapter level

REQUEST A FREE TRIAL
support@taylorfrancis.com

Routledge — Taylor & Francis Group

CRC Press — Taylor & Francis Group

Printed and bound by CPI Group (UK) Ltd, Croydon, CR0 4YY

10/10/2024

01043214-0017